THE CLASSICS
OF WESTERN
SPIRITUALITY

P9-BJA-138

THE CLASSICS OF WESTERN SPIRITUALITY
A Library of the Great Spiritual Masters

ROBERT BELLARMINE
SPIRITUAL WRITINGS

TRANSLATED AND EDITED BY
JOHN PATRICK DONNELLY, S.J., AND ROLAND J. TESKE, S.J.

INTRODUCTION BY
JOHN PATRICK DONNELLY, S.J.

PREFACE BY
JOHN O'MALLEY, S.J.

PAULIST PRESS
NEW YORK • MAHWAH

Cover Art: *St. Robert Bellarmine* by Passarotto Passarotti. Courtesy of the Society of Jesus, Province of Toledo, Spain.

Library of Congress Cataloging-in-Publication Data

Bellarmino, Roberto Francesco Romolo, Saint, 1542–1621.
[De ascensione mentis in Deum per scalas rerum creatorum opusculum. English]
Spiritual writings / Robert Bellarmine ; translated with an introduction by John Patrick Donnelly and Roland J. Teske ; preface by John W. O'Malley.
p. cm.—(Classics of Western spirituality)
Translation of: De ascensione mentis in Deum per scalas rerum creatorum opusculum, and, De arte bene moriendi.
Includes index.
Contents: The mind's ascent to God by the ladder of created things —The art of dying well.
ISBN 0-8091-0389-3 : $18.95 (est.).—ISBN 0-8091-2875-6 (pbk.) : $14.95 (est.)
1. God—Attributes—Early works to 1800. 2. Mysticism—Early works to 1800. 3. Death—Religious aspects—Christianity—Early works to 1800. 4. Christian life—Catholic authors—Early works to 1800. I. Donnelly, John Patrick, 1934– . II. Teske, Roland J., 1934– . III. Bellarmino, Roberto Francesco Romolo, Saint, 1542–1621. De arte bene moriendi. English. 1989. IV. Title. V. Series.
BT100.B4513 1989
248.4'82—dc19 88-38925
CIP

Published by Paulist Press
997 Macarthur Boulevard
Mahwah, New Jersey 07430

Printed and bound in the United States of America

Contents

Translators of This Volume

JOHN PATRICK DONNELLY, S.J., Professor of History at Marquette University, is a specialist in Renaissance and Reformation studies. He received his B.A., Ph.L., and M.A. degrees from St. Louis University, and his Ph.D. from the University of Wisconsin, Madison. He has been associated with Marquette University since 1971. Father Donnelly is the author of *Calvinism and Scholasticism in Vermigli's Doctrine of Man and Grace* (Leiden: E. J. Brill, 1976), and *Reform and Renewal* (Wilmington, N.C.: Consortium Books, 1977), and is the editor of Thomas More's *Utopia* (Milwaukee: Marquette University Press, 1984, rev. ed.). His many other scholarly works include: "Italian Influence on the Development of Calvinist Scholasticism," *The Sixteenth Century Journal* 7 (1976); "Alonzo Rodriguez's *Ejercicio:* A Neglected Classic," *Sixteenth Century Journal* 9, no. 2 (1980); "Peter Canisius," in *Shapers of Religious Traditions in Germany, Switzerland, and Poland, 1560–1600*, edited by Jill Raitt (New Haven: Yale University Press, 1981), and "For the Greater Glory of God: St. Ignatius Loyola," in *Leaders of the Reformation*, edited by Richard De Molen (Selingsgrove, Pa.: Susquehanna University Press, 1984).

ROLAND J. TESKE, S.J., received his B.A., A.M., and Ph.L. from St. Louis University, and his Ph.D. in philosophy from the University of Toronto. He has been acting dean, College of Philosophy and Letters, at St. Louis University and the director of the Honors Program at Marquette University, and is currently an associate professor at Marquette. Father Teske has been the editor of *The Modern Schoolman*, and the Managing Editor of *Theology Digest*. Among his many works are "Time and the World-Soul in St. Augustine," *Augustinian Studies* 14 (1983); "Platonic Reminiscence and Memory of the Present," *The New Scholasticism* 58 (1984); and "Divine Immutability in St. Augustine," *The Modern Schoolman* 63 (1986).

Author of the Preface

JOHN W. O'MALLEY, S.J., is currently Professor of History at the Weston School of Theology, Cambridge, Massachusetts. Father O'Malley, who received his Ph.D. in history from Harvard University, has been Scholar in Residence at the American Academy in Rome and received a research fellowship from the National Endowment for Humanities. His principal publications are *Giles of Viterbo on Church and Reform* (Leiden, 1968), *Praise and Blame in Renaissance Rome* (Durham, N.C., 1979), and *Rome and the Renaissance*. Father O'Malley is a specialist in Italian Humanism, the problem of Church reform, and the history of the early Jesuits.

For
our mothers
Margaret Mary Donnelly
and
Mary Ann Teske

Foreword

This translation is based chiefly on the text found in *Opuscula ascetica autore B. Roberto Bellarmino S.J.* (Regensburg: Friedrich Pustet, 1925), volumes 1 and 3. The translators have also consulted the text in Bellarmine's *Opera omnia* (Naples: G. Giuliano, 1862), volume 6, as well as the first edition of the *Ascent* (Antwerp: Plantin, 1615) and an older edition (Cologne: H. Schlebusch, 1740) of *The Art of Dying Well.* This is the first translation to put either of Bellarmine's books into modern English. Bellarmine's extensive use of biblical quotations presented problems. He, of course, quotes from the Latin Vulgate and his text often pivots on the Vulgate phrasing. Although the better modern translations are from the Greek and Hebrew, the translators have used the Douay version for the Old Testament (while modernizing *thee*, *thou*, *dost*, and the like) and the Confraternity version for the New Testament because both of these are from the Vulgate and are therefore closer to Bellarmine's phrasing. Modern usage is followed in referring to the names of the biblical books and in the numbering of the psalms, although a few of the older biblical names were retained in the text lest Bellarmine sound too anachronistic. Bellarmine's first edition gave biblical references (book and chapter but not verse) in the margin; this translation inserts biblical references including verse numbers into the text. The vast majority of Bellarmine's other references are to the Church Fathers. These are given in the notes with the internal divisions of each work plus a reference to Migne's standard *Patrologia Graeca* and *Patrologia Latina* (*PG* or *PL*). Admittedly there are now better editions for many of the Fathers, but the Migne series still provides a clear, uniform, and simple system of citations to what remains the most widely available edition. The translators wish to thank John Farina and Paulist Press for their encouragement.

Preface

Saint Robert Bellarmine died in 1621, in the chronological center of the historical phenomenon known as the Counter-Reformation or the Catholic Reformation. He was a bishop, a cardinal, and a member of the relatively young Society of Jesus, founded by Saint Ignatius Loyola in 1540. In his own times and for many generations thereafter, he won wide recognition for his writings on the spiritual life, which ran through many editions and translations. He also won recognition for his writings against the Protestants and especially for his opposition to certain ecclesiological ideas espoused by King James I of England.

When he was canonized by Pope Pius XI in 1930, he brought with him into our own century his reputation for skill in religious controversy rather than his fame as a writer on spirituality, which had been part and parcel of the esteem in which he was held in earlier centuries. The two works published in the present volume will help restore to us that latter part of his heritage and help fit him into the general traditions of Western spirituality. This means that he will be more effectively and precisely located within the huge corpus of spiritual writings that flooded the printing presses of Catholic Europe during the era of the Counter-Reformation and that were so tellingly characteristic of it. He cannot be understood, in fact, apart from that "golden age" of Catholic spiritualities.

In English-speaking countries, however, the Counter-Reformation long remained a particularly slighted field of historical interest. Authors of textbooks generally relegated it to a kind of postscript to much more extensive treatments of Luther, Zwingli, Calvin, Henry VIII, and other personages who broke with Roman Catholicism in the sixteenth century. This historiographical fact is rather easily explained. Protestant traditions long dominated the intellectual life of the English-speaking world and naturally focused on persons and issues consonant with those traditions. Catholics insisted, for their part, that their Church represented an unbroken continuity with apostolic, patristic, and medieval Christianity and had rejected all "novelty," a synonym for the supposed outrages committed by the Protestant reformers. They thus promoted the idea that, although the Catholic Church reformed abuses in its practice and structure in the wake of the Reformation, it had not otherwise significantly changed. Since historians have conventionally been more interested in change than in continuity, they received unwitting warrant from Catholics to turn their attention elsewhere.

In recent years the situation has begun to change. Although still in disproportion to their numbers, Catholics have assumed a more active role in academic life. More important, an influential school of historical interpretation, originating in Paris, has for several decades stressed that it is just as important to understand how and why certain historical realities continue somewhat impervious to change as to understand how and why they are transformed or even cease to exist. Many of the historians of this so-called *Annales* school gave special attention to the seventeenth century, the *grand siècle* of French history. They could not ignore Catholicism, nor did they desire to do so, given its immense importance in French life and culture. Historians from Italy soon adopted the aims and methods of their French colleagues, which are now having a decided impact in England and North America as well.

In the meantime, other historians, utilizing more conventional methods and aims, but with techniques of research more precise and objective than those that prevailed in previous generations, have also turned to some aspects of Catholicism in the sixteenth and seventeenth centuries. In 1975 Hubert Jedin of the University of Bonn, perhaps the greatest Catholic Church historian of the twentieth century, completed the four volumes of his monumental *History of the Council of Trent*. Jedin effected almost single-handedly a renewal of interest in the council, and he trained and inspired a large number of disciples in Germany and elsewhere to investigate a wide range of questions about the council's origins, character, and impact. The influence of the *Annales* school and the Jedin school combined to infuse new life into the supposedly moribund field of Counter-Reformation studies. We are beginning to view the Counter-Reformation with new eyes.

Whether earlier historians assessed the Counter-Reformation with sympathy or antipathy, they tended to agree that it was basically a monolithic phenomenon, which was at the same time singularly successful in maintaining continuity with medieval institutions, ideas, and mores. The researches of more recent historians, even those from the *Annales* school, have to a large degree challenged precisely that monolithic and continuous image. The field is still in turmoil, but we are now keenly aware of how variegated Catholicism was and how significantly, despite many continuities, it changed. These realizations obviously have deep significance for the history of spirituality, but they are just beginning to be understood and applied.

Within such a purview Robert Bellarmine does not stand, therefore, for "Counter-Reformation spirituality" or even for "Jesuit spirituality," but represents, rather, a set or sets of trends within both of those larger realities. Up to a certain point, of course, historians have always been ready to grant that much. What we now see to be needed, however, is the setting of him more precisely in his culture, the widely variegated culture of the Counter-Reformation. Setting him in his culture means not simply setting him in the history of ideas, which is how the history of spirituality has long been conceived. It means relating him to literature, art, and the practice of ministry. This is an arduous task, but the translations and Introduction to them in this volume provide the pre-conditions. Other volumes in the series do the same for other authors.

If we look for a moment at the two selections that we have before us, we can begin to perceive what is at stake. In *The Art of*

Dying Well we have an obvious continuity with a medieval tradition that found further expression within both Protestantism and Catholicism in the sixteenth and seventeenth centuries. In the Introduction, Father Donnelly has with admirable precision and erudition located this work within the tradition of the genre and indicated a number of its peculiar features.

Further questions, however, are always suggested by the special context in which Bellarmine was writing. Among the aids for living and dying well, for instance, Bellarmine assigns the sacraments their important and traditional role. One aid for godly living on which earlier generations placed great emphasis, however, is practically missing. Although Bellarmine laces his work with quotations from Scripture, with which he himself obviously had great familiarity, he only in passing commends to his devout audience the reading of the Bible. Nor does he suggest that reading a passage from the New Testament at the bedside might be a suitable remedy for the temptations that assail the dying.

Bellarmine's spiritual writings are remarkably lacking in anti-Protestant polemic and were translated and read by Protestants. In this he was not unique. Even in an age of vicious controversy over religion, we find in much Catholic spirituality an ecumenically acceptable common ground. "In its saints," remarked the Protestant historian A. G. Dickens some years ago, "many of us have found the permanent significance of the Catholic Reformation." Nevertheless, we can perhaps detect in Bellarmine's failure to emphasize the reading of the Bible a subtle shift in the spiritual tradition due to the Reformation.

Perhaps too much should not be made of this fact, however, for other curious omissions also occur in Bellarmine's work. Recent historians have discovered, for instance, that in the Counter-Reformation preaching received an emphasis at least as great as that given it in the Protestant traditions—a discovery that reshapes much of the conventional image of the period. The Jesuits were here in the forefront, and "ministry of the Word" was the central task assigned them in their earliest legislation. Yet Bellarmine fails to stress the hearing of sermons as among primary helps for godly living.

An even more curious slighting regards consideration of the agony of Jesus in the garden and on the Cross as a way of consoling and strengthening the dying—curious because a full "week" of the *Spiritual Exercises* of Saint Ignatius is devoted to the sufferings of

Christ and because those sufferings were represented with new prominence in Italian art during Bellarmine's lifetime. Both of the works in this volume are, in fact, much more theocentric than Christocentric in their orientation. To repeat, therefore, what was stated earlier, Bellarmine presents us with some but not all aspects of Counter-Reformation spirituality.

The point can be further illustrated. Also missing in Bellarmine is recourse to scapulars, indulgences, pilgrimages, prescription by the dying person for the life-style of his heirs, and other features that we know figured in the popular imagination even in Bellarmine's day of how best to assure one's own salvation. In their place Bellarmine recommends a rather stern morality that would draw its strength from prayer and the sacraments. A noted historian of the Art of Dying tradition divides works on the subject into two types: works of consolation and works inspired by what he calls "pastoral terrorism," which stressed almost exclusively the horrors of death, judgment, and damnation. Bellarmine's work fits neatly into neither category, but is, instead, a much more detached, more moralistic—less emotional—consideration. It would seem, then, to fit better into the so-called Stoic rather than Augustinian strains in the spiritualities of the period, but it defies facile categorization.

In Catholic spirituality of the late sixteenth and early seventeenth centuries, the Rheno-Flemish mystics like Tauler, Ruysbroeck, and Suso enjoyed renewed favor, even among some Jesuits, but we find no mention of them in Bellarmine. This fact points to earlier controversies within the Society of Jesus about just how the order was to relate to the broader traditions of Christian spirituality. Everard Mercurian, the fourth general of the society (1573–1580), had forbidden the reading of those mystics as alien to the apostolic character of Jesuit life, and we can detect the ongoing effect of that prohibition in Bellarmine's much more methodical and commonsense approach, closer to the ascetic tenor of the *Devotio Moderna* than to the mystics.

The ascetical tradition did not of itself demand the long hours of secluded prayer each day that were seen as central to the mystical tradition and, hence, as inimical to the ministerial engagement required of Jesuits by their vocation. On the other hand, it also did not of itself promote that engagement, as we see clearly from the failure to deal with it in the most celebrated document of the *devotio moderna*, the *Imitation of Christ*, a work specifically commended by Ignatius in the *Exercises.* The genre of the works contained in this volume and the general readership seemingly envisioned for them perhaps precluded much stress on preaching and other ministries that the Jesuits promoted, but its absence also points to the force of more privatized traditions that continued to dominate writings on spirituality even within the Society of Jesus—and even when they avoided the supposed pitfalls of the more mystical tradition. In other words, close reading of Bellarmine's *The Art of Dying Well* verifies just how much variety existed within the spiritualities of the Counter-Reformation, how much continuity existed with earlier traditions, and how important were some of the shifts one observes.

The Mind's Ascent to God perhaps even better illustrates these phenomena. Father Donnelly points out its intended relationship to Saint Bonaventure's work bearing practically the same title, and he also indicates just how Bellarmine modified the genre. The differences are as important as the similarities. The influence of the *Spiritual Exercises* emerges more obviously here than in *The Art of Dying Well*, for the *Ascent* can be considered almost as a long elaboration of the "Contemplation for Obtaining Love," with which the *Exercises* climax and close.

The most striking difference with Bonaventure, however, consists perhaps not so much in divergences in content and progression as it does in style. In that regard especially, the *Ascent* emerges with features peculiar to the specific culture in which Bellarmine lived and worked. Although many of the ideas in the work derive from both the Fathers and the medieval Scholastics like Bonaventure and Aquinas, the style is decidedly different. The impact of the work is thus different.

Viewed formally, the *Ascent* is a work of epideictic rhetoric, that is, of the art of panegyric. The purpose of panegyric is to hold a person or thing up for praise, with the intention of arousing wonder, admiration, and gratitude. That is precisely what Bellarmine does for us in the *Ascent*, as he contemplates the marvels of the created universe and of God himself. We have here, then, a work quite different from *The Art of Dying Well.* Despite obvious dependencies, it is a work quite different, indeed, from Saint Bonaventure's *Journey of the Mind to God.*

Panegyric was revived in Italy in the fifteenth century, but found full and widespread expression only later, especially in Rome during the next two centuries. The Counter-Reformation had a dour side to it, without doubt, but it also had a more exuberant and joy-filled aspect, reflected in much Baroque art and architecture, which by gradually lifting the eyes to the heavens lifted the heart and mind there as well. The rhetoric of Baroque art and the rhetoric of some spiritual writing in the age of the Baroque have an affinity, here exemplified in Bellarmine's treatise. The form is, therefore, as important as the content for understanding the *Ascent* and the effect it has on the reader.

Bellarmine himself took pleasure in this work, more than in others he wrote, as he tells us in his dedicatory letter to Cardinal Aldobrandini. It is not difficult to see why, even at a distance of several hundred years. The *Ascent* articulates a vision of life and religion that sees all reality as friendly and working unto good. As Bellarmine carries on this lengthy dialogue with his soul, his major task is to remind himself that God wills his good more than he does himself and is active in accomplishing it. The panegyric form thus accomplished its purpose of warming the heart and exciting gratitude, wonder, and praise.

The *Ascent* was born in the Counter-Reformation and can be utilized, like its companion piece, to help us better understand it and its spiritualities. At the same time, it can be validly termed a classic, in that some part of its message transcends the limitations of that culture and has meaning for us today. Gratitude, wonder, and praise recur as constants in the spiritual tradition from the psalms to Augustine's *Confessions* to Bellarmine's *Ascent*, which gives them the pecularly eloquent expression that his culture provided.

Introduction

PART ONE
Bellarmine's Life and Works

Roberto Francesco Romulo Bellarmino was born October 4, 1542, at Montepulciano, an ancient hill town in Tuscany; he was the third son among the twelve children of Vincenzo and Cintia Bellarmino. His father was from an impoverished noble family, but his maternal uncle, Cardinal Marcello Cervini, was a respected and beloved reformer who later presided at the Council of Trent and in September 1555 became Pope Marcellus II, although his pontificate lasted less than a month. Robert Bellarmine was a frail but lively lad who quickly excelled in studies, especially in writing Latin and Italian poetry at the local Jesuit college. His father early marked him for a medical career and opposed his son's request to enter the Jesuits; he relented provided that Robert spend a year at home testing his vocation. The Jesuit General Diego Lainez agreed and even promised to count the year toward Bellarmine's novitiate. For a papal nephew rules could be bent.[1]

The year only steeled Robert's resolve, and on September 21, 1560, he entered the Jesuit novitiate at Rome and simultaneously began philosophical studies at the Jesuit Roman College. Three years later he was assigned to teach classics at the Jesuit colleges of Florence and then Mondovì in Piedmont. In 1567 he began theological studies at Padua. Even before his ordination he preached at both Mondovì and Padua; his frailty, small stature, and cherubic features combined with unusual learning made him seem a boy wonder in the pulpit and created a minor sensation. In 1569 he was sent to complete his theological training at Louvain, where he was ordained a priest in 1570.

That same year the Jesuits opened their own theological college at Louvain with Bellarmine as its first professor. He continued teaching there for seven years, a period in which the Low Countries were racked by rebellion and religious war. Louvain was the region's leading Catholic university, and Bellarmine could not help being sucked into the swirling religious controversies. He increasingly devoted his lectures to defending traditional Catholic teaching, recently reaffirmed by the Council of Trent, from the attacks of Luther, Calvin, and other leading Protestant theologians. While at Louvain he prepared for his students a concise Hebrew grammar, which later went through many editions, and a guide to patristic literature, which gradually evolved into his *Ecclesiastical Writers* [De scriptoribus ecclesiasticis].

The pressure under which he was working at Louvain gradually undermined Bellarmine's health, and turmoil and fighting threatened the university itself. In 1576 the Jesuit General Everard Mercurian recalled Bellarmine to Rome and appointed him to a new chair of controversial theology at the Roman College, the most prestigious school of the growing order. Controversial theology was a new subdiscipline aimed at helping the students at the German and the English Colleges in Rome who would be returning to homelands dominated by Protestants. Bellarmine's lectures to these students were outstanding for their learning, clarity, and comprehensiveness. The lectures became the basis of his most important work, *The Controversies* [Disputationes de controversiis Christianae fidei adversus huius temporis haereticos]. The first volume appeared in 1586, the second in 1588, and the third in 1593. *The Controversies* eventually went through twenty editions and long remained Catholicism's most complete answer to the theological issues raised by the Protestant reformers. His defense of Catholic teaching was remarkably free of the mud-slinging that characterized most of the polemics of the period. What is more important, although he was strongly influenced by Thomas Aquinas, Bellarmine gave theology a more historical and less philosophical orientation than the writings of the medieval Scholastics or the books of his contemporaries in the Second Scholasticism, such as Francisco de Toledo, Francisco Suárez, or Domingo Bañez.

During these years at Rome, Bellarmine also became involved in minor controversies over Henry of Navarre's right to succeed to the French throne and over the censure that the University of Louvain had passed against the teaching on grace and predestination of his Jesuit colleague Leonard Lessius. Although the Holy See employed Bellarmine to edit various patristic and liturgical works, his relations with the headstrong Pope Sixtus V were not altogether happy. Sixtus felt that Bellarmine's *Controversies* limited the pope's temporal jurisdiction too much, and he included the work on a new

Index of Forbidden Books that he was drawing up. The pope's death prevented publication of the new Index, and Bellarmine escaped censure. Another project begun by Sixtus V caused him even more problems. The Council of Trent recognized the need for an official edition of the Latin Vulgate Bible but delegated the arduous task of establishing the text to the papacy. Sixtus V took a personal interest in the project and soon began editing the text with a strong but arbitrary hand; no biblical scholar, he made a thorough mess of the job. After his death Bellarmine warned Pope Clement VIII that the revised Vulgate of Sixtus was an embarrassment, even "a very great danger" to the Church. The new pope put Bellarmine in charge of the immense task of correcting the text; Bellarmine's revision was later published as the Sixto-Clementine Vulgate and remained the official Latin Bible of the Catholic Church for more than three centuries.[2]

In 1590 Sixtus V sent Bellarmine to Paris as theological advisor to Cardinal Enrico Gaetani, a special legate to examine the precarious situation of the French Church, which was engulfed in a civil war and badly divided between the Ultra-Catholic Leaguers and the *Politiques* who recognized Henry of Navarre as Henry IV. Bellarmine's autobiography gives a vivid picture of the hardship of the mission, especially of starvation during the siege of Paris by Henry, which again undermined Bellarmine's health.

Returning to Rome, Bellarmine served as spiritual director for the Jesuit students at the Roman College. Among them was Saint Aloysius Gonzaga. In 1592 he was named superior of the 220 Jesuits at the college, but shortly afterward he was sent off to Naples to serve as Jesuit Provincial for three years. In 1597 Clement VIII appointed him his theological advisor, and the same year Bellarmine published his most popular book, his small catechism entitled *Dottrina cristiana breve*. It remained in use for three centuries and, thanks largely to Jesuit missionaries, was translated into sixty-two languages. In 1598 he published a more advanced catechism that also enjoyed great success. He contributed to the drawing up of the *Ratio Studiorum*, the basic regulations that governed hundreds of Jesuit colleges around the world for centuries.

In 1599 Clement VIII named Bellarmine a cardinal and forbade him to resist the elevation. The pope justified his action, which was against the Jesuit rule, with the words, "We have chosen him because the Church of God has not his equal for learning."[3] Bellarmine was quickly assigned to five Congregations (or administrative departments) in the Roman Curia where his erudition would be most useful. For the rest of his life most of his energy was devoted to the paperwork of the Church's central bureaucracy. The most important of the Congregations that Bellarmine helped to administer was the Holy Office, which supervised the Roman Inquisition. This responsibility later involved him in the most unfortunate chapter of his life, the first trial of Galileo Galilei. In 1616 he personally delivered to Galileo the Holy Office's admonition.[4] As the two treatises printed in this volume make clear, to the end of his life Bellarmine clung to a literal interpretation of biblical passages on cosmology and defended an Aristotelian world view.

Central to the Catholic Reformation was a reformed episcopacy. Saint Charles Borromeo, to whose memory Bellarmine was deeply devoted, provided a model for the new reforming bishops by resigning his posts at Rome and taking up residence in Milan; he devoted the rest of his life to preaching to his flock and visiting the outlying parishes of his sprawling archdiocese. As a curial cardinal Bellarmine worked energetically for the appointment of zealous men as bishops and encouraged their work. In 1602, in a surprise move, Clement VIII appointed Bellarmine archbishop of Capua; within a week of his consecration Bellarmine took up residence in his small archdiocese. Happy to leave behind the bustle and paperwork of Rome, he preached the Sunday sermons in his cathedral and visited the city parishes on weekdays. He averaged one visit per year to rural parishes during his three years as archbishop, and worked hard to strengthen religious fervor in the monasteries and convents under his jurisdiction.[5] He was convinced that people with wealth had a duty of sharing their surplus with the poor. As a cardinal in Rome he kept a frugal household and made a point of distributing his surplus income to the poor at the end of every month. In the Naples region where Capua lay, the problem of poverty was even more pressing; it has been estimated that Bellarmine distributed to the poor of his flock half of the 12,000 ducats that his benefices brought him annually. As archbishop and cardinal he refused to enrich his relatives and to accept gifts from princes, since such gifts might seem to limit his freedom in judging cases on their merits and in demanding reforms that he felt were needed.[6]

Two papal elections in 1605 called Bellarmine back to Rome; in the elections he received many votes from reform-minded friends, but he refused to encourage their efforts and his background as a Jesuit and his reputation for austerity worked against his election. The new pope, Paul V, assigned him various duties at the Vatican; faithful to his convictions on episcopal residency, he quickly resigned as archbishop of Capua. Paul V was soon involved in a bitter quarrel with the Venetian Republic, and Bellarmine wrote several pamphlets defending the papal interdict against Venice. Central to the controversy were church-state relations and the extent of papal powers. Bellarmine became engaged in several other controversies on these touchy subjects. Under a pseudonym he attacked the apology that James I of England had written to defend the oath of loyalty that he was demanding of his Catholic subjects. While most of the oath was innocuous, part of it involved a rejection of the papacy and of Catholic doctrine. The king himself wrote a reply, which Bellarmine answered in his own name (1609). James tired of the controversy and arranged for Bishop Lancelot Andrewes to refute Bellarmine. The cardinal was also engaged in a controversy with the Scotch Catholic William Barclay over church-state relations and with the English Benedictine Thomas Preston, who wrote under the pseudonym of Roger Widdrington to defend James I's oath.

The writings of Bellarmine's last years were more spiritual and serene. In 1611 he published a long commentary on the psalms; although it reveals his weaknesses as a Hebrew scholar, it is rich in insight and piety and was widely read. More popular still were the short ascetical works that Bellarmine wrote during his annual retreats between 1614 and 1619, including *The Mind's Ascent to God* and *The Art of Dying Well.*

By this time Bellarmine was in his late seventies and suffering from various illnesses, especially swelling in his legs. He asked Paul V for permission to retire to the Jesuit novitiate of Sant Andrea in Rome so that he could spend his last days in prayer among his brother Jesuits, but the pope considered his services too valuable and urged him to continue his work in the curia. Bellarmine repeated his request when Gregory XV was elected in February of 1621 and received the same response, but by August he had lost his hearing and was allowed to retire to Sant Andrea, where he took up lodging on August 25. Three days later he contracted a fever and gradually grew worse. His dying words on September 17 were, "Jesus, Jesus, Jesus." Pope Pius XI canonized him in 1930.[7]

PART TWO

The Catholic Reformation and Bellarmine's Ascetical Works

The life of Robert Bellarmine largely coincided with the most important years of the Counter-Reformation or Catholic Reformation. Historians sometimes use the two terms interchangeably, but *Counter-Reformation* is best restricted to the Catholic efforts to block or uproot Protestantism while *Catholic Reformation* designates the positive efforts to deepen religious faith and practice among Catholics. Thus the condemnations of the Council of Trent, the establishment of the Roman Inquisition, the Index of Forbidden Books, and the Spanish Armada were typical actions of the Counter-Reformation. Bellarmine's polemical writings, especially the *Controversies*, were clearly a contribution to the Counter-Reformation. The establishment of new religious orders, such as the Capuchins and Jesuits, the reform of older orders, the founding of seminaries and Jesuit colleges, the disciplinary decrees of the Council of Trent, the reformed papacy, the pastoral visitations and diocesan synods of such bishops as Saint Charles Borromeo, and the striking growth of missionary activity in Asia and the Americas were important aspects of the Catholic Reformation. Bellarmine's spiritual writings and his work as archbishop of Capua were contributions to the Catholic Reformation.

The two movements were closely linked in their results and in the minds of reform-minded Catholics. Saint Ignatius Loyola, for example, urged Saint Peter Canisius to send the best students from the Jesuit colleges in Germany out on Sundays and feast days to teach catechism: "Thus, besides the correct doctrine, they would be giving the examples of a good life, and by removing every appearance of greed they will be able to refute the strongest arguments of the heretics—a bad life, namely, and the ignorance of the Catholic clergy."[8]

In the end, the deepening Catholic life was far more important in checking the spread of Protestantism than were repressive measures such as the Inquisition. At Bellarmine's birth the existence of the Roman Catholic Church was in jeopardy. By his death more than two-thirds of Europeans from Ireland to Poland and from Norway to Sicily were Catholics, and the losses to Protestantism in northern Europe had been largely compensated by Catholic growth in mission countries. But the success of the Catholic Reformation was not chiefly a matter of numbers. The tone of Catholic life was generally higher. The seminaries mandated by Trent were painfully slow in arising, but they gradually began to send out priests who were trained in theology so that they could preach to their congregations on a weekly basis, a task that the untrained parish clergy of the Middle Ages had largely left to friars brought in to preach during Advent and Lent. The better seminaries also tried to develop the prayer-life of their students. The late medieval Church had done little to develop effective catechisms until Luther showed their importance. Catholics such as Canisius and Bellarmine wrote catechisms that were widely used for centuries. Medieval Catholic piety had been shot through with pagan residues and superstitions. Gradually these superstitions gave way to the combined attack of the better-trained local clergy and the parish missions that traveling Capuchins and Jesuits, later joined by Vincentians, conducted in the rural areas of Catholic Europe. It would be hard to overestimate the impact of these missions, which resembled Protestant revivalism in nineteenth-century America, since most Europeans were still peasants living in small villages. Jean Delumeau has gone so far as to argue that the relics of paganism were so strong in rural areas that most medieval peasants were only superficially Christian and that the real Christianization of the countryside had to await the trained clergy, the printed catechisms, and the parish missions of the Protestant and Catholic reformations.[9]

Hardly less important in Catholic efforts at reform was the growth of systematic meditation and mental prayer. Just as the two spiritual treatises printed in this volume look back to medieval sources, so the growth of meditation in the Catholic Reformation has medieval roots, especially in the *devotio moderna* among the Brethren of Common Life. Late medieval writers, especially Florent Redewijns, Gerard of Zutphen, and Jan Mombaer, laid out in an orderly way various methods of mental prayer. Bellarmine, who taught at Louvain, could not have been unaware of this Netherlandish spirituality. Similar ideas were popularized in Spain by the *Ejercitatorio de la Vida Espiritual* of Abbot Garcia Cisneros, whose influence on *The Spiritual Exercises* of Ignatius of Loyola is still debated by specialists.[10] Loyola's little book did more than any other to spread several techniques by systematic meditation and was the fountainhead of the

Jesuit spirituality in which Bellarmine was trained. In 1609 two books appeared that became classic works of Catholic piety and enjoyed hundreds of editions in many languages. The shorter but greater work was St. Francis de Sales's *The Introduction to the Devout Life*. The other was Alfonso Rodriguez's *The Practice of Perfection and the Christian Virtues*. Like Bellarmine in his spiritual writings, both of these authors were writing for serious Christians but avoided a discussion of mysticism. Saint Ignatius Loyola had not obliged the Jesuits to a fixed time for meditation, but the third Jesuit General, Saint Francis Borgia, made an hour of meditation compulsory. Several other orders introduced similar legislation, and the new seminaries tried to inculcate the practice in their students. Perhaps the best indication of the immense appetite of the seventeenth-century Catholics for systematic meditation was the enormous popularity enjoyed by the Jesuit Luis de la Puente's *Meditations on the Mysteries of Our Holy Faith* (1605), whose two hefty volumes were reprinted more than seven hundred times. Obviously the vogue was not confined to monasteries and convents. Nor was it confined to Catholics. Louis Martz, the distinguished scholar of seventeenth-century literature, has argued that these meditation manuals exerted a noteworthy influence on Protestant poets in England.[11]

The practice of meditation described in these manuals, the sermons of the period, and spiritual treatises, such as the two by Bellarmine in this volume, run so closely parallel that passages from one or the other are difficult or impossible to distinguish either in content or presentation. Parts of Bellarmine's *The Mind's Ascent to God* develop ideas that Bellarmine had presented many years earlier in his sermons to young Jesuits at the Roman College. Doubtless these sermons served his hearers as "points" or material for their meditations. All five of Bellarmine's ascetical works were produced in his free time while he was making the meditations of the *Spiritual Exercises*.

In 1607 a General Congregation of the Jesuit Order required all members to make an annual retreat of eight or ten days based on the *Spiritual Exercises* of Saint Ignatius Loyola. Toward the end of his life Bellarmine was accustomed to retire to Sant Andrea, to make his annual retreat, and get a month's rest from his duties during September and October. It was the only vacation that he allowed himself, and he enjoyed exchanging his cardinal's robes for a simple cassock and returning to the routine of Jesuit life. He forbade the superior of the house to make special arrangements for him. Gradually he stretched his retreat until it covered the whole month of his vacation. During September of 1614 he wrote *The Mind's Ascent to God.* In the dedicatory letter he wrote to his friend Cardinal Pietro Aldobrandini and added to the first edition, Bellarmine confessed that he had originally written the *Ascent* for his own use but that he had shown it to friends who urged him to publish it.[12] He agreed, doubtless encouraged by the success of his *Commentary on the Psalms,* whose devotional tone much resembles *The Mind's Ascent to God.* He begged Aldobrandini to "accept this little gift from me . . . a second Benjamin which I have begotten in my extreme old age."[13]

The distinguished Plantin publishing house in Antwerp issued the first edition of the *Ascent* in 1615, but there were five other Latin editions that same year plus an Italian translation by Bellarmine's nephew, Angelo della Ciana. The success was not short-lived; prior to the author's canonization in 1930 there were a total of sixty editions in fifteen different languages (Latin, Italian, English, French, German, Spanish, Flemish, Greek, Hungarian, Slovene, Portuguese, Russian, Czech, Chinese, and Korean). Bellarmine's most distinguished translator was Duke William V of Bavaria. The first English translation appeared in 1616; to mislead government agents the title page gave the translator as T.B., Gentleman, and the place of publication as Douai. In fact it was published by a secret Catholic press in England and the translator was Francis Young. A Protestant translation by Anthony Walker appeared at London in 1703; the translator assured his readers that he had supressed a few passages because of their Romish ring. In fact, there is very little in the *Ascent* that is not the heritage of Protestants as well as Catholics. There was a second Protestant translation by H. Halb published at London in 1703 and a Catholic one by John Dalton in 1844. Far better is the translation published in 1925 at London by an Anglican nun who out of humility signs herself only as *Monialis* (a nun).[14]

The reception of Bellarmine's *Ascent* cannot be measured merely by the number of editions and translations. He was a severe judge of his own work, but he wrote to Pietro Aldobrandini, "I do not read my other books unless I am forced to; this one [the *Ascent*] I have already spontaneously read three or four times, and I have resolved to reread it frequently in the future." The Jesuit poet Mathias Casimir Sarbiewski (1595–1640), rather pompously known as the Polish Horace, wrote a Latin poem extolling the *Ascent.*[15] Another Latin poem came from the pen of Cardinal Maffeo Barbarini, later Urban VIII, who exhorts Christians, "Put away the cares of your soul and direct the pure light of your mind where Bellarmine casts out darkness and reveals a ladder of all creation whose steps mount up to the stars."[16] Pierre Pourrat, the historian of spirituality, hailed the *Ascent* as Bellarmine's most beautiful spiritual work, "wherein his optimistic piety, overflowing with divine love, is best made manifest."[17] Emmerich Raitz von Frentz described it as a "golden book . . . that merits being read again today by all those who love to walk in God's presence."[18] This chorus of praise should be balanced by a critical comment. In his classic *The Great Chain of Being*, Arthur O. Lovejoy finds the *Ascent* "the most celebrated modern elaboration" of the mind's upward movement along the chain of being to the One and commends Bellarmine for avoiding the harshness of Saint Bernard and the extreme contempt of creation encouraged by Saint John of the Cross, but he concludes that for Bellarmine too creatures mainly serve "to remind us of their transiency and insufficiency, or to serve as sensible symbols . . . of deity" so that in the end his ladder "is, after all, only another name for a progressive *contemptus mundi.*"[19]

Bellarmine called the *Ascent* his Benjamin, considering it the child of his old age and his last book, but encouraged by its success he wrote similar books during his retreats of 1615, 1616, 1617, and 1619 so that Benjamin turned out to have four younger brothers. Each book was published the year after its composition.

The second of Bellarmine's five ascetical works was *The Eternal Happiness of the Saints* [De perpetua felicitate sanctorum]. In the preface he outlines the basic structure of the work, which is a series of meditations on twelve scriptural terms for heaven. Four are places: a kingdom, a city, a home, and paradise. Six are taken from Christ's parables in the Gospels: a treasure hidden in a field, a precious pearl, a daily wage, the joy of the Lord, a great banquet, and a royal wedding. Two are taken from Saint Paul: a prize won in a race and a crown. He enriches his reflection on these terms with other passages drawn from the Bible and the Church Fathers, especially Saints Augustine and John Chysostom. This is the most biblical of the five books; in the other works his use of the Bible tends to be ornamental rather than structural.[20]

During his retreat of 1616 Bellarmine wrote *The Mourning of the Dove, or the Value of Tears* [De Gemitu columbae sive de bono lachrymarum]. This book too remained popular throughout the seventeenth century and has appeared in forty-one editions in seven languages. Unlike its brothers, it has never been translated into English, but it became a favorite book of Bellarmine's old antagonist, James I, and of Saint Francis de Sales, who praised it highly. The Lutheran pastor Michael Walther wrote a paraphrase entitled *The Mourning of a Lutheran Dove* [Gemitus Lutheranae columbulae, Hamburg, 1635]. Bellarmine's somber reflections on sin, hell, the persecution of the Church, the sins of the clergy, the miseries of life, and the uncertainty of salvation fitted well with the turmoil of Germany during the Thirty Years' War and with the harshness of life generally in the seventeenth century. Of the five works it is the most dated and least attractive.[21]

The next year Bellarmine wrote *The Seven Words Uttered by Christ on the Cross* [De Septem verbis a Christo in cruce prolatis]. The work enjoyed considerable success with thirty-five editions in nine languages. A series of meditations on Christ's last words on earth, it served Catholic priests for centuries as a quarry for their sermons at Good Friday services.[22]

The book that Bellarmine wrote during his retreat in 1618 does not fit well with the other five although it was written in a popular Renaissance literary genre, the mirror of princes. The Polish Jesuits begged Bellarmine to write a short work of instruction for Prince Ladislas, heir to the Polish throne. He compiled *The Duty of the Christian Prince* [De officio principis christiani] in three books. The first book pulls together passages from scripture and the Church Fathers that teach the virtues and duties of a devout prince toward God, the clergy, his people, and other rulers. The second book takes up biblical leaders, such as Moses and David, to illustrate the themes developed in the first book. The third book does the same with rulers, such as Saints Wenceslaus, Stephan, Edward the Confessor, and Louis IX. The work had restricted interest, and there were only nine editions aside from those printed in Bellarmine's complete works.[23]

During his retreat of 1619 Bellarmine wrote his last work, *The Art of Dying Well* [De arte bene moriendi]. In 1620 deteriorating health prevented him from continuing the series. His thoughts in 1619 were increasingly on his approaching death. *The Art of Dying Well* proved the most popular of the series except for the *Ascent*. It enjoyed fifty-six editions and has been translated into French, Italian, German, Spanish, English, Flemish, Polish, Hungarian, Dutch, and

Czech. In sending a copy to the English convert Sir Tobie Matthew in 1620, Cardinal Bentivoglio, the Nuncio to Paris, admitted that for the most part Spanish spiritual writers were preeminent, but with Bellarmine's little book Italy had produced a rival.[24] The English Jesuit Edward Coffin published a translation at St. Omers in 1621. There was also a Protestant translation in 1720 by John Ball, who dropped "Romish innovations." Bellarmine's book was attacked from a rather different quarter. Hyacinth Petronio, O.P., the Master of the Sacred Palace or official theologian of the pope, objected that Bellarmine's claim that the rich must give all their superfluous wealth to the poor was too rigorous. Perhaps to forestall such objections Bellarmine had buttressed his claim with quotations from the Church Fathers. He avoided the thorny question of whether this was an obligation out of justice or out of charity, observing that it made little difference whether one was condemned to hell for a lack of justice or a lack of charity.[25]

All five works are similar in style and almost identical in length. Bellarmine must have written them very quickly, at a rate of about seven normal modern-sized pages per day, but he was known throughout his life for industriousness and a prodigious memory, and his five works drew on a lifetime of meditation and preaching. Phrases, sentences, and ideas from sermons he had written more than thirty years earlier crop up in the works, but comparison with the sermons suggests that he was drawing on memory rather than lifting passages verbatim from his sermons.[26] Indeed he drew on the sermons less than one might expect. Many of the citations in these works seem also to have been made from memory. We know that he made use of the library at Sant Andrea while he was making his retreats, but there is a carelessness in citation that he would have avoided in a work of controversial theology when enemies would stand ready to pounce on any slip.[27]

If these five books were not written for theologians, what audience did Bellarmine have in mind? In the dedicatory letter to the *Ascent* he told Cardinal Aldorandini, "If some value can be found in my labors, it will be mainly useful for men engaged in public affairs, especially the Princes of the Church." In the Introduction of the same work Bellarmine urged that all Christians have a duty to seek God but the duty is greater for bishops. The immediate success of the five ascetical works (there were at least five editions of each in the first year of its publication) plus the translations that appeared almost immediately must have alerted Bellarmine that he was reaching a far larger audience than bishops and men of affairs. Indeed there is almost nothing in the *Ascent* that is not suitable for any educated, serious Christian man or woman. Several passages in *The Art of Dying Well* indicate that it was written for Christians in all walks of life.

Since Bellarmine wrote his five ascetical works while making an annual retreat according to the *Spiritual Exercises* of Saint Ignatius Loyola, readers might expect a massive influence of the Exercises on his books, but the influence is more often subtle than obvious.[28] At the start of the Exercises Loyola places a prologue entitled Principle and Foundation, in which he teaches those making the Exercises to use creatures "to praise, reverence and serve God our Lord" and thereby to save their souls. Only once does Bellarmine's *Ascent* use phrases that clearly recall this passage from Loyola, but the spiritual atmosphere of the Principle and Foundation pervades the *Ascent*. More important for the *Ascent* is the last and crowning meditation in the Exercises, the Contemplation for Attaining Love, in which Loyola has retreatants reflect on how God dwells in creatures, how he works and labors on our behalf in all created things, and how all good things and gifts descend from God so that created justice, mercy, and other virtues are like rays descending from the sun or waters from a fountain. The influence of the Exercises is perhaps even less clear in Bellarmine's other four works. The third week of the Exercises is devoted to the passion of Christ, and the seven last words of Christ would form part of the meditation material assigned by Loyola for the fifth day. He does not assign the happiness of the saints as a subject for a meditation, but many directors did include it in the Exercises of the fourth week, which centered on Christ's resurrection. Loyola included a meditation on hell in the first week of the Exercises, and other directors often added one on death. These may have influenced Bellarmine's *The Art of Dying Well*, but only in a general way.

If specific meditations from Loyola's Exercises were only of secondary importance for Bellarmine's ascetical works, the Exercises influenced their composition in an important but indirect way. Loyola teaches several methods of prayer, one of which employs the three powers of the soul—memory, intellect, and will—to reflect on religious truths. Loyola develops this method most clearly in his meditation on sin. Another method of prayer advocated by Loyola is the application of the senses; thus in his meditation on hell he tells retreatants to see the great fires of hell, to hear the wailings and blasphemies of the damned, to smell the brimstone and filth, to taste the tears and sadness of the damned, and to feel how the fires touch and burn the soul.

Bellarmine's personal prayer and piety were shaped by the currents of Catholic Reformation spirituality. Certainly his sermons and his five ascetical works reflect this common fund of ideas and attitudes. This Introduction has repeatedly described his five books as ascetical works. Bellarmine's lifetime was a golden age of Catholic mysticism, especially in Spain, but there are few passages in Bellarmine's books that have a mystical tone and none that pretend to give guidance in mystical prayer. Indeed the divisions of the premystical stages of prayer into purgative, illuminative, and unitive ways that figure so prominently in the writings of Bellarmine's Jesuit contemporary Achille Gagliardi play little role in his writings. Like Saint Francis de Sales in *The Introduction to the Devout Life*, Bellarmine is writing for ordinary serious Christians, not for those on advanced levels of prayer. This orientation largely explains his stress on reason and imagination in these works. Although some passages take on an emotional glow, his appeal is more to the head than to the heart. Bellarmine can lay out reasons for us to weigh or sketch images to stir our imagination. He can reason with us, he can teach us why we should love God and our fellow men and women for God's sake, but he cannot feel for us nor elicit acts of love for us. At his prie-dieu he was a saint, but at his writing desk he remained the theologian and rhetorician, the disciple of Aquinas and Quintillian.

PART THREE

Bellarmine's *Ascent* and the Ladder of Ascent Tradition

The thought world that Bellarmine inherited tended to conceptualize God as above and men and women as living below him without, of course, denying that God was also somehow within. The belief that to reach God humans had to climb upward using some sort of ladder is very old, going back before either Christianity or Judaism.

INTRODUCTION

The ladder to God was known among the Egyptians, while the Babylonians gave it striking expression in the building of ziggurats. In China both Confucian and Taoist texts speak of stages of growth and climbing toward perfection. The ladder of salvation was not unknown in the religions of India. Among the Greeks the image of a ladder of ascent toward perfection, often coupled with steps or stages of human development or a graded system of created reality leading to the One or the Ultimate, is found in Pindar and Plato and reached its full development in Plotinus.

The word *ladder* (*sullam* in Hebrew or *climax* in Greek) is found only once in the Bible: Jacob "saw in his sleep a ladder upon the earth and the top thereof touching heaven and the angels of God ascending and descending by it" (Gn 28:12). That single biblical reference to a ladder of ascending to God was often combined with biblical references to stairs, for instance, the six steps of Solomon's throne (1 Kgs 10:19) or the steps leading to Solomon's temple (Ez 40:26, 31). There are also many biblical passages that conceptualize God as above the earth in the heavens, an idea that could easily be combined with the image of steps or a ladder. From these combinations of biblical passages an extremely rich spiritual literature sprang forth. In their article on the spiritual ladder tradition Émile Bertaud and André Rayez discuss more than one hundred Christian authors from the early patristic period to the present who wrote treatises, books, or poems on the subject.[29] Two works in this tradition, *The Ladder of Divine Ascent* by Saint John Climacus and *The Mind's Journey to God* by Saint Bonaventure, have already appeared in the Classics of Western Spirituality.

Bellarmine's title for his book, *The Mind's Ascent to God by the Ladder of Created Things* [De Ascensione mentis in Deum per scalas rerum creatarum], presents a number of difficulties. In his Introduction to the book he states that he had taken Saint Bonaventure's *Itinerarium mentis in Deum* as a model. His title deliberately echoes that of Bonaventure, but substitutes the image of an ascent for that of a journey. At first glance Bellarmine's use of *mind* in his title seems a bit inappropriate, since he seldom uses the term in his text. Rather he is constantly dialoguing with his soul (*anima*), which seems a richer and more Christian term, since it includes both mind and will and implies the whole human person after death, at least until the general resurrection. His choice of *mind* rather than *soul* clearly flows from his desire to honor Bonaventure's work. The use of mind is also appropriate for another reason, although one that Bellarmine might repudiate: His *Ascent* is a "mind trip" in which reason and imagination play a greater role than will and emotion. Modern readers may find a certain intellectualism the least attractive side of his spirituality. Following previous translations, this one translates *scalas* in Bellarmine's title and text as "ladder," but the word in both Latin and Italian can equally mean "stairs" or even "staircase," a meaning still clear in English when we speak of musical scales. Sometimes the terminology that Bellarmine uses with *scalas* (e.g., "primum gradum construximus") suggests that he has stairs rather than mere rungs on a ladder in mind. The final difficulty with his title is that his is to be a ladder of created things. This is accurate enough for the first nine steps (material creation, the human soul, and the angels), but the terminology breaks down in the last six steps, which deal with God's essence, power, wisdom, mercy, and justice.

Bellarmine's ladder or staircase of ascent to God has 15 steps; each step has between four and ten short chapters. In his Introduction he tells us that his ladder has fifteen steps after the pattern of the 15 steps in Solomon's temple (Ez 40:26, 31) and the 15 Psalms (Psalms 120–134) known as the Gradual or Step Psalms, which were among his favorite prayers. In his *Commentary of the Psalms* he gives several explanations of why they were called Gradual Psalms (a point still in dispute among exegetes), but concludes that whether the ascent "originally referred to the return of the Jews from Babylon to Jerusalem or the progress of pilgrims up the steps of Solomon's Temple, they were meant to typify the progress of elect souls who by the steps of the ladder of perfection, and especially the step of charity, ascend from this valley of tears to the heavenly Jerusalem."[30] Among the many authors who wrote books on the ladder of ascent to God, the number of steps varied enormously, from 3 to 190. Twelve was a particularly popular number, but among authors whom Bellarmine knew, Saint John Climacus had 30, Saint Bernard had 12, and Saint Bonaventure had 7. Among those who like Bellarmine had 15 were Saint Hilary of Poitiers, Saint Bruno, and Desmarets de Saint-Sorlin (+1676).[31] Obviously the number was fairly arbitrary, and a biblical pedigree could be found for many different choices.

The first step in Bellarmine's ladder deals with the microcosm, man or the self, since nothing is nearer to humans than themselves.

He proceeds to examine the self according to the four Aristotelian causes: the efficent cause is God, the material cause is nothingness, the formal cause is the image of God, the intrinsic final cause is the beatific vision, and the extrinsic final cause is the person's salvation. The second step examines the macrocosm or the greater world outside the self. The greatness, number, variety, power, and beauty of creatures in the macrocosm show forth the greatness, perfection, goodness, omnipotence, and beauty of God their Creator.

Bellarmine's next four steps are related. Ancient cosmology going back to the pre-Socratics, especially Empedocles, divided the world into four basic elements: earth, water, air, and fire. Bellarmine takes up each of these four in turn and tries to find in each reflections of God. Thus earth provides footing and safe ground for us to stand on, but our minds find rest and safe-grounding in God alone. It is the power of God that causes the earth to produce its fruits and nourish our bodies. The riches of the earth, its precious metals and jewels, are mere shadows of the good things God has in store for his elect. The second element, water, also proves rich in reflecting the goodness of God, who cleanses our sins or spiritual stains, who quenches the flames of evil desires, who assuages our thirst. Bellarmine also devotes four chapters to comparing God to a fountain of grace, being, life, and wisdom. Air is the third element and surrounds us and gives us life, breath, and a means of hearing and speaking; God does the same for our inner life, so that air proves an apt image for God's sweetness and kindness. Because it both destroys and enhances material creation, the fourth element, fire, reflects God, whose hatred for sin is a consuming fire. Just as fire purifies precious metals and brightens iron by making it glow and grow soft, so God by his grace purifies and softens the human heart.

To the earlier tradition of four elements Aristotle and others added a fifth element, which makes up the heavenly bodies. Bellarmine's Step Seven ruminates on the sun, whose lofty place and beauty reflect the Creator; its light and heat are an image of divine wisdom and charity in our minds and hearts. The moon by its subjection to the sun teaches us our relationship to God and by its phases suggests the varying action of divine grace and consolation in our souls. Bellarmine also draws on the order of the stars and the harmony of the spheres to illustrate the joy and order of the city of God, where saints and angels join in singing an endless alleluia to God. The whole of Step Seven is a meditation on David's exclamation (Ps 19:1), "The heavens declare the glory of God and the firmament shows his handiwork." Later Bellarmine briefly compares God to a clockmaker—a simile much developed in the eighteenth century—but his reflections on nature are not a theodicy;[32] rather they assume the existence and attributes of the biblical Creator and go on from there to attempt to stir our admiration and love.

After reviewing Steps One to Seven it is difficult to agree with Lovejoy's contention that Bellarmine's ladder is "after all only another name for a progressive *contemptus mundi.*"[33] By showing how creation reflects the Creator, he has not devalued nature but rather transvalued it. More convincing than Lovejoy are the comments of another philosopher, Paul Kuntz: "Bellarmine starts from delight in the beauty of earth. He shows no contempt for matter when he talks of earth, water, air and fire. There may be a few passages that sound Manichean, but they are very rare and minor. The world has a rich variety of forms and a plenitudinous creation is appropriate to a plenitudinous Creator."[34]

Higher than material creatures are spiritual creatures, the human soul and the angels. To these Bellarmine devotes Steps Eight and Nine. This seems at first sight a breakdown in Bellarmine's orderly ascent, since he has already considered the human soul as the microcosm in Step One, but Bellarmine was a man of the Baroque age, developing anew a schema largely worked out by medieval theologians such as Bonaventure. As Paul Kuntz notes, "In Baroque the fixed number of levels melts into fluidity. If God is above, he also descends. If man is below, he also rises."[35] God is above the angels but becomes man. Bellarmine argues that in the order of grace, which is more important than the order of nature, not only the humanity of Christ and the Virgin Mary, but also many humans will rank higher than many angels.[36] Bellarmine's treatment of the human soul develops a comparison and contrast between its powers and characteristics and those of God that show both the dignity of human nature and its lowliness in comparison with God. Step Nine carries the same comparison over to the angels, then reflects on the graces conferred on the angels and on their duties.

Steps Ten through Fifteen leave created reality and consider God himself. Bellarmine bases all six steps on two verses from the Letter to the Ephesians (3:18, 19): "May you be able to understand with all the saints what is the breadth and length and height and depth and to know Christ's love which surpasses knowledge." This had been a favorite text among the Church Fathers from Saint Irenaeus onward, but Bellarmine draws his inspiration mainly from Saint Bernard's application of breadth and length and height and depth to God in Book 5, chapter 13, of his *De Consideratione*.[37] Bellarmine's application is much more elaborate than Bernard's since it runs through six steps and thirty-three chapters. First he applies the four dimensions in discussing the divine essence, especially as the efficient and final cause of all creatures. He then applies the four dimensions to enrich our understanding of God's power. Two steps use the same *topos* to explore God's wisdom. Next Bellarmine turns to the width, length, height, and depth of God's mercy. The final step deals with God's justice, for example, its height in conferring the reward of heaven and its depth in imposing everlasting punishment.[38]

Generally Bellarmine is more successful in the earlier steps, which deal with the elements, than he is in the last six devoted to the divine essence and attributes. His appreciation of nature and his rhetorical skill in developing vivid but unexpected similarities between the qualities of earth, water, air, and fire and aspects of God's nature and activity are much in evidence. In the last six steps the subject matter is more abstract, but Bellarmine's gift for clear writing does not desert him; at his worst he remains a skillful theologian, and his treatment of the divine attributes bears comparison with any popular contemporary explanation of this difficult subject matter.

The sixfold application of the *topos* of breadth, length, height, and depth may strike the reader as a bit mechanical, but it carries two advantages. It obviously adds to the orderly structure of the book. More important, it shatters the cosmological image that views man on earth as the center from which one rises upward and outward to God whose heaven lies in the outermost sphere—an image that has structured much of the book—and replaces it with the image of the world shot through by God's essence and attributes in height and depth, length and breadth. This correction of one image by another makes it clear that Bellarmine's God is not to be pictured as "out there," without also being thought of as everywhere and especially within. It also suggests that Bellarmine may have been less committed to a Ptolemaic world view than seems indicated by his spiritual writing, which was, as he often tells his reader, not intended as a learned treatise. The use of one image to correct another allows the reader to see that the Creator is at once infinitely above his creatures and yet utterly penetrates all the dimensions of created reality. He penetrates all things not only by his omnipresence, omnipotence, and omniscience in creation and conservation in the order of nature, but also by his infinite wisdom, mercy, and justice, which accompany, guide, and lift us on our ascent in the order of grace until we achieve everlasting union with the Lord, who is no remote God of philosophy but *Deus noster*, God with us, more interior to us than we are to ourselves.

Throughout the *Ascent* Bellarmine's philosophical and theological viewpoint comes chiefly from Aristotle and Aquinas, but his exposition owes little to medieval Scholasticism and much to Renaissance rhetoric and humanist theology. The authorities and authors cited are overwhelmingly the Bible and the Church Fathers. This would have pleased Erasmus. There are many rhetorical questions and frequent exhortations by the author to his soul. Compared with the *Ladder of Divine Ascent* of Saint John Climacus, Bellarmine's *Ascent* lacks colorful anecdotes and earthy aphorisms, but it is more tightly organized and deeper in its theology, although perhaps not in its spiritual psychology. Bellarmine's gift for clear, orderly prose makes him easy to read so that one rarely feels a need to go back and reread a paragraph, but this no more indicates superficiality than obscurity implies profundity.

The spiritual literature on the ladder of ascent to God breaks mainly into two unequal parts. Most ladders deal with the ascent of the soul through various levels of a person's development either in a specific virtue or in the spiritual life as a whole. Three good examples from three different eras of church history are *The Ladder of Divine Ascent* by John Climacus, *The Scale of Perfection* by Walter Hilton, and *The Ascent of Mount Carmel* by Saint John of the Cross. Far fewer are the cosmological ladders such as Bellarmine's *Ascent*. A recent modern example is Gustave Thibon's *L'échelle de Jacob* (Lyon, 1942), which sees the universe as a hierarchy of beings in which each contributes according to its degree to God's glory. The most influential cosmological ladder is clearly Saint Bonaventure's *Itinerarium Mentis in Deum*. As has been indicated earlier, Bellarmine acknowledged that his book was inspired by Bonaventure's work.[39] The *Itinerarium* has only seven steps; two deal with God's vestiges in the material world, one with the natural powers of the human soul, one with the gifts of grace, and two with God's being and goodness.

Bonaventure's seventh and last section has no parallel in Bellarmine. Bonaventure combined his cosmological ladder with degrees of individual spiritual development; his last chapter or step, therefore, deals with mystical ecstasy and the soul's union with God. Several times Bellarmine's *Ascent* approaches the subject of mystical graces and prayer, but each time he turns aside with a statement such as that in his Introduction:

> For us mortal men it seems that no ladder of ascent to God can lie open except through the works of God. Those who by a singular gift of God are admitted to paradise by a different road and hear mysteries of God which it is not lawful for man to utter are better said not to have ascended, but to have been carried up. Blessed Paul openly admits this of himself when he says, "I was carried up to paradise" and I heard "hidden words which it is not lawful for man to utter" (2 Cor 12:4).

There seem to be several reasons why Bellarmine declined to discuss mystical graces. Unlike Bonaventure's book, Bellarmine's *Ascent* makes little effort to dovetail the stages of individual spiritual development with the steps of ascent from the earthly elements, heavenly bodies, and spiritual creatures to the Creator and his attributes. Moreover, Bellarmine was writing for less advanced souls than was Bonaventure, so a treatment of mystical ecstasy may have seemed superfluous. Finally Bellarmine may have shared the uneasiness about mystical prayer that was abroad in Catholic Reformation Rome, not least in Bellarmine's own Jesuit order.[40]

PART FOUR

Bellarmine and the Art of Dying

During the middle years of the twentieth century most Americans tried to pretend that death did not exist. Their futile efforts to ignore or hide the only certain thing in life struck visitors to this country and evoked satirical responses such as Evelyn Waugh's *The Loved One* or Jessica Mitford's *The American Way of Death*. In the late twentieth century this has changed. There are more elderly people among us, our youth broods on nuclear disaster, and college students flock to courses on the psychology of death and dying. Major popular presses turn out distinguished works such as Elisabeth Kübler-Ross's *On Death and Dying* and Philippe Aries's *The Hour of Our Death*. Studies by anthropologists and folklorists on funeral rites and attitudes toward death in primitive and peasant societies have contributed greatly to renewed interest in thanatology. It is then appropriate that the Classics in Western Spirituality contain an example of the literary-spiritual genre, the Art of Dying, that was enormously popular from the fifteenth through the eighteenth centuries.[41]

A growing pessimism and an increased interest in death can be traced to the catastrophes of the mid-fourteenth century, especially the repeated outbreaks of the Black Death and the beginning of the Hundred Years' War, but as a distinct literary genre the Art of Dying began with two writers in the early fifteenth century. One was the famous Chancellor of the University of Paris, Jean Gerson. The third part of his *Opus Tripartitum* (c. 1408), entitled *The Art of Dying* [De arte bene moriendi], pioneered many elements of the later tradition. Even more influential was an anonymous writer whose work went under many similar titles: *Ars moriendi*, *Ars bene moriendi*, *Speculum artis bene moriendi*, and *Tractatus de arte bene moriendi*. It is found in a longer and shorter version. Scholars do not agree about which version was first or on who wrote the book, but there is no dispute about its popularity.

The anonymous *Art of Dying* exists in more than three hundred manuscripts, and there were more than one hundred printed editions before 1500.[42] Thereafter its direct popularity waned, but it continued to influence later writers, not least Saint Robert Bellarmine. The short version especially was frequently illustrated with woodcuts. The finest set of illustrations, which are quite different from the well-known contemporary series on the Dance of Death, is found in the editions by the famous Parisian publisher Antoine Vérard (1493, 1496, 1498); these editions also exemplify how translators and editors did not hesitate to make their own additions to the anonymous *Art of Dying*. The Vérard editions also have a new title, *The Art of Living Well and Dying Well*, which nicely indicates the nature of the additions.[43] Many later editions went much further in this direction. The evolution of the genre is clearly toward prefixing a section on the art of living well to the older art of dying well. A good example is the *Waye of Dyenge Well* (1530) by the English humanist Thomas Lupset, whose first paragraph justifies his expansions with a quotation from Saint Augustine, "If you have lived well, you cannot die badly."[44] Without repeating Augustine verbatim, the first paragraph in Bellarmine's *The Art of Dying Well* seems to be playing with Augustine's statement. Bellarmine's work is divided into two books, one on the art of living well and the other on the immediate preparation for a good death. According to Roger Chartier, Bellarmine's work represents the final stage of the evolution of the Art of Dying genre toward a "humanist exaltation of the dignity of man and a Christian insistence on the necessity to live well in order to die well."[45]

The Art of Dying genre was undoubtedly a characteristic product of the waning Middle Ages, and it might seem that it should disappear with the emergence of Renaissance humanism and the new theological concerns of the Protestant and Catholic reformations. That in fact the genre continued not only to flourish but also to grow in popularity stems from two major factors. One was the concern with personal sin that typified the five centuries from the thirteenth to the eighteenth centuries. One of the greatest historians of early modern Europe, Jean Delumeau, has claimed, "No civilization has accorded so much importance—or value—to guilt and shame as the West from the thirteenth to the eighteenth century."[46] One evidence that he employs to support this claim is the Art of Dying literature.[47] The second factor in the genre's continued popularity is the care that humanists and both Protestant and Catholic theologians took to enrich the medieval tradition with new literary techniques and religious insights so that it continued to answer the tastes and needs of changing times. In this regard we have already noted the humanist Thomas Lupset, but he was a minor figure. The great Erasmus produced two works in the genre: *Declamation on Death* [De morte declamatio, 1517?] and *On the Preparation for Death* [De preparatione ad mortem, 1533]. His second work comes closer to the medieval tradition. His friend Thomas More likewise wrote the *Four Last Things* in 1522 but left it unpublished; his greatest English work, the *Dialogue of Comfort* (1534), which he wrote in prison awaiting execution, also reflects the Art of Dying tradition.[48]

Protestants took up the tradition as early as Luther's *Sermon on Preparation for Dying* [Sermon von Bereitung zum Sterben, 1519].[49] English Protestantism was rich in works of this kind. One of the earliest and most popular was Thomas Becon's *Sicke Mannes Salve* (1561). Becon's book not only teaches a strongly Calvinist doctrine of salvation but goes out of its way to denounce Romish errors.[50] In contrast, Bellarmine's *Art of Dying Well* is clearly the product of Tridentine orthodoxy and contains passages concerning the sacraments with which Protestants will not agree, but it is not overtly polemical. Far less known than Becon's work was *The Treatise on Death* (1579), which the Bible translator Myles Coverdale largely borrowed from the German Protestant Otto Werdmueller.[51] During the seventeenth century three of England's most attractive religious writers produced handbooks to prepare Christians for death. The earliest (sometime before 1626) was Bishop Lancelot Andrewes's *Manual of Directions for the Sick*.[52] Richard Baxter's *Treatise of Death* (1672) and his great work, *The Saint's Everlasting Rest* (1650) are less dependent on the medieval tradition.[53] Beyond question the best English work on the Art of Dying is Jeremy Taylor's *The Rule and Exercises of Holy Dying* (1651), a sequel to his *The Rule and Exercise of Holy Living* (1650). His two works parallel Book I and Book II of Bellarmine's *Art of Dying Well*. Although Taylor tried to move away from the medieval tradition, a close comparison reveals many similarities. His treatise surpasses Bellarmine's or any other on the Art of Dying in the richness of its sonorous prose. Even today Taylor merits reading by three distinct audiences: historians of religious mentalities, connoisseurs of English style, and Christians seeking edification and consolation.[54]

Rich as was the English Protestant tradition in this literary-spiritual genre—and we have noted only the greatest works—the Roman Catholic tradition was richer still, partly because it was more international.[55] Delumeau speaks of a "devout invasion" and notes 130 books on preparation for death published in France alone in the century 1625–1724.[56] No group contributed so much to this flood of literature as the Jesuits. Between their establishment in 1540 and 1700 the Jesuits wrote 159 different titles in the Art of Dying tradition. Among the earliest works was that by Ignatius Loyola's secretary Juan Polanco; his *Method for Helping the Dying* [Methodus ad eos adiuvandos qui moriuntur, 1582] went through several editions.[57] The greatest of all these works by Jesuits was Bellarmine's *Art of Dying Well*.

Bellarmine's work is divided into two books. Book I has sixteen chapters and deals with the remote preparation for death, which is leading a good life. Book II has seventeen chapters and takes up the immediate preparation for death.

Each chapter in Book I examines a rule for dying well by living well. The first two rules are rather general: One must live a good life and die to the world. The third rule is to cultivate the theological virtues of faith, hope, and charity. The next rule explores three passages in the Gospels that teach Christians how to be ready for Christ as their judge—with loins girt for a journey, with lamps lit, and on watch for the return of their master. The fifth rule unmasks the error of heaping up wealth in this world without regard for the needs of God's poor. Here and in his later statements on almsgiving Bellarmine teaches the social obligations of the Christian; although his treatment does not question the social and economic structures of seventeenth-century society, his indictment of superfluous wealth is both compassionate and passionate. To balance the three theological virtues treated earlier he devotes his sixth rule to the role of the moral virtues of piety, justice, and sobriety as he explains Saint Paul's advice to Titus (Ti 2:11–13).

The next three rules deal with the duty of the Christian to pray, fast, and give alms. Bellarmine describes briefly the need for and the fruits of prayer and six conditions of praying well. He develops five reasons for fasting and confirms them with a catena of biblical and patristic quotations. Likewise he points to seven fruits that almsgiving confers on the giver and makes six recommendations for the distribution of alms. His suggestions are directed more toward the spiritual growth of the givers, who were the audience that he was writing for, than toward the temporal welfare of the recipients.

Chapters 10 to 16 of Book I take up the seven Catholic sacraments and relate them to the art of Christian living. His treatment of the seven sacraments here differs from his treatment of them in his larger catechism. There he was speaking to adolescents; here he is speaking to mature Christians and is less concerned to teach doctrine than to stir hearts so that they may profit from the sacraments. Thus his remarks on baptism dwell on the goodness of God in establishing the sacrament, on the recipients' negligence in living up to the pledges made in their name at baptism, and on the spiritual symbolism contained in the ritual. He also reviews the ritual and meaning of confirmation briefly, then asks his readers to examine their consciences on whether their lives have matched the vocation symbolized by the tongues of fire at the first Pentecost.

Bellarmine understandably devotes more space to the eucharist and penance than to baptism and confirmation since they are sacraments that adult Christians continue to receive. During the Reformation era there were more polemics on the eucharist than on all the other sacraments combined, but Luther and Calvin, Loyola and Bellarmine, all agreed on the need for more frequent reception of the eucharist than was the general practice in the medieval church. While noting daily communion in the early church, Bellarmine cautiously encourages weekly communion provided proper preparation and thanksgiving are made. He supports this with quotations from the Church Fathers. In fact many Catholic reformers, especially other Jesuits, had been urging frequent communion for the previous seventy years, but the innovation was gaining ground only slowly. Bellarmine's chapter on penance insists on the need for careful preparation, real contrition, and a genuine commitment to avoiding future sin.

Chapters 14 and 15 take up the sacraments of orders and matrimony. Bellarmine contrasts the dignity of the clerical calling with the often routine performance of sacred duties and tries to stir the fervor of his clerical readers. After recalling the dignity of marriage he reviews its goals: offspring, mutual fidelity, and the grace of the sacrament. He appends a statement on the duty of parents toward their children and of husband and wife toward each other.

The last chapter of Book I, on the sacrament of extreme unction, presents Bellarmine with an organizational difficulty. Unlike the other six sacraments this one was directly related to the immediate preparation for death. Logically Bellarmine ought to postpone discussing it until Book II, but he also wants to round out his discussion of the seven sacraments. He solves the problem by noting that extreme unction involves the anointing of the sense organs and then shows how each organ is a gateway by which sin can enter the soul. Thus his treatment of extreme unction in Book I becomes a sermon on how Christians ought to close the five gates of sight, hearing and speaking, smell, taste, and touch to their specific sins. His explanation draws on stories of how the senses can lead to sin, for example, how David's looking at Bathsheba naked resulted in adultery and murder. Although this is easily the longest chapter in the whole *Art of Dying Well*, it says little about the sacrament of extreme unction.

Book II, on the immediate preparation for death, is rather

shorter than Book I and is closer to the medieval Art of Dying tradition. The first four chapters form a block that reflects on death and its sequels, judgment, hell, and heaven. Bellarmine's reflections on death review its nature, certainty, and importance. He reflects on both the particular judgment immediately after death and the later general judgment. He gives six reasons why there should be a judgment at the end of the world and then describes the general judgment with a wealth of scripture quotations. His chapter on hell does not spare the fire and brimstone, although it is far less gruesome than many such descriptions, for instance, the one that James Joyce put into the mouth of the Jesuit retreatmaster in *A Portrait of the Artist as a Young Man*. Bellarmine locates hell at the center of the earth and emphasizes its crowdedness, flames, and eternal duration. In the *Ascent* Bellarmine devoted two chapters in Step I to explaining how God is the final cause of human beings, but here he says nothing about the loss of God as the chief suffering of the damned. Elsewhere in *The Art of Dying Well* he touches only briefly on this subject. Indications such as this and the many stories and anecdotes in Book II suggest that Bellarmine is writing for a more popular audience than in the *Ascent*. It is a characteristic of the Art of Dying tradition from its beginnings down to Bellarmine and Jeremy Taylor to alternate threats and words of consolation.[58] After hell Bellarmine devotes a chapter to the glory of the blessed in heaven. His orderly discussion of heaven's place, duration, and joys provides a neat antithesis to his discussion of the same points in his chapter on hell. It is worth noting that his description of heaven is considerably longer than that of hell, whereas most writers and preachers find it easier to describe the pains of hell than the joys of heaven.

The fifth chapter urges dying persons to make a will, but Bellarmine does not dwell on the practical need so much as on making restitution and giving alms so that the dying person has a clear conscience before God.

The next three chapters form another block, since each takes up one of the sacraments normally given to the dying. The first is penance. The cardinal's recommendations are more pastoral than theological and urge true sorrow and contrition. His chapter on viaticum devotes considerable space to showing that the early church, contrary to the practice in his own day, gave viaticum after extreme unction. Bellarmine also gives reasons for current practice, but readers may suspect that he was making a point in bringing up the subject. He then turns to more important considerations: the fruits of the eucharist for the dying and the dispositions they should have in receiving it. For Bellarmine, as for contemporary Catholic theologians generally, the key biblical text on extreme unction was James 5:14–15, which suggested that the sacrament had power to forgive sins and (sometimes) to restore health. Bellarmine argues that the second effect is seldom attained because relatives and friends postpone the sacrament too long. He urges that the sacrament should be given much earlier and thereby anticipates recent pastoral practice. His emphasis on the sacraments in both Book I and Book II is not found in the late medieval tradition of the Art of Dying and introduces a theological and ecclesiastical dimension that was typical of Catholicism after the Council of Trent, but it was not restricted to Catholicism. Jeremy Taylor's fifth and last chapter centers on the assistance of the clergy, the confession of sins, viaticum, and the specific prayers to be said by the minister at the bedside.

Chapters 9 to 13 are closely related. The first three deal with three temptations that were seen as particularly dangerous to the dying, namely, unbelief, despair, and the hatred of God. These sins are directly against the three theological virtues of faith, hope, and charity that Bellarmine had discussed in Chapter 3 of Book I. Perhaps nowhere else is his work so clearly dependent on the anonymous *Art of Dying* of the fifteenth century, whose second and longest chapter takes up temptations against faith, hope, and charity but then adds two others, spiritual pride and avarice. Bellarmine combines the temptations of spiritual pride and avarice in his twelfth chapter under the heading "The First Remedy against the Temptations of the Devil." He tries to show how little even scholars can really know and how much has to be taken on human faith about natural phenomena. Why then is it difficult to accept belief in the eucharist or the resurrection? He urges those tempted to despair or the hatred of God to reflect on biblical passages that highlight God's mercy and goodness toward sinners. On the other hand, no one should believe the devil, who is the father of lies. Chapter 13 shows how prayer is the remedy for all the devil's temptations. Here Bellarmine brings in the story of Saint Anthony in the desert. The late medieval *Art of Dying* also introduces Saint Anthony at this point, and the subject was a favorite for artists, especially in Flanders, during Bellarmine's lifetime. Indeed, this chapter mainly consists of three colorful stories about temptation in the lives of the saints borrowed from the writings of Saints Athanasius, Bonaventure, and Gregory the Great.

Bellarmine's next chapter stands somewhat apart and deals with persons who are overtaken by death when they are in full health. This can, of course, happen to anyone, so all Christians must stand constantly on alert, but Bellarmine is chiefly concerned with sailors, soldiers, and condemned prisoners. Following Saint Augustine and the just-war theory he notes that rulers must be certain that their cause is just, while soldiers and sailors may follow their rulers unless they are certain that the war is unjust. He notes that condemned prisoners actually have an advantage in the face of death since they can prepare themselves in full possession of their faculties.

Chapter 15, on the happy death of those who have learned to die well, returns to the theme of consolation. Christians who live and die in God find rest from their labors and reward for their works. Bellarmine refers to eight stories from Gregory the Great to underline the mood of joy that Christians should have in the face of death. The next chapter alternates threats and consolation as it reviews the unhappy deaths of those who have neglected the art of dying, again drawing on Saint Gregory for two stories to drive home the point. These stories and those scattered throughout the closing chapters of *The Art of Dying Well* are similar to the stories frequently used by other spiritual writers of the period, but they are apt to strike modern readers as bizarre. Perhaps because they are so spicy they distract attention from the plain but solid spiritual fare they are meant to enrich.

Bellarmine's last chapter tries to sum up his whole book around Saint Paul's contention (2 Cor 4:17) that "our present light affliction, which is for a moment, prepares for us an eternal weight of glory." He illustrates the theme of threat and promise that runs through his whole book by three pairs of biblical figures: Saul and David, the rich banqueter and the beggar Lazarus, and Judas and Saint Matthias. In each pair the first man experienced a short period of prominence and an eternity of hell; the second for a while endured affliction and labor but won an eternal weight of glory.

Throughout *The Art of Dying Well* Bellarmine stresses the individual's relationship with God. He shows little interest in the family the dying person will leave behind. Men and women gathered around the dying person's bed, who figured prominently in the fifth chapter (out of six) of the late medieval *Art of Dying*, play little role in Bellarmine's work. We might expect that the champion of Tridentine orthodoxy would strongly encourage his readers to set aside money for Masses to deliver their souls from purgatory or to join one of the many confraternities that figured prominently in Catholic Reformation social and devotional life by accompanying the bodies of fellow members to the grave and remembering them in their prayers. On these points and on the spiritual links within the threefold church militant, suffering, and triumphant, Bellarmine has surprisingly little to say.

Bellarmine's spiritual writings are practical and down-to-earth; if they lack the sweetness and geniality of the contemporary writings of Saint Francis de Sales, they possess clarity of organization, vigor of expression, and precision of theology. As was noted above, Bellarmine was writing for serious Christians, but not for advanced souls who needed instruction in mystical graces. He chose, therefore, the safer course of passing over in silence advanced levels of prayer and union with God. His treatises contain no echo of Saint Teresa of Avila or Saint John of the Cross, although he could hardly have been unaware of their writings. Although he wrote in well-established spiritual genres and was obviously influenced by works in both the Ascent to God and the Art of Dying traditions, his treatises seldom refer explicitly to the earlier literature even when its influence is strongly felt. Many other spiritual writers of his era likewise pass over the recent literature in silence. In contrast, frequent reference to biblical and patristic sources was expected, and few contemporary writers could match Bellarmine's familiarity with Scripture and the Church Fathers, especially Saint Augustine.

Hence, the enduring popularity of Bellarmine's treatises rested not so much on any great originality as on his skill in presenting his material. His *Ascent* conjures before us unexpected but convincing analogies between properties and forces of nature and the attributes and activities of a God who is using them to draw our minds and hearts to himself. The final sections of the *Art of Dying Well* sets before us memorable examples and stories that drive home Bellarmine's themes. In places the tone of the *Ascent* becomes philosophical, but Bellarmine allowed no gap to arise between those who reflect on the grandeur of God manifested in the world's created beauty and Christian believers who meditate on the divine attributes revealed in Scripture. Neither is there a dichotomy between the life and death of Christians who have learned the art of dying well, because all life is a preparation for death and the true art of dying well is to live well. For Christians death does not take life away, but rather changes and transforms it.

Any final judgment on Bellarmine's ascetical treatises should recognize that neither individually nor taken together do they try to present a comprehensive spirituality. The *Ascent* largely lacks an ecclesial dimension, but that dimension is more clearly present in *The Art of Dying Well*, especially in the passages dealing with the sacraments. The saving role of Jesus Christ, which should be central to any authentically Christian spirituality, is not prominent in either the *Ascent* or *The Art of Dying Well*, but emerges more clearly in Bellarmine's treatise on Christ's seven last words on the cross. In any case, the two treatises of Saint Robert Bellarmine in this volume provide a solid and fairly typical illustration of spirituality during the mature phase of the Catholic Reformation—a spirituality that remained typical of the Jesuit Order and through it, to a lesser extent, of the whole Roman Catholic Church until the Second Vatican Council in the present century.

NOTES

Notes to the Introduction

1. The best biography of Bellarmine is James Brodrick, *The Life and Work of Blessed Robert Francis Cardinal Bellarmine, S.J., 1542–1621*, 2 vols. (London: 1928); Vol. I, pp. 460–507, reprints Bellarmine's autobiography, the most important single source for his life. Brodrick later revised and condensed his biography as *Robert Bellarmine: Saint and Scholar* (Westminster, Md., 1961). Still valuable is Xavier-Marie Le Bachelet, *Bellarmin avant son Cardinalat (1542–1598)* (Paris, 1911). For Bellarmine's theology, see J. De La Servière, *La Théologie de Bellarmin* (Paris, 1911). There is a good bibliography of Bellarmine studies attached to John O. Riedl's "Bellarmine and the Dignity of Man" in Gerard Smith, ed., *Jesuit Thinkers of the Renaissance* (Milwaukee, 1939), pp. 193–226, 242–254. More recent titles can be found under Bellarmine's name in the annual bibliography of *Archivum Historicum Societatis Iesu*.

2. Xavier-Marie Le Bachelet, *Bellarmin et la Bible Sixto-Clémentine* (Paris, 1911).

3. Brodrick, *Life and Work*, Vol. I, p. 400.

4. Brodrick, *Robert Bellarmine*, pp. 332–378; Jerome Longford, *Galileo, Science and the Church* (New York, 1966).

5. Late in life Bellarmine wrote for his nephew Angelo della Ciana, recently appointed bishop of Teano near Naples, a treatise on the duties of a bishop, *Admonitio . . . quae necessaria sint episcopis.* The first edition (Paris, 1616) was printed without Bellarmine's permission.

6. Brodrick, *Life and Work*, Vol. II, pp. 404–407; Luigi Fiorani, "Religione e povertà: il dibatto sul pauperismo a Roma tra Cinque e Seicento," in Luigi Fiorani, ed., *Ricerche per la storia religiosa di Roma* (Rome, 1979), Vol. III, pp. 54–61.

7. Brodrick, *Life and Work*, Vol. II, p. 452.

8. Loyola to Canisius, August 13, 1554, in William Young, ed. and trans., *Letters of St. Ignatius of Loyola* (Chicago, 1959), p. 347.

9. Jean Delumeau, *Catholicism between Luther and Voltaire: A New View of the Counter-Reformation* (London and Philadelphia, 1977), pp. 154–202.

10. H. Outram Evenett, *The Spirit of the Counter-Reformation*, ed. John Bossy (Cambridge, 1968), pp. 32–35.

11. Louis Martz, *The Poetry of Meditation* (New Haven, 1954), pp. 1–70, 121–132, 146–149.

12. Pietro Aldobrandini was the nephew of Clement VIII, who had raised both him and Bellarmine to the cardinalate. Aldobrandini helped Bellarmine avoid being elected pope, a burden and an honor Bellarmine did not want.

13. Brodrick, *Life and Work*, Vol. II, pp. 376–383.

14. Young's translation has been reissued twice in this century, in London in 1928 and in photo facsimile by Scholar Press, Menston, England, 1970. The editions and translations of Bellarmine's works are given by Carlos Sommervogel, *Bibliothèque de la Compagnie de Jésus* (Paris, 1890) Vol. I, cols. 1231–1247. More recent are the tables of editions and translations given in the volume produced by Caietano Cardinal Bisleti, *Urbis et orbis concessionis tituli doctoris . . . Roberti . . . Bellarmino* (Rome, 1931) p. 167. The same volume prints excerpts (pp. 169–183) from writers down the centuries who have commented on Bellarmine's ascetical works. The best study of the ascetical works is Emmerich Raitz von Frentz, "Les oeuvres ascétiques du B. Cardinal Robert Bellarmin, Notes de Bibliographie critique" in *Revue d'Ascétique et Mystique* 4 (1923): 242–256, and 6 (1925): 60–70. Less useful is H. Monier-Vinard, "Le Bienheureux Robert Bellarmin et Saint François de Sales" in the same journal, 4 (1923): 225–242. Brodrick discusses the ascetical works (*Life and Work*, Vol. II, pp. 381–407.

15. Bisleti, *Urbis et orbis*, p. 168.

16. Pone graues animi tumultus
Huc pura mentis lumina dirige:
Scalam recludit rebus in omnibus
Pulsis Bellarminus tenebris,
Quae gradibus supra astra tendit.

The complete poem is printed in Bisleti, *Urbis et orbis*, pp. 309–310.

17. Pierre Pourrat, *Christian Spirituality*, trans. W. H. Mitchell (Westminster, Md., 1953), Vol. III, p. 253.

18. Bisleti, *Urbis et orbis*, p. 174.

19. Arthur O. Lovejoy, *The Great Chain of Being: A Study of the History of an Idea* (New York, 1960), pp. 91–92.

20. Brodrick, *Life and Work*, Vol. II, pp. 391–397; Frentz, "Les oeuvres ascétiques," pp. 247–249.

21. Brodrick, *Life and Work*, Vol. II, pp. 398–399; Frentz, "Les oeuvres ascétiques," pp. 250–251.

22. Ibid. p. 252.

23. Ibid. pp. 253–254.

24. Bisleti, *Urbis et orbis*, p. 170.

25. Brodrick, *Life and Work*, Vol. II, pp. 404–407; Frentz, "Les oeuvres ascétiques," pp. 254–256.

26. Most of Bellarmine's sermons remained unpublished until Sebastian Tromp's edition, *Roberti Bellarmini Opera Oratoria Postuma*, 9 vols. (Rome, 1942–1948).

27. Brodrick, *Life and Work*, Vol. II, p. 377.

28. The most detailed study of Bellarmine and the Exercises is Xavier-Marie Le Bachelet, *Bellarmin et les Exercises Spirituels de S. Ignace* (Paris, 1912).

29. Émile Bertaud and André Rayez, "Échelle spirituelle," in *Dictionaire de spiritualité* IV, cols. 62–86.

30. Quoted by Brodrick, *Life and Work*, Vol. II, p. 383.

31. Bertaud and Rayez, "Échelle spirituelle," cols. 65–78.

32. See p. 189.

33. Lovejoy, *Great Chain of Being*, p. 92.

34. Paul G. Kuntz, "The Hierarchical Vision of St. Roberto Bellarmino," in *Acta Conventus Neo-Latini Turonensis* (Paris, 1980), Vol. II, p. 963.

35. Ibid. This essay is reprinted (pp. 111–130) together with many other essays on the ladder of ascent in *Jacob's Ladder and the Tree of Life: Concepts of Hierarchy and the Great Chain of Being*, ed. Marion Leathers Kuntz and Paul Grimley Kuntz (Bern and New York, 1986).

36. See Step 13, ch. 2.

37. *De Consideratione Libri Quinque* V, 13; *PL* 182, 804–807. On the history of the *topos* of length, breadth, height, and depth, which was often tied in with the tree of the cross, see E. S. Greenhill, "The Child in the Tree: A Study of the Cosmological Tree," *Traditio* 10 (1954): 323–371, especially pp. 332–333.

38. Steps Ten to Fifteen of the *Ascent* have a more proximate and important source than Saint Bernard's *De consideratione*. From November 1593 to August 1594 when Bellarmine was superior of the Roman College, he delivered a series of thirteen exhortations to his community under the title *De cognitione Dei*. The best edition of these exhortations is Tromp's *Opera oratoria postuma* IX, 289–351. This material was first published by Justin Fèvre in his edition of Bellarmine's *Opera omnia* (Paris, 1873) VIII, 627–651; Fèvre found this material in manuscript, but his introductory remarks (p. 627) suggest that he knew nothing about the date or circumstances of its composition. Steps Ten to Fifteen of the *Ascent* clearly parallel the *De cognitione Dei* and expand it by almost 50 percent. The basic phrases from *De cognitione Dei* are found in the *Ascent*, but a close comparison of the two texts indicates that whole sentences are very rarely

found in both works. The two works are independent developments of the same ideas by the same author more than twenty years apart, the *Ascent* being somewhat more popular in tone.

39. The sources for Bellarmine's *Ascent* are discussed by Eusebio Hernandez, "Las Fuentes principales del opusculo belarminiano 'De ascensione mentis in Deum per scalas rerum creatarum,' " *Estudios eclesiasticos* 10 (1931): 235–243.

40. For a fuller discussion of Bellarmine and mysticism, see O. Marchetti, "Di alcuni passi delle opere bellarminiane riguardanti la mistica," *Gregorianum* 11 (1930): 579–597.

41. An important guide to early modern attitudes toward death is the issue of *Annales: Economies, Sociétés, Civilizations* entitled *Autour de la mort:* 31/1 (1976). It devotes two articles to the Art of Dying literature: Roger Chartier, "Les arts de mourir, 1450–1600," pp. 51–75, and Daniel Roche, " 'La Mémoire de la Mort': Recherche sur la place des arts de mourir dans la libraire et la lecture en France aux XVIIe and XVIIIe siècles," pp. 76–120.

42. Chartier, "Les arts de mourir," pp. 53, 61–63; Mary Catherine O'Connor, *The Art of Dying Well: The Development of the Ars Moriendi* (New York, 1942), pp. 1–2; she lists the manuscripts and early printed editions on pp. 61–171; Nancy Lee Beaty, *The Craft of Dying: A Study of the Literary Tradition of the Ars Moriendi in England* (New York, 1970), pp. 1–53.

43. On the Vérard editions see O'Connor, *The Art of Dying Well*, pp. 150, 153–156; and Émile Mâle, *L'art religieux de la fin du moyen age en France* (Paris, 1931), pp. 382–387, which reprints six of the woodcuts.

44. For Lupset's use of Saint Augustine, see Beaty, *The Craft of Dying*, p. 61. Beaty devotes pp. 54–107 to an analysis of Lupset's book.

45. Chartier, "Les arts de mourir," p. 51.

46. Jean Delumeau, *Le péché et la peur: La culpabilisation en Occident, XIIIe–XVIIIe siècles* (Paris, 1983), pp. 9–10.

47. Ibid., pp. 64–97, 389–415.

48. For Erasmus and More, see O'Connor, *The Art of Dying Well*, pp. 180–181, 185–187.

49. Ibid., p. 190.

50. Ibid., p. 195; Beaty, *The Craft of Dying*, pp. 108–156.

51. O'Connor, *The Art of Dying Well*, pp. 197–198.

52. Ibid., pp. 202–203.

53. Ibid., p. 210.

54. Ibid., pp. 208–210; Beaty, *The Craft of Dying*, pp. 197–270.

55. O'Connor, *The Art of Dying Well*, pp. 180–189; Beaty, *The Craft of Dying*, pp. 157–196; Henri Bremond, *Histoire littéraire du sentiment religiuex en France* (Paris, 1968) IX, pp. 331–380.

56. Delumeau, *Le péché*, p. 389.

57. Roche, "La Mémoire," pp. 94, 114; Carlos Eire, "Ars moriendi," *The Westminster Dictionary of Christian Spirituality* (Philadelphia, 1983), p. 22. Sommervogel, *Bibliothèque* Vol. X, cols. 510–519, lists Jesuit books on the art of dying.

58. Beaty, *The Craft of Dying*, p. 9.

The Mind's Ascent to God by the Ladder of Created Things

by

Saint Robert Cardinal Bellarmine, S.J.

DEDICATION

To Pietro Aldobrandini,[1] illustrious cardinal of the Holy Roman Church, Robert Cardinal Bellarmine sends greetings. During last September I wrote as best I could with God's help a short book on the ascent of the mind to God by the ladder of created things. With the permission of our Holy Father and Lord I chose that month to put aside other cares and devote myself to God. Although I wrote the book for my own use, I was advised and urged by friends that I allow its publication, and I wanted it to appear in your name above all. If some value can be found in my labors, it will be mainly useful for men engaged in public affairs, especially the Princes of the Church. Among the Princes of the Church you are particularly burdened with a mass of business as cardinal, archbishop, chamberlain of the Holy Roman Church, and a member of the universal Inquisition, besides the strain and care of being Cardinal Protector for many important organizations. I have another reason for dedicating this book to you, namely, that I should provide for posterity an acknowledgement of your great benefits to me and my regard for you. I trust in your kindness that the smallness of the gift will not make it less welcome. Books are judged not by the number of pages, but by their usefulness and results.

I do not know how others will judge this book, but I have found it very useful compared to my other smaller works. I do not read my other books unless I am forced to; this one I have already gladly read three or four times, and I have resolved to reread it frequently in the future. Perhaps I am more fond of it, not because of its merits, but because I love it as a child, a second Benjamin, which I produced in my extreme old age.

Therefore, dear Cardinal, accept from me this little gift which offers testimony of the regard I owe. May it also serve as a sort of counselor. Should your crowd of business commitments overwhelm you and try to keep you from your usual zeal in devoting certain hours to God in prayer, may this book gently advise you to block out that crowd for a short time and recall to mind your accustomed interior joy. And taking time for reflection or reading, you will see that the Lord himself is God, that is, the only true, supreme, and eternal good, whose possession gives man complete happiness and whose loss brings utter misery.

INTRODUCTION

The Need to Seek God by The Ladder of Created Things The Title of This Work

Holy Scripture frequently warns us to seek God diligently. Although God "is not far from anyone of us, for in him we live and move and have our being," as the Apostle[1] says (Acts 17:27–28), still we are far from God, and unless we carefully set our hearts on rising up and build ourselves a ladder to heaven and seek God with great effort, we feed the swine with the prodigal son in a distant land far from our Father and fatherland (Lk 15:11ff.).

So that I can briefly explain how it is not contradictory that God is not far from us and we are, nevertheless, distant from him, I answer that God is not far from us since he sees us continually because all things are present to his eyes. Likewise he thinks about us continually "because he cares for" us (1 Pt 5:7), and he is in contact with us continually because "he upholds all things by the word of his power" (Heb 1:3). On the other hand, we are distant from God because we do not see God and cannot see him because "he dwells in light inaccessible" (1 Tm 6:16). "Not that we are sufficient of ourselves to think anything, as from ourselves, but our sufficiency is from God" (2 Cor 3:5). Far less can we touch him and cleave to him with holy affection unless his right hand grasps us and draws us to himself. This is why when David said, "My soul has stuck close to you," he immediately added, "Your right hand has received me" (Ps 62:9). Not only are we far from God because we can neither see nor easily think about him nor cleave to him in affection, but being worried about worldly goods which surround us and overwhelm us from all sides, we easily forget God and can scarcely bring our tongue and dried-up heart to speak God's name in psalms and holy prayers. This is the reason why the Holy Spirit in Sacred Scripture, as we just said, urges us so often to seek God. "Seek God, and your soul shall live" (Ps 68:33). "See his face evermore" (Ps 104:4). "The Lord is good to them that hope in him, to the soul that seeks him" (Lam 3:25). "Seek the Lord while he may be found" (Is 55:6). "Seek him in simplicity of heart" (Wis 1:1). And "When you shall seek there the Lord your God, you will find him, if you seek him with all your heart" (Dt 4:29).

Although this zeal in seeking the Lord should be common to all believers, it is even more fitting for churchmen, as the Fathers, Saints Augustine, Gregory, and Bernard among others testify. They write quite explicitly that a bishop cannot help himself and others unless he earnestly applies himself to meditating on the divine mysteries and to renewing his soul. Saint Augustine in his *City of God* says, "Love of truth seeks holy leisure; the needs of charity take up rightful duties. But the enjoyment of truth ought not to be so completely put off that its pleasure is destroyed and duty becomes oppressive."[2] Again it is Saint Augustine who, speaking in his *Confessions* of himself and his frequent meditations on how creatures reveal God, says, "I often do this. I enjoy it and take refuge in this pleasure from all the things that need doing so I can get as much relaxation as possible."[3] Saint Gregory in his *Pastoral Care* says, "Let the bishop be near the faithful by his compassion and go beyond others in his contemplation so that he takes upon himself the weakness of others by his feelings of devotion, and may he surpass himself by the loftiness of his contemplation in seeking unseen reality."[4] In that same place Saint Gregory notes the example of Moses and of Christ. "Moses frequently went in and out of the Tabernacle. He entered to consider the mysteries of God; he went out to carry the infirmities of his neighbors. And Christ himself devoted his days to the salvation of his neighbors by preaching and performing miracles, but he spent his nights awake in prayer and contemplation. As Saint Luke says, "He continued all night in prayer to God" (Lk 6:12). One can read many similar statements in the last chapter of the same book.

Next, Saint Bernard earnestly warned Pope Eugenius, his former student, against giving himself over completely to business; rather he should recollect himself daily at a set time and enjoy some holy leisure and heavenly repast. He wrote his five books, *On Consideration*, in which he not only urges the pope to persistent meditation on heavenly subjects, but also teaches him a method and way of meditating and by meditation of ascending and by ascension of uniting himself to God in mind and heart. Nor does he allow him the excuse, which he could have offered and which many people today do offer, that the vast business of the papal office does not allow enough leisure for a churchman to devote himself to meditation on spiritual subjects.[5] Certainly nobody is bound to become so absorbed in external business that he allows himself no time to restore his body with food and drink and to take some rest in sleep. If the body rightly demands sustenance and rest, how much more does the spirit demand its food and sleep for the best reasons? For without this sustenance the soul cannot in any way rightly do its duty amid its mass of crucial business. Moreover, prayer is the food of the soul, and contemplation is its sleep by which the rising up of the heart is set in motion so that "the God of gods is seen in Sion" (Ps 84:7), as he can be seen in this vale of tears.

For us mortal men it seems that no ladder of ascent to God can lie open except through the works of God. Those who by a singular gift of God are admitted to paradise by a different road and hear mysteries of God which it is not lawful for man to utter are better said not to have ascended, but to have been carried up. Blessed Paul openly admits this of himself when he says, "I was caught up into paradise" and heard "secret words that man may not repeat" (2 Cor 12:4). The Book of Wisdom (Wis 13:1ff.) and the Apostle's Letter to the Romans (Rom 1:19–20) teach that man can ascend through the works of God, that is, through creatures, to a knowledge and love of the Creator. Reason itself confirms this well enough since an efficient cause can be known from its effects as can an exemplar from its images. There can be no doubt that all created things are the works of God, and the Holy Scriptures teach us that a man and an angel are not only works, but also images of God.

These arguments moved me, as did the example of Saint Bonaventure, who wrote his *Journey of the Mind to God* during some leisure time, so that during the short vacation granted me from public business I tried to build a ladder from the consideration of creatures by which one can somehow ascend to God. I divided it into fifteen steps to correspond with the fifteen steps by which people ascended to Solomon's temple and with the fifteen psalms which are called the Gradual Psalms.[6]

STEP ONE

The Consideration of Man

CHAPTER ONE

The General Causes under Consideration

Anyone who really wants to build a ladder to God should start by considering himself. Each of us is a creature and an image of God, and nothing is closer to us than ourselves. Therefore, Moses says with good reason, "Consider yourself." Basil the Great has written a superb sermon on those two words.[1] He who examines his whole self and considers what lies hidden within will find the whole world in shortened form, from which he will ascend without difficulty to the maker of all things.

I have determined to investigate on the present subject nothing but the usual four causes:

1. Who is my maker?
2. From what material did he make me?
3. What nature did he give me?
4. For what end did he create me?

For if I seek my maker, I find God alone. If I seek the material from which he made me, I find absolutely nothing. From this you can conclude that whatever is in me was made by God and wholly belongs to God. If I ask about my nature, I find that I am the image of God. If I ask about my end, I find God himself, who is my supreme and total good. Therefore, I will recognize that I have a great bond with and need for God, as he alone is my creator, my maker, my father, my exemplar, my happiness, my all. And if I understand this, what can happen except that I seek him ardently, that I think of him, that I yearn for him, desire to see and embrace him? Should I not be horrified at the dense darkness of my heart which for so long has considered, desired, and sought anything other than God, who alone is my all?

CHAPTER TWO

God Our Creator

But let us look a little more closely at the individual points. I ask you, my soul, who gave you your existence, since a little time ago you were nothing? Certainly the parents of your flesh did not beget you, because "that which is born of the flesh is flesh" (Jn 3:6), but you are a spirit. Neither did heaven, nor earth, the sun nor the stars make you. They are bodies, and you are immaterial. Neither the angels nor archangels nor any other spiritual creature could have been the creator of your existence because you are not created out of any material, but out of absolutely nothing. Only almighty God can make something from nothing. When he wanted to, he alone without assistant or helper created you by his own hands, which are his intellect and will. But perhaps not God himself but created things produced your body so that your soul should acknowledge God as its maker, but your body should acknowledge your parents? That is not the case. Although he used human parents to bring forth flesh, as one uses lowly workers to build a house, still he wishes to be and to be called the architect, the maker, the true father not only of the soul, but also of the body and, therefore, of the whole man. For, if the producers of your flesh were the real makers and quasi-architects of your body, they would surely know how many muscles there are in the human body, how many veins and sinews, how many bones large and small, how many fluids and innards and many similar things of which they are wholly ignorant unless they might have learned about them in anatomical studies. Besides that, when the body becomes sick or a limb dries up or is cut off, certainly they could use that skill by which they first produced it to restore it, if they were your true makers, just as those who make watches or build houses know how to modify or restore them. But parents cannot do these things and know nothing about them. In addition, the union of the soul with the body, which is the main part of the making of human nature, could be achieved by nobody except a craftsman of infinite power. By what skill, except God's, could spirit be joined to flesh by such a close bond that they make up one substance? Body has no similarity or proportion with spirit. Therefore, he made it "who alone does great wonders" (Ps 135:4).

Truly then does the Spirit of God speak through Moses in Deuteronomy: "Is not he your father, who possessed you, and made you, and created you?" (Dt 32:6). So also through Job, "You clothed me with skin and flesh. You put me together with bones and sinew" (Jb 10:11), and through the Royal Prophet, "Your hands have made me and formed me" (Ps 118:73), and again "You formed me, and laid your hand upon me" (Ps 138:5), and through that very wise woman, the mother of the Maccabee brothers, "I know not how you were formed in my womb, for I neither gave you breath, nor soul, nor life, neither did I frame the limbs of every one of you. But the Creator of the world, that formed the nativity of man, and that found out the origin of all" (2 Mc 7:22–23). Hence, Christ our Lord, the Wisdom of God, said, "Call no one on earth your father; for one is your Father who is in heaven" (Mt 23:9). With this in mind Saint Augustine spoke to God about his son, Adeodatus, whom he begot by fornication, "You made him well, for I had no part in the boy except my sin."[2]

Consider now, my soul, if God is the maker of your body and your soul, if he was father to you, carried and nourished you, if whatever you are, you are his, whatever you have, you have it from him, whatever you hope for, you hope for from him, why then do you not boast of such a great parent? Why do you not love him with your whole heart? Why do you not hold in contempt all earthly things for his sake? Why do you let vain desires become your master? Lift up your eyes to him. Fear not what your enemy on earth may do to you, since you have an almighty Father in heaven. With how much confidence and feeling, do you think, David used to say, "I am yours, save me" (Ps 118:94)? O my soul, if you would consider what it is that the almighty and eternal God, who needs not your goods and loses nothing if you perish, still does not turn his eyes away from you and so loves, so protects, so directs, and so nurtures you as if you were his great treasure, then you would put all your trust in him, you would fear him as Lord, love him as

Father, and there would be no temporal good or evil however great that would pull you away from his love.

CHAPTER THREE

God Created Man From Nothing

We now turn to the material from which man is formed. It is base indeed, but the more base it is, the better foundation it gives us for building up the virtue of humility in ourselves. No virtue is more useful in our life than this, none more rare and, therefore, more precious and to be sought with greater eagerness.

As for the material of the soul, there can be no doubt. It is nothingness itself, than which nothing lower or more worthless can be imagined or thought of. What is closest to the material of the body if not the menstrual blood, a thing so vile that the eyes avoid looking at it and the hand refuses to touch it and even the mind shudders to think about it? What was the material from which the first man was formed—what else but sterile clay or dust or mud? "God formed man," Scripture says, "of the slime of the earth" (Gn 2:7). And again, God told man, "You are dust, and into dust you shall return" (Gn 3:19). Hence, Abraham, aware of his lowliness, said to God, "Seeing I have once begun, I will speak to my Lord, whereas I am dust and ashes" (Gn 18:27). But this is not the extent of the baseness of the human material, for the slime or dust was not formed out of some other material but out of nothing. For in the beginning God created heaven and earth, and he clearly made them not from some other heaven and earth, but from nothing. Therefore, the origin of this proud animal called man goes back to nothingness, whether you wish to consider either his soul or his body. There is nothing in man that he can boast about, as if he had not received it from God. The works of man, whatever they are, whether they come from his genius or labor, always have something from themselves so that, had they understanding, they could boast against their maker; for instance, a golden bowl, a wooden chest, and an ivory or marble house, if they could speak, would say to their craftsman, "I owe my shape to you, but not my material. What I have of myself is more precious than what I received from you." But man, who has nothing from himself and who in himself is absolutely nothing, has nothing to boast about. The Apostle says very rightly, "For if anyone thinks himself to be something, whereas he is nothing, he deceives himself" (Gn 6:3). "What have you that you did not receive? But if you received it, why do you boast as if you had not received it?" (1 Cor 4:7). Saint Cyprian agrees with this in saying, "There is nothing to boast about when there is nothing of your own."[3]

But, you say, men do many outstanding deeds for which they are rightly praised so that praise may increase virtue. It is true that men do many outstanding deeds for which they are praised and honored, but in the Lord and not in themselves, as is written, "But he who boasts, let him boast in the Lord" (2 Cor 10:17) and "My soul finds priase in the Lord" (Ps 34:2). For I ask, when a man makes something notable, from what material does he make it or by whose power or with whose guidance and help? Certainly he does it from material created by God and not by man himself. The power by which he acts is given him by God and is not something he produced. God guides and helps what man does, and without his guidance and help man would accomplish nothing good. God accomplishes many good things in man without man, but man does nothing good which God does not bring about, as is stated in the Second Council of Orange, Chapter 20.[4] Therefore, God deigns to use man's help in doing good works, which he could do by himself, so that thereby man might the more confess himself God's debtor and not in order that he grow proud of himself, but that he glory in the Lord.

Therefore, my soul, if you are wise, always take the last place, do not steal the glory of God either in the smallest or in the greatest matter. Go down to your own nothingness—that alone is yours—and the whole world will not be able to lift you up to pride. And because this precious virtue of true humility had already disappeared from the world and could not be found either in the books of the philosophers or in the customs of the nations, the Teacher of humility came down from heaven and, though he was by nature God, equal to the Father, he "emptied himself, taking the nature of a slave," and "he humbled himself, becoming obedient to death" (Phil 2:6–8). And he said to the human race, "Learn from me, for I am meek and humble of heart, and you will find rest for your souls" (Mt 11:29). Therefore, my soul, if perhaps you are ashamed to imitate the lowliness of men, you will not be ashamed to imitate the lowliness of God, who can neither deceive nor be deceived and "who resists the proud but gives grace to the humble" (Jas 4:6).

CHAPTER FOUR

Man Was Created in the Image of God

We next examine the form, which is the third of the causes. Just as the material from which man is made is base, so the form which man is given appears precious and excellent. I pass over the external form of the body, namely, the shape of the human body, which is superior to the shapes of all the other animals, for this is not the substantial, but only the accidental form. The substantial form of man, which makes him a man and distinguishes him from the other animals, is his immortal soul endowed with reason and free choice; it is the image of God modeled on the pattern of the supreme Godhead. Thus we read that God said when he wanted to form man, "Let us make man to our image and likeness; and let him have dominion over the fishes of the sea, the fowls of the air, and the beasts of the whole earth, and every creeping creature that moves upon the earth" (Gn 1:26). Man is therefore the image of God not because of his body, but because of his spirit, for God is a spirit and not a body. "The image of God," says Saint Basil, "lies in that which commands the other animals."[5] But man commands the beasts not by the body's limbs, which are stronger in many beasts than in man, but by his mind, which is endowed with reason and freedom. Man has charge of the other animals not by what he shares with them, but by that which distinguishes him from them and makes him similar to God.

Lift up your mind, my soul, to your exemplar and consider that the whole excellence of an image lies in its similarity to its exemplar. If the exemplar should be as deformed as the devil's is usually imagined to be, then the excellence of the image lies in representing skillfully the deformity of the exemplar. The deformity of the exemplar remains a deformity, but deformity in its image will be beauty. If the exemplar is also beautiful, the image will be very precious if it imitates as far as possible the beauty of the exemplar. If the image has understanding, it will hope for nothing more than always to gaze at its exemplar and perfect its imitation and become as similar to it as it can.

Your exemplar, O soul, is God—infinite beauty, "light, and in him is no darkness" (1 Jn 1:5), at whose beauty the sun and moon gaze in awe. So that you may more easily imitate the beauty of such an exemplar and desire to mirror it and achieve this by every means (in this lie all your perfection, all your usefulness, all your honor, all your joy, all your rest, and all your good), consider that the beauty of God your exemplar consists in wisdom and holiness. Just as the beauty of a body arises from the proportion of its parts and the harmony of its color, so in a spiritual substance the harmony of color is the light of wisdom and the proportion of the parts is justice, but here justice means not just some particular virtue, but that universal virtue which includes all the virtues. The spirit is most beautiful whose mind glows with the light of wisdom and whose will is strong with the fullness of perfect justice. I say, my soul, that God your exemplar is wisdom itself, is justice itself, and is thereby beauty itself. And since the Scriptures designate both these goods by the name "holiness," in Isaiah the angels praise God as "Holy, holy, holy, the Lord God of hosts" (Is 6:3), and God says to his images, "Be holy because I, the Lord your God, am holy" (Lv 11:44), and our Lord in the Gospel says, "Be perfect, even as your heavenly Father is perfect" (Mt 5:48).

If you, my soul, wish to be a true image of God, as close to your exemplar as possible, you must love wisdom and justice above all things. True wisdom consists in judging everything by its highest causes. The highest cause is the divine will or the law which makes the will of God clear to men. Therefore, if you love wisdom, you must not listen on any question to what the law of the flesh dictates or what the senses judge good or what the world approves or your relatives urge, much less to what flatterers propose. Turn a deaf ear to all these and give your attention to the will of the Lord your God alone. You must regard as useful, glorious, desirable, and good for you in every respect that which agrees with the will and law of God. This is the wisdom of the saints, about which the Wise Man writes, "I loved her above health and beauty, and chose to have her instead of light, for her light cannot be put out. Now all good things come to me together with her" (Wis 7:10–11).

Next, justice, which is the second part of spiritual beauty, embraces all the virtues which adorn and perfect the will, but especially charity, which is the mother and root of all virtues, about which Saint Augustine says in the last book of his *On Nature and Grace*, "Once charity begins, justice begins; as charity increases, justice increases; when charity is perfect, justice is perfect."[6] For "he who loves his neighbor has fulfilled the law," because "love does no evil," and therefore "love is the fulfillment of the law," as the Apostle taught (Rom 13:8, 10). Conversely, "he who keeps his word," that is, his commandments, "in him the love of God is truly perfected," as Saint John says (1 Jn 2:5). Those who wish to become like their divine exemplar must obey him who says, "Be you, therefore, imitators of God, as very dear children and walk in love" (Eph 5:1, 2). A child is the image of his Father, and the perfection of an image, as we said above, consists in being just like the exemplar.

O my soul, if you had fully understood this and if, having become like your exemplar by the beauty of true wisdom and true justice, you had been pleasing to the eyes of the supreme king, how much peace would you have enjoyed! How you would have exulted in joy! How easily you would have spurned all the enticements of the world! In contrast, think how terribly angry God becomes when he sees his image stripped of the light of wisdom and the splendor of justice, defiled, disfigured, and darkened, and man, established in such honor that he was like God, now "is compared to senseless beasts, and is become like to them" (Ps 48:13). Certainly you would shudder and quake and you could find no way to rest until you had washed away your stains with rivers of tears flowing from bitter contrition and until you had recovered the likeness of your beauteous exemplar. Because you are a pilgrim away from God "for we walk by faith and not by sight" (2 Cor 5:6–7), you always need God's help both to retain the likeness you have acquired and to make yourself daily more like him, that is, more beautiful and shining. Cry to God with all your heart and tell him, "O holy and merciful Lord, who was pleased to make my soul after your image, I beg you, improve your faint likeness, increase my wisdom, increase my justice, hide my soul in your hidden tabernacle so that the mud of fleshly desire and the smoke of worldly honor and the dust of earthly thoughts may not defile her." So much for the formal cause.

STEP ONE

CHAPTER FIVE

Man's Intrinsic End Is the Blessed Vision of God

There remains the last of the causes, called the final cause. The end for which man was created is none other than God himself. But there is a twofold end: one intrinsic, the other extrinsic. We will examine both briefly, one at a time. The intrinsic end of each thing is the perfect state to which the thing can attain. The intrinsic end of a palace is to be a complete and perfect palace. It is then said to have achieved its end when it lacks nothing that the building of a palace requires. The intrinsic end of a tree is the perfect state which its nature requires; a tree can be said to have attained its end when it has stretched out its branches and produced leaves and is covered with blossoms and when a little later it is seen weighed down with ripe fruit. Man, who is created for the most lofty end, can be said to have attained his end when his mind sees God as he is. This vision brings with it the knowledge of all things, and the will enjoys the supreme good, which it has ardently loved and desired, and the body endowed with immortality and impassibility and other glorious gifts possesses eternal peace and happiness. The essence of this final beatitude is the vision of God by which the images of God, we ourselves I say, attain our perfect state and perfect similarity to our divine exemplar; for this reason Blessed John writes, "Now we are the children of God, and it has not yet appeared what we shall be. We know that, when he appears, we shall be like to him, for we shall see him just as he is" (1 Jn 3:2).

O my soul, if you could imagine what this means, "We shall be like him because we shall see him as he is," how quickly all the clouds of worldly desires would disappear. God is completely happy, and completely happy because he always sees himself as he is and enjoys himself, the supreme good, clearly seen and ardently loved from all eternity without any interruption. He wanted to make you, together with the holy angels, a partaker of this priceless good. For this sublime and lofty end he created you. The verse "Enter into the joy of your master" (Mt 25:21) means that you become a partaker of the joy by which God himself rejoices. "And I appoint to you a kingdom, even as my Father has appointed to me, that you may eat and drink at my table in my kingdom" (Lk 22:29–30) likewise means that I will make you participants in my kingdom and royal table so that you may enjoy the honor, the power, and the pleasure which I enjoy and which God my Father enjoys. Who can imagine the greatness of this honor, this power, this pleasure, and this happiness of the King of kings and the Lord of lords, the Lord our God? Surely the person who has raised his thought and hope to the great height of our end would be absolutely ashamed to quarrel over the ownership of the earth or be downcast by any loss of temporal things or rejoice over temporal gains. He would be ashamed, I say, to covet the pleasures that cattle covet, who has been made the companion of angels and a partaker of God's friendship and of his priceless goods, since friends share all in common.

CHAPTER SIX

Man's Extrinsic End Is God's Glory and His Own Eternal Salvation

The extrinsic end of each thing is the person for whose sake a thing is made. The end of a palace is its inhabitant; the end of a tree is its owner; the end of man is the Lord his God alone. He made man, made him for himself. He conserves him, feeds him, and pays his salary. Therefore, he rightly commands and says, "You shall fear the Lord your God, and shall serve him only" (Dt 6:13). Note carefully, my soul, that other things which were made for man's sake are useful for man, but not for God. Beasts of burden work for man, not for God. The fields, vineyards, and gardens fill man's storehouse, barn, and purse, not God's. Finally, labor, sweat, and weariness belong to servants; to the master belongs profit, rent, and pleasure. But the Lord your God, who lacks nothing, does indeed want man to serve him, but wants the use, gain, and reward to belong not to himself, but to man his servant.

"O Lord, sweet and mild and plenteous in mercy" (Ps 85:5), who will not serve you with his whole heart if he begins to taste only a little the sweetness of your fatherly rule? What, Lord, do you command your servants? "Take my yoke," you say, "upon you." Of what sort is your yoke? "My yoke," you say, "is easy, and my burden light" (Mt 11:29–30). Who would not gladly bear a yoke that does not press down but helps and a burden that does not weight down but refreshes? Rightly then you add, "and you will find rest for your souls" (Mt 11:30). What is your yoke which does not weary but gives rest? Surely it is the first and greatest commandment: "You shall love the Lord your God with your whole heart." What is easier, gentler, and sweeter than to love goodness, beauty, and love, all that you are, Lord my God? Your servant, David, was right in judging when he concluded that your commandments are "more to be desired than gold and many precious stones, and sweeter than honey and the honeycomb" (Ps 18:11–12). He added that "in keeping them the reward is great." How is this, Lord, that you promise a reward to those who keep commandments which are more desirable than much gold and sweeter than the honeycomb? You absolutely promise a reward and an extremely rich reward, as your apostle, James, says that God has prepared "the crown of life for those who love him" (Jas 1:12). And what is this crown of life? A greater good than we can conceive or desire. Thus Blessed Paul quotes Isaiah, "Eye has not seen or ear heard, nor has it entered into the heart of man, what things God has prepared for those who love him" (1 Cor 2:9; cf. Is 64:4). Truly rich is the reward for those who keep the commandments. Not only is the first and greatest commandment useful for the man who obeys it rather than for God who commands it, but also the other commandments of God perfect, enhance, teach, enlighten, and make good and happy the man who obeys them. If you would be wise, recognize that you were created for God's glory and your own eternal salvation, that this is your end, this the center of your soul, this the treasure of your heart. If you reach this end, you will be happy. If you fall short of it, you will be wretched. Judge therefore that your true good is that which leads to your end. That is true evil which makes you fall short of it. Wealth and poverty, abundance and shortage, health and sickness, honor and dishonor, life and death, are not of themselves to be sought or avoided by the wise man. If they lead to God's glory and your eternal happiness they are good and desirable. If they hinder that, they are evil and must be avoided.

STEP TWO

The Consideration of the Macrocosm

CHAPTER ONE

The World's Greatness and God's Greatness

We built the first step in our ladder of ascent to God by considering human nature, which is called the microcosm. We now plan to add the second step by reflecting on that enormous mass that is commonly called the macrocosm. In his Second Sermon for Easter, Saint Gregory Nazianzen writes that God created man as the macrocosm in miniature.[1] That is true if we separate the angels from the world, for man is greater than the corporeal world, not in his mass, but in his power. If, however, the angels are included in the world, as we are including them here, then man is the microcosm set in the macrocosm. In this macrocosm which includes all things, many objects are clearly wonderful, especially their size, number, variety, power, and beauty. If we reflect carefully under God's enlightenment, these creatures will have no little power to raise up our heart so that it will be overcome in admiration at their immense size, number, variety, power, and beauty and returning to itself it will despise whatever it sees outside of God as nothing and worthless.

The earth is surely great, so great that Ecclesiasticus says, "Who has measured the breadth of the earth, and the depth of the abyss?" (Sir 1:2). This can also be seen from the fact that in the many thousands of years which have flowed by since the foundation of the earth the whole surface of the earth—what Ecclesiasticus calls the breadth of the earth—has not yet become known to us men, despite our careful explorations. And what, I ask, is the size of the earth in comparison with the vastness of the heavens above? Astronomers claim that it is like a mere point, and they are right. We see that even when the earth comes in between, the sun's rays reach to the stars at the end of the firmament as if the earth were nothing at all. And if every star of the firmament is greater than the whole earth, as scholars generally believe, and still these stars seem tiny specks to us because of the almost infinite distance, who can grasp in thought the size of the heavens where so many thousands of stars shine? Therefore, if Ecclesiasticus says about the surface and depth of the earth, "Who has measured the breadth of the earth, and the depth of the abyss?" (Sir 1:2), what, I ask, should be said about the outside surface of the heavens and the depth of the whole universe from the top of heaven down to hell? The size of the material universe is absolutely so great that no mind or thought can grasp it. Please consider now, my soul, if the world is so great, how great is he who made the world? "Great is the Lord, and of his greatness there is no end" (Ps 144:3). Listen to Isaiah: "Who has measured the waters in the hollow of his hand and weighed the heavens with his palm? Who has poised with three fingers the bulk of the earth?" (Is 40:12). Following Aquila's translation, Saint Jerome says the "hollow of his hand" means his little finger,[2] so that it really means that all the waters, which are less than the land, are measured by the little finger of God, the weight of the earth by three fingers, and heaven, which is greater than the waters and the earth combined, is weighed by the palm. But this is metaphorical since God is a spirit and, strictly speaking, has neither fingers nor palms, but Scripture still shows clearly enough by these comparisons that God is much greater than his creation. Solomon indicates this more precisely when he says, "Heaven and the heaven of the heavens do not contain you" (2 Chr 6:18). This is so true that, if another world were created, God would fill it too, and if there were many worlds or even an infinite number of worlds, God would fill them all. Do not think, my soul, that your God fills the world so that part of God is in part of the world and that he is complete in the whole world. God does not have parts. He is complete in the whole world and complete in every part of the world. Therefore, he is present everywhere by his omnipotence and his wisdom. Hence, if you are faithful to him, even if an armed camp lies against you, your heart will not fear. What should it fear, when it has with it an almighty Father, friend, and spouse who sees all and is aflame with love? But if God is your wrathful judge, rightfully because of your guilt, and your almighty enemy who sees all and detests sin with an implacable hatred, then you ought to fear with dread and terror and give no rest to your eyes and your feet until you appease him through true penitence and breathe again in the light of his mercies.

CHAPTER TWO

The Multitude of Created Things and the Infinity of God's Perfections

Who shall count the multitude of creatures of our God, who alone is creator of heaven and earth? Ecclesiasticus says, "Who has numbered the sand of the sea, and the drops of rain?" (Sir 1:2). But putting aside all these minute things, how many metals, gold and silver, brass and lead, precious stones, gems and pearls, are found on land and sea? How many types and species and individual grains, shrubs, and plants are there on earth? How many parts in each of them? How many types, species, and individual animals, perfect and imperfect, which run, crawl, and fly? How many types and species and individual fish in the sea? Who can count them? What about the races of men, of which it is written, "According to your highness you have multiplied the children of men" (Ps 11:9)? Finally, how many are the stars in the sky? How many angels above the heavens? As we read of the stars in the trustworthy Scriptures, "Number the stars, if you can" (Gn 15:5). Elsewhere Scripture compares the number of the stars with the number of the sands of the sea, which everybody agrees are uncountable (Jer 33:22). Rightly does Daniel say of the angels, "Thousands of thousands ministered to him and ten thousand times a hundred thousand stood before him" (Dn 7:10). And Saint Thomas[3] agrees with Saint Dionysius[4] that the number of the angels is so great that it surpasses the number of all material creatures. Consequently, this nearly infinite number of things which our almighty God alone has created shows that the perfections of the divine essence are completely infinite.

God wanted man to know him somehow through his creatures, and since no creature could fittingly reflect the infinite perfection of the Creator, he multiplied his creatures and gave a certain goodness and perfection to each of them so that from them we could judge the goodness and perfection of the Creator, who embraces infinite perfection in the perfection of his one and utterly simple essence, just as a gold coin contains the value of many copper coins. My soul, when anything that seems wonderful strikes your eye or your thought, make it a ladder to recognize the Creator's perfection which is incomparably greater and more wonderful. This way created objects which have become "a snare to the feet of the unwise" (Wis 14:11), as the Book of Wisdom teaches, will not mislead you but will teach you; they will not cast you down but direct you upward toward better things. Therefore, if you encounter gold or silver or jewels, you will say in your heart, "My God is more precious, who promised to give me himself if I despise these things." If you marvel at kingdoms and earthly empires, say in your heart, "How much greater is the kingdom of heaven which endures forever and which God, who does not lie, promised to those who love him." If pleasures and delights begin to titillate your sensuality, say in your heart, "The pleasure of the spirit is much more enjoyable than the pleasure of the flesh, and intellectual delights are much more enjoyable than those of the belly." The first come from a perishable creature, the second come from the God of all consolation. He who tastes the latter can say with the Apostle, "I am filled with comfort, and I overflow with joy in all our troubles" (2 Cor 7:4). Finally, if you are offered something beautiful, new, unusual, great, or wonderful on condition that you desert your God, answer serenely, "Whatever good they possess and much more and better are beyond doubt to be found in God." Therefore, it would be useless to trade a gilded coin for gold, glass for a precious gem, little for much, the uncertain for the certain, and the temporal for the eternal.

CHAPTER THREE

The Variety of Created Things and God as Infinite Font of All Good

The multitude of creatures is wonderful and suggests the manifold perfection of the one God, but much more wonderful is the variety of things which are seen in that multiplication and which more easily lead us to the knowledge of God. For it is not difficult for one sign to express many numbers which are identical and for countless letters to be printed from the same type, but to vary natures in the almost infinite way that God has done in his creation of things, this is clearly a divine work worthy of wonder. I pass over the genera and species of things which are commonly agreed to be extremely different and varied. How much variety there is in the individual grains, plants, flowers, and fruits! Do not their shapes, colors, odors, and tastes differ in almost infinite ways? Is this not equally true among the animals? But what can I say about men, when you can hardly find two men really alike in a vast army? The same is found among the stars and the angels, for every "star differs from other stars in glory" (1 Cor 15:41), as the Apostle states, and Saint Thomas asserts that the angels, even though they are more numerous than material beings, differ not only regarding their individuality, but also in the form that determines their species.[5]

My soul, raise the eyes of your mind to God in whom are the patterns of all things and from whom as from a font of infinite richness there flows that nearly infinite variety. Even God could not have endowed created things with their countless natures unless he contained in the breast of his being their natures in a most high and exalted way. Rightly the Apostle cries out, "Oh, the depth of the riches of the wisdom and of the knowledge of God" (Rom 11:33). Truly it is a well of infinite depth in which hide the treasures of riches, the wisdom, and the knowledge which was able to produce such a variety of things. Rightly again Saint Francis, illumined by divine light, used to say to the Lord, "My God and my all," because the various goods which are found scattered and divided in creatures are found collected in one God in a higher and better way. My soul, you may object, "These assertions seem true, but we see created goods with our eyes, touch them with our hands, taste them with our mouth, possess them physically, and enjoy them. We do not see God, touch him, taste him, possess him; we can barely apprehend him in thought as a faraway object. So it is no wonder if created things touch us more than God." But, my soul, if your faith is strong and vigilant, you cannot deny that after this life, which flits away like a shadow, if you remain firm in faith, hope, and love, you will see God clearly and truly as he is in himself and you will possess him and enjoy him far better and more intimately than you now enjoy created things.

Hear the Lord himself, "Blessed are the clean of heart, for they shall see God" (Mt 5:8). Hear the Apostle Paul, "We see now through a mirror in an obscure manner, but then face to face" (1 Cor 13:12). Hear Saint John, "We shall be like to him, for we shall see him just as he is" (1 Jn 3:2). Moreover, how much of the world, I ask you, is yours? Certainly not the whole world nor a half nor a third nor a fourth, but barely a particle is yours, and you will be forced to surrender it after a short time, whether you like it or not. But you will totally possess God in whom are all things, and you will possess him forever. For the saints and blessed "God will be all in all" (1 Cor 15:28) without any end. He will be your life, food, clothing, housing, honor, riches, delight, and all else.

In addition, your God is gentle and mild. He does not command that while you are a pilgrim on earth you must utterly forgo creaturely consolations; indeed he created all things to serve you. But he did command that you use them with moderation, sobriety, and temperance, that you share them cheerfully with the needy, that your possessions be not your master but you theirs, and that you use them to attain God. Think carefully then, is it not better for you not to lack created things in this life insofar as they are necessary and to enjoy in the other life the Creator himself in whom are all things, as I have often said? Or is it better to strive mightily in this life to acquire temporal possessions, never to be satisfied with their amount, and in the next life suddenly to be stripped of all your temporal goods and never attain eternal goods? Moreover, God is not far from those who love him, so that even in this life he gives them great joys, greater joys than lovers of the world find in created things. The Scripture speaks the truth: "I remembered God, and was delighted" (Ps 76:4), and "Delight in the Lord, and he will give you the requests of your heart" (Ps 36:4), and "I will take delight in the Lord" (Ps 103:34), and "give joy to the soul of your servant, for to you, O Lord, I have lifted up my soul" (Ps 85:4). I can skip other passages since the Apostle says, "I am filled with comfort, I overflow with joy in all our troubles" (2 Cor 7:4). Certainly he does not mean that tribulation gives birth to consolation or suffering to joy, for thorns do not produce grapes nor thistles produce figs. Rather he means that to ease tribulation God fills his friends with such pure, clear, and solid consolations that worldly joys cannot be compared with them. Make this your firm conviction, my soul: Whoever finds God, finds all; whoever loses God, loses all.

CHAPTER FOUR

The Power Implanted in Created Things and God's Omnipotence

Our next task is to ascend from the strength that God has given creatures to an understanding of the infinite strength of the Creator. There is no creature without exception which does not have wonderful strength or power or efficacy. Earth or a lump of mud, if it falls from on high, crushes with great impact. Is there anything it cannot break? What can resist it? When the Holy Spirit in the Book of Revelation wishes to describe the tremendous force with which Babylon the great, that is, the whole group of the damned, will be hurled into the deep abyss on the judgment day, he speaks thus, "A strong angel took up a stone, as it were a great millstone, and cast it into the sea, saying, 'With this violence will Babylon, the great city, be overthrown, and will not be found any more' " (Rv 18:21).

Water which soft and smooth flows gently over the face of the earth, when it swells wrathfully in rivers and torrents, smashes down and destroys everything in its path; we have seen it demolish not only the houses of country folk, but also the gates and walls of cities and marble bridges. Next the winds. Sometimes they blow very gently, but they also smash great ships against the rocks and root up and knock down aged oak trees. I myself saw something that I would never have believed unless I had seen it, a great mass of earth dug up by a tremendous wind and dumped on a village so that a deep crevice could be inspected where the earth had been ripped out. The whole village was covered where the earth had fallen and remained as if buried. What shall we say about fire? How fast a little fire spreads into a conflagration which devours and burns down homes and forests in a matter of minutes. "Behold," says Saint James, "how small a fire—how great a forest it kindles" (Jas 3:5).

What various powers lie hidden in plants! What strange powers are found in stones, especially magnetic stones and amber. What strength do we see in animals, such as lions, bears, bulls, and elephants. How clever, although tiny, are ants, spiders, bees, and flies. I pass over the power of the angels and the might of the sun and stars, which are far away from us. Finally, how great is human genius, which has invented skills such that we wonder whether nature surpasses art or art surpasses nature! Now lift up your eyes to God, my soul, and reflect on how great is the strength, efficacy, and power of the Lord your God, of whom Scripture truthfully says, "Who is like you among the strong" (Ex 15:11), and "You alone perform great wonders" (Ps 135:4), and "The Blessed and only Sovereign, the King of kings and Lord of lords" (1 Tm 6:15). All the powers that created things possess come from God, and they possess them only as long as God pleases. Who wrought it that Jonah, shut up in the belly of a whale, went unharmed either by the waters of the sea or the teeth of the whale, except God (Jn 2:1ff.)? Who closed the mouths of hungry lions so that they touched not Daniel, except God (Dn 6:16)? Who kept unharmed the three young men in the fiery furnace, except God (Dn 3:33ff.)? Who said to the raging wind and the seething sea, " 'Peace, be still!,' and the wind fell and there came a great calm"? (Mk 4:39). Who, except Christ who is true God? God does not have his strength and power from another, but his will is power, a power nothing can resist. He has infinite power and has it always and everywhere. All human power compared to God's is not small or puny, but nothing whatsoever, as Isaiah says, "All nations are before him as if they had no being at all, and are counted to him as nothing and vanity" (Is 40:17). Are they not silly who are fearful of created things, but do not fear almighty God? Likewise those who trust in their own strength and that of their friends and do not trust in almighty God? "If God is for us, who is against us?" (Rom 8:31). And if God is against us, who is for us?

If you are wise, my soul, "Humble yourself under the mighty hand of God" (1 Pt 5:6); cleave to him in true devotion, and you will not fear what man or demon or other creature may do to you. But if you have fallen away from devotion and provoked God to wrath, give your days no rest until you make peace with your God, for it is an exceedingly "fearful thing to fall into the hands of the living God" (Heb 10:31).

CHAPTER FIVE

The Beauty of Created Things and the Uncreated Beauty of God

The last subject we will examine is the beauty of created things. On this the Prophet said, "You have given me, O Lord, a delight in your doing" (Ps 91:5). Certainly everything that God has made is beautiful as well as good, if we rightly reflect on it. Passing over other things, let us consider those which everyone judges and agrees are beautiful. Certainly there is great beauty in a green pasture or a well-kept garden, a pleasant wood, a tranquil sea, a serene sky, fountains, streams, cities, and the heavens adorned and glittering with countless jewel-like stars. And how much do we delight in the beauty of a tree clothed in blossoms or laden with apples? Or the beauty in the shapely bodies of the different four-footed animals, in the flight of birds, the darting of fish? What shall I say of the beauty of the stars and moon and especially the great and brilliant light of the sun, whose rising delights the whole world? It is human beings that we are really talking to, and nothing gives them more pleasure than their own beauty and appearance. "Many have perished by the beauty of a woman" (Sir 9:9), says Ecclesiasticus. Often we have seen with sorrow men otherwise wise so captivated by love for the beauty of women and, conversely, serious and honored women reduced to such madness by the beauty of men that they prefer the love of human beauty to their family life, their dignity, their children, their parents, even to life itself and their eternal salvation. Well known are the stories in Sacred Scripture about David, Solomon, and Samson. History is full of similar examples.

So, my soul, if the Creator has lavished such beauty on created things, how great and marvelous do you think is the beauty of the all-beautiful Creator? No one can give what he does not have. If the appearance of the sun and the stars has so enchanted men that "they took to be gods" those luminous bodies, the Wise Man said, "let them know how much the Lord of them is more beautiful than they: for the first author of beauty made all those things" (Wis 13:3). The greatness of God's beauty not only is known with certainty from the fact that the beauty of all creatures is gathered together and found on a higher level in him, but also from the fact that since he is invisible to us while we are pilgrims far from him and is known only by the testimony of the Scriptures and to a degree in the mirror of his creatures, still many saints so burned with love for him that some hid themselves in desert places, wishing to devote themselves entirely to contemplation. Examples of this are Saints Mary Magdalene, Paul, the first hermit, Anthony the Great, and countless others who can be looked up in Theodoret's *Religious History*.[6] Others giving up wives, children, and all earthly possessions chose to live in monasteries under the command of others so that they could enjoy God's friendship. Others yearned to risk freely their lives amid bitter suffering in order that they might merit to attain the vision of infinite beauty. Listen to one of them, namely, Saint Ignatius the Martyr in his *Letter to the Romans*, "May I endure fire, the cross, beasts, the breaking of bones, dismemberment, the crushing of the whole body, and all the torments of the devil, if only I can enjoy Christ."[7] If, therefore, the divine beauty not yet seen, but only believed in and hoped for, stirs such fiery desire, what will he do when the veil is removed and he is seen as he is in himself? Then he will certainly bring it about that, "drunk by a torrent of his pleasure" (Ps 35:9), we will neither wish to nor be able to switch our eyes even for an instant from his beauty. It is not surprising that the angels and blessed souls always look on the face of the Father who is in heaven without finding any tedium or surfeit. For God is himself always gazing on his beauty from eternity and finds total peace in that vision and from it is happy and wishes nothing else. He is like someone who has entered a wine cellar or a garden of all delights which he never leaves nor shall ever leave for all eternity.

My soul, seek this beauty and aspire to it day and night. Say with the Prophet, "My soul has thirsted after the strong living God; when shall I come and appear before the face of God?" (Ps 41:3). Say with the Apostle, "We even have the courage to prefer to be exiled from the body and to be at home with the Lord" (2 Cor 5:8). Do not fear that the mighty love of this beauty will defile you. Love of the divine beauty perfects the heart without wounding; it sanctifies without defiling. The holy virgin and martyr Agnes rightly said, "I love Christ, whose mother is a virgin, whose Father knows not woman. When I love him, I am chaste; when I touch him, I am pure; when I receive him, I remain a virgin."[8] If you really desire the uncreated beauty of the Lord, you ought to fulfil what the Apostle adds in that passage; he says, "And therefore we strive, whether in the body or out of it, to be pleasing to him" (2 Cor 5:9). If God is pleasing to you, you ought also to be pleasing to God. Beyond doubt we will please him in the land of the living when we shall be present and illuminated by his brightness, as the Prophet sings, "I will please the Lord in the land of the living " (Ps 114:9). But in this pilgrimage we become soiled so easily, and we are defiled with the dirt of sin, as the Apostle James said, "In many things we all offend" (Jas 3:2). The prophet David, to show how few remain stainless on the way, claimed that this was part of beatitude in saying, "Blessed are the undefiled in the way" (Ps 118:1). If you desire, my soul, to please your loved one even while you are distant and on pilgrimage, it is not enough to desire to please him, but, as the Apostle says, you must strive to please him, that is, by constant and intense work you must avoid sins which make ugly the face of the soul. And if some stains cling there, you must strive to cleanse them with no less effort and work. Do you not see how many hours young women who want to please their husbands spend in setting their hair, putting on makeup, and removing stains from their clothes—this to please the eyes of mortal man who in a little while must be turned into dust and ashes? What then should you do to please the eyes of your immortal spouse, who sees you always and wants to find you without spot or wrinkle? Certainly you must work at it with all your strength, so that you may walk "in holiness and justice before him" (Lk 1:75). You must energetically remove or cut out everything that blocks true holiness and true justice. Pay no attention to flesh and blood and ignore what men say and judge since you cannot please both God and the world, as the Apostle says, "If I were still trying to please men, I should not be a servant of Christ" (Gal 1:10).

STEP THREE

The Consideration of the Earth

CHAPTER ONE

As Our Body Rests on Earth, So Our Mind Can Rest in God Alone

We have examined the physical world as a whole. Now we come to consider its principal parts so that we can build from them a ladder for us to contemplate the builder, as far as we can.

The first subject is earth, which, although it lies in the lowest place and seems less important than the other elements, in fact is not less important than water and surpasses all the other elements in dignity and value. Throughout the Holy Scriptures we read that God made the heavens and the earth as the principal parts of the world, to which the other parts are subordinated. He made heaven as a sort of palace for God and the angels; earth he made as a palace for men. "The heaven of heaven is for God," says the Prophet, "but the earth he gave to the sons of men" (Ps 113:24). This is the reason why heaven is full of glittering stars and the earth abounds with the immense riches of metals, precious stones, grasses, trees, and many kinds of animals. Water has only fishes. Air and fire are barren and almost empty elements. Let us pass over these. Three aspects of the earthly globe are most worthy of consideration. If our mind is alert, we can ascend from them to God without difficulty.

First, earth is the firm foundation of the whole world, and if we did not have it, man could neither walk nor rest nor work nor carry on life at all. "He has established the earth," says David, "which will not be moved" (Ps 93:2). "You have founded the earth upon its own bases, and it shall not be moved forever and ever" (Ps 103:5). Second, earth is a good nurse for men and other animals, steadily producing grain, crops, fruit, herbs, apples, and countless other products. Thus God speaks, "Behold I have given you every herb-bearing seed upon the earth, and all trees that have in themselves seed of their own kind, to be your meat, and to all the beasts of the earth" (Gn 1:29–30). Third, earth produces stone and wood for building homes, and copper and iron for various uses, and gold and silver from which coins are minted, in short, the instruments for procuring easily all the things needed for human life.

The first property of earth is obviously its location, in which our bodies find rest since they cannot rest in water, air, or fire. It is a symbol of the Creator, in whom alone the human soul can find rest. "You have made us for yourself, O Lord," says Saint Augustine, "and our heart is restless until it rests in you."[1] If anyone sought rest in power, riches, and pleasure, it was King Solomon. He possessed a vast and peaceful kingdom so that the Scripture testifies that he "had under him all the kingdoms from the river to the land of the Philistines, even to the border of Egypt: and they brought him presents, and served him all the days of his life" (1 Kgs 4:21). Besides he had incomparable wealth so that he kept up forty thousand stalls to stable his chariot horses and twelve thousand riding horses and, as we read in the same book, Solomon's fleet brought gold and precious gems from Ophir in such quantity that silver was counted as worthless, and the quantity of silver in Jerusalem equaled the cobblestones (1 Kgs 4:24, 9:28, 10:27). He indulged himself in pleasures that seem incredible; in his lust for women he took seventy wives as queens and had three hundred concubines, as we read in the same book (1 Kgs 11:3). Let us now hear how he described himself. "I made me great works," he said, "I built me houses, and planted vineyards. I made gardens, and orchards, and set them with trees of all kinds, and I made me ponds of water, to water therewith the wood of the young trees. I got me menservants, and maidservants, and had a great family, and herds of oxen, and great flocks of sheep, above all that were before me in Jerusalem. I heaped together for myself silver and gold, and the wealth of kings, and provinces. I made me singing men, and singing women, and the delights of the sons of men, cups and vessels to serve to pour out wine. And I surpassed in riches all that were before me in Jerusalem. My wisdom also remained with me. And whatsoever my eyes desired, I refused them not. And I withheld not my heart from enjoying every pleasure, and delighting itself in the things I had prepared; and esteemed this my portion, to make use of my own labor" (Eccl 2:4–10). This is his statement, and he surely had complete satisfaction if it can be found in created things. He lacked nothing, not kingdom, not riches, not that human wisdom which is regarded as having the greatest worth, and finally not peace and tranquillity in possessing and holding onto so many goods for a long time.

Let us now ask whether he found rest in all these goods and whether they could fill the capacity of his soul. "And when I turned myself to all the works which my hands had wrought, and to the labors wherein I had labored in vain, I saw in all things vanity, and vexation of mind, and that nothing was lasting under the sun" (Eccl 2:11). Therefore, Solomon did not find peace in his many riches and pleasures and wisdom and honors, nor could he have, even if they had been much more and greater, because the human spirit is immortal and such things are mortal and cannot last long under the sun. It is impossible for the human spirit, which is open to infinite goodness, to be satisfied with finite goods—just as the human body cannot find rest in the air regardless of its breadth nor in water regardless of its depth, because its center is the earth, not air or water. Thus the human spirit can never find rest in airy dignities or dirty or watery riches, that is, soft and filthy pleasures, or in the false glitter of human knowledge, but only in God, who is the center of our souls and their true and only resting place. How truly and wisely did Solomon's father speak out and say, "What have I in heaven? and besides you what do I desire upon earth? You are the God of my heart, and the God that is my portion forever" (Ps 72:25–26). What he was trying to say is, "I find nothing either in heaven or on earth or in any other created thing under heaven or on earth that can bring me true rest. You alone are the solid rock for my heart." The word *God* in the Hebrew text in this context signifies rock. Therefore, you alone are the most solid rock for my heart; I rest only in you, you alone are my portion, my inheritance, all my good. Everything else is nothing and can do nothing to fill and satisfy me, not merely for a day or two or a year, but for eternity.

Only you satisfy me for eternity, and all other things do not satisfy even for one day.

Have you as yet recognized, my soul, that God alone is your rock on which you rest? All other things are vanity and trouble for your spirit and have no real existence, but are phantoms. They bring not solace, but trouble because they are acquired with labor, held onto with fear, and lost with sorrow. Be wise and spurn all things that are passing lest they snatch you away with them. Stay with him, chain yourself to him by love, who remains forever. Lift your heart to God in heaven lest it grow rotten upon earth. Learn that true wisdom which is folly to the multitude in whose name the Wise Man says, "We have erred from the way of truth, and the light of justice has not shined unto us. We wearied ourselves in the way of iniquity and destruction, and have walked through hard ways, but the way of the Lord we have not known. What has pride profited us? Or what advantage has the boasting of riches brought us? All those things are passed away like a shadow, but we are consumed in our wickedness" (Wis 5:6–9, 13).

CHAPTER TWO

We Are Securely Grounded in God

There is another reason why a solid rock is a symbol of the Lord our God. The wisdom of God explains this symbol to us in his Gospel where he said that the house built on solid rock remains unmoved if the rains fall from above and the winds rush in from the side or streams strike it from below. But the house built on sand cannot stand up to any of these, but collapses at the first attack of rain or wind or stream, and great is the ruin of that house (Mt 7:24–27).

Your home, O soul, has its various powers and virtues as its rooms and halls. It will be secure if it is based on God as on a rock, that is, if you trust God absolutely, if all your confidence is in God, if rooted and based on the love of God, you can say with the Apostle, "Who shall separate us from the love of Christ?" (Rom 8:35). Then neither wicked spirits who are above us, nor carnal desires which are within us, nor the enemies of our own household who attack us from the side, that is, our relatives and friends, will ever prevail against you in their machinations. Great indeed are the forces and great is the cleverness of the spiritual powers, but greater is the power and greater the wisdom of the Holy Spirit who presides over the house which is based on God. The flesh fights most stubbornly against the spirit, and carnal desires usually subdue even the strongest souls, but the love of God easily conquers the love of the flesh, and the fear of God easily casts down the fear of the world. Finally, "a man's enemies are those of his own household" (Mi 7:6; Mt 10:36), and they try by evil suggestions to draw souls to their fellowships of sinners. But the soul, which trusts that she has her Lord and Father and her brother and spouse in heaven, knows without great effort not only how to condemn her fleshly friends and relatives, but also how to hate them and can say with the Apostle, "For I am sure that neither death, nor life, nor any other creature will be able to separate us from the love of God, which is in Christ Jesus our Lord" (Rom 8:38–39). But it is truly an unhappy soul whose house is founded on sand and cannot last long, and it will soon utterly collapse since she believes in a lie and relies on a reed for a staff and has either her belly or money or the smoke of honor for her God. All these pass away and perish very quickly and drag the soul that clings to them down to eternal destruction.

CHAPTER THREE

The Earth Nourishes Our Body by God's Power, Who Alone Nourishes the Whole Man

Another property of the earth lies in the fact that the earth like a good nurse pours forth grain and other crops abundantly to feed man and the other animals. But this property leads us to the Creator as the true nourisher, for it is God, not the earth, who produces all the good things on earth, as the Holy Spirit says through the mouth of David. "He makes grass to grow on the mountains, and herbs for the service of men" (Ps 147:8), and again, "All expect of you that you give them food in season. What you give to them they shall gather up; when you open your hand, they shall all be filled with good" (Ps 104:27–28). Our Lord in the Gospel says, "Look at the birds of the air; they do not sow, or reap, or gather into barns; yet your heavenly Father feeds them" (Mt 6:26). Likewise the Apostle Paul says that God "did not leave himself without testimony, bestowing blessings, giving rains from heaven and fruitful seasons, rain and harvest time, filling our hearts with food and gladness" (Acts 14:17). Also true is the statement at the beginning of the Book of Genesis, "Let the earth bring forth the green herb, and such as may seed, and the fruit tree yielding fruit after its kind" (Gn 1:11). And the earth does produce grasses and fruit trees, but by the power God gave them, while God himself produces and conserves and gives the increase through that power. Hence, when he invited all creatures to praise the Creator, David added fruit trees and all cedars along with the rest (Ps 148:9), and the three young men in Daniel urged all things that grow in the earth to join the other creatures in blessing the Lord and praising and exalting him forever (Dn 3:51–90).

Since all things praise God in their own way, with what intensity should you, my soul, bless and praise him for all the benefits you continually enjoy? You should acknowledge in them God's hidden hand which gives everything and the fatherly and pure love of your God which shows itself not as something hidden, but clear and manifest. He never ceases to benefit you from heaven and provide you with everything! But in the eyes of the Lord your God this is too little. He it is who produces in you as in his spiritual field the noble shoots of love. Love comes not from the world but from God, as the beloved disciple says in his Letter (1 Jn 4:7). From love as from a divine and heavenly tree there spring forth bright flowers fragrant with holy thoughts, green leaves useful for the salvation of the nations, and the fruits of good works which glorify God, help the neighbor, gather merit, and remain unto eternal life.

Woe to those who like stupid oxen think to satisfy themselves with the fruits of the earth and eagerly collect and hide them away without thinking of the Creator or giving him thanks. Their souls are like the earth cursed by God which gives forth thorns and thistles. What fills the mind of those God does not sow with chaste thoughts, except fornication, adultery, murder, sacrilege, theft, treachery, and the like? What do they speak about except blasphemies, perjuries, curses, heresies, abuse, insults, false testimonies, lies, and the like, which they have learned from their father, the devil? And finally what fruits do they produce except the poisoned fruits about which, we have said, they continually think and which the Apostle Paul calls the works of the flesh? (Gal 6:7). These indeed are the thorns which first pierce the souls who nurture them with the bitter punctures of fears and cares, then pierce the reputation, bodies, and spirits of their neighbors with serious and often incurable wounds which later inflict much grievous harm on others.

But passing over this, my soul, if you are the little garden of the heavenly farmer, take care that thorns and thistles are never found in you but that you foster with great care the tree of love, the lily of chastity, and the nard plant of humility. Keep watch so that the conviction never creeps into you that it is from yourself that these heavenly buds of virtues spring and not from the Lord your God, who is the Lord of virtues, the sower of chaste thoughts. Do not attribute to yourself the conservation, growth, and ripening of the fruits of good works; entrust them to him, and may your strength always be in him.

CHAPTER FOUR

The Treasures of the Earth, as a Shadow of God's Eternal Goods

The last glory of the earth that remains is the gold and silver and precious stones which it contains in its lap. Earth certainly does not produce such a precious variety of things by its own power; rather he made them who says through Haggai, "The silver is mine, and the gold is mine" (Hg 2:9). O Lover of men, did it also please your sweetness that you provide the human race not only with stone and wood, copper and iron, and all other such materials needed for constructing houses and ships and making various tools, but also with gold, silver, and precious stones for ornament and decoration? And if you gave this to earthly pilgrims and often even to your enemies who blaspheme your name, what will you give to your loved ones who will bless you and reign with you in heaven? You will give them not a crust of gold and silver or a few precious gems, but the city about which John the Apostle spoke in Revelation when he said, "And the material of its walls was jasper; but the city itself was pure gold, and the foundations of the wall of the city were adorned with every precious stone. And the twelve gates were twelve pearls" (Rv 21:18, 19, 21). But let us not imagine that supernal city, the heavenly Jerusalem, as built and decorated with gold, gems, and pearls, as cities are here. We know that the Holy Spirit uses these words because he speaks to us who have seen nothing better or greater. Beyond any doubt that city, which is the fatherland of God's elect, will be much more splendid than all the cities of this pilgrimage, even as a city of gold and gems surpasses all peasant villages which are made of mud and straw.

Raise the eyes of your mind to heaven, my soul, and mull over how greatly the blessings given there should be esteemed, since the luster of gold, silver, and precious stones, which here count for so much, when compared with those goods will hardly be granted the name of mud and straw. Moreover, gold, silver, and pearls, which are here considered valuable, are perishable, but those that shine in the heavenly city are imperishable and eternal. But if you want to transfer through the hands of the poor the same perishable gold and silver that you have here to the heavenly city, which you would gladly do if you were wise, then they would become imperishable and remain yours for eternity. For the Truth cannot lie, which says, "Sell what you have and give to the poor, and you shall have treasure in heaven" (Mt 19:21), and elsewhere, "Sell what you have and give alms. Make for yourselves purses that do not grow old, a treasure unfailing in heaven, where neither thief draws near nor moth destroys" (Lk 12:33). Oh, the unbelief of the sons of men! A liar who promises to give 10 percent interest and to return the whole capital to the lender is believed. God, who cannot lie, promises that he will return to the almsgiver treasure in heaven and a hundredfold besides and life everlasting, but the greedy man is fearful and cannot be brought to believe and prefers to hide his treasure where rust corrodes and thieves break in and steal rather than lay up his treasure in heaven where a thief cannot creep up nor rust corrode. Even if sometimes thieves do not carry off and moth or rust do not destroy what you have gathered and saved by great effort, whose will they be, O unhappy man? They certainly will not be yours, but they could have been yours if you had transferred them into heavenly treasures through the hands of the poor. Experience indeed teaches that possessions heaped up by greedy rich men go to their prodigal heirs, who quickly run through what their greedy parents gathered. Meanwhile, the sin of avarice remains and will remain forever, and the worm of conscience will not die nor will the fire of hell be extinguished.

Let the folly of others teach you, my soul, and listen to your Lord and Teacher who cries out, "Take heed and guard yourselves from all covetousness, for a man's life does not consist in the abundance of his possessions" (Lk 12:15). The greedy man gatheres and guards so that he can have possessions with which to live a long life, but the opposite happens. He dies when he least expects it, and the possessions that he greedily gathered and guarded beget the worm that dies not and feeds the fire which is not extinguished. O unhappy miser, did you heap up money with such care to prepare fuel for the fire of hell so that it will never go out? Listen to Saint James, who says at the end of his Letter, "Come now, you rich, weep and howl over your miseries which will come upon you. Your riches have rotted, and your garments have become moth-eaten. Your gold and silver are rusted; and their rust will be a witness against you, and will devour your flesh as fire does" (Jas 5:1–3). Because you are rich, Saint James says, you are considered and called happy, but in truth you are wretched, more wretched than all the needy, and you have great cause for weeping and wailing over the enormous misery which will certainly overtake you, namely, your superfluous wealth which you have hoarded and which you allowed to rot when you ought to have given it to the poor, and your superfluous clothing that you possess or rather that you allowed the moths to eat rather than allow the poor to use for clothing, and the gold and silver which you prefer rust to corrode rather than give it away as food for the poor. All these, I say, will give witness against you on the day of judgment, and the moths and rust from your riches will become a burning fire which will eat your flesh through endless time and never finish it, just as the fire will not go out nor the pain cease. Therefore, we close with the Royal Prophet, the foolish "called people happy, that has these things," that is, wealth in abundance, but in truth, "happy is that people whose God is the Lord" (Ps 144:15).

STEP FOUR

The Consideration of Waters and Especially Fountains

CHAPTER ONE

Water Cleanses Bodily Stains, but God Cleanses Spiritual Stains

The second of the world's elements is water. Rightly considered, it can provide a step in our ascent to God. We will consider water in general, then that special ascent to God that we draw from fountains.

Water is moist and cool and, therefore, has five characteristics. For it washes and cleans away stains, it puts out fires, it refreshes and restrains burning thirst, it brings together many diverse things into one, and finally it descends to the depths just as it ascends on high. All these are clear symbols or footprints of God, the Creator of all things. Water washes away physical stains, God washes away spiritual stains. "Wash me," says David, "and I shall be made whiter than snow" (Ps 51:7). Although contrition and the sacraments and priests and almsgiving and other works of piety all wash away the stains of the heart, that is, our sins, still all these are instruments or predispositions. It is God alone who really does the cleansing. "I am," God says through Isaiah, "I am he that blots out your iniquities for my own sake" (Is 43:25). And, therefore, the pharisees who murmured against Christ kept saying, "Who can forgive sins, but God only?" (Lk 5:21). They were not wrong in attributing to God alone supreme power to forgive sins, but rather in believing that Christ was not God. For this reason they were blaspheming and telling the truth at the same time.

Not only does God wash away the stains of the heart in a way similar to water, but he also wanted to be called water. Thus Saint John writes, "He who believes in me, as Scripture says, from him there shall flow rivers of living water. He said this, however, of the Spirit whom they who believed in him were to receive; for the Spirit had not yet been given, since Jesus had not yet been glorified" (Jn 7:38). Therefore, the Holy Spirit, who is indeed God, is living water. It is of this water that Ezechiel speaks, "I will pour upon you clean water, and you shall be cleansed from all your filthiness" (Ez 36:25). And since this heavenly and uncreated water far surpasses earthly and created water in power, we should note three differences in the cleansing power of created and uncreated water.

Created water cleans physical stains, but not all kinds. It cannot remove many stains without the help of soap and other aids. Uncreated water cleans away absolutely every stain. Thus we read in the passage cited a moment ago, "And you shall be cleansed from all your filthiness" (Ez 36:25).

Created water rarely gets out all stains without leaving some trace or sort of shadow from the stain. Uncreated water washes so that it leaves the object cleansed brighter and more beautiful than before it was dirtied. "You shall wash me," says David, "and I shall be made whiter than snow" (Ps 51:7). The Lord speaks through Isaiah, "If your sins be as scarlet, they shall be made as white as snow; and if they be red as crimson, they shall be white as wool" (Is 1:18).

Lastly, created water cleans natural stains which do not resist the cleaner. Uncreated water cleans voluntary stains, which cannot be washed away unless the soul itself wishes it and freely consents to the cleaner. But the power of this water is so great and wonderful that it gently penetrates even stony hearts and, therefore, is not rejected by a hard heart because it brings it about that it is not rejected, as Saint Augustine rightly tells us.[1] Lord, who can grasp the wonderful way you inspire faith in faithless hearts and pour humility into proud hearts and instill love into the hearts of your enemies so that those who were moments before breathing out threats and slaughter and persecuting you in your disciples suddenly change and gladly bear threats and slaughter for the sake of you and your Church (Acts 9:1)? It is too much for me to penetrate these secrets of yours; I would rather experience than delve into the efficacy of your grace. And since I know that your grace is a voluntary rain, restricted to your inheritance, as your Prophet sang (Ps 68:9), therefore, I humbly beg and plead that I may have part in your inheritance, and may it be pleasing for your grace to come down upon the soil of my heart lest it remain for you like waterless soil, baked and sterile, for it has not power of itself even to think of anything good. Let us move on to remaining considerations.

CHAPTER TWO

Water Puts Out Fire, but God Extinguishes the Blaze of Concupiscence

Water puts out fire, and heavenly water, that is, the grace of the Holy Spirit, puts out the fire of carnal desires in a wonderful way. Fasts and bodily austerities help greatly to restrict the blaze, but only as helps to the grace of the Holy Spirit. Otherwise by themselves they are of little help. Love controls the affections and drives of the spirit; it rules all and all obey it. Love cannot be forced, and if its way is blocked in one direction, love breaks out in another. Love fears nothing and dares all, conquers all and thinks that nothing is hard or impossible. Finally, a lesser love yields only to a greater and stronger love. Thus a completely fleshly love, whether it seeks riches or the pleasures of the world, yields only to the love of God. As soon as the water of the Holy Spirit begins to enter into the human heart, fleshly love immediately begins to grow cold. A good example for us is Saint Augustine, who was accustomed to give in to lust and thought that he could not get along without living with a woman, but when he began to taste the grace of the Holy Spirit, he exclaimed at the beginning of the Ninth Book of his *Confessions*, "How sweet it suddenly became for me to do without the pleasures of those playthings, and what I had feared to lose was now a joy to dismiss. You cast it out of me, you true and highest sweetness; you cast it out and you, sweeter than all pleasures, although not to flesh and blood, entered in their place. You are brighter than any light, but more inward than any secret; you are higher than any honor, but not to those who are high in their own esteem."[2]

CHAPTER THREE

Water Alleviates Thirst, but God Satisfies the Heart's Desires

Water also alleviates thirst, and heavenly water alone can put an end to the varied, vexing, and nearly infinite desires of the human heart. Truth taught this to the Samaritan woman when he said, "Everyone who drinks of this water will thirst again. He, however, who drinks of the water I will give him shall never thirst" (Jn 4:13). That is exactly the way things are. "The eye is not filled by seeing, neither is the ear filled by hearing" (Eccl 1:8). Nothing man encounters can satisfy his desire since he has a capacity for infinite good and all created things have their set limits. But the person who begins to drink heavenly water, which contains all things, looks for nothing more and needs nothing more. We have talked about this above when we were speaking about the spirit's rest in God alone as its true center.

CHAPTER FOUR

Water Joins Material Things Together, but God Establishes a Union of Spirits

Water simultaneously joins and makes one things that it seems hardly possible to unite. Thus many grains of flour are made into one loaf of bread by mixing with water, and bricks are made by adding water to many particles of earth. Much more easily and permanently does the Holy Spirit cause many men to be "one heart and one soul," as the Acts of the Apostles says of the first Christians (Acts 4:32), upon whom the Holy Spirit had just descended. This unity which the water of the Holy Spirit brings about was predicted and praised by the Lord when he was about to go to the Father, "Yet not for these only do I pray," he said, "but for those also who through their word are to believe in me, that all may be one, even as you, Father, in me and I in you" (Jn 17:20–21). And a bit later, "That they also may be one, even as we are one: I in them and you in me, that they may be perfected in unity" (Jn 17:22–23). The Apostle also urges us to this union and says in his Letter to the Ephesians, "Careful to preserve the unity of the Spirit in the bond of peace: one body and one spirit, even as you were called in the one hope of your calling" (Eph 4:3–4).

O happy union, which makes many men into the one body of Christ, which is ruled by its one head (1 Cor 10:16), eats of one bread, drinks of one chalice, and lives by one spirit and, by clinging to God, becomes one spirit with him. What more can a servant desire than to be not only a partaker in all his Master's goods, but also to be united indissolubly by a bond of love to his all-powerful, all-wise, and all-beautiful Lord? The grace of the Holy Spirit like living and life-giving water achieves all this when it is devoutly received into the heart and is guarded with all diligence and care.

CHAPTER FIVE

Water Comes Down and Goes Back Up; the Fountain of God's Grace Springs Up to Life Everlasting

Lastly, water ascends on high, just as it falls from on high. Since the Holy Spirit comes to earth from the height of heaven, he becomes for the man who receives him into his heart "a fountain of water springing up unto life everlasting," as the Lord says to the Samaritan woman (Jn 4:14). In other words, man is reborn by water and the Holy Spirit, and he who bears the same Spirit dwelling in his heart builds up merit toward the goal whence grace came down to him.

Taught and moved by the words of Scripture, my soul, tell your Father again and again with unutterable groans, "Give me this water which cleans away every stain, which quenches the heat of passion and satisfies all thirst and all desires, which makes you one spirit with your God, which becomes in you a fountain of water springing up to eternal life so that you may send merits before you to the place where you hope to dwell forever." With good reason the Son of God said, "If you, evil as you are, know how to give good gifts to your children, how much more will your heavenly Father give the good Spirit to those who ask him?" (Lk 11:13). He did not say that he will give bread or clothing or wisdom or love or the kingdom of heaven or life everlasting; rather he said, "He will give you the good Spirit," because everything is contained in him. Do not stop reminding the Father daily about the promise of his Son and tell him with great love and the certain hope of being answered, "Holy Father, I pour out my prayers to you not because of my merits, but because of the promise of your only begotten Son. He said to us, 'How much more will your Father give the good Spirit to those who ask him?' Your Son is assuredly the Truth, who does not deceive us. Therefore, fulfill the promise of your Son who glorified you on earth and was obedient to you even to death, death on a cross. Give the good Spirit to one who begs you, give the Spirit of fear and love of you so that your servant may fear nothing except offending you and love nothing except you and his neighbor in you. 'Create a clean heart in me, God, and renew a right spirit within me. Cast me not away from your face, and take not your holy spirit from me. Restore unto me the joy of your salvation, and strengthen me with a perfect spirit' " (Ps 51:10–12).

CHAPTER SIX

A Fountain of Water Reflects God as the Fountain of Being

Now I come to the analogy which fountains have with God. From this analogy the spirit can be raised to contemplate the wonderful excellence of the Creator. With good reason the Holy Scriptures call God "the fountain of life" (Ps 36:9) and "the fountain of wisdom" (Sir 1:5) and "fountain of living water" (Jer 2:13). The words of God himself to Moses suggest that he is the font of being, "I am who am." "He who is, has sent me to you" (Ex 3:14). The Apostle seems to have summed all this up, when he says, "In him we live and move and have our being" (Acts 17:28). For in him we have our being as in a fountain of being, and in him we live as in a fountain of life, and in him we move as in a fountain of wisdom, because "wisdom is more active than all active things, and reaches everywhere by reason of her purity" (Wis 7:24), as is said in the Book of Wisdom.

Here among us a fountain of water has as its characteristic that it gives birth to streams, and if they stop flowing from the fountain, they immediately dry up. The fountain, however, does not depend upon the streams because it does not get its water from them, but possesses water in itself and gives it to others. This is a true symbol and trace of the divinity. God is the truest fountain of being since he receives being from no other being and all receive from him. God receives being from no being because existence stems from God's essence, and his very essence is his existence so that it cannot be or be thought that God has not always existed or does not always exist. Other beings can exist for a time and not exist for a time because existence is not necessarily part of their essence. As an example, it is part of man's essence to be a rational animal; therefore, a man cannot be without being a rational animal. If it were also part of man's essence to exist, he could not not exist forever, but because it is not part of his essence to exist, therefore, he can exist and not exist. God is, therefore, the fountain of being because he includes in his essence actual existence forever. This is the meaning of the words "I am who am" (Ex 3:14), that is, I am existence itself, and I do not receive existence from outside, but have it in myself. The property that my essence is to exist belongs to me alone. For the same reason eternity and immortality are also properties of God, as the Apostle says, "To the King of the ages, who is immortal, the one God" (1 Tm 1:17), and "who alone has immortality" (1 Tm 6:16). Thus all other things truly receive their existence from God so that unless they always depend upon him and are conserved by a certain influx from him, they at once cease to exist. Hence, the same Apostle says, "He upholds all things by the word of his power" (Heb 1:3). Unless created things are sustained by God they indeed stop existing.

Look up in wonder, my soul, at the infinite goodness of your Creator, who carries and conserves all things so lovingly despite his not needing their works. No less should you admire and imitate the patience of your same Creator who "is kind toward the ungrateful and evil" (Lk 6:35) so that he bears with those who blaspheme him and conserves them who are worthy of annihilation. Nor should you consider it a heavy burden if sometimes you are commanded to bear the weakness of your brothers and do good to those who hate you.

The greatness of the fountain of being does not consist only in the fact that it receives being from no other fountain and communicates being to other things. Among us water from fountains and water from streams are basically the same. Even though the waters in fountains do not take water from other fountains, they still have a cause for their being, namely, mists, and for these there are other causes and so on, until we reach the first cause, which is God. God your Creator, O soul, is not of the same kind as created things, but stands apart from them by an infinite distance of dignity, nobility, and excellence. He is the true and proper fountain of being because he alone does not receive his being from another fountain of being, but knows no cause whatsoever. The fountain of created waters, as we said, derives not from other waters, but from other causes. The uncreated fountain of being has nothing prior to itself, depends on nothing else, and lacks nothing else; nothing can harm it, but all things depend on it, and it can "utterly destroy the whole world at a beck" (2 Mc 8:18), as the brave Maccabee said. Marvel, my soul, at this loftiness, this beginning without beginning, cause without cause, infinite being, limitless, immense, absolutely necessary, while everything else is contingent by comparison. Perhaps it was of this that Truth said, "But one thing is necessary" (Lk 10:42). Therefore, cling to him alone, serve him alone, delight in the love and desire of him alone. Despise everything else in comparison with him, or certainly do not worry yourself too much about many things, when one thing is necessary and it alone is enough for you and mankind. Let your one worry be that you never fall away from his grace and that you try to please him alone, always and everywhere.

CHAPTER SEVEN

God Is the Fountain of Being with Life in Himself

God is rightly called the fountain of life because he lives and has life in himself. Indeed, he is eternal life. "He is the true God and eternal life" (1 Jn 5:20), says Saint John, and all living things receive life from him, and should he cease to supply life, they would fail and would turn back to dust, as the holy prophet David sings (Ps 104:29). It is the property of living things to beget offspring similar to themselves. God begets a Son similar to himself, God begets God, and the living God begets living God. "For as the Father has life in himself, even so he gave the Son also to have life in himself" (Jn 5:26), as Saint John states in his Gospel. But the Father has life in himself because he is the fountain of life and does not receive life from another. He gave the Son to have life in himself, because he gave the same life that he has himself and through this the Son is also the fountain of life, but a fountain of life from the fountain of life, just as he is God from God and Light from Light. Who will explain or even understand what is the life of God and how he is the fountain of life from which all living things, whether on earth or in the sky, draw their little drops? Realize that life for us in this exile is nothing but having an internal principle of motion. We say things are alive which move themselves in some way. Thus by analogy we commonly call living waters those in streams and dead waters those in ponds, because the first seem to move themselves and the second cannot move unless they are stirred up by the winds or some other outside force.

Your God, my soul, truly lives and is the author and fountain of life. He teaches this himself throughout the Scriptures. "As I live, says the Lord" (Nm 14:28). The prophets frequently repeat, "The Lord lives, the Lord lives" (2 Kgs 3:14; Jer 4:2). In Jeremiah God complains about the people, "They have foresaken me, the fountain of living water" (Jer 2:13). Still he is not moved either by himself or by another. "I am the Lord," he says, "and I change not" (Mal 3:6). And elsewhere, "God is not as a son of man that he should be changed" (Nm 23:19). Daily we sing in the Church's hymn.

O God, Strength who holds all things,
Remaining in yourself unmoved,
You nonetheless mark off the times,
By the succession of the light of day.[3]

If God begets a son, he does so without changing. If he sees, hears, speaks, loves, has mercy, and judges, he does all these without change. Even if he creates and conserves things, then destroys and disperses them, and then again renews and changes them, he himself works while at rest and changes without changing. How is he living if he cannot move? And how can he not be alive if he is the fountain and author of life? This problem is easily solved. Strictly speaking, it is enough if a living thing acts of itself and is not moved from outside for it to be counted as having life. At most life in creatures is an internal principle of motion because creatures are imperfect and need many things for carrying out the actions of life. But God is infinite perfection and needs nothing outside himself. Therefore, he acts by himself and not by a push from another. He has no need for a push or a change. Creatures need to change in order to beget and be begotten because they beget outside themselves, and the thing that is begotten has to change from nonbeing to being. God, however, begets his Son within himself and produces the Holy Spirit within himself. The Son and the Holy Spirit do not have to change from nonbeing to being because the being that they receive has always existed, and they received it not in time, but in eternity. Creatures need the change of growth because they are born imperfect. God the Son, in contrast, is born absolutely perfect, and God the Spirit is spirated and produced absolutely perfect. Creatures need to be changed or modified so that they may acquire the various qualities that they need. God, in contrast, needs nothing since he has a nature of infinite perfection. Creatures need a change in place since they are not everywhere. God is totally present everywhere. Creatures need many things so that they can see, hear, speak, and work because, while they have life, it is an imperfect and impoverished life. God, in contrast, needs nothing outside of himself in order to see everything, hear everything, speak to everybody, and work everything in all things, because he not only has life, but life in utter abundance and happiness and is life itself and the fountain of life.

Let us give one example from the act of seeing. For a man to see he needs the power of sight, which is distinct from the soul which properly speaking lives. He needs an object, that is, a colored body existing outside of himself. He needs the light of the sun or of some other luminous body. He needs a medium, that is, a transparent body. He needs a sensible species which comes from the object to his eyes. He needs the bodily organ, that is, the eye complete with its various liquids and covering membranes. He needs sensitive spirits and optic nerves by which the spirits are transferred to him. He needs a proportionate distance, and he has to apply his faculties. Behold all the little instruments men and the other animals need so that they can carry out a simple action of life! God, in contrast, who has life complete in himself, needs nothing. His infinite essence supplies him with faculty, object, species, light, and everything else. By himself, through himself, and in himself God sees all things that are, that were, and that will be. He clearly knows all that could be. Before the world existed God was seeing all things, and nothing new has come before his sight or knowledge from the creation of things. What will you be, my soul, when you become a partaker of his life? Does God ask something great of you when he asks you to sacrifice this corporeal and animal life, indeed this imperfect and impoverished life, for your brothers and for God himself so that you may become a partaker in an eternal life which is very rich and happy? And if he does not command something great, when he commands you to despise life, how little and light ought it to seem when he orders you to give generously your dead wealth to the poor and to abstain from fleshly desires and to renounce in earnest the devil and his pomps and to yearn with your whole heart for that life which alone is true life.

CHAPTER EIGHT

God Is the Fountain of Wisdom

Now is the time for us to go up as well as we can to the fountain of wisdom. Ecclesiasticus says, "The word of God on high is the fountain of wisdom" (Sir 1:5). He rightly says "on high," because the fountain of wisdom richly and profusely flows out not only to the holy angels and to the souls of the blessed who live in heaven, but to us who are engaged as pilgrims in this desert, there comes not wisdom but a certain mist or scent of wisdom.

For this reason, my soul, do not for now seek higher than you should. Do not be "a searcher of majesty" lest you "shall be overwhelmed by glory" (Prv 25:27). Wonder at his wisdom about which the Apostle Paul says, "God who alone is wise" (Rom 16:27). Congratulate the blessed spirits who drink from the fountain of wisdom, and although they cannot fully grasp God, which is a property restricted to the very fountain of wisdom itself, still they look into the face of God, the first cause, not covered by any veil, and understand aright all things in the flashes of his splendor. In that noonday light of wisdom they do not fear the darkness of error nor the obscurity of ignorance nor the fog of opinions.

Aspire after this happiness; to obtain it with certainty, love with your whole heart the Lord Jesus Christ, "in whom are hidden all the treasures of the wisdom and knowledge" of God (Col 2:3). He himself said in his Gospel, "He who loves me will be loved by my Father, and I will love him and manifest myself to him" (Jn 14:21). What does "I will manifest myself to him" mean except that "I will manifest all the treasures of the wisdom and knowledge of God which lie within me"? Certainly every man by nature desires to know,[4] and although in many people fleshly concupiscence now in a way puts this desire to sleep, still when we shall have put aside our body which decays and which now weighs down the soul, then the fire of this desire will blaze out beyond all other desires. How great will be your happiness, O soul, when Christ your beloved and lover shows you all the treasures of the knowledge and wisdom of God? Strive to keep the commandments of Christ so that you do not cheat yourself of this great hope. He said, "If anyone love me, he will keep my word" and he "who does not love me does not keep my word" (Jn 14:23, 24). Meantime, let your wisdom be that which holy Job describes when he says, "The fear of the Lord, that is wisdom, and to depart from evil is understanding" (Jb 28:28). Recognize that any good you see in creatures flows from God, who is the fountain of goodness, so that you can learn with Blessed Francis to taste that fountain of goodness as it flows in individual creatures as in streamlets. On this point, see chapter nine of St. Bonaventure's *Life of St. Francis*.

STEP FIVE

The Consideration of Air

CHAPTER ONE

The Body Lives by Breathing Air; the Soul Lives by Praying

The element of air can be an outstanding teacher of behavior for men if its nature is considered. It proves very effective not only in teaching moral philosophy, but also in revealing the mysteries of sacred theology and in raising our minds to God, if we are willing to examine the various services which, under divine guidance, the air continually provides the human race.

First, in providing breath, the air preserves the life of the animals of the earth and of man himself. Second, it is crucial for the working of our eyes, ears, and tongues. If it were taken away, we would all immediately be struck blind, deaf, and dumb, even though all our other needs were provided for. Finally, air is so necessary for the movement of men and the other animals that without it all movement would be blocked and all the arts and almost all human activity would be forced to stop. Let us start with the first point.

If men realized that their souls need to breathe no less than their bodies, many people who are now perishing would be saved. The body needs constant breathing because our natural heat, which causes our heart to beat through the lungs' sucking in cool air and breathing out warm air, is controlled so that it preserves our life, which cannot be preserved without breathing. This is why living and breathing are commonly considered the same thing. Everyone is alive who is breathing, and anybody who has stopped breathing has also stopped living. You, my soul, need the continual breath which is God's grace to live a spiritual life. You do this by emitting sighs to God in prayer and receiving from God the fresh grace of the Holy Spirit. What else do the words of your Lord mean, that you "must pray always and not lose heart" (Lk 18:1), except that you ought always to be sighing out and receiving in fresh breath so that your spiritual life is not suffocated. The Lord repeats this when he says, "Watch, then, praying at all times" (Lk 21:36). In his First Letter to the Thessalonians the Apostle reenforces this, "Pray without ceasing" (1 Thes 5:17). The Apostle Peter in his First Letter agrees with him, when he writes, "Be prudent therefore and watchful in prayers" (1 Pt 4:7). True prudence implies that we who are always in need of God's help should always be asking for it. True, our Father knows what we need and is prepared to supply it generously, especially everything that relates to our eternal salvation. But he wants to give it by means of prayer, since this does him more honor and is more useful for us than if he were to give everything to us while we slept and did nothing. Our generous Lord begs and urges us to ask him when he says, "I say to you, ask, and it shall be given to you; seek, and you shall find; knock, and it will be opened to you. For everyone who asks receives; everyone who seeks finds; and to him who knocks it shall be opened" (Lk 11:9). A moment later he explains what it is that we should especially seek and what he will give without hesitation. "If you, evil as you are, know how to give good gifts to your children, how much more will your heavenly Father give the good Spirit to those who ask him?" (Lk 11:13).

The good Spirit is the most important thing for us to keep praying for, and it will be given to us without hesitation if we ask in the right way. This is the Spirit by which we breathe in God and preserve our spiritual life by this breathing. Holy David did this, as he said in the Psalms, "I opened my mouth and I drew breath" (Ps 119:131). That is, I opened my mouth in desire, in sighing, in demanding with indescribable groans, and I drew in the gentle air of God's Spirit. It cooled my seething passion and strengthened me in all good deeds. Given this, who would claim that they are living according to God who throughout whole days or even months and years do not sigh out to God and do not aspire to God? A clear sign of death is not breathing. If this breathing is prayer, not to pray is a sign of death. The spiritual life, by which we are children of God, is rooted in love. Saint John says in his Letter, "Behold what manner of love the Father has bestowed upon us, that we should be called children of God; and such we are" (1 Jn 3:1). Who loves without wanting to see the person he loves? Who desires something without asking for what he wants from the person who he knows will give it, if asked? Hence, anyone who does not ask regularly to see the face of his God does not desire to see him. Anyone who does not desire him does not love him, and anyone who does not love is not alive. Therefore, it follows that we must consider those people dead to God even if they are alive to the world, since they do not seriously devote themselves to prayer. A person should not be said to pray and, hence, to breathe and live, who pours forth prayers with only his physical voice. Wise men define prayer as the raising of the mind to God, not raising the voice to the sky.

Do not fool yourself, my soul, into thinking that you are living for God if you do not earnestly seek God with your whole heart and sigh after him day and night. Do not say that your other business prevents your taking time for prayer and conversation with God. The holy Apostles were extremely busy precisely in working for God and the salvation of souls, so much so that one of them said, "Besides those outer things, there is my daily pressing anxiety, the care of all the churches. Who is weak and I am not weak; who is made to stumble, and I am not inflamed?" (2 Cor 11:28). Still it was he who besides noting his frequent prayers wrote to the Philippians, "Our citizenship is in heaven" (Phil 3:20), which means that even in the midst of business he was living in heaven in his desire. Nor did he ever forget his Beloved; otherwise he would not have said, "With Christ I am nailed to the cross. It is now no longer I that live, but Christ lives in me" (Gal 2:20).

CHAPTER TWO

The Air Considered as a Means of Seeing, Hearing, and Speaking

The second property of air is its role as a medium through which the species of colors reach our eyes and species of sound reach our ears. Without these we could neither see nor hear nor even speak. In this regard we ought first to thank God that he wished to bestow such an outstanding benefit on our nature. Then it is right for us to admire the wisdom of our Creator in a creature so subtle and delicate since the air is a true body. But it is so large that it fills an almost measureless space, yet so unbelievably fine that it cannot be seen or felt. Antiquity admired the subtlety of a single line that Apelles painted with his brush, but that line was seen and touched and, therefore, could in no way be compared with the fineness of the subtle veil that wraps and touches us all, but that nobody notices because of its marvelous subtlety. Our admiration is increased by the fact that, although air is a most subtle and fine body, when it is cut, it comes back together and closes up as if it had never been cut. No craftsman could sew back together a spider's web or a cut in a very thin veil so that the previous cut would not show.

Besides that, there is something worthy of all admiration and characteristics of God's wisdom alone, namely, that the countless species of colors are mixed and transmitted together through the same body of air. A person who stands by night in the moonlight in an open and elevated spot and surveys the stars of the sky, the fields on earth full of flowers, and at the same time the homes, trees, animals, and many other similar things could not deny that the air next to him contains and contains intermixed the species of all these things. Who can understand this? How can it be that a thing so thin can contain at the same moment such a variety of images? And what if the singing of the birds from one side, various musical instruments from another, and the murmur of falling water from a third side reechoed at the same time and place? Would not the same air have to hold all those sounds and all the species of those sounds together with the many kinds of color? Who does this, my soul, except your Creator, "who alone does great wonders" (Ps 136:4)? If his works are so marvelous, how much more so is he himself?

There is another advantage to the wondrous fineness of the air—it does not hinder but helps the motion of all things that move from place to place. We all know how much effort goes into moving a ship through water, even though it is liquid and easily cut. Sometimes neither wind nor oars are enough, and the strength of horses and oxen must be added. If perchance a path has to be opened through mountains or hills, how much sweat and how much time it takes to cut even a short roadway! But horses run, birds fly, and spears and missiles are thrown through the air without effort and with the greatest ease and extreme swiftness. Men go up and down in performing their various jobs, they walk, they run, they move their feet, their arms, and their hands up and down and to right and left; the air is diffused everywhere, but it blocks them no more than if it had a spiritual rather than a corporeal nature or than if it were nothing at all.

CHAPTER THREE

How Air Symbolizes God's Sweetness and Kindness

Last is the reflection that the nature of air makes way for everything and changes itself into any shape and allows itself to be cut and torn apart so that it serves human needs and seems to be a gift to teach men humility, patience, and love. What ought greatly to ignite and inflame the love of your Creator in you, my soul, is the fact that here the air itself represents the unbelievable gentleness and enormous kindness of the Creator to men. Reflect on and think over carefully, I beg you, my soul, how your Lord is always present to all his creatures, how he is always working, and—a mark of infinite gentleness—how he adapts his cooperation to the nature of each of them as if he were saying with the Apostle, "I became all things to all men" (1 Cor 9:22) so that I might help and perfect all. He cooperates with necessary agents so that they act with necessity, with voluntary agents so that they act voluntarily, and with free agents so that they act freely. He helps and moves fire to move upward, earth to tend downward, water to flow to low spots, air to move wherever it is driven, stars to turn forever in a circle, grains, bushes, and plants to bear fruit according to their natures, land animals, fish, and birds to act as their nature demands.

If the gentleness of God is so clear in his cooperation with his creatures in the works of nature, how should we regard it in the works of grace? God gave man freedom of the will but in such a way that he could rule him by command, terrify him by destruction, and allure him by benefits. God wills all men to be saved (1 Tm 2:4), but he wills it in such a way that he wants them to will it too. Therefore, he gently anticipates them, urges them on, leads and conducts them in a quite wonderful way. These are the works of God's wisdom of which Isaiah says, "Make his works known among the people" (Is 12:4). Now he indeed utterly terrifies the wicked, now he encourages them lovingly, now he warns them in a kindly way, now he mercifully corrects them as he judges is best suited to their individuality and behavior. Listen how gently the Lord dealt with the first sinner. "Adam," he said, "where are you?" When he answered, "I heard your voice in paradise; and I was afraid, because I was naked, and I hid myself," the Lord continued with equal kindness, "Who told you that you were naked, unless you have eaten of the tree whereof I commanded you that you should not eat" (Gn 3:9–11). Adam, warned by this correction, repented without hesitation, as the Scriptures indicate. "She [the Wisdom of God] preserved him, that was first formed by God the father of the world, and she brought him out of his sin" (Wis 10:1).

Listen again how gently and kindly through his angel he corrected and urged all the children of Israel to repent. Scripture says, "An angel of the Lord went up from Gilgal to the place of weepers, and said, 'I made you go out of Egypt, and have brought you into the land for which I swore to your fathers, and I promised that I would not make void my covenant with you forever, on condition that you should not make a league with the inhabitants of this land, but should throw down their altars and you would not hear my voice. Why have you done this?' When the angel of the Lord spoke these words to all the children of Israel, they lifted up their voice, and wept. That place was called the place of weepers or of tears. And there they offered sacrifices to the Lord" (Jgs 2:1–5). The new name given the place bears witness to the massive weeping and unanimous sign of true repentance so that posterity will remember it forever. Hence, the place was called "the place of weepers or of tears" (Jgs 2:5).

What shall I say now about the prophets? They certainly teach this in all their sermons and cry out that God does not want the death of sinners, but that they turn from their ways and live (Ez 18:23). The Lord says through Jeremiah, "It is commonly said: 'If a man put away his wife and she go from him, and marry another man, shall he return to her any more?' 'You have prostituted yourselves with many lovers. Nonetheless return to me,' says the Lord, 'and I will receive you' " (Jer 3:1). Likewise in Ezekiel, "Thus have you spoken, 'Our iniquities and our sins are upon us, and we pine away in them. How then can we live?' Say to them: ' "As I live," says the Lord God, "I desire not the death of the wicked, but that the wicked turn from his way, and live. Turn, turn from your evil ways. And why will you die, O house of Israel?" ' " (Ez 33:10–11). Let us now leave sinners aside.

There is no way to explain how great is the goodness and kindness, more than that of father or mother, of the Lord our God toward those who fear him and trust in him. David says in the Psalms, "For according to the height of the heaven above the earth, he strengthened his mercy toward them that fear him." Later he adds, "As a father has compassion on his children, so has the Lord compassion on them that fear him." Still later, "The mercy of the Lord is from eternity and unto eternity upon them that fear him" (Ps 103:11, 13, 17). And elsewhere, "Taste, and see that the Lord is sweet; blessed is the man that hopes in him" (Ps 34:8). And again, "How good is the God of Israel to those who are of upright heart" (Ps 73:1). Who will explain the greatness of the Lord's goodness, gentleness, and sweetness to devout and upright souls? The Lord also says through Isaiah, "Can a woman forget her infant, so as not to have pity on the son of her womb? And if she did forget, yet will I not forget you" (Is 49:15). In Lamentations Jeremiah says, "The Lord is my portion, said my soul, therefore will I wait for him. The Lord is good to them that hope in him, to the soul that seeks him. It is good to wait with silence for the salvation of God" (Lam 3:24–26).

Should I wish to add what the apostles preach in their Letters about the fatherly mercy of the Lord our God for devout men, I would never find an end. Let what the Apostle Paul wrote at the beginning of the Second Letter to the Corinthians stand for all these citations, "Blessed be the God and Father of our Lord Jesus Christ, the Father of mercies and the God of all comfort, who comforts us in all our afflictions so that we also may be able to comfort those who are in any distress" (2 Cor 1:3). He does not describe God as a God of comfort, but a God of all comfort. He does not say that he consoles us in some affliction, but in all our afflictions. He could not have emphasized more how gentle and sweet God is to those whom he loves and who love him.

It is appropriate to conclude with the words of Saint Prosper, who explains that God is kind not only to good men, but also to bad ones so that he can make them good. He says, "Grace mainly stands out amid all his justifications in persuading by exhortations, warning by example, terrifying by dangers, urging by miracles, giving understanding, inspiring counsel, enlightening the heart, and encouraging a mentality of faith. The human will is subordinated and joined to grace. The will is stirred to this task by the aids just mentioned to cooperate with God's work within it and to begin to work toward the reward which it began to seek by a heavenly inspiration. If it fails, it attributes this to its own inconstancy; but if it succeeds, to the help of grace. This help is employed by all in countless ways, some hidden, some clear. It is due to their own wickedness if many are refused; it is due to divine grace and the human will if many accepted it."[1] Thus he ends.

CHAPTER FOUR

The Soul Is Urged to Imitate God's Kindness

Ah my soul, if your Creator is so gentle and meek to his servants, so incredibly good in tolerating sinners in order to convert them, and consoles the upright so that they can make progress in justice and holiness, should you not deal kindly with your neighbors and become all things to all to win all to your God and Lord? Mull over within yourself the lofty excellence to which the Apostle Paul urges you when he says, "Be imitators of God, as very dear children, and walk in his love as Christ also loved us and delivered himself up for us as an offering and sacrifice in fragrant odor" (Eph 5:1). Imitate God the Father, "who makes his sun to rise on the good and the evil, and sends rain on the just and the unjust" (Mt 5:45). Imitate God the Son, who, after assuming human nature for us, did not spare his own life to rescue us from the power of darkness and from eternal death. Imitate God the Holy Spirit, who pours forth abundantly his precious gifts to change us from carnal to spiritual men.

STEP SIX

The Consideration of Fire

CHAPTER ONE

God's Hatred of Sin Is Like a Consuming Fire

Fire is an element so pure and noble that God wanted himself called a fire, as Moses and Paul say, "Our God is a consuming fire" (Dt 4:24; Heb 12:29). When God first appeared to Moses, he wanted to be seen in a fire that filled but did not burn up a bush. "The Lord appeared," says Moses, "in the flame of fire out of the midst of a bush, and he saw that the bush was on fire and was not burnt up" (Ex 3:2). When the same God came to give his law to the people, he came in the form of fire. Here is Moses again, "All Mount Sinai was smoking because the Lord had come down upon it in fire" (Ex 19:18). The proclamation of the new law was similar to this mystery, since the Holy Spirit appeared to the apostles in tongues of fire. Lastly, those closest to God in heaven, the Seraphim, are called the fiery ones because more than the other angels they take their fervor and ardor from the intense fire of God. Given all this, it is not difficult for us to build a step from the element of fire, its nature and properties, by which we ascend to God in meditation and prayer. Certainly, it will be less difficult to go upward with Elijah in a fiery chariot than to build a ladder with earth or water or air.

Let us proceed to examine the properties of fire. It is the nature of fire to work in different and opposite ways on different materials. It immediately burns up wood, hay, and stubble. It makes gold, silver, and precious stones more pure and beautiful. Iron by nature is black, cold, hard, and heavy; fire changes it into the opposite characteristics so that it is quickly made clear, hot, soft, and light so that it shines like a star, burns like fire, becomes liquid like water, and becomes light so that a blacksmith can lift and move it about with great ease.

It is fairly obvious how all this applies to God. First, the Apostle in his First Letter to the Corinthians uses wood, hay, and stubble to signify evil deeds which cannot withstand the fire of divine judgment (1 Cor 3:12–13). It is indeed unbelievable how tremendously all sins displease God, who is fire most pure, and how zealously he burns up and destroys them if they cannot be destroyed by repentance, that is, if the person who sinned is in a state which allows him to repent. Repentance destroys all sin. But if the sinner is incapable of repentance, for instancc, the demons and men after this life, then the divine wrath turns against these sinners. As the Wise Man says, "But to God the wicked and his wickedness are hateful alike" (Wis 14:9). The devil is a witness to how great and severe is this hatred. He sinned once. According to Saint Gregory he was the noblest of angels, the leader of the first choir of angels and God's most outstanding creature.[1] He was immediately cast down from heaven, stripped of all beauty and supernatural grace, and transformed into a hideous monster and enslaved in eternal ruin.

Christ is a witness. He came down from heaven to destroy the work of the devil, that is, sin (1 Jn 3:8). This is why he is called "the Lamb of God, who takes away the sins of the world" (Jn 1:29). Who can explain or even imagine all that Christ suffered to destroy the work of the devil and to satisfy perfectly the justice of God? "Though he was by nature God, he emptied himself, taking the nature of a slave" (Phil 2:6). "Being rich, he became poor for our sakes" (2 Cor 8:9). He "had nowhere to lay his head" (Lk 9:58), although he made heaven and earth. "He came into his own, and his own received him not" (Jn 1:11). "When he was reviled, he did not revile, when he suffered, did not threaten, but yielded himself up to him who judged him unjustly; who himself bore our sins in his body upon the tree" (1 Pt 2:23–24). "He humbled himself and became obedient unto death, even death on the cross" (Phil 2:8). "By his stripes we were healed" (1 Pt 2:24). At last mocked, spit upon, scourged, crowned with thorns, crucified in complete shame and excruciating pain, he poured out all his blood and his life. He bore all this to destroy the works of the devil and wipe out our sin.

The law of God is witness which forbids and punishes every sin and does not leave unpunished even an idle word (Mt 12:36). How much does he hate crimes and wicked deeds if he cannot allow an idle word? The law of the Lord is spotless and the precept of the Lord is bright, and they oppose stains and darkness (Ps 19:8). There can be no union of light with darkness or of justice with sin (2 Cor 6:14). The final witness is hell itself, which God has prepared for the wicked and sinners who could have washed themselves in the blood of the Lamb, but refused or neglected to do so. It is quite right that those whose sin will last forever should be punished forever. The nature and amount of punishment in hell is terrible even to think about. We will say more about this in our last step.

Since God has such great hatred for sin, my soul, if you love God above all things, you ought to hate sin more than anything else. Be careful that they do not lead you astray who explain away or excuse sin. Take care that you do not deceive yourself with false arguments. If sin does not displease you, whether in yourself or others, you do not love God. If you do not love God, you are lost. Moreover, if you are not displeasing to Christ, how much do you think you owe to his love? To his labors? To his blood and death? He washed you from sin and reconciled you to his Father. Will it be hard for you in turn to suffer something for Chirst or to resist sin unto blood for his grace and with his grace? Finally, if you cannot bear patiently a hell of eternal fire, neither should you under any conditions bear sin patiently, but rather step aside from it as from a snake (Sir 21:2), and from the occasion, even the slightest suspicion of sin. Therefore, you ought to have a firm and determined hatred of sin joined to a total love of God.

CHAPTER TWO

Fire Purifies Precious Metals; God Crowns Human Good Works

The same fire does not destroy, but perfects and makes gold, silver, and precious stones shine brighter because, as the same Apostle explains in the same passage, these metals symbolize good and perfect works which come through the fire of divine judgment successfully and will receive a great reward. God tests these works because they are his gifts, as Saint Augustine says, "When he crowns our merits, he crowns his own gifts."[2] They were done at his command and with his help. He gave us the power to perform them, and he guided us by the law he gave and the rules he established. Gold symbolizes the works of love. How can the works of love fail to please God when God himself is love (1 Jn 4:8)? Silver symbolizes the works of wisdom of those poeple "who instruct many to justice" (Dn 12:3). God also greatly approves and is pleased with these works, as the Wisdom of God says, "Whoever carries them out and teaches them, he shall be called great in the kingdom of heaven" (Mt 5:19). Precious stones are the works of the chaste soul, about which Ecclesiasticus says, "No price is worthy of a continent soul" (Sir 26:15). This is the reason why the Gospel read at Lauds in the Church's Office for Holy Virgins is about finding a single precious pearl. The Prophet Isaiah suggests how pleased God is by virginal purity, when he speaks in God's name to eunuchs, namely, to those who have castrated themselves for the kingdom of heaven, "I will give them a place in my house and within my walls and a name better than sons and daughters. I will give them an everlasting name which shall never perish" (Is 56:5). Saint Augustine shows in a magnificent passage in his book *On Holy Virginity* that this text should be applied to holy virgins, both men and women.[3] The doctors agree that there are three works which merit a golden crown in the kingdom of heaven. Golden crowns, that is, a certain reward beyond life everlasting, are given to martyrs, doctors, and virgins. To martyrs because of their outstanding love, for "greater love than this no one has, that one lay down his life for his friends" (Jn 15:13). To doctors because of their outstanding wisdom; of these Daniel says, "They that instruct many to justice shall shine as stars for all eternity" (Dn 12:3). To virgins because of the matchless price of purity, on account of which the virgins in Revelation are seen singing the new song which nobody else can sing. "These are they," says John, "who were not defiled with women; for they are virgins. Those follow the Lamb wherever he goes" (Rv 14:4).

But it is not just the love of martyrs, the wisdom of doctors, or the purity of virgins that will be tested by the fire of divine judgment and will receive full reward. Good works of whatever kind, as long as they are done in love, will be counted among the golden vessels and undergo the divine fire and will receive their reward.

The Lord will say to them at the last judgment, "Come, blessed of my Father, take possession of the kingdom prepared for you from the foundation of the world" (Mt 25:34). These are the people who offered bread to the hungry, drink to the thirsty, hospitality to travelers, clothing to the naked, and encouragement to the sick and to prisoners. The Lord also promised that no one would be deprived of this reward who gave even a glass of cold water out of charity to someone because he was a disciple (Mt 10:42).

Do you understand, my soul, how much difference there is between different works? What is more foolish and wretched than to gather dry wood, hay, and stubble with considerable effort—where and when you can, if you are wise, easily acquire gold, silver, and precious stones? May you be wise and intelligent and provide for the last times (Dt 32:29), for, when they come, all things will be examined and tested in the fire of God's judgment. The first category will earn praise and reward; the second will be burned and turned into ashes and smoke. Why do you now choose what you will surely regret having chosen? Why not condemn now while it is to your advantage what you will condemn in a short while to no advantage? If perhaps you do not see this now and a veil of present things cloaks your eyes, so that they do not see the pure and obvious truth, pray to God and say earnestly to the Lord with the blind man in the Gospel, "Lord, that I may see" (Lk 18:41) and with the Prophet, "Open you my eyes, and I will consider the wondrous things of your law" (Ps 119:18). It is absolutely wonderful that works done out of love become gold, silver, and precious stones, while those not done out of love are changed into dry wood, hay, and stubble.

CHAPTER THREE

Fire Brightens Black Iron; God Leads the Sinful Soul to a Knowledge of Truth

We now take under consideration a second property of fire. So far we have learned from fire what God does to those who leave this life with evil works and to those who reach the end of life with good works. I will draw another comparison based on fire which will help us understand what God accomplishes in persons he draws from sin to repentance.

A sinful man is like iron because, while it is away from fire, it is black, cold, hard, and heavy, but if it should be put into fire, it becomes bright, hot, soft, and light. Every sinner lacks inner light and walks in darkness, and in this he resembles the blackness of iron. Even if he seems to enjoy intelligence and also good judgment in the areas of scholarship and human affairs, nonetheless, he is blind and worse than blind in discerning between good and evil. The blind man sees nothing and, therefore, does not move without having a guide. The sinner thinks he sees what he does not see or sees one thing for another and judges good to be evil and evil good, large to be small, and small large, long to be short, and short long. For this reason he is always making mistakes in choosing. This is what the Apostle says about the gentiles who worship idols; they have "their understanding clouded in darkness, through the ignorance that is in them, because of the blindness of their heart" (Eph 4:18). This is what our Lord himself in the Gospel so often criticized in the scribes and pharisees, that they were blind and guides for the blind (Mt 15:28). This is what the prophet Isaiah says to the Jews of his time, "Hear, you deaf, and you blind, behold that you may see" (Is 42:18). He predicted to them that Christ will come and open the eyes of the blind. Speaking in the person of God about the New Testament he added, "I will lead the blind into the way which they know not, and in the paths which they were ignorant of I will make them walk. I will make darkness light before them, and crooked things straight" (Is 42:16). Lastly, will not sinners admit this after this life when punishment begins to open the eyes of their mind which guilt has closed? "We have erred," they will confess, "from the way of truth, and the light of justice did not shine on us, and the sun of understanding did not rise upon us" (Wis 5:6). It is not surprising that those who have turned away from God in their will and understanding are blind. "God is light, and in him is no darkness" (1 Jn 1:5). The same Apostle concludes from this, "He who hates his brother is in darkness, and walks in darkness, and does not know whither he goes, because the darkness has blinded his eyes" (1 Jn 2:9, 11).

The fact that they have turned away from God, who is light, is not the only cause for the blindness of sinners. Besides that, "their own malice blinded them," as the Wise Man says (Wis 2:21). The passions of the mind, love, hate, anger, envy, and the others which are included under the term "malice"—so blind the mind that they prevent it from discerning truth, but they work like tinted lenses which make white seem red or lenses designed to make small things appear large or large things small or things far away appear close or things close appear distant. A person violently in love judges that the object he loves is beautiful, useful, wonderful, and absolutely necessary for him, and so he must get hold of it at the cost of neglecting or throwing aside everything else. Conversely, when a person hates something violently, he considers it ugly, useless, evil, and even dangerous to himself and, hence, absolutely to be pushed away even at the cost of losing everything else. But if this black and dark iron be put in the fire, that is, if the sinner begins to be turned away from sin and turned toward God, then, as the Prophet says, "Come to him and be enlightened" (Ps 34:6), he begins little by little to gain light and to see the plain truth of the matter in that light, as the same Prophet said, "In your light we shall see the light" (Ps 36:9). Then when the tinted glasses of the passions have been broken and the crystal clear glasses of pure love have been put on, he will judge that eternal possessions are more important and temporal ones count for little and almost nothing, as is really the case, and he will see clearly that created splendor and beauty cannot in any way be compared with the light of wisdom and truth which is in God and is God. He then will exclaim with Saint Augustine, "Late have I loved you, beauty so ancient and so new, late have I loved you."[4] Christ says, "You shall know the truth, and the truth shall make you free" (Jn 8:32). The man who is enlightened and freed by the light of truth from the shackles of concupiscence, greed, ambition, and the other passions will rejoice with the Prophet and say, "Lord, you have broken my bonds; I will sacrifice to you the sacrifice of praise, and I will call upon the name of the Lord" (Ps 116:16–17).

STEP SIX

CHAPTER FOUR

Fire Makes Cold Iron Glow;

God's Grace Makes Man's Works and Deeds Effective

Fire not only changes iron from dark to bright, but also changes it from cold to hot, and not only to hot but makes it so fiery and burning that it seems to be fire itself. Great is the Lord and great his power. Man by nature is cold and fears and trembles at everything and dares not speak or put himself forward to try anything which is a bit difficult, but as soon as God kindles in him the fire of love, he makes him braver than a lion who terrifies everybody with his roar and conquers everybody in combat. For him nothing seems difficult, nothing hard, and he says with the Apostle Paul who had been set ablaze by that fire, "I can do all things in him who strengthens me" (Phil 4:13).

Let us talk about the efficacy of fire under different headings. We can first briefly discuss the efficacy of words, then that of deeds. There are many preachers of God's word in the Church today, and there always have been. What then is the reason that all their exhortations and shouting convert so few? In large cities twenty, thirty, and even forty preachers give sermons every day during Lent, but when Lent has passed there seems to be no change in the morals of the city. The same vices, the same sins, the same indifference, the same dissoluteness, are seen. The only reason I can find is that regardless of all the learned, elegant, and flowery sermons that are poured out, there is no soul, no life, no fire. In short, that great love is missing which alone can give life and fire to the words of the preachers and inflame and change the hearts of the hearers. I do not say that many preachers lack energetic delivery or gyrations of the whole body. Cannons let out a mighty roar even when they have no iron or stone shot, but they produce no result. What is needed is this, that preachers have a great love for God and the salvation of souls. It must be genuine, not put on; it must flow out of the fountain of the heart naturally and not seem strained. Saint Peter had not mastered the art of speaking; he was skilled only at steering a boat and repairing and casting nets. But when the Holy Spirit came down on him in fiery tongues and filled him with a burning love, he at once began to speak in the middle of Jerusalem so powerfully, so fervently, so effectively that in one sermon he converted many thousands to repentance and faith (Acts 2:14). Still we do not read that he used a lot of shouting or wore himself out by gyrations of his whole body. Saint Bonaventure tells of Saint Francis that he was not greatly learned and had not studied rhetoric, but when he gave a sermon to the people, he was listened to like an angel from heaven. For, he says, his speech was like burning fire piercing the inmost heart.[5] Chapter 30 of *The Chronicle of the Order of Friars Minor* narrates that, when he made a few unprepared remarks after dinner to the people, there was such a great movement toward repentance among all the people that it seemed as if the day was Good Friday.[6] Why did these few words cause such a stir and produce so much fruit? For this reason, namely, that the holy preacher was like a glowing coal and his word was a blazing torch, as Ecclesiasticus (Sir 48:1) wrote about Elijah.

We have in writing the sermons of Saint Vincent, Saint Bernardine, and several other saints which some people would hardly deign to read because the style found in them is so simple. Yet we know that many thousands of people were converted to God by their sermons and that they were always listened to attentively by incredible crowds, clearly because they uttered their simple words from hearts afire and glowing. Moreover, that divine fire showed its power no less in deeds than in words. God decided to subject to himself the city of Rome, the head of the empire and the mistress of the nations, through the Apostle Peter. He decided to send forth the other apostles, some to Ethiopia, others to India, others to Scythia, others to distant Britain, and through them to destroy the idols of the world and raise the standard of the cross, to change laws and ceremonies, and to overturn the tyranny of the devil. Had anybody predicted this to the apostles on Lake Gennesareth or when they were looking for a place to hide during the Lord's passion, all this would have seemed like dreams or old wives' tales. But all this came true a short time later and by no other power than the power of burning love which the Holy Spirit set afire in their hearts. "Love casts out fear" (1 Jn 4:18); it "bears with all things, hopes all things" (1 Cor 13:7). He thinks that he can do all things and cries out with the Apostle, "I can do all things in him who strengthens me" (Phil 4:13). We see how the work and effort of these men, armed only with love, quickly overthrew idolatry throughout the world; how they founded churches everywhere and raised up the standard of the cross in all kingdoms and did it without an army of soldiers and without military equipment.

CHAPTER FIVE

Fire Makes Hard Iron Soft; God's Grace Conquers a Stubborn Heart

Next, fire has the property of changing iron from hard to soft so that it can be easily thinned and lengthened into blades and can be adapted to any shape by a craftsman. Fire has great power over iron, but far greater is the strength of our God in the stubborn and obstinate hearts of mortals. Listen to Saint Bernard, who says in his book *On Consideration*, "The only hard heart is one which is not aghast at itself because it feels nothing. What is a hard heart? It is one which is not torn by regret nor softened by devotion nor moved by prayers. It does not yield to threats and is hardened by scourging. It is ungrateful for benefits and heedless of advice." And further on, "This is the one who neither fears God nor respects men."[7] Pharaoh proves that all this is true. The more he was scourged by God, the more he became hardened, and the more God's kindness shined upon him in removing the scourge, the more spirited he became in scorning and despising God.

But if it sometimes pleases God to light a spark of the fire of true love for him in even the hardest heart, it at once softens and becomes like molten wax. No stubbornness, although old and hard, can resist his power. Immediately the heart that was stony becomes fleshy, and under the breath of the Holy Spirit waters flow from the icy snow. In the Gospel we have the example of the woman who was a public sinner. Neither the warnings of her brother nor the rebuke of her sister nor family honor nor her own disgrace could move her to stop from sinning, yet a single beam of Christ penetrated her heart and lit in it a spark of divine love. This suddenly changed her into another woman so that, even though she was a noblewoman, she was not ashamed to go to Christ's feet at a public banquet. And totally dissolved in tears, she made a bath for Christ's feet from her tears and dried the same feet with her own hair as a towel, and she kissed his feet in the intensity of her love and anointed him with expensive and fragant ointment so that she could signify that she wished henceforward to dedicate herself and all her possessions to him. Thereby she merited to hear these words of the Lord, "Her sins, many as they are, shall be forgiven her, because she has loved much" (Lk 7:47).

I would like to bring up a much more recent example, William, Duke of Aquitaine, in the time of Saint Bernard. He was stubborn and persistent beyond all others in defending Anacletus the anti-pope and attacking Innocent the legitimate pope. He drove the Catholic bishops out of his territory and bound himself by an oath never to make peace with them. Because everybody knew how his heart was hardened in evil and feared his ferocity and pride, there was nobody who dared correct him. It pleased God through his servant Bernard to visit the heart of this stubborn man and kindle no small spark of divine love in it. Instantly he was changed from a lion into a lamb, from a proud man to a humble one, from a stubborn man to a very obedient person. At a single suggestion from Saint Bernard, he embraced the Bishop of Poitiers lovingly and with his own hand gave him his throne. What seemed to pass all wonder came about when he asked a certain hermit about curing his soul from the sins he had committed. He ordered him to put on his bronze breastplate over his naked flesh and have it locked with a key so that he could not take it off. The duke agreed immediately and then obeyed the command when the hermit sent him off to the supreme pontiff to receive absolution. When the supreme pontiff suspected that in his heart he had not repented or wanted to test his repentance, he ordered him to make a pilgrimage to Jerusalem and request absolution from the patriarch of that city. William shortly undertook the journey and carried out the pontiff's command. Finally, becoming a humble monk after being a powerful prince, he surpassed practically everybody of his age in modesty, patience, poverty, devotion, and piety.[8] Clearly, "This is the change of the right hand of the most High" (Ps 77:10); it is the power of divine fire which no stubbornness of the heart can resist.

CHAPTER SIX

Fire Lightens Heavy Objects; God's Grace Lifts Souls to the Path of Justice

There remains the last property of fire—it lightens heavy burdens and lifts them up with ease. This is why men who do not burn with divine love are heavy of heart. To them the Prophet says, "How long will you be heavy of heart? Why do you love vanity and seek after lying?" (Ps 4:2). This is certainly the reason that "the corruptible body is a load upon the soul" as the Wise Man says (Wis 9:15). "And a heavy yoke is upon the children of Adam, from the day of their coming out of their mother's womb until the day of their burial into the mother of all," as Ecclesiasticus puts it (Sir 40:1). A little later the same author explains what this heavy yoke is which weighs down the soul in a mortal body. He mentions anger, envy, inconstancy, fear, wrath, and other things usually called the passions of the mind. These weigh upon a man so that he looks at nothing except the earth and clings to it lying flat and does not arise to seek God and cannot run freely in the way of God's commandments. But when the divine fire from above starts to inflame the human heart, those passions immediately grow weak and begin to die and the heavy burden begins to become lighter. And if the fire increases, it is not hard for the human heart to drop its burden so that it takes wings like a dove and can say with the Apostle, "Our citizenship is in heaven" (Phil 3:20). With a heart enlarged by the fire, it says with David, "I have run the way of your commandments when you have enlarged my heart" (Ps 119:32). Indeed, the Savior said later, "I have come to cast fire upon the earth, and what will I but that it be kindled" (Lk 12:49). We have seen many made so light that they have put aside all love of honor, flesh, and riches and have said to Christ, who was going off toward heaven, "Draw us after you" (Sg 1:3). For this reason many monasteries were built, many deserts began to be inhabited, and many choirs of virgins were established for whom it was not only easy to run in the path of the commandments, but also to climb up the path of the counsels and follow the Lamb wherever he goes (Rv 14:4).

O blessed fire, you do not consume but enlighten, and if you do consume, you consume our harmful disposition so that it cannot destroy life. Who will grant me to be seized by this fire, which cleans and removes the blackness of ignorance and the darkness of an erroneous conscience with the light of true wisdom, which changes the coldness of laziness, distraction, and carelessness into the fire of love, which never allows my heart to become hardened, but always softens it by its warmth and makes it devout, which finally removes the heavy yoke of earthly cares and earthly desires and lifts up my heart on the wings of holy contemplation that nourishes and increases charity so that I can say with the Prophet, "Lord, Give joy to the soul of your servant, for unto you, O Lord, do I lift up my soul" (Ps 86:4)?

STEP SEVEN

The Consideration of the Heavens, the Sun, the Moon, and the Stars

CHAPTER ONE

How the Sun Is the Dwelling Place of God, Who Is High and Beautiful

Here we will not have to work hard to build ourselves a step to God from the consideration of the heavens since we have a predecessor in the Royal Prophet who sings in the psalms, "The heavens show forth the glory of God, and the firmament declares the work of his hands" (Ps 19:1). There are two times—day and night—by which we ascend from heaven to God on the wings of contemplation. He writes in the psalm about the first, "He has set his tabernacle in the sun, and he, as a bridegroom coming out of his bride chamber, has rejoiced like a giant to run the way. His going out is from the end of heaven, and his circuit over to the end thereof, and there is no one that can hide himself from his heat" (Ps 19:5–6). In another psalm he writes of the second, "I will behold your heavens, the work of your fingers: the moon and the stars which you have founded" (Ps 8:4).

Let us begin with the first time. The Holy Spirit by the mouth of David praises in song four features of the sun which we see during the day: the first that it is the tabernacle of God, the second that it is very beautiful, the third that it is always running tirelessly and extremely fast, and the fourth that it mainly shows its power in illuminating and warming. For all these reasons Ecclesiasticus writes that it is "an admirable instrument, the work of the Most High; great is the Lord that made him" (Sir 43:2, 5).

First, God the Creator of all things placed his tabernacle in the sun as in the most noble of things; this means that God chose the sun out of all bodily things so that he might dwell in it as in a royal palace or a divine sanctuary. God, of course, fills heaven and earth (Jer 23:24), and heaven and the heaven of heavens do not contain him (2 Chr 2:6). Still he is said more appropriately to dwell where he manifests greater signs of his presence in working marvels. Since the Hebrew text says that he placed his tabernacle at the sun in them, that is, the heavens, we gather from this verse of the psalm another excellence of the sun which does not contradict the first one. The sun is large, and for it God made a vast, beautiful, and noble palace. He wished that the sky itself be the palace of the sun in which it might roam freely and do its work and that the sun itself might be the palace of God, the highest prince. Just as we know the greatness and eminence of the sun from the fact that its tabernacle is the sky, so we know the greatness and eminence of God from the fact that his tabernacle is the sun, clearly a marvelous instrument, and nothing more wonderful than it is found among bodily things.

To show from things we know the outstanding beauty of the sun, David compared it to a groom leaving his bridal chamber. Men never dress themselves up more and never desire more to show off their beauty and handsomeness than when they marry. They want beyond measure to please the eyes of the bride whom they love intensely. If we could fix our gaze on the sun and if we were closer to it and if we could see it in all its size and splendor, we would not need the analogy of the bridegroom to grasp its incredible beauty. The whole beauty of colors depends on light, and the whole beauty of colors vanishes if light disappears. Nothing is more beautiful than light, and God himself, who is beauty itself, wanted to be called light. Saint John says, "God is light, and in him is no darkness" (1 Jn 1:5). Furthermore, there is no bodily object more luminous than the sun and, therefore, nothing is more beautiful than the sun. Besides that, the beauty of lower creatures and especially human beauty fade quickly, but the sun's beauty is never extinguished, never lessened, and always gives joy to all things with equal splendor. Do we not feel that somehow everything seems to rejoice at sunrise? Not only are men happy, but gentle breezes whisper, flowers open, the grain crops up, and the little birds sweeten the air with their song. When the angel said to the blind old man, Tobit, "May joy be to you always," he answered, "What manner of joy shall be to me, who sit in darkness and see not the light of heaven?" (Tb 5:11–12).

Come, my soul, and think over within you, if the created sun makes all things so happy at its rising, what will the uncreated sun do, which is incomparably brighter and more beautiful, when it rises in pure hearts to be seen and contemplated, not for a short time but forever? How unhappy and sad will that hour be, when condemned men are turned over for burial in everlasting darkness where the rays of neither the uncreated nor the created sun ever penetrate? What will be the joy of the soul to whom the Father of lights says, "Enter into the joy of your master" (Mt 25:21)?

CHAPTER TWO

The Sun's Course Shows God's Greatness

Later the same Prophet celebrates the truly marvelous course of the sun: "He has rejoiced as a giant to run the way" (Ps 19:5). He is certainly a powerful giant, if he stretches his stride to match the size of his body and runs with a speed to match the strength of his forces, for he covers an absolutely immense space in a short time. The Prophet, since he had compared the sun to a bridegroom to explain as well as he could the beauty of the sun, later compared it to a giant man so that he could explain as well as possible the sun's speedy course by using the same analogy. Even if he had compared the sun to flying birds, arrows, winds, and lightning bolts instead of to men, however large and strong, he would still have fallen far short of the truth. If what we see with our eyes is true, the sun runs the whole circumference of its orbit in twenty-four hours. And if the route of the sun surpasses by an almost infinite distance the circumference of the earth, and if the circumference of the earth measures about twenty thousand miles—and all this is absolutely true—it undoubtedly follows that the sun completes a run of many thousands of miles every hour. What am I saying, every hour? Rather every quarter hour and almost every minute. Anybody who wants to observe the rising or the setting of the sun, especially above a clear horizon as is found on the sea or a flat plain, will realize that the sun's whole body rises above the horizon in a shorter span of time than an eighth of an hour, and yet the diameter of the sun's body is much greater than the diameter of the earth, which measures seven thousand miles.

Once I myself out of curiosity wanted to find out how much time it would take for the whole sun to set into the sea. At the beginning of its setting I started to read the psalm "Have mercy on me, O God" (Ps 51:1). I had barely read it through twice when the sun had already entirely set. Hence, the sun in that short time in which the psalm "Have mercy" is read twice had to traverse in its course a distance much greater than seven thousand miles. Who would believe that, unless it had been demonstrated by certain argument? Should some person now add that the body which moves so fast has a mass much greater than the whole earth and that the movement of such a large body at such speeds goes on without any pause or weariness and, if God were to command it, could last for eternal time, certainly that person could not help admiring the infinite power of the Creator unless he was a dunce or a blockhead.[1] Ecclesiasticus wrote accurately that this was a wonderful instrument, the work of the Most High, and the Lord who made it was great indeed (Sir 43:2).

CHAPTER THREE

The Sun Gives Light and Heat, but God Gives True Wisdom and Charity

There remains the efficacy of light and heat to consider. David says about it, "There is no one that can hide himself from his heat" (Ps 19:6). This one luminous body stationed in the middle of the universe illuminates all the stars, all the air, all the seas, and all the earth. Everywhere on earth it makes all the buds, all the plants, and all the trees become green and leafy by its life-giving warmth, and it makes all the crops ripen. It even spreads its power beneath the earth and produces every kind of metal. This is why Saint James at the beginning of his Letter compared God with the sun: "Every good gift and every perfect gift is from above, coming down from the Father of lights, with whom there is no change, nor shadow of alteration" (Jas 1:17). The sun is the father of bodily lights, while God is the father of spiritual lights, but God differs greatly from the sun in three ways. First, the sun must be constantly changing in order to fill the whole earth with light and heat, but God who is totally present everywhere needs no change. For this reason Saint James says, "In him there is no change." Second, because the sun is always changing its place, it brings day in turn to place after place, leaving some in night, shining on others, bringing shadows elsewhere. But God never moves and is always present to every place. Hence Saint James adds, "In him there is no shadow of alteration." Finally, the greatest boon of all from the sun as father of bodily lights is all the gifts and benefits which are born from the earth. But these good things are not supreme or perfect but rather poor, temporary, failing, and they do not make man good and can be misused by those who so wish, and many turn them to their damnation. But "every good gift and every perfect gift" comes down from the Father of spiritual lights, and these make their possessor very good and perfect. Nobody can misuse them, and they lead him who perseveres in them to the state of true happiness, a state made perfect by the accumulation of every good.

Investigate, my soul, what are these best gifts and perfect boons which are from above, coming down from the Father of lights so that when you discover them, you will be on the alert for them and will strive to obtain them with all your strength. It is not that you have to go far away—the nature of the sun will show you that well enough. The sun achieves all its effects by heat and light, and these are the gifts and boons of the father of bodily lights, light and heat. So too the best gifts and the perfect boons which are from above and come down from God, the true Father of lights, are the light of wisdom and well-ordered love. The light of wisdom, which makes a person truly wise, which no one can misuse, and which leads to the fountain of wisdom which lies in our heavenly fatherland, is the light which teaches us to scorn temporal things and esteem eternal things. It teaches us "not to trust in the uncertainty of riches, but in the living God" (1 Tm 6:17); it teaches us not to make this exile our fatherland and to endure rather than love this pilgrimage; lastly it teaches us to bear patiently this present life, which is full of dangers and temptations, and see death as desirable, for "blessed are the dead who die in the Lord" (Rv 14:13).

What is well-ordered love except to love God, who is the end of all desires, without end or limit, and to love other things, which are means to the end, within limits and only to the degree to which they are necessary for the end, that is, for attaining happiness? Nobody among the sons of men would turn things upside down in taking care of his body so that he would love health within limits and love a bitter medicine without limit since he knows that one is the end and the other the means. How comes it then, that so many who want to pass for wise can set no limit in heaping up riches, in seeking the pleasures of the flesh, and in acquiring titles of honor, as if these goods were the end for the human heart? But in loving God and seeking eternal happiness they are content with narrow limits, as if these were means to an end and not the end of all means. This above all is the reason why they have the wisdom of this world and not the wisdom which is from above coming down from the Father of lights and why they do not have a well-ordered love and, therefore, do not have true love, which cannot exist without being well-ordered. Rather they are full of covetousness, which does not come from the Father but from the world. While you are a pilgrim, my soul, away from your fatherland and sojourning among enemies who plot against true wisdom and true love and substitute guile for wisdom and covetousness for love, sigh with your whole heart for the Father of lights that he make the best gifts and perfect boons, namely, the light of wisdom and the passion of well-ordered love, come down to your heart so that filled with them you may run with a sure foot the path of the commandments and reach the fatherland where one drinks from the very fountain of wisdom and lives on the pure milk of love.

STEP SEVEN

CHAPTER FOUR

The Moon Is Subject to the Sun; the Soul Attains True Glory When United with God

I now come to nighttime, when the heavens through the moon and the stars provide us a step for climbing up to God. David says, "I will behold your heavens, the work of your fingers: the moon and the stars which you have founded" (Ps 8:4). If we could see heaven itself, the Prophet would not have said as an explanation of his earlier words, "the moon and the stars which you have founded." Indeed, if our senses could reach out to heaven itself or we could investigate its nature and qualities with exact knowledge, we would undoubtedly have a splendid ladder to God.

We are aware that there have been some persons who on the basis of the stars' movements have defined the nature of the heavens as a fifth element which is simple, incorruptible, and eternally moving in a circle. We know that there have also been others who have urged that heaven was made of the element of fire, which does not move in a circle but is incorruptible in its parts,[2] but we are not seeking opinions but certain knowledge or the teaching of the faith so that out of it we may build ourselves a solid ladder to the knowledge of God. With the Prophet we will be content to build a ladder from the moon and the stars which we see, as we just did from the sun, which is the prince and leader of the other lights.

The moon has two properties which can help us to ascend to and attain our God. The first is that, the more the moon draws near the sun, the more it is illumined in its higher part, which looks toward heaven, and the more it falls into shadow on its lower part, which looks toward earth. And when it is wholly beneath the sun and is wholly in conjunction with it, then it is totally bright toward heaven and darkened toward earth. Conversely, when the moon is opposite the sun, people living on earth see it as completely bright, but it has no light on its upper part, which is seen by heaven's inhabitants. This property of the moon can be seen as a fine illustration or example for mortal men so they can understand how careful they should be about their closeness, subordination, and union to God, the true Father of lights. The moon stands for man; the sun stands for God; when the moon is opposite the sun, then the light borrowed from the sun looks only at the earth and in a way turns its back on heaven. Hence, it appears very beautiful to earth's inhabitants but very ugly to heaven's inhabitants. In exactly the same way mortal men, when they wander far from God, are like the prodigal son who left his father and went to a distant country. They misuse the light of reason, which they received from the Father of lights; examining only the earth they forget God, think only about the earth and love only the earth and devote themselves wholly to acquiring earthly goods. The children of this world describe them as wise and happy, but those who dwell in heaven judge them poor, naked, blind, deformed, wretched, and miserable.

On the other hand, when the moon is in conjunction with the sun, it is perfectly subordinated to the sun; it is entirely bright on its upper side and looks toward heaven alone and turns its back after a fashion on the earth and disappears completely from human eyes. Just so the sinner begins to turn toward holiness and through perfect conversion is subordinated in humility to God, the true sun of souls, and is joined to him in charity. The soul then fulfills the Apostle's urging to seek things that are above where Christ is at God's right hand and to relish the things that are above, not those of earth (Col 3:1–2). Fools look down on such a person and account him as if dead. Such a person is indeed dead to the world, and his life is hidden with Christ in God. But when Christ, who is his life, appears, he also will appear with Christ in glory, as the Apostle adds in the same text.

This is why, as Saint Augustine notes in his *Letter to Januarius*, the Passover of the Lord in both the Old and the New Law cannot be celebrated properly except after a full moon, that is, when the moon, which is opposite the sun at full moon, begins to turn and to come back into conjunction with the sun. God wanted to show by this heavenly sign how it happens through the passion and resurrection of the Lord that a man who is opposed to God by his sinfulness begins to turn toward God and through the merits of Jesus Christ to hasten to grace and union with him.[3]

If you, my soul, under the inspiration of his grace find yourself subordinated to the Father of lights by true humility and joyfully joined to him by burning charity, do not imitate fools who change like the moon. Rather imitate the wise who stand firm like the sun, as Ecclesiasticus testifies (Sir 27:12). As fast as the moon advances toward conjunction, it also retreats from conjunction. If you are wise, once you have attained grace, do not desert it, do not depart or go back. Nowhere will you find anything better, nor do you know whether you will have a chance to come back if you go away of your own choice. He who promises pardon to the penitent and grace to those who turn back does not promise you a longer life or the gift of repentance. Turn your back confidently on the earth and look toward your sun. Rest in him. Delight in him, remain in him. Say with the Apostle Peter, "It is good for us to be here" (Mt 17:4). Say with the martyr Ignatius, "It is good for me to live with Christ rather than to rule over the ends of the earth."[4] Pay little attention to what the worldly wise think of you. "For he is not approved" whom the world commends, "but whom God commends" (2 Cor 10:18).

CHAPTER FIVE

The Moon, which Illuminates but Sometimes Leaves the Night in Darkness, Symbolizes Divine Grace

The moon has another way of acting which God also employs with his elect. The moon rules the night as the sun rules the day, as Moses says in Genesis (Gn 1:16) and David in the psalms (Ps 136:8–9). The sun illuminates the whole day with continuous brightness, but the moon illuminates the night now with much light, now with very little, and sometimes it does not relieve the darkness of night with any light at all. In the same way God, like the sun, brightens with everlasting brilliance the holy angels and the souls of the blessed, for he is their everlasting day. Saint John says, "For there shall be no night there" (Rv 21:25). God like the moon visits the night of our pilgrimage and exile here in which we walk by faith and not by light (2 Cor 5:7) and we heed the Holy Scriptures as a lamp shining in a dark place, as Saint Peter says in his Second Letter (2 Pt 1:19); by turns he illuminates our hearts but sometimes leaves them in the darkness of desolation.

You ought not, my soul, become too downcast if you do not enjoy the light of consolation nor be too elated if shortly after you breathe in the light of consolation and devotion. God acts like the moon, not like the sun, in the night of the world. Not only does God now appear to us who are weak and imperfect as a moon full with the light of consolation, and now lacking all light leave us in the terror and utter darkness of night. The Apostle Paul, "a vessel of election" (Acts 9:15) who "was caught up into paradise and heard secret words that man may not repeat" (2 Cor 12:2, 4), once said, "I am filled with comfort, I overflow with joy in all our troubles" (2 Cor 7:4). Sometimes, however, he groans and says sorrowfully, "I see another law in my members warring against the law of my mind and making me prisoner to the law of sin that is in my members. Unhappy man that I am! Who will deliver me from the body of this death?" (Rom 7:23–24). Likewise in the Second Letter to the Corinthians, "We would not, brethren, have you ignorant of the affliction which came upon us in Asia. We were crushed beyond measure—beyond our strength, so that we were weary even of life" (1 Cor 1:8). It is this that Saint John Chrysostom warns about: God works in all his saints so that he allows them to have neither continued troubles nor joys; rather he weaves the life of the just with a marvelous variety of adversity and prosperity.[5] So much for the moon.

CHAPTER SIX

The Order and Harmony of the Stars Mirror the Hierarchy of Heaven

Among the ornaments of the heavens there are also the stars. Ecclesiasticus says of them, "The glory of the stars is the beauty of heaven," and immediately adds, "The Lord enlightens the world on high" (Sir 43:10). Just as with the sun and the moon, whatever beauty the stars have comes totally from the Father of lights. The sun does not illumine the world by day nor the moon and the stars by night; rather it is the Lord who dwells above and illumines the world by the sun, the moon, and the stars. As the Prophet Baruch says, it is he who "sends forth light and it goes; he has called it and it obeys him with trembling; and the stars have given light to their watches and rejoiced. They were called and they said, 'Here we are' and shined forth with cheerfulness to him who made them" (Bar 4:33,34). These words signify God's infinite power which instantaneously produced, beautified, and set to work the vast and beautiful bodies with incredible ease. What for us is the word *to call* is the word *to create* for God. "He calls things that are not" (Rom 4:17) and by his calling makes them exist. When the stars say "Here we are" this means nothing other than their existing and working instantly at his word of command. "With cheerfulness they shined forth to him that made them" suggests that their prompt and ready obedience to their maker brought them great happiness and joy in obeying.

What is utterly wonderful in the stars is how, even though they move with extreme speed and never stop from their rapid course, some moving in slower and others in faster orbits, still they always keep their measure and proportion with the others so that they give rise to a sweet and melodious harmony. God speaks of this harmony in the Book of Job when he says, "Who can declare the order of the heavens, or who can put the harmony of heaven to sleep?" (Jb 38:37). This is not the harmony of voices and sounds which our bodily ears hear but the harmony of the proportions in the stars' movements which the ear of the heart recognizes. For the stars of the firmament all race together through the whole circle of the sky at the same speed during twenty-four hours; for those seven stars which are called planets or wandering stars are hurled with differing movements, some faster, some slower, so that the stars of the firmament seem to represent the bass notes (to use the common expression) and the planets play a sort of eternal and sweet counterpoint. But they are above us and that harmony is hearable only to those who live in heaven and grasp the order of their movement. Since the stars keep their proper distances and never tire in turning in their orbit, they seem to behave like a joyous chorus of noble virgins who are ever dancing skillfully through the sky.[6]

Do you, my soul, climb a bit higher if you can and reflect on the utter brilliance of the sun, the beauty of the moon, the great number and variety of the other lights, the marvelous harmony of the heavens and the happy chorus of the stars. What will it be to see God above the heavens, the sun "who dwells in light inaccessible" (1 Tm 6:16); to gaze on the Virgin, the Queen of heaven, who is "beautiful as the moon" (Sg 6:9), who gives joy to the whole city of God; to watch the choirs and ranks of many thousands of angels who, more numerous and brighter than all the stars, add beauty to the heaven of heavens; to see the souls of holy men mingling with the choirs of angels as planets mixed among the stars of the firmament? What will it be to hear the songs of praise and sing sweetly that eternal alleluia with harmonious voices in the streets of that glorious city? May it come about that even the beauty of the sky may not seem great to you and the things beneath the sky be accounted utterly puny and almost nothing and hence contemptible and despicable.

STEP EIGHT:
The Consideration of the Rational Soul

CHAPTER ONE
The Soul Is a Created Spirit; God Is an Uncreated Spirit and Creator of All Things

So far we have passed in review of all material things, while we tried to ascend to the Creator by reflecting in our mind about created things. Now we come to human souls, which surpass the dignity of all material things. Human souls are acknowledged as belonging to the lowest genus of spiritual beings, and there is no intermediate stage that we know of between them and God except the hierarchies and orders of angels.

The human soul has so much likeness to God its Creator that I surely know of no other way by which one can more easily mount to a knowledge of God than from reflection on one's own soul. God wished man to be without excuse if he lacked a knowledge of God since with God's accompanying aid he could draw this knowledge of God from an understanding of his own soul (Rom 1:20).

First the human soul is a spirit, as the holy Fathers explain regarding the words of Genesis (Gn 2:7): "The Lord God formed man of the slime of the earth and breathed into his face the breath of life." Likewise regarding the statement of Tobit (Tb 3:6): "Command my spirit to be received," and Ecclesiastes (Eccl 12:7): "The dust shall return into its earth from whence it was and the spirit shall return to God who gave it." Although the word *spirit* also means wind, as is said in the psalms, "the wind of storms" (Ps 148:8), and in the Gospel, "The wind blows where it wills and you hear its sound" (Jn 3:8), still there is no doubt that the wind of storms is a very thin body which by its extreme subtlety imitates more closely a spiritual nature than does any other body. The human soul is properly a spirit, not a body. It is not made of matter but is created by God. On this point all Catholics agree.

Here is where the excellence of the soul and its likeness to God begins. God is a spirit, as our Savior states plainly, "God is a spirit, and they who worship him must worship in spirit and truth" (Jn 4:24). Although God is a spirit and the human soul is a spirit, still God is an uncreated spirit and the Creator, while the soul is a created spirit. There is then an infinite distance between the spirit which is the soul and the spirit who is God. Just as the soul can rejoice that it belongs to the genus of spiritual substances and is thereby higher than the sky and the stars by the nobility of its nature, so it ought to abase and submit itself before God its Creator since it is made from nothing and is nothing of itself.

CHAPTER TWO

The Soul Is Immortal; God Is Eternal

Next, the human soul is also immortal because it is simple. It has nothing in itself that could divide or kill it. Although the human soul can boast greatly since it is above the souls of brute animals which perish with the body, it should equally look up to and admire the excellence of its Creator, who is not only immortal but also eternal. At one time the human soul did not exist, and it came to exist only through God's will, and it could also be reduced to nothing by God's will, even though it does not have of itself a principle of corruption. Rightly the Apostle says of God, "He alone has immortality" (1 Tm 6:16), and he alone can be destroyed by no force, no accident, and no cause since he is existence itself, life itself, and the font of being and life.

CHAPTER THREE

The Soul Is Endowed with Reason; God Is Light and Intelligence

Third, the human soul is endowed with the light of intelligence. It knows not only colors, flavors, odors, and sounds, heat and cold, hard and soft, and other similar qualities which are accessible to the bodily senses. It also judges about substance and not merely about individual objects, but also about universals. It not only knows things present but conjectures about the future and in thought climbs above the heavens, penetrates the abyss, searches out effects from their causes, and reduces effects back to their causes. Finally, by the keen edge of the mind it reaches God himself, "who dwells in light inaccessible" (1 Tm 6:16). It is about this light that Saint John speaks in his Gospel, "It was the true light that enlightens every man who comes into the world" (Jn 1:9). David adds in the psalms, "The light of your countenance, O Lord, is signed upon us" (Ps 4:7) and "Do not become like the horse and the mule, who have no understanding" (Ps 31:9).

Great is the dignity of the soul since by it man is like God and unlike the beasts. From it man can and should calculate how high and sublime is the Lord his Creator. The soul is endowed with the light of understanding, but God is light and intelligence. The soul reasons from causes to effects and from effects to causes and pursues knowledge by this reasoning, but only with great effort. God knows all things perfectly at the same moment by a single, simple intuition. The soul knows things which exist and, therefore, its knowledge depends on its objects. God makes things exist by his knowing them and, therefore, the existence of things depends on God's knowledge. The soul can somehow guess about future events. God sees all future events no less clearly than past and present events. The soul needs many things for it to carry on the work of understanding: the object, the species, the phantasm, and other things.[1] God needs nothing. For him his essence is all these things; indeed his essence is his understanding. Finally, while it is in the body the soul not only does not see God but does not see the angels or itself, and it does not properly speaking see any substance, even bodily ones, and makes many mistakes, is ignorant of much, and has opinion about many things and true knowledge about very little. God is ignorant of nothing, has no mere opinion, is never mistaken, and never errs. As the Apostle says in his Letter to the Hebrews, "All things are naked and open to his eyes" (Heb 4:13). Therefore, if a man is so proud of his knowledge that the Apostle says "Knowledge puffs up" (1 Cor 8:1), how much should he admire the knowledge of his Creator, compared to which all our knowledge is not knowledge but ignorance?

CHAPTER FOUR

The Soul Has Practical Knowledge; the Supreme Law of Right and Justice Is in God's Mind

Fourth, another kind of knowledge flourishes in the human soul, which deals with action rather than speculation. What is the source of all the books of the philosophers about virtues and vices, of all the laws of princes and briefs of legal experts, of all the manuals and exercises about the art of living well? These wonderfully indicate the light of reason in man, the one thing that sets us far, far above the beasts.

All these things are nothing compared to the eternal law which exists in the mind of the Creator, from which as from an abundant fountain flow all law and all rights. Saint James says in his Letter, "God is the one Lawgiver and Judge" (Jas 4:12). He is truth and justice and wisdom, through whom "kings reign and lawgivers decree just things" (Prv 8:15). For this reason you will never discover the art of living rightly and happily until you are enrolled in the school of Christ, who is the one true teacher (Mt 23:8) and you learn from his word and example that justice which surpasses the justice of the scribes and pharisees (Mt 5:20), as well as that of the philosophers; "its purpose is charity from a pure heart and a good conscience and faith unfeigned" (1 Tm 1:5).

STEP EIGHT

CHAPTER FIVE

The Human Soul Invents the Arts; God Is the Font of the Genius and Wisdom That Invents Things

Fifth, the human soul possesses a third kind of knowledge, which is the gift for inventing things. True, spiders know how to spin webs, birds how to build nests, bees how to make honey, and foxes how to search out burrows for their dens, but these animals by a certain natural instinct do the same thing in the same way. The human soul is endowed with reason and judgment and invents countless skills by which it commands and dominates all animals whether they like it or not. Birds are not helped by their wings, nor fish by watery depths, nor lions and bears by their singular strength, nor horses and mules by their fierceness, nor deer and goats by their agility. Even boys capture birds with traps, birdlime, and nets. Fishermen catch fish by hooks and nets. Men by their genius and skill have learned how to lock up and parade around lions and bears in iron cages, how to net goats and deer with ropes and stab them with iron, and how to tame horses and mules with a bridle and make them obey their commands. What shall I say about the arts of navigation? How the light of ingenuity glows in the human soul when it teaches massive ships laden with heavy cargo to run the liquid sea not only with oars for feet but also with sails for wings! What about agriculture? Who is not amazed at human ingenuity when he examines the grainfields, vineyards, apple orchards, gardens, fishponds, and the various watercourses designed to irrigate the gardens and water the fields? What about architecture? Who does not admire palaces, temples, cities, citadels, towers, sports arenas, pyramids, and obelisks? I pass over the arts of painting and sculpture, which sometimes express the faces of men and other objects either by colors in pictures or by a chisel in marble so true to life that they are believed to be real rather than painted or sculpted. I pass over the other arts developed by human ingenuity either for the needs of life or convenience or pleasure. They are so many that they can scarcely be counted.

Give thanks to God, my soul, that he has wished to put such a great distance between your nature and that of the other animals, but at the same time lift up the eyes of your mind to your Creator in whom is the true fountain of genius and wisdom which creates things. Whatever genius has flowed down to your nature comes from this fountain. If you admire human genius which teaches how to master by work and skill the animals who lack reason, you should admire God more since not only animals but also all inanimate creatures serve and obey him. If it seems to you great that man has developed so many skills for sailing the seas, cultivating fields, and building houses, why should it not seem greater that God in his wisdom has built heaven, earth, the seas, and all that is in them and controls and directs them all? Finally, if you can stand in awe at the art of painting pictures and bringing almost living faces out of marble, why should you not be awestruck at the art of your Creator, who formed a true and living man out of mud and built up a true and living woman from his rib (Gn 2:21–22), especially if you also consider that what men make would not happen without God's cooperation, but what God makes is done by him alone without anybody else's cooperation?

CHAPTER SIX

Human Free Choice Compared to God's Freedom

Sixth, man's soul is endowed with the free choice of the will, which he shares with God himself and the angels and by which he stands completely apart from other created things. This is a great nobility and a wonderful excellence.

But the liberty in God, the Creator of all things, is so much greater that compared with it the freedom of the soul seems hardly a shadow of it. First, the freedom of the human will is weak and easily inclined to choose things which are evil and harmful to it. The freedom of the divine will is extremely strong and in no wise can fail or be inclined toward evil. Just as the possibility of dying is a weakness of the mortal body and the impossibility of dying pertains to the health of the glorified body, so the ability to sin is a weakness of free choice and the impossibility of sinning pertains to the health of the same choice. In our heavenly fatherland God will give us as a grace this gift which he possesses forever by nature. While our freedom of choice is indeed free to will or not to will, to decide for or against, it is not powerful enough to make what it wants or not to have happen what it does not want even in itself, much less in other objects. Listen to the Apostle's lament in his letter to the Romans, "It is not what I wish that I do, but what I hate, I do" (Rom 7:15). Is there any of us who has not experienced this? I want to pray intently to God, and I order my imagination not to wander while I am busy praying and not to draw me to other thoughts. But I cannot make it do its duty, and when I am less careful about this I find that I am tricked by my imagination and, forgetting about prayer, I fall into other thoughts. I do not want to desire or get angry beyond a reasonable extent. I give orders by my free choice to my irascible and concupiscible faculties, which are within me and ought to be wholly subject to reason, that they do not allow themselves to be led astray by the bodily senses in any way. But there is often disobedience, and I get not what I want but what I do not want. What is really marvelous and miserable is that the mind commands the body and gets instant obedience; the mind commands itself and meets resistance. "Where does this monster come from?" asks Saint Augustine. "The mind commands the hands to move, and there is such ease that the command can hardly be distinguished from its execution. And the mind is mind, though the hand is body. The mind commands the mind to will, and though it is not something else, it does not act. . . . But it does not will completely, so it does not command completely. Therefore, it is not a monster, . . . but a sickness of the mind that being weighed down by habit, it does not completely arise when lifted up by truth."[2] In contrast, free choice in God our Lord is joined with full and absolute power, as has been written in this regard, "He does whatever he wills" (Ps 115:3), and "There is none that can resist your will" (Est 13:9). Therefore, my soul, be wise and boast not about the powers of your free choice until you reach the glorious freedom of the sons of God (Rom 8:21), when the heavenly physician will heal all your sicknesses and fill your desires with good things (Ps 103:5). Meanwhile, keep up your sighs and urge God with the Prophet: "Be my helper, forsake me not" (Ps 27:9). Repeat not merely in body and out of routine but urgently with your whole heart what you say more than seven times daily, "O God, come to my assistance; O Lord, make haste to help me" (Ps 69:2).[3]

CHAPTER SEVEN

The Will of the Rational Soul Can Seek Spiritual Goods; God, Who Is the Highest Good, Is Himself Charity

Seventh, the human soul has a rational will with which it can seek not only the present, particular, and material goods that brute animals seek; it can also seek absent, universal, and spiritual goods which faith and reason show it, and therefore it can seek the highest and infinite good, which is God. This is what makes men capable of great virtues, especially charity, the queen of all virtues.

Brute animals love, but do so with a love of concupiscence; they know nothing at all about the love of friendship. But God made you, my soul, capable of that gift, bright and beautiful charity, which is the font of all gifts and which links you to God, the highest good, so that he remains in you and you in him. "God is love and he who abides in love abides in God, and God in him" (1 Jn 4:16).

If the good of the created will is so great, how great will be the good which fills the uncreated will? Only God's will is capable of the infinite love. The infinite goodness of God is worthy of being loved by such a love. His will needs no virtues, nor does it need the guidance of the intellect since his will and intellect are the same, just as wisdom and charity are a single reality in God.

CHAPTER EIGHT

The Presence of the Soul in the Body Mirrors the Existence of God in Created Things

Eight, the human soul is in the human body, but in a far different way than the souls of brute animals are in their bodies. The souls of brute animals are material, and they are extended to the extent of their bodies so that they exist partially in the parts and wholly in the whole body. But the human soul, which is an indivisible spirit, in a marvelous way is whole in the whole body and wholly in each part. And since it fills the whole body, it occupies no single place within the body, and when the body grows, the soul does not grow, but begins to be where it did not previously exist. And if a member of the body is cut away or withers, the soul is not lessened or dried up, but ceases to be in that member where it was before but without itself being hurt or mutilated.

This is a true mirror of God's existence in created things. God is an indivisible spirit; he nonetheless fills the whole world and all of its parts without occupying any place. Rather he is whole in the whole world and whole in every part of the world. And when a new creature is produced, God begins to be in it, though he does not move. When a creature for some reason is destroyed or dies, God is not destroyed and does not die, but he ceases to be there though without changing his position.

In this God and the soul are similar, but in many other things, as is fitting, God is far superior. For the soul to be in the body and to rule and move the body, it has to become the form of the body and to be joined with the body so that a single man is made of soul and body. God does not need to be the form or soul of the world or that there be one substance made up of him and the world. But he has from his own immensity that he exists everywhere and from his indivisible unity that he is whole everywhere, and from his omnipotence that he rules all things, carries all things, and moves all things. Furthermore, although the soul is said to be in the whole body, still it really exists only in the living or animated parts, so that it does not exist in the fluids, the hair, the nails, or in dried up or dead limbs. God is in absolutely everything, not only in bodily things but also spiritual beings; nothing can come into existence without God being in it. Moreover, the soul exists only in its own body, an object rather narrow and small whose parts are all joined together at one time. If any part is separated from the others, the soul can no longer be in it. But God is whole in the universe of objects, although the universe is very great and its parts are not bound together, although they are contiguous, and even if a second and third world were created, God would be in them all. Therefore, it is written, "Heaven and the heaven of heavens do not contain you" (2 Chr 6:18). Hence, if other heavens and another earth came to be, he would also be in them; and further if new heavens and new earths were multiplied endlessly, he would fill them all, and where he was not, there would be nothing at all.

CHAPTER NINE

The Soul Is Somehow an Image of the Holy Trinity

Ninth, beyond what has been said, the human soul contains within it, although obscurely, an image of the divine Trinity, because it has a strong memory, and the power of understanding and the power of loving, and also because, when the mind understands, it forms a word of its own, and love proceeds from the mind and its word because that which is known by the mind and is represented by the word as a good is immediately loved and desired by the will.

In a much higher and more divine way God the Father begets God the Word, and the Father and the Word breathe forth God the Holy Spirit, who is living love and the living font of every chaste love. For this reason the mystery of the Trinity surpasses our natural way of knowing so that no philosopher, however learned, can attain a knowledge of it without supernatural light. Still the human soul produces a word and love, which are accidents rather than a substance and, therefore, are not persons. But God the Father begets a Word which is consubstantial with him, and the Father and the Word breathe forth the Holy Spirit who is likewise consubstantial with both of them so that the three persons are rightly called the Father and the Son and the Holy Spirit. Moreover, the word produced by the human soul does not last long, and the love produced by the will does not last long, but God the Father begets the eternal Word, and the Father and the Word breathe forth the eternal Holy Spirit. Nor can God exist without his Word and Holy Spirit. Finally, the human soul represents each thing by a single word and therefore multiplies words both in thought and in speech, and the human will has to produce many acts of love if it wants to love many things. God by his single Word says all true things and by a single act of love loves all good things.

STEP EIGHT

CHAPTER TEN

The Soul Gives the Body Natural Gifts; God Gives the Soul Heavenly Gifts

Lastly, the human soul is neither seen nor heard nor moves and is scarcely recognized as existing in the body, and when it leaves nothing seems to be missing from the body; still it belongs to the human soul while it is in the body to provide the body with all things good—sensation, movement, speech, subsistence, beauty, and strength. How is it that while a man lives, he can see, hear, speak, walk, subsist, and be strong, handsome, and lovable? The only reason is that a soul is in his body. How is it that after death he neither sees nor hears nor speaks nor moves but lies ugly, useless, and detested? Because the soul from which all these good properties flowed has departed.

Your God, O my soul, when he lives in you through his grace, brings it about that you see what faith shows you, that you hear what the Lord speaks within you, that you walk in the way of the commandments to the heavenly Jerusalem, that you speak in prayer to God and to your neighbor with holy encouragement, that you subsist by continuing in your good works, that you are strong in the battle against invisible enemies and beautiful in the eyes of the invisible God and his angels. Beware that if God's grace, which is the life of your soul, should be withdrawn, you suffer the losses which the first death carries with it, and then you will be snatched away to the second death from which no resurrection is granted (Rv 20:5–6). Oh, that God would open the eyes of your mind and you could see the surpassing beauty and extreme splendor which adorns a soul which is pleasing to God and is joined to him by true charity and that you could see with what eyes God beholds the soul, what a place he prepares for her, what joys he promises her, and what yearning the angels and the other blessed spirits have in awaiting her. Then you could certainly never bear that such beauty be defiled by even a small stain, and should that somehow happen, you would at least strive to wash away these stains, however small, with streams of tears.

Saint Bonaventure reports that, because Saint Francis saw that he could not follow the stainless Lamb without some stain, he at least made an effort to cleanse his soul daily with copious showers of tears and to wipe away all stains, even the smallest.[4] If by this same grace of God your interior eyes were opened and you could see how ugly a sinful soul is, how it gives off a foul odor like a rotting corpse, and how God and the holy angels shrink to look at it even though it may dwell in a beautiful, handsome, and very attractive body in the eyes of men, then beyond any doubt you would be so terrified that you would not allow yourself for any reason to become such or long remain in such a state.

STEP NINE:

The Consideration of Angels

CHAPTER ONE

An Angel Is Wholly a Perfect Spirit and Is Created; God Is an Uncreated Spirit and Is Most Perfect

We now reach the top step in the ascent to God which created substances can provide. No created substance is higher than the angelic as long as we are talking about natural perfection. We shall reflect on angels regarding first the excellence of their nature, then the loftiness of their grace, and finally the duties they perform. We do not plan to present a full-scale treatise on the angels but only to touch on those points that can help us lift our mind to God.

If an angel is compared to the rational human soul, he can be rightly enough called a perfect soul just as a soul can be called an imperfect angel. Thus the Prophet speaks of man by reason of his soul when he says, "You have made him a little less than the angels" (Ps 8:6). An angel is a complete and perfect spiritual substance; the human soul is a diminished and imperfect substance because it is the form of the body and, therefore, is a part of man.

Hence, an angel is wholly spirit; man is part spirit and part flesh, or part angel and part beast, just as one might say that an angel is wholly golden, while man is part gold and part mud. Hence, what the Prophet says is true, that man is a little less than the angels; and it is also true that the human soul, because it is part of man, is a little less than an angel. From this it follows that an angel is more like God than is man or his soul because God is spirit and not a body or the form of a body. But this greater likeness of an angel to God does not mean that God is not a spirit elevated above angelic substance by an infinite distance of honor, for God is an uncreated spirit, eternal, immense, alone mighty, alone wise, alone good, and alone most high.

If you agree, my soul, that you should esteem angelic nature, how much more should you esteem and admire the divine nature, which utterly surpasses angelic dignity beyond all measure.

CHAPTER TWO

The Intelligence and Knowledge of the Angels

An angel can be called a perfect man and a man an imperfect angel not only in nature and substance, but also in intelligence and knowledge. Man or the human soul works hard to understand things since he has to use the help of the senses and, moving from causes to effects and from effects to causes, he gradually gains knowledge of himself; therefore, he often remains doubtful and often makes terrible mistakes and rarely attains certain understanding. An angel by a single glance intuits an object and at the same moment sees its causes and effects and penetrates not only to its accidents but also to its substance. He sees not only physical objects but also spiritual ones.

As long as he is a pilgrim on this earth, man is as regards his intelligence not only a little less than the angels, but is so much less that, however much talent he enjoys and however much he devotes himself to the pursuit of wisdom, when compared to an angel, a man can rightly be called a child or an infant and suckling. The Prophet was not wrong when he sang about us mortals, "Out of the mouth of infants and sucklings you have perfected praise" (Ps 8:2). Listen to how the wise Solomon rates our wisdom that so puffs us up, "All things are hard; man cannot explain them by word" (Eccl 1:8), and again, God "delivered the world to their consideration so that man cannot find out the work which God has made from the beginning to the end" (Eccl 3:11).

If man finds everything difficult and unexplainable and if man understands nothing about this visible world from the first thing created to the last, if he understands nothing perfectly, I say, so that he can explain its nature or the properties, accidents, forces, and so forth that lie within it, how many errors will he not get caught in if he tries to investigate things which are above the heavens? So be wise, my soul, and seek the science and wisdom of the saints which consists in this, that you fear God and keep his commandments. May you find more delight in prayer than in disputation, in charity that builds up than in knowledge that puffs up. This is the way that leads to life and the kingdom of heaven where we children will be given equality with the angels, who "always see the face of my Father who is in heaven" (Mt 18:10; cf. Lk 20:36).

CHAPTER THREE

The Power of Angels over Bodies and The Omnipotence of God

There is a third way that the human soul is not a little but very much less than an angel. This is its power and control over bodies. The human soul can move only its own body by a command of the will; it cannot move other bodies this way, and it moves its own body across the earth by progressive steps, but it cannot hold it up on water or lift it above the air and carry it off where it wishes. Angels by the mere movement of spirit, that is, by a command of their will, lift aloft and carry about heavy bodies wherever they wish; thus one angel snatched Habakkuk and in a moment carried him to Babylon to bring lunch to Daniel and then carried him back to Palestine. Man cannot fight with his enemies by his spirit alone but needs hands and weapons. An angel without hands and without weapons can fight against and conquer a whole army by the force of his spirit alone; thus a single angel once killed 185,000 Assyrians. And if an angel can do this, what can the Creator and Lord of the angels do? Surely he who created everything from nothing can turn back everything to nothingness.

The human soul can by the art of painting and sculpture through work and labor make images of men which represent living men that seem to breathe and be alive. Angels can without effort and without hands and instruments and in scarcely a moment of time mold a body for themselves so that intelligent men would judge it a human body seeing that it walks, speaks, eats, drinks, and can be touched, felt, and even washed. Thus Abraham prepared food for angels and even washed their feet (Gn 18:2ff.). As the Apostle explains, he received angels as guests thinking that he had received men (Heb 13:2). The same thing happened to his nephew, Lot, when he welcomed into his home two angels as though they were men on a journey (Gn 19:1ff.). So too Raphael spent many days with young Tobit, walking, talking, eating, and drinking as if he were a truly and rightly a man. And yet when he was later about to depart he said, "I seemed indeed to eat and drink with you, but I use an invisible meat and drink" (Tb 12:19), and he suddenly vanished from their sight.

Indeed great and wonderful is the power to mold instantly a body which seems to differ from a human and living body in no respect and dissolve it instantly at will so that no trace of it can be found. But if the power of the angels is so great and wonderful, how great will be the power of the Creator of the angels who both made them and gave them as much power as he wished? Just as our knowledge and that of the angels is utter ignorance when compared with the knowledge of God, and our justice and that of the angels is injustice compared with the justice of God, so all our power and that of the angels is weakness compared to the power of God. Therefore, our God is rightly called alone wise, alone good, and alone powerful (1 Tm 6:15).

CHAPTER FOUR

The Place and Movement of Angels and God's Omnipresence

If we reflect on the place of angels and men, we will find that in this respect man or his soul is not slightly, but very much less than an angel—I gladly use the terminology that the Apostle uses (Heb 2:7). God has given the human soul its place on the earth and the angels their place in heaven, that is, in his palace. "The heaven of heaven is the Lord's, but the earth he has given to the children of men" (Ps 115:16). Hence in Matthew the Lord calls them "angels of heaven" (Mt 24:36) and says in Luke, "There will be joy in heaven over one sinner who does penance," and shortly later, "There will be joy before the angels of God over one sinner doing penance" (Lk 15:7, 10). Moreover, God so bound the soul to the body that without the body it cannot change its place, but God did not bind the angels to a body but gave them the power to travel at enormous speeds from heaven to earth and from earth to heaven and anywhere they wish. Thus the angels are next to God in the dignity of their nature and by their subtlety imitate to a degree God's omnipresence. God is always everywhere by the immensity of his nature and has no need to change his place since he is everywhere; an angel by the speed of his motion moves so easily from place to place and manifests his presence in all places that he seems somehow to be everywhere.

If you are willing to listen to the Lord of the angels, my soul, you will have no reason to envy the angels their lofty place or how they move at tremendous speeds without tiring. For you will not only be equal to the angels when you are freed from the body, but also, when you return to the body that Christ "has made like to the body of his glory" (Phil 3:21), you will possess together with your body heaven as your own home. And your body, once made spiritual (1 Cor 15:44), will without effort or weariness be immediately there where you its soul wish and command it to be. Your Lord does not deceive you when he says in the Gospel, "In my Father's house there are many mansions," and "I go to prepare a place for you," and "If I shall go and prepare a place for you, I will come again and will take you unto myself, that where I am, you may also be" (Jn 14:2–3). "Father, I will that where I am they also may be with me; that they may see my glory which you have given me" (Jn 17:24). You are not ignorant of where Christ is and the sort of body he has since you daily profess and say, "The third day he arose from the dead and ascended into heaven."[1] You know that after the resurrection his body used to come to the disciples through closed doors (Jn 20:19). And when he went away, he used to leave them not by walking away but by vanishing (Lk 24:31), that is, he used to move his body from place to place by a motion so swift as to seem a spirit and not a body. If you wish to share this glory, you must first conform your body to the body of Christ's humility. Then you must follow his footsteps. "Christ has suffered for us, leaving us an example that we may follow his footsteps," as Saint Peter says. What are his footsteps? He continues, "Who did not sin, neither was guile found in his mouth. Who when he was reviled did not revile; when he suffered, he threatened not" (1 Pt 2:21–23). Christ has two footsteps; if you step out of them, you have lost the way and will never reach your fatherland; do not do evil but suffer it, and what follows from this, do good without expecting good here below. It all comes down to this: You must love your neighbor for God's sake with the true and pure love of friendship and not out of gain, gratuitously and not for the sake of human reward, content with a reward from God which surpasses all measure.

CHAPTER FIVE

The Kind of Grace Given to the Angels and the Kind Given to Men

We now come to the dignity of the angels in the order of grace. Here too man is more than a little less than the angels. At the beginning God so created the individual angels that he simultaneously created their nature and infused them with grace, as Saint Augustine states in his work *The City of God*.[2] Soon afterward, when their minds first turned to God and they joined themselves to him by charity, they were crowned with happiness and glory, after the reprobate had fallen. Thus their pilgrimage was very short and their stay in their fatherland has been eternal, if that very short delay which came between creation and happiness should be called a pilgrimage. We men received grace with nature at creation, but in our first parent and not in ourselves so that we all fell when he fell; "in him all sinned," as the Apostle says (Rom 5:12), although we are reconciled to God through Christ Jesus, the mediator of God and man (1 Tm 2:5). Still we were condemned to long exile and, while we are in the body, we are pilgrims away from God, for we walk by faith and not by sight. What greatly saddens holy men who desire their fatherland is that we meanwhile dwell among savage enemies and that there is the danger that, surrounded and taken prisoner by them, we may end by being cut off from the possession of that dearest fatherland. This gives rise to the cry "Woe is me that my sojourning is prolonged! I have dwelt with the inhabitants of Cedar; my soul has long been a sojourner" (Ps 120:4).

Although in this regard we are less than the angels, God's goodness wonderfully consoles us men both because he has placed a man and a woman from our race, Christ and Mary, ahead of all the angels in the kingdom of heaven and because he has wished not a few of us men, although inferior to the angels in all the gifts of nature, to be superior to many angels in the gift of grace and he has made some equal to the highest angels. Saint John Chrysostom in explaining the Letter to the Romans certainly did not hesitate to place the princes of the apostles, Peter and Paul, in the zone where the seraphim fly and glorify God.[3] It is a holy belief that the same applies to Saint John the Baptist and some others. Moreover, the good angels achieved glory after their first merit, and the evil angels were delivered over to eternal punishment after their first sin; men should, therefore, not complain about their longer journey since they can again and again correct their failures and attain pardon through repentance.

CHAPTER SIX

The Duties of the Angels are Considered

Our remaining task is now to say a few words about the duties of the angels. The angels have five duties. The first is to continually sing hymns and praise to their Creator. To understand how highly God values this service we must note that the highest angels are assigned to this duty; all the choirs of angels follow their lead in singing with harmonious voices and incredible delight. Listen to Isaiah (Is 6:1–3), "I saw the Lord sitting upon a throne high and elevated, and his train filled the temple. Upon it stood the seraphim; the one had six wings and the other had six wings; with two they covered his face, and with two they covered his feet, and with two they flew. And they cried out one to another and said, 'Holy, Holy, Holy, the Lord God of hosts, all the earth is full of his glory!' " (Is 6:1–3). Here you hear the name, seraphim, who are the leaders of the highest order; you see them cover his face and feet, which is a sign of reverence, as if they did not dare to gaze on his face or touch his naked feet; you see them constantly flying as they sing, which signifies their desire and eagerness to come always closer and closer to God. Two things are necessary for those who wish to please God while they sing his praises, namely, that they join love with reverence and reverence with love. The Prophet David pointed this out when he said, "Serve the Lord with fear and rejoice unto him with trembling" (Ps 2:11).

From this you should learn, my soul, how much veneration God deserves, since these supreme leaders of heaven who always stand beside him and always see his face never dare while reciting his praises to slacken in fear and reverence because of their lofty station or their long familiarity. And you, dust and ashes, what will you answer when you are charged at the judgment with sleepiness and mind-wandering in the divine task which you were unworthy to undertake? Then at least learn, taught by this great example, to perform the hymns and praises you owe your God with fear and trembling, with attention and zeal, and with love and desire.

The second duty of the angels is to present the prayers of mortals to God and commend them with their petitions. Thus the angel Raphael says in the Book of Tobit (Tb 12:12), "When you prayed with tears and buried the dead and left your dinner, . . . I offered your prayer to the Lord." In Revelation John saw an angel standing in front of the altar with a golden censer and said, "And there was given him much incense that he might offer it with the prayers of all the saints upon the golden altar which is before the throne of God" (Rv 8:3).

Here we see the truly incredible kindness and mercy of our God, for he was not content to encourage us to pray and make requests, first through the prophets and then through his Son, but he also added a promise to give us whatever we requested: "Ask, and it shall be given to you" (Lk 11:9); and elsewhere, "If you ask the Father anything in my name, he will give it to you" (Jn 16:24). Not content with this promise either, he added also that he would give a reward to those who asked. He said, "When you pray, go into your room, and closing the door, pray to your Father in secret; and your Father, who sees in secret, will reward you" (Mt 6:6), namely, with a reward beyond what you had requested. For in the same passage the Lord speaks this way of almsgiving and fasting, "Your Father, who sees in secret, will reward you" (Mt 6:4, 18). Not content with this proof of his fatherly care, God appointed angels as his personal attendants to take care of prayers, the petitions of the poor as it were, and to present and read them in his presence lest even a single petition of the poor be overlooked. What earthly prince ever promised a reward to those who came to him seeking a favor or justice? Still, those who come to the princes of the earth are men, just as the princes are also men formed out of the same mud and subject to the same supreme prince, God. If it is a burden to give a reward to those who ask, it should surely not seem a burden to admit petitioners freely and appoint a trusted attendant to preserve carefully the humble petitions of one's subjects and present them and see to their swift dispatch.

The third duty of the angels consists in their being sent as messengers to declare what God wants to declare, especially matters related to redemption and eternal salvation. Thus the Apostle speaks to the Hebrews (Heb 1:14), "Are they [the angels] not all ministering spirits sent for the service, for the sake of those who shall inherit salvation?" Thus we see throughout the Old Testament that angels appeared to the patriarchs and prophets and declared to them what God ordered them to declare (e.g., Gn 18:2; Dn 9:21). We also read in the New Testament that the Archangel Gabriel was sent as a messenger to Zachary and to the Virgin Mother of God (Lk 1:11, 26), then angels were sent to the shepherds (Lk 2:9), to Saint Joseph (Mt 1:20, 2:13, 19), and after the Lord's resurrection to the women going to his tomb (Mt 28:2ff.), and after his ascension to all the disciples (Acts 1:10).

The reason why God, who is everywhere and can easily speak to the hearts of men by himself, should wish nonetheless to send angels seems to be so that men may understand that God has a care for human affairs and that he rules and directs everything, for men can easily persuade themselves that divine inspirations are their own reasonings and plans. But when they see and hear that angels are sent by God and that the things that the angels predict come true as they foretold, they cannot doubt that God oversees human affairs and especially directs and arranges those which relate to the eternal salvation of his elect.

The fourth duty of the angels is protecting men whether as individuals or groups. It pleased the kindness of God our Father to entrust to his most powerful servants the weakness of mortals and place them as guardians over children, as tutors over youngsters, as patrons over clients, as shepherds over sheep, as doctors over the sick, as protectors over orphans, and as defenders over those who cannot defend themselves, unless they take refuge under the wings of the mighty. David gives witness about the protection and guardianship of individual men: "For he has given his angels charge over you to keep you in all your ways" (Ps 91:11). Christ himself is a witness, and a most trustworthy one: "See that you do not despise one of these little ones, for I tell you their angels in heaven always behold the face of my Father in heaven" (Mt 18:10). Daniel is witness to provinces and kingdoms having protectors; he calls the angel-protector of the kingdom of the Persians, the king of the Persians; he gives the name of the king of Greeks to the protector of the kingdom of the Greeks, and calls the protector of the sons of Israel by the name Michael (Dn 10:5ff.). John in Revelation writes about the protectors of the churches where he mentions the angel of the church of Ephesus and the angel of the church of Smyrna and of others as well (Rv 2 and 3). Therefore, in each kingdom there are two kings, one a man and visible, the other an angel and invisible; and in each church there are two bishops, one a man and visible, the other an angel and invisible; and in the universal Catholic Church there are two supreme pontiffs established under Christ the Lord, one a man and visible, and one an angel and invisible, who we believe is the Archangel Michael. As once the synagogue of the Jews revered him as a patron, so now does the Church of Christians.

Do you see, my soul, how caring about us his servants is that majesty, who has no need for our goods? What could he have done to show his great love that he has not done? He has overwhelmed us with gifts so that we should gladly remain near him; he has walled us round with guards lest we flee; he has surrounded us with protectors lest we be snatched away. What would he do were we his treasure, as he is indeed our great and only treasure? Now at last, my soul, yield to his love and, conquered by the love of such a mighty lover, sell, hand over, and make a gift by an irrevocable oath and vow your whole self, holding back no part of yourself, to his service and will. Be not moved by anything that can be seen. Think of things invisible and aspire to them: "For things that are seen are temporal, but things that are not seen are eternal" (2 Cor 4:18).

The last duty of the angels is to serve as soldiers and armed leaders "to execute vengeance upon the nations, chastisements among the people" (Ps 149:7). It is the angels who burned up the wicked cities with fire and brimstone (Gn 19:13), killed the firstborn of all Egypt (Ex 12:12ff.), and destroyed many thousands of Assyrians at a single blow (2 Kgs 19:35); it will be the angels who on the last day "will separate the wicked from the just and will cast them into the furnace of fire" (Mt 13:49, 50). Let good men love their fellow citizens, the angels; let wicked men shudder at the power of the angels, servants of the wrath of almighty God, from whose hands no one can snatch them.

STEP TEN:

Reflection on God's Essence in Comparison with Bodily Greatness

CHAPTER ONE

General Considerations on God's Greatness Drawn from the Four Dimensions of Bodily Things

We have ascended as far as we could through created substances, but we have still not reached the full knowledge of God that can be achieved by reflection even in this vale of tears. There remains for us to see whether through the dimensions of bodily greatness, which we know, we can ascend to the breadth and length, the height and depth of God's invisible essence. Among creatures those are called great that have four great dimensions. In the psalms and elsewhere generally it is said that God is great and that his greatness has no limit (Ps 47:1, 94:3, 146:5, 144:3; Dt 10:17; Tb 13:17). Certainly that outstanding contemplative, Saint Bernard, made himself a ladder for understanding God from these dimensions in the book *On Consideration*, which he wrote for Pope Eugenius.[1] He was not the inventor of this kind of ladder, but rather learned this way of ascent from the Apostle, who penetrated to the third heaven and to paradise; thus the Apostle speaks in his Letter to the Ephesians, "that you may be able to comprehend with all the saints what is the breadth and length and height and depth" (Eph 3:18).

Anyone who considers carefully will surely find that nothing is full and solid outside God, but all things are narrow, short, lowly, empty, or superficial. But in God there are true breadth—his immensity; true length—his eternity; true height—his lofty nature; true depth without bottom—his incomprehensibility; and again true height—his omnipotence; true depth—his infinite wisdom; true breadth—his heart full of mercy; true length—his severe judgment, that is, his full and perfect justice.

It is not enough to touch on these ideas lightly if one wants to ascend and find what he is seeking. One must understand fully, as the Apostle says, "that you may be able to comprehend with all the saints what is the breadth and length and height and depth" (Eph 3:18). He really comprehends who giving close attention is completely convinced how things stand and is so convinced that he hurries off to sell all his possessions and buy the treasure he has found (Mt 13:44–46). This is why the Apostle includes the phrase "with all the saints." Only the saints fully understand this, or nobody understands this as he ought without being made a saint. What we have said is not in disagreement with Saint Augustine, who writes in his *Letter to Honoratus* that the cross of Christ is depicted by the Apostle when he describes the breadth, length, height, and depth; as he himself teaches, the cross beam to which the hands of the crucified were nailed corresponds to breadth; the vertical beam to which the body of the crucified was attached corresponds to length; the wooden bar put above the cross holding the title corresponds to height; the wooden part which was stuck into the ground and hidden corresponds to depth.[2] Saint Augustine, I say, does not disagree with our meaning but rather wonderfully enriches it, for the cross of Christ is the way to attain real breadth, length, height, and depth. Although the cross seems to the eyes of men narrow and short, lowly and not very deep, still it truly extends its arms from east to west and from north to south, that is, it has spread its glory far and wide by the preaching of the apostles and lifted its top to the highest heaven, which it opened like a key for the elect, and it reached to the bottom of hell, which it shut forever on those so destined.

CHAPTER TWO

The Breadth of God's Being Is the Immensity of His Perfections

Let us begin with his essence and then go on to his attributes. God's essence can rightly be called most broad in many ways. First it is in itself most broad and indeed immense because it includes all the perfections of creatures and of things that could be created which are still more numerous beyond any number; everything that has been made, will be made, or can be made are beyond doubt contained in God in a higher degree and mode. Other things are good with qualification, that is, a good man, a good horse, a good house, good clothes, and so on for everything else. But God is all good, for when Moses said, "Show me your glory," God answered, "I will show you all good" (Ex 33:18, 19).

Suppose that somebody had a single thing at home that contained all the objects of the senses in the highest degree so that he would not want to ever leave his home to see or hear or smell or taste or feel anything since he had at home every delight in that one object that the greatest pleasure-seeker could hope for. Would not that object be enormously precious? Suppose too that the object contained in itself so great an abundance of every sort of riches as an utterly greedy person could desire so as not to go out of his house to acquire anything else. Would not that object be very rich and precious? And again, if that object could offer its owners honors and awards such as the mind of a most ambitious man could conceive of—would it not seem to surpass any price? And if that object could fulfill the desire not only of man but also of an angel, which is as much greater and more extensive as the angels know more and better things than men, what would you say? Yet the goodness of this object would still be far inferior to the goodness of God, which is so great that it can satisfy and fill the infinite desire or rather infinite capacity of God.

How wonderful is the breadth of the perfection of God's essence which includes such an immensity of goods that it fully satisfies the infinite capacity which is in God! God never goes outside himself because he is all good in himself. Before the world came to exist he was as rich and happy as he was later because nothing was made by God which was not always in God to a higher degree.

My soul, do you understand what sort of good you will enjoy in your fatherland if you love God on the path to it and what a good you will lose if you do not love him? God offers himself, that is, all good to be enjoyed, to those who love him when he will say to his good and faithful servant, "Enter into the joy of your master" (Mt 25:23).

CHAPTER THREE

The Breadth of the Divine Essence Is God's Immensity by Which He Fills All Things

God is immense in another way because he completely fills all that exists in created things: "I fill heaven and earth" (Jer 23:24). If there were many worlds, he would fill them all, says David, "If I ascend into heaven, you are there; if I descend into hell, you are present" (Ps 139:8). I also add that if I go above heaven or below heaven or outside of heaven, I will not be alone because you will be there, nor can I exist unless I exist in you and you uphold me who uphold all things by the word of your power (Heb 1:3). Not only does God fill all bodies by his immensity, but he also fills spirits, hearts, and minds. How can he search hearts (Ps 7:9) unless he is in hearts? How could he hear the prayers of hearts (Ps 27:8) unless he had his ears at our hearts? How could the Prophet say "I will hear what the Lord God will speak in me" (Ps 85:8) if God did not move his mouth to the ears of our hearts? Happy is the soul that loves God because she has her Beloved always within her and cherishes him on her lap and is cherished on his. "He who abides in love abides in God and God in him" (1 Jn 4:10).

God fills all things not only by his presence but also by his glory. As the seraphim exclaim, "All the earth is full of his glory" (Is 6:3), and David adds, "O Lord our Lord, how admirable is your name in the whole earth. For your magnificence is elevated above the heavens" (Ps 8:1), as if he were saying: Your name, your fame and glory have not only filled the whole earth with admiration but also they have gone up to heaven and been lifted above the heavens.

Finally Ecclesiasticus adds, "Full of the glory of the Lord is his work" (Sir 42:16). There is no creature in heaven or on earth who does not continually praise God. This is the reason why David in the psalms and the three children in Daniel urge all creatures to bless and glorify the Creator with praise. They were not ignorant that by their nature many creatures could not heed the voice urging them; rather because they understood that all works of God are good and hence praise their maker by their specific makeup, they congratulated them and urged them to do what they were doing.

Certainly anyone who had inward eyes would see that all the works of the Lord are like censers sending upward a sweet smell to the glory of God. If they had inward ears they would hear like a mixed harmony of every sort of musical instrument those praising God and saying, "He made us and not we ourselves" (Ps 100:3). Although they all are sinners who curse God and blaspheme his name, still these also, however unwillingly, are forced to praise God in the way that a product praises its maker, for in them too there shines forth marvelously the power by which he made them, the wisdom by which he governs them, the goodness with which he preserves their life despite their ingratitude and evil, and the mercy and justice by which he either justly directs them toward punishment or awaits mercifully their repentance. Many on earth are deaf to hearing the voices of these creatures, but they still do not stop crying out. The innumerable ears of angels and holy men are not lacking who listen to these praises and delight in them, and they too continuously celebrate God their maker in hymns and songs.

CHAPTER FOUR

The Length of the Divine Essence Is Its Eternity

The length of the divine essence is indeed its eternity, which has no beginning of duration and will never have an end and will always remain the same without any change: "But you are always the selfsame, and your years shall not fail," says David and Tobit and the Apostle after him (Ps 102:27; Tb 13:6; 1 Tm 1:17). They call God the King of ages because he alone is not subject to ages but is over the ages and rules the ages, who alone has come before all ages.

Other things either have a beginning and an end and never remain in the same state, or they have a beginning without an end or without a change in substance, but they could cease even to be if that would please their creator. Therefore, eternity is so proper to God that it belongs to no created thing, nor has any prince ever been so arrogant as to presume to take for himself the title of eternity among the many titles that princes usurp, unless perhaps with a different meaning as when Constantius was called eternal emperor because he was not emperor for a fixed time but for life.

You, my soul, can be counted among both types of creatures, for you have a body which began to be when it was conceived and born and gradually grew to the greatness that God had predetermined for it; then it began to grow less and a little after death ceases to be and, therefore, never remains in the same state but is subject to change in every part and at every hour. The Prophet stated this idea by a comparison with grass: "In the morning man shall grow up like grass; in the morning he shall flourish and pass away; in the evening he shall fall, grow dry and wither" (Ps 90:6). Thus in the morning, that is, in childhood, the human body grows like grass but soon passes to youth; in the noonday of youth it flourishes and suddenly passes to old age; in the evening of old age it dies, continues on in death, dries up in the grave, and returns to its dust. See, my soul, how far your body is away from eternity! You were created in time since you previously were nothing. In this you are very unlike your eternal Creator. But once created you will not see an end to your duration—this you have in common with your Creator. But because you are changeable while you live in the body you go from vice to virtue and from virtue to vice, and you will be judged in the state you are found when you leave your body either to reign forever with God or to suffer torments forever with the devil. There is nothing you should have more care for than fleeing vice and seeking virtue. Beware lest the allures of your flesh seduce you to its everlasting loss and yours. Rather crucify your flesh with its vices and desires (Gal 5:24) so that a little later not only you may live happy forever, but your flesh may arise in glory and it too may continue forever joined to you in the eternity of your God.

The souls of the blessed like the holy angels will participate in the eternity of God in that lofty and happy union with God through a beatific vision and love. This union will not only not have an end but will always remain the same, stable and unchanged; still in other ways your thoughts, affections, and location will be able to change and vary. They will always stand in awe and look up above themselves at God's eternity in which no change of mind or will or place is possible, and yet he lacks nothing but rather always has everything which he could gain for himself by various changes through eternal time. Hence, the length of eternity is something infinite and proper to God no less than the breadth of his immensity.

CHAPTER FIVE

The Height of God Signifies the Nobility of the Divine Nature, Which Is the First and Highest, the Efficient, Exemplary and Final Cause of All Things

The height of God next comes under consideration. This is why God is acclaimed, "You alone are the most high" (Ps 83:18). God is alone most high in the nobility of his nature, for things are noble and lofty to the degree that they are more pure and withdrawn from matter. We see this first in bodily things: Water is higher than earth, because it is purer; for the same reason air is higher than water, fire than air, and heaven than fire. We see the same thing in spiritual things: The intellect is higher than a sense faculty because a sense faculty has a bodily organ which the intellect does not need. An angelic intellect is higher than a human intellect because the latter needs the help of the imagination and phantasms which the former does not need. Among the angels those are higher that understand more things with fewer species. Hence, God alone is pure act and needs nothing outside of himself, neither organ nor imagination nor species, and not even the presence of some object outside himself. His own essence is for him everything, and he can have nothing which he has not always had in act and the very having in act is always his pure and simple actual existence. Therefore, his nature is most high and sublime, nor can he have an equal in any way. Hence, he who said "I will be like the most High" (Is 14:14) was suddenly cast down and fell into the lowest depths of hell, as Isaiah relates. Christ our Lord says of him, "I was watching Satan fall as lightning from heaven" (Lk 10:18).

God is most high in another way, because he is the first and highest efficient, exemplary, and final cause of all things. He is the highest efficient cause because no created thing would have any power at all to make anything unless it had that power from God. But God has this from no one. Again, there is no cause that can exercise its power unless it is moved by God, but God is moved by no one. Finally, in created things those other causes are called higher which are universal. Particular causes depend on them, as the heavens and the angels that move the heavens, but God made both the heavens and the angels. Therefore, he alone is the first and highest efficient cause. He is likewise the first exemplary cause because God made all things according to the forms or ideas which he has in himself. Finally, he is the first final cause because he created all things for himself, that is, to manifest his glory, as the Wise Man says in Proverbs (Prv 16:4). He is very rightly called and is the most high God because he sits in the highest throne: "I saw the Lord," says Isaiah, "sitting upon a throne high and elevated" (Is 6:1). Since a throne has two uses, one for judging, the other for resting, we should consider each of them separately.

CHAPTER SIX

God Has the Highest Throne, for He Is the Supreme King and Judge Who Gives Favor to the Lowly

First, God has the highest throne because he is the supreme judge, for Abraham says to God, "You judge all the earth" (Gn 18:25), and David adds, "He judges gods" (Ps 82:1), that is, God judges the judges themselves who are called gods in Scripture (Ex 22:28; Ps 82:6). Saint James says openly, "There is one giver and judge" (Jas 4:6), that is, God alone is properly the lawgiver and judge because he alone gives laws to everyone and receives them from nobody, he judges all and is judged by nobody. Besides, God is not only a judge, but he is also king and, therefore, judges not as a judge appointed by a king but as a king and supreme prince. Hence, he is called "King of kings" (Rv 19:16), and "a great King above all gods"

(Ps 95:3), and "terrible with the kings of the earth" (Ps 76:12), clearly because, when he wishes, he transfers kingdoms and empires from nation to nation and, when he wishes, he takes away the life of princes. Lastly God is not only the supreme Judge and King but also the absolute Lord, which is the greatest of all titles. Kings are not masters of their subjects to the degree that they can strip them of goods and life at their whim. King Achab can serve as a witness of this. He wanted to have the vineyard of Naboth but could not get it except through the trickery and calumny of his wife (1 Kgs 21:2ff.), with the result that both perished miserably. But God is a true and proper Lord, and all things serve him, and he serves nobody; he can if he wishes reduce everything to nothing since he made everything from nothing.

Consider then, my soul, how much fear and trembling we worms of the earth owe to him who sits upon that throne so high that it has nothing at all above it. He says through Malachi, "If I am a master, where is my fear?" (Mal 1:6), and if those supreme princes of heaven attend him with fear and trembling, what is fitting for us weak mortals that dwell on the earth with the beasts?

It seems a wonderful thing that the most high God does not love lofty and sublime creatures like himself but humble and poor ones. Thus does God speak through Isaiah, "To whom shall I have respect, but to him that is poor and little and of a contrite spirit and that trembles at my words?" (Is 66:2). David says, "God is high . . . and looks down on the low things" (Ps 113:4, 6). God does indeed love high and sublime things which are therefore like himself, but things truly sublime, not things that seem so but are not. Therefore, God does not love the proud, who should be called elated and puffed up, not high and sublime; he truly loves the humble and those who fear his words because the more they humble themselves, the more they are exalted by God himself, and those whom God exalts are truly high. Therefore, these are both lowly and lofty, lowly in their own eyes but lofty in the eyes of God. If anyone were to look not only with the eyes of the body but also with eyes of a heart which God had enlightened at the rich banqueter clothed in linen and purple and reclining at a table loaded with all sorts of expensive food and surrounded by many waiters eagerly carrying out their duties, and if he also at the same time were to look at Lazarus half-naked and full of sores sitting at the door of the rich man and desiring to be filled with the crumbs that fell from the rich man's table, he would surely see that the rich man, whom the world believed to be truly happy, was utterly hateful and wretched in the eyes of God and the angels, indeed like the mud and dung of the ground: "For that man which is exalted in the sight of men is an abomination before God" (Lk 16:15), says the Lord in the same passage in which he describes the banqueter. On the other hand, he would see the poor and lowly Lazarus as noble and honored in the eyes of God and the angels like a precious pearl. The outcome makes this clear: Angelic hands carried Lazarus as one dear to God to Abraham's bosom; the rich man as one hateful to God the demons snatched off for the hell of fire (Lk 16:19–31). But why do I speak about Lazarus? Nobody is higher before God than our Lord Jesus Christ, even according to his humanity, yet nobody was found more humble than he in heaven or on earth, as he said so truly, "Learn from me for I am meek and humble of heart" (Mt 11:29). As his holy soul understood more clearly than all others the infinite loftiness of the divinity, so much the more did it recognize the vileness of the creature, which is made from nothingness. Therefore, since it was a creature, it subjected itself more than any other creature to God, humbled itself and exalted God, and was in turn exalted by God above all creatures, even angelic ones. We can say the same about the angels and saintly men: None are more humble than those who sit high in heaven because they who are closer to God see by that fact more clearly what a distance separates the greatness of the Creator from the smallness of the creature.

Then love humility, my soul, if you want to be truly exalted. Imitate the spotless Lamb, imitate the Virgin Mother, imitate the cherubim and seraphim. All of them are the more humble the higher they are.

CHAPTER SEVEN

The Throne of the Most High Signifies God's Blessed and Beatifying Rest

God has a lofty throne not only because he judges all men but also because he rests more than all others and he gives rest to those in whom he is enthroned. The lofty throne of God is his lofty rest.

Although he rules the whole world, in which there are constant wars and the conflicts among the elements, beasts, and men, he still judges in tranquillity, as is said in the Book of Wisdom (Wis 12:18), and always rejoices in the highest peace. There is nothing that can disturb his rest and contemplation of himself in which is his eternal delight. He is, therefore, also called the King of Jerusalem (Tb 13:11; Sir 24:15), which means the vision of peace. His proper throne is the blessed spirits so that he is called he "who sits upon the cherubim" (Ps 80:1, 99:1). God is said to sit upon the cherubim rather than upon the seraphim because "cherubim" signifies the vastness of knowledge, but "seraphim" signifies the ardor of charity. Rest follows upon wisdom, but care and anxiety follow charity unless it be joined to wisdom. For this reason the soul of the just man is called the seat of wisdom (Prv 8:12). Finally when Isaiah says "Heaven is my throne" (Is 66:1), and David says "The heaven of heaven is the Lord's" (Ps 115:16), by the heaven of heaven is understood the spiritual heavens dwelling above the corporeal heavens, that is, the blessed spirits, as Saint Augustine explained in his exposition of [the Vulgate's] Psalm 113.[3] God makes these heavens rest in such a wonderful rest that this is that "peace which surpasses all understanding" (Phil 4:7). Saint Bernard in his *Sermons on the Canticle* draws an apt comparison to explain this quiet with these words: "The God of peace gives peace to all, and to gaze on this rest is to grow quiet. It is to look upon a king who sends the crowds away from him after the day-long controversies of the law courts, puts aside the troubles of his office, seeks his quarters in the evening, and enters his quarters with a few companions whom he honors with his privacy and familiarity; there he rests the more securely as he is more private and becomes the more serene as his gentle glance falls only on those whom he loves."[4] With these words he rather openly shows that God does not show himself to the blessed spirits as their judge or lord but as their friend and companion.

Truly incredible is the intimacy which God shows in this life to the pure of heart; it completely fulfills the statements "My delights were to be with the children of men" (Prv 8:31) and "his communication is with the simple" (Prv 3:32).

For this reason the saints, although they suffered oppression in this world, had peace in their heart where God was, and they were accordingly always happy and appeared to be and were always serene, for the Truth had told them, "Your heart will rejoice, and your joy no one shall take from you" (Jn 16:22).

CHAPTER EIGHT

On the Multiple Depth in God's Essence

The fourth dimension of greatness remains. It is called depth. Depth in God's essence is manifold: The divinity is in itself most profound, for it is not superficial and rarified but extremely full and solid. The deity is not like a gilded object which has gold only on its outer surface, but is inwardly made of bronze or wood. Rather it is like a solid gold mass, a huge and immense mass, or rather like a gold mine so deep that it can never be exhausted by digging. Thus God is so utterly incomprehensible because just as a gold mine whose bottom is not reached is never exhausted by digging, so also God, of whose "greatness there is no end" (Ps 145:3), is never so perfectly known by a created mind that it cannot be known better and better. Only God comprehends that infinite depth because he alone has an infinite power of understanding.

Second, God is deep by reason of place. Just as he is most high because he presides over all things and is above all, so God is most deep because he underlies all things to hold them up and is below all things to carry them; as the Apostle says, he carries "all things by the word of his power" (Heb 1:3). Therefore, God is the foundation and the roof of the building in which we all "live and move and have our being" (Acts 17:28). Rightly then did Solomon say, "heaven and the heavens of heavens do not contain you" (Prv 6:18) because God rather contains the heavens and what is beneath heaven, for he is above the heavens and beneath the earth.

Finally, God's depth is his invisibility. God is indeed light, but light inaccessible (1 Tm 6:16). He is truth, but very inward truth more interior than our interior: "He made darkness his covert" (Ps 18:11), says David. As Isaiah says, "Verily you are a hidden God" (Is 45:15). When Saint Augustine was seeking after God he sent his eyes as messengers from earth up to heaven and all things answered back, "We are not what you seek, but he made us." Not finding God by ascending through outward things, he began to make his journey through inward things, and he recognized that through them he could indeed more easily come close to God. He knew that the soul was better than the body and that internal sense was better than external sense, and the intellect, which is still more inward, is better than internal sense. Hence, he concluded that God, who is more inward than the intellect, is better than the intellect, and that whatever we understand or think is not God, but something less than God, since God is better than we can understand or think.[5]

Consider, my soul, if you are better than your body to which you give life, because it is a body and you are a spirit, and the eye of your body does not see you because it is outside and you are within. Then by all means recognize that your God is better than you are because he gives you an intellect and is like a soul to you, and therefore you cannot see him because he is a higher and more inward spirit than you are, and you somehow remain without and he remains within, in his own most secret and deep recess. Will you never be admitted to that secret place? Quite the contrary. Your God does not lie, who says, "Blessed are the clean of heart, for they shall see God" (Mt 5:8). Nor does his Apostle who says, "We see now through a mirror in an obscure manner, but then face to face" (1 Cor 13:12), nor the holy Evangelist John, who wrote, "We know that when he appears, we shall be like to him, for we shall see him just as he is" (1 Jn 3:2). What joy that will be when admitted to his secret sanctuary, you will see and possess that light, that beauty, that goodness! Then it will be clear how vain and fleeting and almost non-existent were the temporal goods of this world on which men become drunk and forget true and eternal goods. If you really thirst for the living God and if tears are your bread day and night and the challenge comes, "Where is your God?" (Ps 42:3), be not slow in cleaning your heart by which God is to be seen nor weary in raising up your heart until it sees the "God of gods in Sion" (Ps 84:7). Grow not cold in loving God and your neighbor and do not love with word and tongue but in deed and truth for that is the way that leads to life (1 Jn 3:18).

STEP ELEVEN: On the Consideration of The Greatness of God's Power by Comparison with Bodily Greatness

CHAPTER ONE

The Breadth of God's Power

Great is the Lord and there is no measure or end to his greatness. He is great not only because his omnipotence is his height, his unfathomable wisdom is his depth, his mercy which reaches everywhere is his breadth, his justice which is like a rod of iron is his length, but also because each of these attributes is great with the magnitude of infinite breadth, length, height, and depth.

Let us begin from his power or rather from his omnipotence. The power of God has its breadth, which consists in the fact that it extends to things that are clearly infinite. First it extends to everything that has been made. There is nothing in this whole universe of beings from the first angel down to the last little worm and from the summit of heaven to the lowest depth which was not made by God's power. Saint John says, "All things were made through him and without him was made nothing" and further on, "and the world was made through him" (Jn 1:3, 10).

Second, it extends to all things which will come to exist even unto eternity. Just as nothing could have come to be except through him, so also nothing will come to be except through him, for as the Apostle says, "From him and through him and unto him are all things" (Rom 11:36).

Third, it extends to all things that could be but will never be, for thus speaks the Angel, "Nothing shall be impossible with God" (Lk 1:37) and the Lord himself says, "With God all things are possible" (Mt 19:26).

Fourth, it extends to the complete destruction of all created things. Thus God was able to kill simultaneously all men and animals that were on the earth by the waters of the flood except the few that he wished to save in Noah's ark (Gn 1:7ff.). Thus he will be able at one time by the flood of fire to destroy not only all men and all animals which are found alive on the last day but also all trees and all cities and everything else which is on earth. The Apostle Peter says in his Second Letter, "The day of the Lord will come as a thief; at that time the heavens will pass away with great violence, and the elements will be dissolved with heat and the earth and the works that are in it will be burned up" (2 Pt 3:10).

Great indeed is the breadth of God's power, which nobody can wonder at enough unless he can count the multitude of things, some of which God has made, some of which he will make, and some of which he can make. But who can count such a great multitude except him whose knowledge is infinite? Moreover, the magnitude of his power increases when one reflects how mighty it is to destroy with complete ease in barely a second, or as Judas Macchabaeus says to destroy at a nod (2 Mc 8:18), everything accomplished by so much power over so many centuries. Let us say with Moses, "Who is like to you among the strong, O Lord?" (Ex 15:11).

CHAPTER TWO

On the Length of God's Power

The length of God's power is seen in the fact that it constantly cooperates with everything that God has made, nor does it grow weary in this cooperation, nor will it ever grow weary since this power of God cannot be lessened or weakened or broken in any way because it is joined to true eternity, or rather it is itself the eternity of true divinity.

Many people wonder how the sun and moon and stars can move for so long and at such speed from their rising to their setting and return in their orbits without any pause. This would indeed be a matter most worthy of wonder unless we knew that they are carried by almighty God, who carries "all things by the word of his power" (Heb 1:3). Others wonder how it can be that the fire in hell is not used up by burning through eternal time or that the burning bodies of these unhappy people are not dissolved through eternal time. This could be judged not only surprising but also impossible unless it was God almighty and eternal who made that fire burn forever so that it never goes out and preserves the bodies of those wretches in that fire so that they are always tormented and never consumed. Finally, others wonder how God carries and sustains everything but never wearies in carrying and sustaining such a giant load of nearly infinite weight. A strong man or a horse or an ox or an elephant can carry a great weight for a fairly long period or hold up a very great load for a short time, but to carry a maximum weight for eternity without weariness surpasses the strength of all created things. They rightly wonder whether God has strength in weight and measure as all created things have, but since God's strength exceeds all measure and he is infinite in every respect, it is not surprising if an infinite strength can uphold a weight however heavy for eternity without weariness. Let us say with the holy prophet Moses, "Who is like to you among the strong, O Lord?" (Ex 15:11).

CHAPTER THREE

On the Height of God's Power

The next topic is the height of God's power, which especially consists in two things. First his omnipotence can be called most high because he alone made the highest objects. God alone made the objects which are under the moon in the first creation of things, but they can be generated, changed, and corrupted by the action of creatures. The elements work on one another according to their natures. Grasses and trees grow from the earth; animals beget animals; fish are born in water, clouds and rain in the air, comets in fire. God alone created, alone conserved the sky and the stars, which are the highest bodies; no creature can have any role in making or changing or destroying or preserving them. The Prophet says, "I will behold your heavens, the works of your fingers; the moon and the stars which you have founded" (Ps 8:3). The Most High has reserved for himself alone his highest works; he began to build them from their foundations and carried on right up to their summit. The Most High alone by his infinite power established, conserves, and will conserve without interruption right into eternity spiritual beings, the angels and human souls, which are the most noble and sublime of all his works. In making these no creature had any part. Even if all creatures got together, they would never be able to make or destroy a single angel or a single soul.

Second, the height of divine power is most clearly shown in miracles, which, as Saint Augustine teaches, are actions outside the usual course and pattern of nature and strike all of nature and even the angels as wonderful and stupendous.[1] Who of the angels was not awestruck when at Joshua's command the sun and the moon, which travel at enormous velocity, stood motionless (Jos 10:12ff.). Lest we should think that this happened by mere chance—and no one could suspect that such an unusual event could be caused by a mortal man located on earth—the Holy Spirit speaks and says, "the Lord obeying the voice of a man" (Jos 10:14). Nor did Joshua really speak to the sun and the moon themselves, which he knew could not hear his command; rather he invoked the Lord, as though he was speaking by command of the Lord, "Move not, O sun, toward Gabon, nor you, O moon, toward the valley of Ajalon" (Jos 10:12). The Lord did obey the voice of a man, that is, he brought it about that those luminaries obeyed the voice of a man.

Often in sacred Scripture the Lord is said to do those things which he causes to happen; thus in Genesis the Lord says to Abraham: "Now I know that you fear the Lord" (Gn 22:12). These words mean: I have now brought it about that you and others know that you really fear God. Such also was the work that signified the height of the divine power when in the Lord's passion the moon, which was at its maximum distance from the sun, approached the sun by a move of extreme speed and occluded it and for three hours caused darkness on the earth and after those three hours by the same move of incredible speed it returned to the place it had left. Saint Dionysius the Areopagite testifies that he had seen and observed all this in his *Letter to Saint Polycarp*.[2] This is indeed a sign opposite the first one but no less wonderful since it is equally new and unusual and beyond the forces of all nature to make the moon stand still or move it out of the usual course. I omit giving sight to the blind, the raising of the dead, and many other miracles of that sort which God has done and still does through the prophets and apostles and his other faithful servants. All these cry out, "Who is like you among the strong, O Lord?" (Ex 15:1). But I cannot omit that supreme and greatest miracle that God will show on the last day when all the dead will arise at once, although the bodies of many men have been reduced to ashes and dispersed or eaten by beasts or turned again and again into other bodies or even disappeared after burial in gardens and fields by being transformed into various sorts of plants. Which of the angels will not be awestruck when he sees in the blink of an eye at the command of the Almighty so many millions of men take up their own bodies even though they have been hidden for many centuries and dispersed and destroyed in the most diverse ways? This then is the height of God's power, about which one can equally ask, "Who is like you among the strong, O Lord?" (Ex 15:11).

CHAPTER FOUR
On the Depth of God's Power

Lastly there is depth, which seems to me to consist in the way that God uses in making things. Who can penetrate how something is made from nothing? Those who have fixed it as an established and certain principle that nothing comes from nothing could not direct their eyes at this depth. On this point we too believe what we do not see (Jn 20:29; Heb 11:1), but we trust securely in God who cannot lie. We believe, I say, that heaven and earth and what is in them have been created by God since earlier nothing at all had existed out of which they could have come to be, nor would God have made everything that has been made if something had preexisted out of which they were made. But how something came to be before which nothing had existed is a deep abyss which we cannot search or investigate.

Second, not only did God make all things from nothing, but he made them in nothing, that is, without a preceding space or place in which to put what came to be—something that is hardly possible to understand, especially about bodily things. Hence, this abyss too is impenetrable. Saint Augustine says in his *Letter to Dardanus* that, if one takes stretches of space away from bodies, they will be nowhere, and because they will be nowhere, they will not be.[3] If then there was nothing before God created heaven and earth, where did God place heaven and earth? They certainly could not be placed in nothing, and yet they were created and were their own place because he could and did will it so, who can do all things even if we cannot understand how such things are done. God himself referred to this when he wanted to show holy Job his omnipotence and said, "Where were you when I laid the foundations of the earth? Tell me if you have understanding. Who has laid the measures thereof, if you know it? Or who has stretched the line upon it? Upon what are its bases grounded? Or who laid the cornerstone thereof?" (Jb 38:4–6). That we may understand that these works of God almighty are worthy of all praise the same Lord immediately added, "When the morning stars praised me together, and all the sons of God made a joyful melody" (Jb 38:7). The holy angels were created at the same time with heaven and earth and are like certain bright, spiritual stars so that they can be called the sons of God; when they saw heaven and earth come forth from nothing and stand on nothing and still rest most firmly on their own stability, they doubtless praised the omnipotence of the Craftsman with immense awe and rejoicing.

It is no less profound to understand that God raised up such immense masses by the mere command of his will. We know how incomparably smaller buildings need much equipment, many tools, and many helpers for the architect. Who by reflection can follow how it came about that such immense and varied works came to be by a single internal wish which did not go outside the one willing? God spoke, clearly within himself, for the Word of God is in God and is himself God; he spoke, I repeat, in ordering and expressing the command of his will: "Let heaven be, and heaven was made. Let earth be, and earth was made. Let light be, and the sun was made, let the stars be, let the trees be, let the animals be, let men be, let the angels be, and all were made." Moreover, God could, if he wished, "at a beck utterly destroy" (2 Mc 8:18) all these things and the whole world, as we read in the books of Maccabees.

What adds to that depth is that God made in a moment all these many and great things which are composed of so many units and parts. For us art and nature require a long time-span to bring their works to perfection. We see that plants are sown long before they are born, trees often need many years to fix their roots, stretch out their branches, and produce fruit. Animals carry their offspring a long time in the womb and later feed them for a long time before they grow up. I say nothing about art because it is well known that our craftsmen take their time, a rather long time, in finishing anything. How great then is God's power which finishes great things faster than saying the word.

I am not going to get into an argument over whether God completed heaven and earth and all that is in them in a single stroke or took six whole days in the first creation of things. I have not undertaken a scholarly inquiry but the construction of a staircase to God by reflecting on his creatures. What I add and admire is that the almighty Creator completed the individual things in a moment. Nobody has doubts about the earth, water, air, and fire all being made together in a moment, but the angels were also made in the same moment. Regarding the firmament and the division of the waters, it is known that all were made solely by the power of the Word, saying, "Let the firmament be made amid the waters," and they were all made in an instant, for there follows, "And it was so" (Gn 1:6, 7). Here Saint John Chrysostom says that he only spoke and the work followed; the same author asks on the words "Let the earth bring forth green herb . . . and it was so" (Gn 1:11ff.), who would not be awestruck in considering how the word of the Lord, "Let the earth bring forth," adorned the face of the earth with various flowers like a wonderful robe? You would suddenly see the earth, which previously was shapeless and uncultivated, rivaling heaven in glory and decoration.[4] Later he speaks thus on the words "Let there be light" (Gn 1:14), "He merely spoke and that marvelous element was produced, I mean, the sun. Add to that at the same time and with the same word the same Creator made the moon and all the stars."[5] On the words "Let the waters bring forth" and so on (Gn 1:20), he says, "What tongue is sufficient for the praises of the craftsman? Just as he said about the earth only, 'Let it bring forth,' and soon a varied and complex abundance of flowers and plants appeared, so here he said, 'Let the waters bring forth,' and immediately so many species of reptiles and birds were created that they cannot be counted in language."[6] "Who," therefore, "is like you among the strong, O Lord?" (Ex 15:11).

CHAPTER FIVE

The Soul Is Urged to Fear God and Keep His Commandments

Now, my soul, you understand clearly how great is the power of your Creator which by its breadth reaches all things, by its length endures forever and carries and rules all things without weariness, by its height attains to the creation of things which seem impossible and are indeed impossible for anybody else except him alone, by its depth makes things so that their way of being made surpasses all created intelligence since he makes them out of nothing and in nothing, using no instruments or time but only his word and command; the Prophet says, "He spoke, and they were made; he commanded, and they were created" (Ps 148:5). If you are wise, you can gather how much it matters whether he is angry or pleased, whether you have him for foe or friend, for if you have him for a foe and angry, he can instantly strip you of all your goods and fill you with all misery. There is none who can deliver you from his hands. Who dares contend with the Almighty? What would you do alone and naked if you come up against your implacable foe who is looking for you with a sharp sword? You would break out in a sweat, become pale and tremble, throw yourself at his knees, and beg for mercy! But he is a man, and maybe you might save yourself from death by fleeing or fighting back and wresting his sword from his hands. But what will you do with an angry God, whom you cannot flee since he is everywhere, or resist since he is almighty, or try delaying tactics since he acts instantly on his mere decision? Not without reason did the Apostle say, "It is a fearful thing to fall into the hands of the living God" (Heb 10:31).

On the other hand, if you please God and have him for a friend, who could be happier than you? If he wishes something, he can do it. If he is a friend, he wants to fill you with every good and free you from every evil. It is up to you, while you are leading this life, to have God angry and an enemy or a friend who is pleased with you.

STEP ELEVEN

In the Sacred Scriptures God is continually crying out through the prophets and then through his Son and through his apostles, inviting sinners to repentance and the just to the observance of the commandments so that he may thus have both groups as friends, or better as dear sons and heirs of his eternal kingdom. Listen to Ezekiel, "As I live, says the Lord God, I do not desire the death of the wicked, but that the wicked turn from his way and live. Turn, turn from your evil ways, and why will you die, O house of Israel." And later, "The wickedness of the wicked shall not hurt him in what day so ever he shall turn from his wickedness" (Ez 33:11, 12). And what Ezekiel cries out, Isaiah, Jeremiah, and the rest of the prophets also proclaim. The same Spirit was in them all and kept crying through them all. Hear the Son of God at the beginning of his preaching, "Jesus began," says Matthew, "to preach and to say, 'Repent, for the kingdom of heaven is at hand' " (Mt 4:17). Hear the Apostle Paul who says, speaking about himself and his co-apostles in the Second Letter to the Corinthians, "On behalf of Christ, therefore, we are acting as ambassadors, God as it were appealing through us. We exhort you, for Christ's sake, be reconciled to God" (2 Cor 5:20). What could be clearer, what more sweet? In Christ's name the Apostle begs us to be willing to be reconciled with God and have him pleased rather than angry with us. Who can have doubts about God's mercy if he seriously returns to him? He will certainly welcome those who return as the loving father welcomed his prodigal son (Lk 15:20–32). When we have returned and received his forgiveness, what does he ask of us so that we continue to be his friends and sons, except that we keep his commandments? The Lord said, "If you wish to enter into life, keep the commandments" (Mt 19:17). Do not argue that the commandments cannot be kept without God's help; listen to Saint Augustine in his explanation of Psalm 56, where speaking on the most difficult of all the commandments, that is, laying down one's life for one's brothers, he says, "God would not have asked us to do this if he thought it impossible for it to be done by man; if considering your own weakness you faint under this command, draw comfort from his example; his example is also important for you, for he who gave you an example is present also to give you aid."[7] And "that on the word of two witnesses every word may be confirmed" (Mt 18:16), listen to Saint Leo, who says, "God justly insists on this commandment because he comes ready in advance with his help."[8] Why then do you fear, my son, to advance confidently in the way of the commandments when he comes ready in advance and with the mighty help of his grace makes "the crooked straight and the rough ways plain" (Is 40:4)? Since he certainly comes ready in advance with his help, the Lord's yoke becomes "easy and his burden light" (Mt 11:30). The Apostle John exclaims, "His commands are not burdensome" (1 Jn 5:3). But if they seem burdensome to you, think how much more so will be the torments of hell! Unless you are mad, you would not dare to want to experience them. Think this over and over and never forget it: Now is the time for mercy, later for justice. Now one is free to sin, but later one must pay the heaviest penalties. Now a man can easily square accounts with God and with the small effort of of repentance obtain great forgiveness and by a brief mourning avoid eternal wailing. On the other hand, any good work done now out of charity can obtain the kingdom of heaven; later the riches of the whole earth will not gain a single drop of cold water.

STEP TWELVE:

On the Consideration of The Greatness of God's Wisdom in Comparison with Bodily Greatness

CHAPTER ONE

The Breadth of God's Wisdom Consists in the Perfect Knowledge of All Things

How truly did the Apostle write at the end of his Letter to the Romans that God alone is wise (Rom 16:17). If anybody cares to pay close attention, he may easily understand the breadth, length, height, and depth of God's wisdom.

Let us begin with breadth. God's wisdom is recognized as very wide because God distinctly and perfectly understands everything that is in the universe from the first angel down to the last little worm. He not only knows substances as a whole but also their parts, properties, powers, accidents, and actions. This is behind the words "You have indeed numbered my steps" (Jb 14:16), and "The Lord beholds the ways of man and considers all his steps" (Prv 5:21). If he counts and considers every step, how much more every act of the mind, whether good or bad. If God has all our hairs numbered according to the saying of our Lord "The very hairs of your head are all numbered" (Mt 10:30), how much more does he know all the limbs of your body and the powers of your soul? If he knows the number of the sands of the sea and the drops of rain, as Ecclesiasticus suggests (Sir 1:2), how much more should he be thought to know the number of the stars and angels? If as the Lord himself testifies he will bring up every idle word of every man for judgment, certainly his ears hear simultaneously all the voices of all men, not only the voices of the body but also those of the soul, that is, our thoughts and desires. How great and how immense is the breadth of his wisdom that understands simultaneously all that is, that was, that will be, and that can be!

Nonetheless, the divine mind is not cheapened by such a variety of individual and minor matters, as the foolish wisdom of some philosophers thought. We might hold this opinion if God's knowledge were dependent on things as our is, but since he sees everything in his essence, there is no danger of cheapening. Just as it is far better to go around seeking knowledge, which is man's lot, than to lack knowledge entirely, which is the lot of brute animals, so it is higher to be blind, which is proper to beings with souls, than not being blind but being without the capacity to see, which is the situation of stones. The other parts of the body are not more noble than the eyes because they cannot be blind; rather the eyes are more noble since they have the faculty of sight even though they also can be blind, as Saint Augustine rightly argues in the books of his *City of God*.[1]

Hence, you should always and everywhere be careful, my soul, over what you do, what you say, and what you think since nothing that you ever do, say, or think will be without God's seeing, hearing, or observing it. If you would not dare to do or speak something evil, although urged by the strongest desire, if you thought that you were being seen or heard by a man, how do you dare to consider such things with God looking on and growing angry? In his rule for holy nuns Saint Augustine says, "Granted that no human sees you, what will one do about that heavenly spectator from whom nothing can hide?"[2] Saint Basil in his book *On Virginity*, speaking to a virgin alone and shut in her chamber, warns her to reverence her Spouse who is present everywhere and his Father and the Holy Spirit and the countless multitude of angels and with them the holy spirits of the fathers: "There is none of these," he says, "who does not see everywhere."[3] O my blessed soul, if you were always aware that you are on this stage even amid the darkness and silence of night, how perfectly you would spend your life, how carefully you would avoid all lightheadedness and distractions. This is indeed what the Lord once spoke to the Patriarch Abraham, "Walk before me and be perfect" (Gn 17:1), that is, remember that you are always seen by me and without any doubt you will be perfect.

CHAPTER TWO

The Length of God's Wisdom Reveals Itself in the Knowledge of Future Events

The length of God's wisdom reveals itself in the knowledge of future events. God sees so sharply that from eternity he has seen what will happen at the end of time and beyond that unto eternity. Nothing of greater length can be thought of than that. David said in the psalms, "You have understood my thoughts from afar," and a bit later, "You have known all things, the last and those of old" (Ps 139:2, 5), that is, every future event and every past event. The books of the prophets are full of clear and accurate predictions which they did not speak by themselves but, as Zachary sings, God "spoke by the mouth of his holy prophets who are from the beginning" (Lk 2:70).

This foresight and prediction is so characteristic of God alone that God himself says through Isaiah, "Show the things that are to come hereafter and we will know that you are gods" (Is 41:23). That we may consider a few of many examples, Isaiah speaks thus, "Thus says the Lord to my anointed Cyrus, whose right hand I have taken hold of, to subdue the nations before his face and to turn the back of kings" and so forth (Is 45:1). There the empire of the Persians is predicted, and Cyrus is correctly named as first king of the Persians, and a reason is provided why God wanted to exalt Cyrus, namely, because he would relax the Babylonian captivity. All these events were fulfilled about two hundred years later.

Daniel too clearly predicted by the image of an immense statue with its head of gold, its breast silver, its stomach and thighs bronze, and its feet partly of iron and partly of clay (Dn 2:31ff.) the four monarchies of the Babylonians, Persians, Greeks, and Romans and in the time of the last monarchy the kingdom of Christ, that is, the

Christian Church, which is greater than all these kingdoms. Then he describes (Dn 11:5ff.) the wars of the successors of Alexander the Great so clearly that some unbelievers have suspected that these passages were written after those wars were finished.[4] To pass over other instances, Christ himself in Luke bewailed the destruction of Jerusalem, which was many years in the future, and described all the particulars as clearly and individually as if he wanted to relate the past rather than the future (Lk 19:41ff.). I omit all the other predictions of which, as I said, the books of the prophets are full.

Astrologers and all other diviners, who want to appear like apes of God, deserve total contempt. It is impossible for them to predict the truth about future contingent events, especially free acts, unless they sometimes stumble on the truth by accident. Since the will of God foresees and presides over all future causes—necessary, contingent, and free—and can block lower causes whenever he wishes, no one can predict the truth unless God wants to manifest to him his will, as he often did manifest it to his prophets. This is so true that the demons wanted to be taken for gods mainly because they poured out oracles and foretold the future, as Saint Augustine testifies in the books of *The City of God*.[5] The same distinguished Doctor of the Church proves clearly in his book *On the Divination of Demons* that their divination is as false as their divinity.[6] They say nothing clearly except what they themselves are going to do, or using their natural speed report what has already happened as if it were the future to those who are far away, or using their long experience conjecture about what will happen just as sailors are given to predictions about the winds, farmers about the weather, and doctors about diseases. When questioned about the future, the demons give ambiguous or equivocal answers about things of which they are ignorant, and if things turn out wrong, they put the blame on interpreters or soothsayers.

Only the Lord our God, "of whose wisdom there is no number" (Ps 147:5), gives forth true oracles and foretells the truth about future events, even those that are contingent and free.

CHAPTER THREE

On the Multiple Height of God's Wisdom

The height of the divine wisdom is very lofty and far surpasses every pinnacle of human and angelic wisdom. The height of wisdom is calculated by the nobility of its object, its power, its species, and its act.

The divine essence itself is both the natural and proportionate object of God's wisdom. It is so sublime that it is a proportionate object for neither a human nor an angelic intellect. Therefore, not even the highest angels can climb to see God unless they are lifted up by the light of glory. This is the reason why God is called invisible in the Holy Scriptures. "The King of the ages, who is immortal, invisible, the one only God" (1 Tm 1:17), the Apostle says in his First Letter to Timothy, and he adds later, that God "dwells in light inaccessible" (1 Tm 6:16).

Second, the power which in us is an accident is in God his divine substance, and for this reason is far more sublime and lofty than in us. A species is higher to the degree that it represents more things; therefore, angels are said to have higher knowledge depending on whether they have fewer and more universal species. How much greater then is the height of God's wisdom, who has no species other than his own essence, which is single and alone suffices for God to represent and know God himself and all things created, to be created, or even which can be created.

Last, the knowledge or wisdom is called more noble or higher which knows more things by fewer acts. By one unique intuition which always goes on in him and remains unchanged God knows perfectly himself and all other things. Therefore, only the wisdom of God ought to be called more noble and high.

Lift up your eyes now, my soul, and see what a gulf separates your knowledge from the wisdom of your Creator. By many acts, running here and there you hardly know one thing perfectly, but your Creator by one act intuits all things and himself most clearly and distinctly. Still you who now lie in darkness can if you wish climb on the wings of faith and charity so high that after shucking off this mortal body and having been transformed from glory to glory you may see the God who is light in the light of God (Ps 36:9; 2 Cor 3:18). Made like unto God, you too by a single intuition, one which remains forever, may see at once God in himself and yourself and all created things in God. "What does he not see," asks Saint Gregory in his *Dialogues*, "who sees him who sees all? What will be that pleasure" that glory, that abundance of all things, "when you are admitted to that inaccessible light and become partaker of all the goods of your Lord!"[7] When the Queen of Sheba had heard the wisdom of Solomon and saw the wise ordering of his palace servants, she was so astonished that her breath was taken away (so Scripture puts it), "and she said: Blessed are your men and blessed are your servants who stand before you always and hear your wisdom" (1 Kgs 10:8). What is there in common between the wisdom of Solomon and the wisdom of God, who alone is wise and is wisdom itself? What is the order of his servants compared to the nine orders of God's angels, whose thousands of thousands minister to him and whose tens of hundreds of thousands serve him (Dn 7:10)? If you have tasted this only a little, certainly you will try anything and do anything and suffer anything most gladly so that you can deserve God. Humble yourself meantime "under the mighty hand of God, that he may exalt you in the time of visitation" (1 Pt 5:6). Bow your intellect to faith that you may be lifted up to vision; bow your will to obeying the commandments that you may be lifted up to "the freedom of the glory of the sons of God" (Rom 8:21); bow your flesh to patience and labor so that God may lift it up glorified to rest eternal.

CHAPTER FOUR

The Depth of God's Wisdom Consists in Knowing Our Thoughts, Especially Our Future Thoughts

Our remaining task is to consider the depth of God's wisdom, which seems to consist mainly in searching loins and hearts, that is, in knowing human thoughts and desires, especially future ones. On this we read, "Man sees those things that appear, but the Lord beholds the heart" (1 Sm 16:7); and "You alone know the hearts of the children of men" (2 Chr 6:30); and "You have understood my thoughts from afar; my path you have searched out, and you have foreseen all my ways" (Ps 139:2, 3); and "He knows the secret of the heart" (Ps 44:21); and "The heart is perverse above all things and unsearchable. Who can know it? I am the Lord, who searches the heart and proves the reins" (Jer 17:9, 10). The Septuagint translators rendered this passage: "The heart of man is deep and inscrutable." In explaining the passage, Saint Jerome notes that Christ is rightly proved to be God because he saw the thoughts of men, which only God can see: "Jesus, knowing their thoughts" (Mt 9:4), "But he knew their thoughts" (Lk 6:8), and "Why are you arguing these things in your hearts?" (Mk 2:8).[8]

All human thoughts and desires, even when present and really existing, are very profound so that neither angels nor demons nor men can penetrate to investigate them. Much more profound are future thoughts and desires, for men and angels are not only unable to penetrate them, but they are not able to penetrate the way that God, who alone knows them, comes to know them. This seems to be what David meant to say in the psalm when he said, "Your knowledge has become wonderful to me" (Ps 139:6). The expression "to me" in Hebrew signifies "in front of me" or "above me" so that its sense is: Your knowledge is more wonderful than I can understand how it exists. Therefore, he adds, "It is high and I cannot reach it" (Ps 139:6), that is, it is raised above my comprehension and there is no way I will be able to climb up to an understanding of it. He is speaking about a knowledge of future thoughts, for he had said, "You have understood my thoughts afar off; and you have foreseen all my ways" (Ps 139:2, 3). About foreknowledge of these thoughts and ways he says, "Your knowledge has become wonderful to me; it is high and I cannot reach it" (Ps 139:6).

Somebody may object: God sees these future thoughts in his eternity to which everything is present or in the predetermination of his will; but if that were so, his knowledge would not be wonderful, for even we can easily know what we are going to do or what is present to us. But Scripture says: God searches reins and hearts and there sees what man desires and thinks or what he will later desire and think. This is truly wonderful, how God in searching reins and hearts sees what does not yet exist there and what depends on the freedom of the will whether it will happen sometime. Hence, as it pertains to the height of God's power to make something from nothing and call forth those things which are not as those which are (Rom 4:17), so it pertains to the depth of God's wisdom that in searching reins and hearts he sees what is not yet there as if it already existed because undoubtedly it will exist.

CHAPTER FIVE

Raising the Soul to the Divine Physician Who Searches and Heals Hearts

Because I have undertaken to stir the soul and raise it to God and not stir up scholarly arguments, do you, my soul, rise up and lift yourself above yourself, as Jeremiah encourages us (Lam 3:28), and consider that deep abyss of God's wisdom which searches the inmost heart and sees there many things the heart itself does not see.

O blessed Peter, who kept saying to the Lord, "Even if I should have to die with you, I will not deny you" (Mt 26:33, 35; Mk 14:30, 31), you were certainly not speaking from a duplicitous heart, but sincerely and correctly. In your heart you did not see that weakness which your Lord saw in it when he said, "Before the cock crows twice, you will deny me three times" (Mk 14:30). That skilled physician was aware of the weakness in your heart which you could not see, and the prediction of the physician, not the boasting of the sick man, came true. But give thanks to the physician who both foresaw and predicted the future sickness and divinely inspired your soul with the powerful medicine of repentance and quickly cured your sickness.

O good, holy, wise, and powerful Physician, cleanse me from my hidden ills (Ps 19:12)! How many are there that I do not regret or wash with tears because I see them not? May your grace with which you search my reins and heart be with me. Show me the evil desires and evil works that you see but I do not. Look down kindly and open a fountain of tears so that while there is time they may be washed away and blotted out by your grace. Amen.

STEP THIRTEEN:
On the Consideration of Practical Wisdom

CHAPTER ONE
The Breadth of Practical Wisdom Shines forth from the Creation of Things and their Disposition in Measure, Number, and Weight

We have considered God's theoretical wisdom. Now we have to consider his practical wisdom, which we can also call his constructive wisdom. This wisdom has its own breadth, length, height, and depth. Its breadth is seen in creation, its length in the conservation of created things, its height in the work of redemption, and its depth in providence and predestination.

Let us start with creation. God made all things in his wisdom, as is said in the psalms (Ps 104:24), "and he poured her out on all his works," as Ecclesiasticus writes (Sir 1:10). Just as we recognize the power of the maker in the creation of all things from nothing, so from the marvelous craftsmanship which we notice in individual things we admire the wisdom of the Creator, for he has ordered each and every thing by measure and number and weight, as the Wise Man says (Wis 11:21). This is the seasoning with which God has seasoned all things so that by that seasoning we may recognize how savory is the wisdom itself and how lovable and desirable.

All created things have a fixed measure, number, and weight for two reasons. One is to distinguish them from God, who has no measure because he is immense, no number because he is wholly one and simple in essence, and no weight because his worth and price surpass all worth and price. The second reason is that they may be good and beautiful, as Moses said most truly, "God saw all the things that he had made, and they were very good" (Gn 1:31).

All things have that measure which they need to attain the end for which they were made. Nothing can be added to or subtracted from that measure without making the thing deformed or useless and, therefore, less good. God "made all things good in their time," says Ecclesiastes. "We cannot add anything, nor take away from those things God has made that he may be feared" (Eccl 3:11, 14). Therefore, God gave heaven a very ample measure because it has to hold all lower things in its embrace. The air received much less than heaven but much more than earth and water, which make up the one globe and are surrounded on all sides by air. He gave the elephant massive bodily size so he could carry huge burdens and even towers filled with men. Horses got less because they were made to carry only one rider. He made birds tiny so that they could hang their nests in the branches of trees. He made bees and ants very tiny so that they might hide in the openings of beehives or of the ground.

We can say the same thing about number. God created one sun because one sun was enough to brighten the whole earth and bring day with its splendor. He also made one moon because one was enough to light up the night. He wanted many stars to exist so that when the sun and moon were absent, as happens during a conjunction of the sun and moon, they might dispel a bit of the darkness of the night. He assigned a necessary number not only to all things in general, but also set up the number of parts in each individual thing so that nothing could be added or taken away. God granted men two eyes, two ears, two hands, two feet, one nose, one mouth, one chest, one head, and the outcome was very beautiful and well proportioned. Turn the order upside down and give a man one eye, two noses, one ear, two mouths, one hand, one foot, two chests and two heads—nothing more ugly or useless could exist.

Finally, God gave each thing weight, that is, the worth which its nature required. By the term *weight* or *worth*, we mean the qualities that make things good and precious. These three qualities perfect all objects: the number of parts that is necessary that nothing at all be lacking, proportion or the right relationship of the parts, and lastly the internal or external qualities such as a pleasing color on the outer surface of the body and internal strength which is useful or necessary for various actions. It is absolutely wonderful how much power God has given to certain tiny little things so that he seems to have wished to display his power in big things and his wisdom in small things. Who would conceive how much power there is in a grain of mustard? It is the smallest of all the seeds, so that the eye can hardly see it, and yet a mighty tree lies hidden in it so that even the birds may live in its branches, as Truth himself says in the Gospel (Mt 13:31–32). This is not unique to mustard seed, but is common to all seeds in whose power lie hidden the roots, trunks, branches, leaves, flowers, and fruits of the biggest trees. If we had not learned from clear experience this fact, men would not easily be persuaded that such a great mass of different things could ever spring from such a tiny seed. Likewise, who could conceive that ants, flies, fleas, and other tiny insects have legs which move them quickly about, have a head, have a heart, have external and internal senses, and have in their own way prudence and judgment, although very imperfectly? Finally, who would conceive that these and other similar wee and tiny animals have such ability to pierce and enter living flesh so that they are not only extremely troublesome to men, but so that gnats terrify elephants and lions?

Great then is the Lord and great his wisdom both in the biggest things and also in the tiniest. Although he was a pagan, that prince of doctors once admired the craftsmanship of God which is seen in the human hand and cried out in praise of its Creator.[1] O Christian, what should you do, who have no doubt that not only the bodies of men and the rest of the animals, but also the sky and the stars and the angels and the immortal minds of men were created with incredible wisdom by the same most wise Creator?

CHAPTER TWO

The Length of God's Practical Wisdom Shines forth in the Conservation of Things

The length of his practical wisdom does indeed shine forth in the conservation of things, just as we said earlier that its breadth was manifest in creation. God's great and wonderful wisdom is clear in the conservation and duration of created things, especially of those that are corruptible.

First, anybody who reflects on how God gives food and growth to grasses, plants, animals, and the bodies of men so that they can be conserved as long as possible will be wholly struck with astonishment and will not be able to admire God's wisdom enough. Out of earth and water he nourishes grasses and plants and causes their food to travel from their roots to their trunk and from their trunk it is borne upward by a certain force to their branches, leaves, and fruit and penetrates them all in a truly wondrous order and way. So, also, he nourishes many animals and even men with grains and fruits and the flesh of animals and causes the food to enter and penetrate all the internal and external parts of the body with such ease and gentleness that it seems incredible. God acts like a learned and humane doctor who knows how to mix drugs so that sick people take them not only easily but gladly. Food is certainly a medicine, and unless mortals take it often they cannot avoid death. Our God, who is a loving and wise doctor, first added seasoning to our food so that it would be eaten with pleasure; then he varied it in infinite ways to take away boredom; finally, by the various changes that take place in the mouth, the stomach, the liver, and the heart, he converts food into a juice so thin and subtle that without cutting or pain it enters through all the veins, capillaries, and pores of the body and penetrates to all parts of the flesh, bones, and nerves without our feeling anything and even while we are sleeping. When they examine these things, philosophers wonder at the ingenuity and art of nature, but what ingenuity can there be in inanimate things that lack sense and reason? It is not the ingenuity of nature, but the wisdom of the Creator that deserves admiration. His wisdom made nature and discovered the way in which these marvels happen. Listen to the Wisdom of God speaking in the Gospel: "Consider how the lilies of the field grow; they neither toil nor spin . . . and God so clothes" them (Mt 6:28, 30). Therefore, it is not the ingenuity of nature, but God that causes the lilies to grow and put on such beauty like a robe. The Apostle gives witness that the same is true of the nourishment and increase of all living things; he says, "Neither he who plants is anything, nor he who waters, but God who gives the growth" (1 Cor 3:7).

If God's wisdom feeds, nourishes, and conserves in their mortal life plants and animals in such a wondrous way, consider, if you can, my soul, how God will feed the minds of angels and men in life everlasting. On earth we are fed with earthly foods, although they were created by divine wisdom. In heaven that wisdom itself is the food and drink for those who live forever. Blessed would you be, if you penetrate inwardly what this means: God will be all in all (1 Cor 15:28); what this means, I say, that God, the highest and infinite good, will be for all the saints food and clothing and life and all. Then you would certainly grow tired of all things present and relish and seek only things that are above. But let us go on to the other considerations.

It is also like a miracle the way God gives long, continuous, and tireless motion to very delicate things in conserving and propagating the life of mortals. Men put in enormous labor in building a clock in which the force of weights make the wheels spin for twenty-four hours without stopping. How much wisdom does God employ so that the nutritive power operates constantly without ever stopping throughout the whole time that plants and animals live and keeps lungs and arteries working without a halt for seventy or more years? It is necessary that the nutritive power operate and the lungs and the arteries keep working from the beginning of life to the end. Hence, in those who continue to live for eighty or ninety years, their lungs and arteries have to keep moving for the same length of time. Before the Flood, when men lived for nine hundred years, the lungs and arteries, which are clearly fragile and delicate, had to keep going without any halt or lasting rest for nine hundred years. Clearly, everyone who does not marvel at these facts and is not led by them to esteem and worship God's wisdom must wholly lack the light of wisdom.

There is a third side to God's wisdom. Although it can produce and conserve grain and trees so that all living things may have their food prepared without any work by men or the other animals and even without the help of the sun and other secondary causes, still his wisdom wished to use the help of secondary causes and the labor and work of men and the other animals so that, instead of languishing in idleness, they all might use their forces. He also wished that among men some might be rich and others poor so that all might have an opportunity to cultivate virtue and be linked by a bond of charity. Thus it happens that the rich exercise their generosity and mercy and the poor their patience and humility. The rich need the work of the poor to cultivate their fields and feed their cattle and develop various skills that all depend on. The poor need the work of the rich to provide them money and equipment so that they can obtain food, clothing, and other necessities. There is no reason for the poor to complain about the divine wisdom. God, who knows everything and loves everybody, gives to each what he foresees is more useful for obtaining everlasting life, just as doctors on earth order fasting for some patients and open a vein, while they indulge others with wine and meat and order them to enjoy themselves. Surely many poor people now attain eternal salvation who, if they had been rich, would have perished forever. Although the rich too can be saved, if they try to be rich in good works and give easily and freely what they receive from a common Lord for sharing and not for hiding away, still it cannot be denied that poverty is a safer, smoother, and more direct way to eternal life than riches. The divine Teacher does not deceive us in saying, "Amen I say to you, with difficulty will a rich man enter the kingdom of heaven" (Mt 19:23), and again, "Blessed are you poor, for yours is the kingdom of heaven," and "Woe to you rich! For you are now having your comfort" (Lk 6:20, 24). Neither does the Apostle deceive us when he says in his First Letter to Timothy, "But those who seek to become rich fall into temptation and a snare of the devil and into many useless and harmful desires, which plunge men into destruction and damnation" (1 Tm 6:9). What the Lord and the apostles taught by word they confirmed by their example. The Lord says of himself, "The foxes have dens, and the birds of the air have nests, but the Son of Man has nowhere to lay his head" (Lk 9:58). The Apostle says of himself and his fellow apostles, "To this very hour we hunger and thirst, and we are naked and buffeted, and have no fixed abode" (1 Cor 4:11), that is, we do not have our own home. We cannot doubt that the wisdom of God the Son and the disciples of wisdom have chosen the smoothest and safest road to life. But because "the number of fools is infinite" (Eccl 1:15), few freely choose this road while many turn aside from it with all their heart and strength.

The last thing in which the length of divine wisdom is seen is the fact that since it is itself eternal it has implanted in all things a vivid instinct for self-preservation and for prolonging their lives and existence as long as they can. We see men when they recognize that their lives are in danger try everything and spare no resources or efforts; we see that all animals fight beyond their strength with stronger animals to save their life. We see a burning candle when it is almost burnt out flare up two or three times and let out a large flame so that it seems to be fighting against extinction with all its forces. We see drops of water sometimes hang on wood or stone and gather themselves into a sphere and hold themselves up as long as they can to keep from falling and perishing. We see heavy objects rise against their nature and light objects fall against their nature; otherwise a vacuum would form, and they could not continue to exist, being cut off from other things. More marvelous still so that it seems wholly unbelievable is the tremendous affection that God implants in parents for their children so that the species may go on. We see a mother hen grow weak for the sake of her chicks, but despite being weak and feeble she fights bravely against hawks, dogs, and foxes. Everybody knows how much pain and work women gladly accept in bearing and educating their children. The reason for this is the plan of God's wisdom; that he might foster this propagation like a shadow of eternity, he implanted an intense love for their offspring in all animals, even brute and savage animals. There are many animals that all men make a determined effort to kill, either for their own advantage, for example, rabbits, boars, deer, thrushes, quail, partridges, and almost all fishes, or to prevent their doing harm, for example, wolves, foxes, snakes, and countless others of the same sort. Many species of animals would easily have died out already unless God's wisdom provided for their conservation and propagation through this instinct.

If all living beings have by nature within them so much love for this life which is short and full of troubles, how much love should we have toward a life that is happy and eternal! Oh, the blindness and folly of the human race! All things work beyond their strength for a very short life, a shadow of eternity. Man, who is endowed with reason, disdains to work for a true eternity of blissful life, not,

I say, beyond his strength, but using normal strength. All things fear temporal death by a natural instinct and flee it more than all other evils. Man, instructed by reason and taught by faith, neither fears eternal death nor flees it, at least to the degree he usually flees and fears temporal evils. Ecclesiastes was right in saying, "The number of fools is infinite" (Eccl 1:15), and Truth said truly in the Gospel, "How narrow the gate and close the way that leads to life; and few there are who find it" (Mt 7:14).

CHAPTER THREE

The Nature of the Height of God's Practical Wisdom Is Seen in the Work of the Redemption

The height of God's practical wisdom is seen in the work of redemption: "I could not get enough," says Saint Augustine, "of the marvelous sweetness of reflecting on the height of your plan for the salvation of the human race."[2]

High indeed was the plan to repair by the ignominy of the cross all the damage which the craftiness of the devil did by the sin of the first man and so repair it that the restored work was more beautiful than it had been before it began to need restoration. The sin of the first man gave birth to four evils: the injury to God by the pride and disobedience of Adam; the punishment of the first man and the whole human race, that is, the privation of God's grace and eternal happiness; the sorrow of the angels, who were extremely displeased by God's injury and men's misery; the joy of the devil and all the evil spirits, who were delighted that they had conquered and cast down man. The wisdom of God took away all these evils and turned them into greater goods by the mystery of the cross, so that the Church not without reason sings: "O happy fault that merited to have such and so great Redeemer!"[3] Certainly if a tailor were to repair by his work and the addition of some ornament a new and precious robe which had been accidently cut and torn so that it turned out more beautiful and precious, one could rightly speak of a lucky cut which provided the opportunity for such beauty.

The first man, puffed with pride by the craftiness and envy of the devil, pretended to be like God, disobeyed God, and transgressed his commandment. Thus he somehow stole away the honor he owed to God. But Christ, the second Adam, who is the Wisdom of God, "humbled himself, becoming obedient to death, even to death on a cross" (Phil 2:8); he restored to God an honor much greater than was that which the first Adam had taken away by his pride and disobedience. Adam was a mere man, and had he obeyed God, he would have obeyed in a very easy matter. What sacrifice was it for the first humans to abstain from the fruit of one forbidden tree when they had an abundance of many excellent fruits? Therefore, their sin was very serious, and that much more serious as obedience would have been easier since it involved no effort. Christ was God and man and humbled himself to obey God his Father in the greatest and hardest of all things, namely, in death on a cross, full of suffering and shame. Taking into consideration the eminence of the person and the depth of humility and obedience, nothing greater or more meritorious or more filled with hónor for God can be thought of than that humble obedience of Christ. Therefore, the Lord was telling the truth in the Gospel: "I have glorified you on earth" (Jn 17:4). Before the angels of God and before all the holy minds of the prophets and others to whom these things were known, Jesus Christ glorified God the Father with a glory clearly ineffable, and if the angels at Christ's birth sang "Glory to God in the highest" (Lk 2:14), because of the humility of the crib, much more did they sing the same hymn with greater exaltation because of the humility of the cross.

Had he not sinned, man would have at most obtained equality with the angels; now through the redemption which is in Christ Jesus the human race has obtained that one man, raised above all the angels, sits at God's right hand, and is head and Lord of angels and men. The Apostle Peter writes thus of Christ in his First Letter: "He went into heaven, angels, powers, and virtues being made subject to him" (1 Pt 3:22). His fellow Apostle Paul writes to the Philippians, "Therefore, God has also exalted him and has bestowed on him the name that is above every name, so that at the name of Jesus every knee should bend of those in heaven, on earth, and under the earth" (Phil 2:9, 10). The son ineffably glorified the Father by the humility of his passion, and the Father also ineffably glorified his Son by lifting him to his right hand. This glorification flowed down to the whole human race so that they are total ingrates who do not acknowledge this immense benefit and do not give thanks to God for it. Indeed, not only Christ, who is God and man, but his Mother is exalted above all the choirs of angels, although she is only human, not God. Over the great increase of glory added to that which they would have had, if the first man had not sinned, men can rightly exclaim, "O happy fault that merited to have such and so great redeemer!"

The holy angels, who were so saddened by the fall of the first man, as by a terrible accident to their younger brother, were equally touched with great joy by the full redemption that Christ accomplished. If "there will be joy in heaven among the angels of God over one sinner who repents" (Lk 17:7, 10), how much more should we believe there will be great joy among the same angels when they see that through Christ, a man, God's justice is fully satisfied for the human race and the kingdom of heaven has been opened to believers by the key of his cross? It is not to be thought that the angels bear it ill that God has exalted the man Christ and the blessed Virgin above the eminence of the angels themselves. The angels cherish no envy or jealousy; they are full of true and burning charity. Charity is not envious, is not puffed up, it is not sad over another's good but is delighted and rejoices with all good persons over the good of others as if it were its own (1 Cor 13:4, 5). Hence the Church sings, "Mary is assumed into heaven, the angels rejoice."[4] She does not say that the angels are sad, but that they rejoice because they see the Virgin Mother of God exalted above the angel choirs in the heavenly kingdom. They recognize that this has been done most fairly by God, who never acts except wisely and fairly; at the same time they have their will joined with God's will by an inseparable and unbreakable bond of love so that what pleases God also pleases them and can in no way displease them.

But the devil, who for a time rejoiced that he had defeated and cast down the first man, drew much greater sorrow from the victory of the man, Christ, than had been his earlier rejoicing. The result of Christ's victory was that now not only men such as Adam was, but also women and children mock the devil and triumph over him. It would not have been shameful for the devil to have been conquered by Adam in paradise when he lacked ignorance and weakness and was armed with original justice which subjected his lower part to his reason so that it could not rebel unless the mind itself was first in rebellion against God. But now it is the greatest disgrace for the devil to be conquered by a mortal man, who is a pilgrim subject to ignorance and concupiscence. But he is conquered by the grace of Christ, and so conquered that many raise aloft their trophies of chastity, patience, humility, and charity, even though the devil keeps throwing his fiery spears of temptation and persecution. In this respect the height of God's wisdom deserves boundless admiration. God sees that against the tricks of the devil the human race must have contempt for worldly goods, fleshly pleasures, an abundance of wealth, earthly glory, and the like, which are the snares of the devil and plunge those they have trapped "into destruction and damnation" (Tm 6:9). Was it not, therefore, his strategy that these things should grow bitter for men and that the contrary, namely, chastity, poverty, humility, patience, and contempt for the world should become sweet? He himself came down from heaven and, taking the form of a servant, made the bitter and repugnant medicine that man's sickness required so sweet and pleasant by his own example that now many men prefer fasting to feasting, poverty to riches, virginity to marriage, martyrdom to pleasures, obeying to giving orders, being condemned to being honored, being a subject to being a superior, and being humbled to being praised. Who would not be inspired and stirred to imitation when he sees God in human form, full of wisdom and grace, who can neither deceive nor be deceived, poor, humble, patient, pure, and, what is more, wonderful, nailed to a cross to redeem the human race and dying voluntarily with burning charity by the shedding of his precious blood?

This was the high and wonderful strategem of God's wisdom; it is of these works that Isaiah sings, "Make his works known among the people" (Is 12: 4). But even this highest wisdom of God seems folly not only to the wise of this world, as Paul says in his First Letter to the Corinthians (1 Cor 1:21), but also to carnal and sensual men who believe in Christ but refuse to follow in Christ's footsteps. The Apostle called these the enemies of the cross of Christ (Phil 2:18). Make the effort, my soul, to suck the honey from the rock and oil from the hardest stone (Dt 32:13), that is, wisdom from folly, the wisdom of God from the folly of the cross. Examine carefully and diligently who he is who hangs on the cross and why he hangs there. And when you find out that it is he "who sits on the cherubim" (Ps 99:1), indeed he has "taken his seat at the right hand of the Majesty on high" (Heb 1:3), you will easily understand that he does not hang on the cross because of his faults or his weakness or the power of others, but voluntarily, because of his burning desire to satisfy the divine justice for the sins of the whole world, for the sake of the honor and glory of God the Father, to gain the eternal salvation of all the elect, and, as the Apostle says, "in order that he might present to himself the Church in all her glory, not having spot or wrinkle" (Eph 5:27). Finally, he hangs on the cross because of love for you, for he loved you and delivered himself up for you as an offering and a sacrifice to God in the odor of sweetness (Eph 5:2). When, I say, you discover these truths, rise up with inward love for so great a benefactor and, imitating him, begin to thirst ardently for the glory of God, for the salvation of all nations, and especially for the beauty and glory of the whole Church and for your own salvation. Begin to thirst after a perfect hatred for sin, after purity of heart, and perfect justice so that some day you may also begin to thirst to share the cross of your Lord and to rejoice in tribulation and suffering so that later you may come to share the resurrection with the just unto glory and not unto punishment with the wicked.

CHAPTER FOUR

The Depth of God's Practical Wisdom Lies in His Providence and Predestination

The depth of God's practical wisdom, which lies in providence, predestination, and his judgments, remains for treatment. It is written: "Your judgments are a great deep" (Ps 36:6).

First, the fact that God rules all created things immediately and directs them toward their ends indicates that God's providence is indeed admirable: The Wise Man says, "He has equally care of all" (Wis 6:8), that is, God takes care of all things without any exception so that not even a sparrow falls to the ground without God's providence, as our Savior says (Lk 12:6). Could someone count the number of things in the whole universe, he might make a sort of estimate of the greatness of God's wisdom, which rules and directs each and every thing. A single supreme pontiff might rule the whole Christian world with a general providence, but not with a particular one which reaches to individual Christians, and so he calls many bishops to share in this care. A single king can govern many provinces with a general providence but not a particular one which includes individual citizens, and therefore he employs many viceroys, officials, and deputies. But God takes care of one as all and all as one: Not even a sparrow "is forgotten before God" (Lk 12:6). "The very hairs of" our "head are all numbered" by him (Mt 10:30), and his providence watches over us always lest even one of them perish. Even the chicks of the raven, deserted by their parents, are not deserted by God (Ps 147:9).

Therefore, my soul, you can rest secure in the embrace of your great Father, even in the midst of darkness, amid the jaws of the lion and dragon, amid the countless hosts of countless spirits. Only cling to him with sincere love, holy fear, steady hope, and undoubting faith.

God's providence has care not only for present individual things but also "it reaches therefore from end to end mightily and orders all things sweetly (Wis 8:1). God is called the king of ages (1 Tm 1:17) because he himself established the order of the ages and has arranged the succession to kingdoms and the twists and turns of history from all eternity. Nothing new, nothing unforeseen, nothing unexpected can happen to God. As the Wise Man says, "For the thoughts of mortal men are fearful, and our counsels are uncertain" (Wis 9:14), because we have nothing but misleading conjectures about the future. But God knows all future events as certainly as he knows the past and the present, and before the foundation of the earth he arranged in his own mind the succession and order of all events. This is why our mother the Church publicly and confidently proclaims in song that God's providence in guiding her does not err.[5]

But because the scheme of divine providence is hidden and his "judgments are a great deep" (Ps 36:6), it happens that many people, seeing the many evils that happen among men and go unpunished, rush headlong into believing that human affairs are not governed by God's providence or certainly that all evils are committed by God's wish. Either of these conclusions is wicked, but the second is the worse, as Saint Augustine writes.[6] They rush into these rash errors because they see one part of divine providence but do not see another part of it, and when they ought to await the outcome of things, which will be clear to all at the last judgment, they prematurely dare to make rash judgments and fall into serious errors. Hence the Apostle cries out in his First Letter to the Corinthians, "Pass no judgment before the time, until the Lord comes, who will both bring to light the things hidden in darkness and make manifest the counsels of hearts" (1 Cor 4:5). Saint Augustine illustrates this with a superb metaphor: "If somebody," he says, "could look at the arrangement of only one panel in a mosaic floor, he would criticize the artist as an incompetent in arrangement and composition because he sees a small part of his work and does not see the biggest part. If he looked at all the parts and their relationship, he would undoubtedly highly praise the work and its craftsman."[7] Thus many men see that the wicked prosper and that the upright, in contrast, are oppressed and afflicted; they do not know what future God has in store for the crime of the wicked or for the patience of the upright, and therefore they break out in words of blasphemy or agree with those who argued in Job that God "does not consider our things, and he walks about the poles of heaven" (Jb 22:14), or with those who said in Malachi, "Every one that does evil is good in the sight of the Lord and such please him" (Mal 2:17). Saint Augustine used to put forward in several places another metaphor taken from poetry. Should somebody when he began to hear an epic poem say at the beginning or in the middle that it was not a good poem, he would rightly be considered a fool. Let him wait till all the syllables are recited and finished, then let him make his criticism if the poem does not please him.[8] Thus they are utter fools who dare to vilify God's carefully ordered providence before the whole order of providence has run its course.

My soul, you will be wise to strive as hard as you can that evils do not happen; for God has given you this command. But leave to his judgment why he permits evil. His judgment may be hidden, but it cannot be unjust.

CHAPTER FIVE

On the Mystery of Predestination and Reprobation

Although the arrangement of God's providence in governing human affairs is a great abyss, still the arrangement of eternal predestination and reprobation is an incomparably deeper abyss. Why God heaps temporal goods on many wicked persons and leaves their sins unpunished in this life, and on the other hand why he permits many innocent people to be oppressed by poverty and unjustly afflicted, scourged, and killed, is a question that we cannot examine in individual instances, but we can give with probability a general explanation. God often makes the wicked abound in temporal goods so that he may reward their few good moral acts since he is not going to give them eternal life or so that he may coax them by temporal benefits to conversion from their sins and lead them to hope for and desire eternal benefits. Sometimes he does not punish their sins in this life since he will punish them enough in hell. The just, however, he permits to be afflicted with want, shame, and various troubles both so that they may wipe away their minor sins in this life and so that he may crown their patience, humility, and other merits more gloriously and splendidly in eternal life. Who shall find the answer to why God loved Jacob and hated Esau before they had done anything good or evil? This is what caused the Apostle to wonder in his Letter to the Romans; they were twin brothers, sons of the same father and mother, but God loved and predestined one and hated and reprobated the other (Rom 9:10ff.). Nor should anyone say that God foresaw the future good works of one and the evil ones of the other; the Apostle anticipates this argument and says that this happened "in order that the selective purpose of God might stand" and adds the words given by Moses, "I have mercy on whom I have mercy, and I show pity on whom I show pity" (Rom 9:11, 15; Ex 33:19). Who will not be astonished that one person who perseveres a long time in good works falls away at the end of life and perishes, as did Judas the traitor, and that another perseveres a long time in evil works and at the end of life changes and immediately goes up to paradise like the good thief? You may say: "But Judas betrayed Christ and the thief confessed him." That is true, but Christ could have looked upon Judas as he looked upon Peter and have given Judas the sort of efficacious grace which is not rejected by the hardest of hearts. Could not Christ have given faith and repentance to both the thieves that were hanging with him, as he gave it to one, or have permitted both to finish their lives in sin, as he allowed one? Who can give the reason why God carries off some so that evil does not change their mind, as the Wise Man says about Enoch, and does not carry off many, but permits them to change from good to evil and end their days in evil? What shall we say about whole regions? Some are called early to the faith without which nobody can be saved, and others very late. "He who does not believe is already judged" (Jn 3:18). And as the Apostle says, "For whoever calls upon the name of the Lord shall be saved. How then are they to call on him in whom they have not believed? But how are they to believe him whom they have not heard? And how are they to hear, if no one preaches? And how are men to preach unless they be sent?" (Rom 10:13–15).

These are the lofty and deep secrets that the Father hid in the abyss of his wisdom which the Apostle does not disclose, but marvels at when he says, "Oh, the depth of the riches of the wisdom and of the knowledge of God! How incomprehensible are his judgments and how unsearchable his ways! For who has known the mind of the Lord, or who has been his counsellor?" (Rom 11:33, 34). We are allowed to know only this: In God there is no iniquity and on the last day there will be no one who cannot rightly say, "You are just, O Lord, and your judgment is right" (Ps 119:137). Moreover, this secret is useful for all of us because it provides a reason so that no sinner should despair of salvation and no upright person should presume that his salvation is certain and that upright men should not lose heart about the conversion of any sinner but pray for all and work for the salvation of all. Conversely, no one, however good and holy, may get careless since no one knows what tomorrow may bring, but all should work out their salvation "with fear and trembling" (Phil 2:12).

Having reflected on all this, my soul, strive to make your calling and election certain through good works as the Apostle Peter warns you in his Second Letter (2 Pt 1:10). The Apostle John teaches what are the good works which make certain one's calling and election when he says, "My dear children, let us not love in word, neither in tongue, but in deed and in truth" (1 Jn 3:18). This means charity, with which no one is damned and without which no one is saved. But charity is shown by works, namely, when one gives alms to the poor or forgives enemies for injuries, not out of hope of temporal retribution or from a disordered attachment to a creature, but out of a pure and inward love for God and the neighbor. Making a start is not enough; rather "he who has persevered to the end will be saved" (Mt 10:22). That is why the Apostle says, "Strive" (2 Pt 1:10), that is, give yourself to the business of your eternal salvation with seriousness, care, and diligence. If there is a probable sign of divine election, it is that a man is more careful about his salvation than anything else and never stops begging God for the gift of true repentance, true humility, perfect charity, and perseverance to the end. And not content with prayer alone, he hastens to seek and find "the kingdom of God and his justice" (Mt 6:33) with all his strength, as our Savior warned us.

STEP FOURTEEN:

On the Consideration of God's Mercy

CHAPTER ONE

God Bears Our Miseries with the Breadth of His Mercy

In Scripture the Holy Spirit highlights God's mercy with striking praise so that he does not hesitate to extol it above all God's works. Thus the Prophet David sings, "The Lord is sweet to all, and his tender mercies are over all his works" (Ps 145:9). We will easily grasp the greatness of this divine attribute if we study a bit more closely its width, length, height, and depth.

The breadth of the divine mercy consists in the fact that God and God alone can take away all miseries, and he does take away some from all things and does it out of the love with which he loves all creatures and not for any advantage of his own. Created things can take away some miseries. Bread takes away hunger, drink takes away thirst, clothing takes away nakedness, knowledge takes away ignorance, and so forth, but no creature can take away all misery. Moreover, there are certain miseries, which weigh more heavily as they are more hidden and inward, for which only God can provide a cure. These include the snares of the devils, who are numerous, crafty, powerful, and full of malice toward us. They include the error and blindness of mind and of warped conscience, which we do not notice in ourselves since we often see ourselves as being in good spiritual health when we are in critical and dangerous condition. Who can save us from this sort of misery except the one omnipotent doctor? Because God without our knowing it often frees us from these miseries in his mercy, all men can rightly be called ungrateful toward God, as our Lord himself witnesses when he says that our heavenly Father is kind toward the ungrateful and the wicked (Lk 6:35). We are barely aware of the smallest part of God's benefits, and even for those we do not give thanks with the devotion and humility we owe.

Created things do not take away all miseries, but only a few, and those they do not take away from everybody but only from a few people. Only God is able take away all miseries from everybody; and although he does not take away all of them from everybody, still there is nobody who does not have some share in God's mercy. Rightly then did the Prophet sing, "The earth is full of the mercy of the Lord" (Ps 33:5). In her prayer the Church says, "God, whose property it is to be merciful,"[1] because it pertains to him to take away misery who has no misery, and it pertains to him alone to take away all miseries from everyone who alone has no miseries at all. Who has no misery at all except God alone, who is pure act and the highest good and whose happiness is part of his essence?

My soul, had you attained in thought to what is the life of your Lord and Father which, raised above all misery, is pure and total happiness, how heartily you would yearn for his embrace, so that it could be said of you too, "There shall no evil come to you, nor shall the scourge come near your dwelling" (Ps 91:10). You may object: If God is able to take away all miseries from all things, why does he not do it since he is "the Father of Mercies" (2 Cor 1:3), that is, a most merciful Father? Why do so many miseries afflict the human race under the rule of the Father of mercies? Why is it said, "The earth is full of the mercy of the Lord" (Ps 33:5), and not the opposite, that the earth is full of every misery? God can indeed take away all miseries, but he takes away only those that his wisdom judges should be taken away. Divine wisdom judges that it is not good for man that all be taken away and that it is sometimes mercy not to take away some misery to make room for a greater mercy. Three times the Apostle asked the Lord to deliver him from a thorn of the flesh, and he was not heard, "for strength is made perfect in weakness" (2 Cor 12:9). God did not take away from Lazarus the misery of poverty and sores so that the angels might carry him with greater mercy to Abraham's bosom (Lk 16:19ff.). How could there be the works of mercy which are so necessary for the merit of the rich if nobody was poor, hungry, thirsty, naked, sick, homeless, or imprisoned? If there were no temptations and struggles with the demons, how could there be the triumphs and crowns of the virgins and confessors? If there were no labors and sufferings, how could there be a crown for patience? If there were no persecutors, how could there be a palm of martyrdom? Therefore, in this exile both statements are true: The earth is full of miseries because our sins by themselves are giant miseries, and the earth is full of the mercy of the Lord. For what else are the conversion of sinners, the merits of the saints, and the other nearly infinite spiritual and temporal benefits of God except the great and continued mercies of God our Creator? Let us then give thanks to our good God because just as our tribulations abound in this pilgrimage, so also our consolation abounds by his mercy (2 Cor 1:5). "O Lord, your mercy is in heaven" (Ps 36:5), says David, because there his mercy will exist without misery because his mercy will completely take away all misery.

CHAPTER TWO

The Length of God's Mercy Is His Long-suffering or Patience

The length of mercy is long-suffering or patience, which Scripture usually joins with mercy as one of its parts or types. Thus David says, "The Lord is compassionate and merciful; long-suffering and plenteous in mercy" (Ps 103:8), and again, "The Lord is gracious and merciful; patient and plenteous in mercy" (Ps 145:8).

Wholly admirable is the long-suffering or patience of God our merciful Father toward the human race since it is such as we do not find among masters toward their servants or parents toward their children, even though they are all human beings.

First, God is long-suffering toward sinners, waiting for them with incredible patience, sometimes from their early childhood till extreme old age, allowing them to break his law and insult his name and meanwhile "bestowing blessings, giving rain from heaven and fruitful seasons, filling hearts with food and gladness" (Acts 14:16), as the Apostle says. Is there among men a master or parent so meek and mild that, if he were to see his servant or child insulting and injuring him and keeping up this evil behavior for a long time, he would still not throw him out of his house? But God's mercy is not conquered by human malice; he is "long-suffering, not wishing that any should perish but that all should turn to repentance" (2 Pt 3:9), as Saint Peter asserts in his Letter. And the Wise Man says, "But you have mercy upon all, . . . and overlook the sins of men for the sake of repentance" (Wis 11:24).

Secondly, his patience is seen even more in the fact that many sinners have not only been pulled from the lake of misery and the muck of dung and been transformed from sons of darkness into sons of light and called from deserving eternal death to adoption as sons of God and to the hope of the heavenly kingdom. But after they again and again, many, many times have fallen back into vileness and ingratitude, they still are not abandoned by the long-suffering of God, who kindly awaits and invites their conversion. And if they do repent from the heart, the merciful Father receives them back like prodigal sons to the kiss of peace and to their former honors and dignity. It was not without reason that, when Saint Peter asked how many times he should forgive a brother who had sinned against him, even as many as seven times, the Lord answered, "I do not say to you seven times, but seventy times seven" (Mt 18:20). He wants us to act exactly the way he acts in offering forgiveness to penitents. He sets no limit to reconciliation except the end of this life. As long as a sinner lives, even if he reaches a hundred years or more, falling and falling again, the kind Father welcomes him to the remission of his sins. No repentance is too late for the Father of mercies provided that it be serious and from a heart truly contrite and humble (Ps 51:17). But no one should, therefore, take advantage of God's kindness and put off conversion from day to day since no one knows what hour or day he will leave his body and be summoned before the tribunal of that most just judge. Rather the great and incredible goodness of God should invite and encourage all to conversion; for if the Lord is so kind to sinners who have repeatedly fallen, how great will be the Father's sweetness toward those who after one taste of God's grace can never again be induced to be separated or torn from it by the poundings of any temptation!

There is another aspect of God's long-suffering that is extremely marvelous and lovable, which he uses in tolerating the offenses of the just. By his infinite kindness God changes us from enemies into friends, from servants into sons, from men condemned to eternal death to heirs of his kingdom. Despite this our ingratitude is so great that we daily return him evil for good; if the Apostle James said, "in many things we all offend" (Jas 3:2), what should we say who come far short of the holiness of the apostles? For example, in praying we are speaking with God, and suddenly we are pulled away to other thoughts by our imagination and we turn our back on God. Would any master on earth allow his servants who are standing in his presence and talking with him suddenly to ignore him and turn to chat with other servants? What shall I say about idle chatter, vain thoughts, fruitless actions, excesses in food and drink or sleep and games, the neglect of religious services, failure to make fraternal correction, or the other countless offenses by which we all are continually offending him? Still our God, "sweet and mild and plenteous in mercy to all that call upon" him (Ps 86:5), bears this boorishness and impoliteness—if I may put it so—and rudeness of his sons, which men would not put up with from other men. Saint Augustine notes this in his treatise on Psalm 85 at the verse "You, Lord are sweet and mild" (Ps 86:7) where he decries our human weakness in warding off distractions during prayer and extols God's mercy in putting up with many injuries from his servants.[2] "For he knows our frame" (Ps 103:14) and deals with us as a mother with her little baby whom she cherishes and nurses even if it strikes out at her. Although God puts up with so many of our offenses, since he does not break off his friendship over them or deprive us of the right to our inheritance, still he will not let them go unpunished at the judgment where we will have to render an account of every idle word unless he finds that they previously have been washed away by tears or prayer or some other kind of satisfaction.

To keep you, my soul, from thinking that these are light offenses and therefore from beguiling yourself and neglecting them, listen to what Saint Bonaventure writes in his biography of Blessed Francis, a man much enlightened by divine light. He says, "He thought that he had offended greatly if sometimes when engaged in prayer his mind wandered in vain distractions. When this sort of thing happened, he did not fail to confess it, but expiated it right away. This zeal had the result that he was very rarely bothered by such flies. In Lent he was making a little basket to occupy spare moments lest they be wholly wasted. While he was saying Terce this popped into his memory and distracted his mind for a moment; moved by fervor of spirit, he burned the little basket and said, 'I sacrifice this to the Lord, in whose sacrifice it interfered.'"[3] A wandering mind during prayer or the praises of God is not such a minor fault as many people think. But great is the mercy and long-suffering of God our Father that he does not become greatly angry nor punish us for it immediately.

CHAPTER THREE

The Cause That Moves God's Mercy Indicates Its Height

Next, the height of God's mercy is related to the cause that moves God to pity. This is very high and is lifted above all the heavens, as the Psalm has it: "O Lord, your mercy is in heaven" (Ps 36:5) and, "Mercy shall be built up forever in the heavens" (Ps 89:2).

Some men have mercy on other men because they need their help; this is the lowest grade of mercy since it does not go above one's own advantage, as when we deal kindly with our horses, dogs, and cattle. Others have mercy because of kinship or friendship, because they are sons or brothers or acquaintances or friends, and this grade is a little higher and begins to have a dimension of virtue. Others have mercy, finally, because they are neighbors, that is, men like themselves, created by the same God from the same earth. Hence, they do not distinguish whether they are friends or enemies, good or evil, local people or foreigners, but have mercy on all, who they know were created in God's image. This is the final grade to which mortals can ascend. But God has mercy on all things because they are his creatures and has a special mercy on men because they are his images and has a still more special mercy on the just because they are his sons, the heirs of his kingdom and co-heirs with his Only-Begotten. You may ask: Why did God create the world, why did he make man in his image, why did he justify sinners, why did he adopt men as sons, why did he make them heirs to his kingdom? Absolutely no answer can be given except this: because he wanted to. Why did he want to? Only because he is good. Goodness pours itself out and freely communicates itself. Mercy was made in heaven, and from the highest abode, namely, the heart of the supreme Father, it descended to and filled the earth, so that the Prophet might sing, "the earth is full of the mercy of the Lord" (Ps 33:5). Therefore,

God found within himself his reason for being merciful to us; in us he found reason for punishing us.

Now, my soul, lift up the eyes of your mind to that lofty font of mercy. See that highest purity unmixed by any intention of personal advantage. When you hear the Teacher of all urging you and saying, "Be merciful, therefore, even as your Father is merciful" (Lk 6:36), strive as hard as you can not only to be merciful to your fellow servants, but to be merciful with that pure love with which the heavenly Father has mercy on us. If you forgive someone who insults or tells lies about you, forgive with a true heart, casting every offense into lasting oblivion, for our Father forgets our sins, as the prophet Ezekiel writes (Ez 18:22). And David says, "As far as the east is from the west, so far has he removed our iniquities from us" (Ps 103:12), so that they cannot harm us any longer. If you give alms to the poor, understand that you are receiving more than giving since "he that has mercy on the poor lends to the Lord" (Prv 19:17), and therefore give with humility and reverence, not like alms to the poor man, but like a gift to a prince. If you should suffer some disadvantage in helping a needy neighbor, reflect how much you differ from your Lord, who gave his life and blood to help you. Thus it will come about that without any hope of earthly reward and without any motive of vainglory, but only out of pure love for God and your neighbor, you will make progress in the virtue of mercy.

CHAPTER FOUR

The Depth of God's Mercy Is Seen in Its Effects

Our remaining consideration deals with the depth of God's mercy. Just as the height of mercy shines forth best in its cause, so its depth, it seems, should be sought out in its effects.

A mercy that goes no deeper than mere words should be called wholly shallow and superficial. Deeper is the mercy which raises and refreshes the suffering not only with consoling words but also with benefits. The deepest mercy is that which helps the suffering not only with words and gifts but also by undergoing and shouldering their trials and sufferings. Our God, whose mercies are beyond counting, has mercy on us in all these ways. First, he sends letters of consolation to us; these are the divine Scriptures, of which the Maccabees say, "We have for our comfort the holy books that are in our hands" (1 Mc 12:9). God speaks to us and promises aid and protection not only by writing but also by the sermon of preachers, who work as ambassadors of Christ during our pilgrimage (2 Cor 5:19, 20), and by inward inspirations. David says, "I will hear what the Lord will speak in me; for he will speak peace to his people and to his saints and to them that are converted to the heart" (Ps 85:8). Second, the benefits of God's mercy against our manifold miseries, both spiritual and temporal, are so many that they cannot be counted, for everywhere he crowns us "with mercy and compassion" (Ps 103:4), that is, he surrounds us on all sides with the benefits of his mercy. Third, by the mystery of the incarnation God's mercy comes down to trials and sufferings, to hunger and thirst, to shame and reproach, to stripes and wounds, to the cross and death in order to redeem us from all sin and the eternal death which is due to sin. Is there any deeper abyss into which God's mercy could have descended? Indeed there is. He did this gratis, not because he owed something. "He was offered because it was his own will" (Is 53:7). Who forced the Son of God, who did not think it theft to be equal to the Father, to empty himself and take the form of a servant, becoming poor for us so that he might enrich us by his poverty, to be humiliated even to death, death on a cross, so that he could give us life and lift us up (Phil 2:8; 2 Cor 8:9)? Surely only love forced him, only mercy drove him.

But there is something still deeper: He wanted to share with us the glory and honor of the work of our salvation. That angelic division seemed good enough: "Glory to God in the highest, and on earth peace" (Lk 2:14), honor to God, benefit to men. But God's mercy wanted all the benefit to be ours and part of the glory to be his and part ours. He wanted to give us the grace by which we ourselves cooperate in our salvation and truly merit the eternal life which Christ merited for us, not because the merit of Christ was insufficient, but to share with us the praise and glory of our own salvation. Thus, the Gospel says, "Pay them their wages" (Mt 20:8), and the Apostle glories in saying, "There is laid up for me a crown of justice" (2 Tm 4:8).

Finally, God has a deepest mercy toward men, especially toward holy men who fear God, which surpasses the love of a father and mother, which is as great as any we know on earth. Listen to the prophet Isaiah, "Can a mother forget her infant, so as not to have pity on the son of her womb? And if she should forget, yet I will not forget you" (Is 49:15). Hear David, "As a father has compassion on his children, so has the Lord compassion on them that fear him" (Ps 103:13). Lest you object that there are parents whose love for their children sometimes turns into hatred, David adds about God's mercy toward his children, "The mercy of the Lord is from eternity and unto eternity upon them that fear him" (Ps 103:17). The Apostle makes us certain about its duration when he calls God "the Father of all mercies and the God of all consolation" in his Second Letter to the Corinthians (2 Cor 1:13). Therefore, God is not only a Father to those who fear him but a most merciful Father very prepared to console, for he takes away the miseries of troubles and tribulations from his children when he judges removing them is to their advantage. In this he shows himself the "Father of mercies."

He also provides ineffable consolation so that they may easily bear those miseries which he judges would not be to their advantage to take away, and in this he proves himself to be "the God of all consolation" (2 Cor 1:3). The Apostle speaks of "all consolation" for two reasons: first because God knows how to console his own in every kind of trouble, which the world surely cannot do because it often does not understand the cause of the troubles. Thus the friends of Job were "troublesome comforters" (Jb 16:2ff.), as he himself says, because they did not know the cause of his sickness and they applied their medicine in the wrong place. Or sometimes the trouble is so serious that no human consolation can equal it. But God, the most wise and omnipotent doctor, can cure absolutely every disease, and hence the Apostles says, "who comforts us in all our afflictions" (2 Cor 1:4). Second, he is called the "God of all consolation" because he knows how to console so fully and richly that one prefers to suffer tribulation when united with such a consoler than to be without both. This actually happened to Theodorus when he was a young man and a confessor during the persecution of Julian the Apostate. For ten full hours he was tortured with such cruelty and so many shifts of torturers that no epoch records its like, and still during the whole time he joyfully sang the psalms of David; he first became sad when he was ordered cut down because of the tremendous consolation he received from the presence of an angel while he was being tortured, as Rufinus recorded.[4] This is not surprising given the Apostle's statements, "I am filled with comfort, I overflow with joy in all our troubles," and at the beginning of the Letter, "who consoles us in all our afflictions, so that we also may be able to comfort those who are in distress" (2 Cor 7:4, 1:4).

What do you think, my soul, about that mercy, which is so ample, so lasting, so pure, and so immense, of a Lord who has no need for our goods and yet, because of his overflowing charity, is as helpful to his little servants as if his every good depended on them? What thanks can you give to him? What can you ever offer to avoid being ungrateful for so much kindness? At least try to do as much as you can to please him and carry out what pleases him. Since it is written: "Be merciful, therefore, even as your Father is merciful" (Lk 6:36) and "Have pity on your own soul, pleasing God" (Sir 30:24), begin carefully above all to examine the miseries of your own soul, for the miseries of the body are clear, nor is there need to warn a man to take care of his body. If the body goes without food and drink for even one day or spends a single sleepless night or suffers from a fall or a wound, it immediately weeps and lets out a roar, and there is a great rush to bring it help. But the soul fasts for whole weeks from its food, or languishes under wounds received, or even lies dead, and no one takes care of it or shows sympathy. Therefore, visit your soul more and more often; check whether all its faculties are in good health, whether they are making progress in the knowledge and love of true good or instead labor under ignorance and languish with various evil desires. See whether the mind is blinded by malice and the will is corrupted by the disease of envy or pride. If you find such things, cry out to the Lord, "Have mercy on me, O Lord, for I am weak" (Ps 6:2). Seek out doctors of the spirit and take suitable remedies. Second, have mercy on other souls, an infinite number of which perish, and yet Christ died for them. My soul, if you really understood the price of souls, namely the precious blood of the Son of God, and likewise the terrible slaughter they suffer from the wolves of hell and the demons roaring like lions, you surely could not fail to have wholehearted compassion on them and work for their liberation both by praying to God and any other way you could. Finally, have compassion on the bodily needs of your neighbors, "not in word, neither with the tongue but in deed and in truth" (1 Jn 3:18), remembering the words of the Lord, "Blessed are the merciful, for they shall obtain mercy" (Mt 5:7).

STEP FIFTEEN:

On the Consideration of God's Justice By Comparison with Bodily Greatness

CHAPTER ONE

The Breadth of God's Justice Is Universal Justice

The justice of God has four meanings in Scripture. First it stands for universal justice, which includes all virtues and is identical with holiness or uprightness; thus in the psalms, "The Lord is just in all his ways and holy in all his works" (Ps 145:17). Second, it stands for truth or fidelity, as in another psalm, "that you may be justified in your words" (Ps 51:4). Third, it stands for distributive justice in rewards, as in the Second Letter to Timothy, "There is laid up for me a crown of justice, which the Lord, the just Judge, will give me in that day" (2 Tm 4:8). Last, it stands for justice that avenges sins, as in another psalm, "He shall rain snares upon sinners, fire and brimstone and storms of winds shall be the portion of their cup, for the Lord is just and has loved justice" (Ps 10:7, 8). We can get some notion of the greatness of divine justice if we consider the breadth of his universal justice; the length of his justice, that is, the length of his truth and fidelity; the height of his justice that distributes rewards in heaven; and the depth of his justice which scourges sinners in hell with eternal punishments.

Let us begin with breadth. Men call that justice universal which disposes a man so that in all his actions he conducts himself in accord with all the laws. It, therefore, includes all the virtues, both theological and moral; but there is one virtue, called charity, which includes in her bosom all the virtues and commands and directs the acts of all the virtues to their last end. This virtue, although it is a particular virtue and one of the theological virtues, still can rightly be called universal justice because it disposes man to conduct himself properly toward God and his neighbor and thereby to fulfill the law. The Apostle puts it this way, "Love does no evil" and "He who loves . . . has fulfilled the law" and "Love therefore is the fulfillment of the Law" (Rom 13:8, 10). In his book *On Nature and Grace*, Saint Augustine says, "Charity begun is justice begun, advanced charity is advanced justice, great charity is great justice, perfect charity is perfect justice."[1] In God are all the virtues that do not presuppose some imperfection and in place of those which do presuppose imperfection there is something far better and higher. Hence, he lacks no goodness, but instead in him goodness and holiness are so great and so infinite that he merits on the highest grounds to be called alone good and alone holy (Mt 19:17). Therefore, God does not have the theological virtues of faith because faith deals with things that are not seen, whereas God sees all things. Neither does God have hope because hope is the expectation of things to come, whereas God expects nothing since he possesses all things from eternity. God has no sorrow for sin since God cannot sin. He has no humility because humility restrains man from foolishly climbing above himself and keeps him in his place, but God has nothing above him toward which he might want to climb since he is the Most High. Yet God does have the queen of all the virtues, full and immense and clearly infinite charity, for he loves himself with an infinite love because he alone perfectly knows the infinite good, which is his essence. He also loves all the things that he has made, for the Wise Man says, "For you love all things that are, and hate none of the things which you have made" (Wis 11:25). By his wisdom God knows how to separate evil from good, that is, the defect from the nature; even in the demons and the most wicked men he loves the nature which he made and hates the defect which he did not make.

Moreover, charity exists so truly in God that God himself wanted to be called charity. Saint John speaks this way when he says, "God is charity" (1 Jn 4:16). Our love is very narrow when compared to divine love; there are many things that we do not love because we do not know them. We do not love many of the things we know because we do not easily distinguish in them the good from the evil. We also do not love well many good things and, hence, do not love them with true charity because we are evil and serve cupidity more than charity. Indeed we love God with imperfect charity, not only because we do not love him as much as his goodness deserves, a level to which not even the angels attain, but also because we love him less than we ought and less also than we could, if we devoted ourselves more alertly and diligently to prayer and meditation.

The queen of virtues in the Lord of virtues has as companions singular magnificence, effusive liberality, incredible kindness and generosity, unheard-of patience and long-suffering, a more than fatherly affection and sweetness, never-failing truthfulness and fidelity, a mercy that fills heaven and earth, upright and unswerving justice, and lastly a pure and bright holiness in whose sight the stars are not clean (Jb 25:5) and the seraphim, overcome with awe, cry out, "Holy, Holy, Holy, the Lord, God of hosts" (Is 6:3).

If you examine these things closely, my soul, you will serve God with great fear and trembling in praise and prayer; above all at the holy altar with great reverence and humility in the sight of the angels you will offer to the eternal Father his only-begotten Son for the salvation of the living and the dead!

CHAPTER TWO

The Length of God's Justice Is Revealed by His Truth and Fidelity

Let us proceed to the remaining points. The length of God's justice is revealed in his truth and fidelity. The Prophet says, "The Lord is faithful in all his words" (Ps 144:13; Vulgate), which means: The promises of the Lord, even those announced centuries ago by the mouth of the prophets, never will be or have been frustrated; they are more stable and firm than heaven and earth. Thus the Lord says, "It is easier for heaven and earth to pass away, than for one tittle of the law to fail" (Lk 16:17). Our Lord understands by the law the truth of not only the commandments but also of all the promises. What God has commanded absolutely must be fulfilled or result in punishment. What he has promised is built on an eternal foundation. Therefore, the same Lord says, "Heaven and earth will pass away, but my words will not pass away" (Mt 24:35); Isaiah adds, "The word of our Lord endures forever" (Is 40:8); David adds, "All his commandments are faithful, confirmed forever and ever" (Ps 111:8); and the Apostle, "For God is true, and every man is a liar" (Rom 3:4) and "It is impossible for God to deceive" (Heb 6:18). The reason for these statements is that he cannot be deceived since he is wisdom, nor can he deceive since he is goodness, nor fail since he is omnipotence. But men, however wise, good, and strong, can deceive and be deceived because they neither know everything, nor can accomplish all they wish, and even if they are good when they promise, they can shortly afterward become bad and not wish to live up to their promises.

Be wise, my soul, and trust in God alone, cling to him alone, and cast all your cares on him alone. Walk carefully with the Lord your God and he will take good care of you. Guard with all your strength against offending his justice, and his mercy will always protect you, and you will not fear what man or devil may do to you.

CHAPTER THREE

The Height of God's Justice Is Seen in the Bestowal of our Heavenly Reward

The height of God's justice is seen in the bestowal of the heavenly reward which God as supreme and just judge has prepared for those who have lived holy and just lives.

We may recognize the greatness of this justice first, if we compare God as judge with human judges and, second, if we compare reward with reward, that is, the reward that God will give with what men usually give.

Human judges, even princes or prelates, who have subordinates or servants for many reasons do not usually give a just reward to those to whom it is due. Either they cannot because they do not have such great resources sufficient for rewarding the merits of everybody, or they do not know all the merits of their subordinates. Or they do not know with certitude the just value of their merits since these depend on the mind's sincerity and devotion. Or they do not want to give their subordinates a just reward for their honest labors because of their own dishonesty or avarice or some other vicious inclination. Or, finally, they themselves are prevented by death from giving the reward that they owe, or those to whom they owe the reward depart from this life before they can begin to enjoy the reward of their labors. But for all their good works God gives to all the just not only a reward that is just, but one that surpasses their merits. What more lowly and hidden merit could be imagined than to offer a cup of cold water to a thirsty person? Still the Lord promised a reward even for this deed (Mt 10:42), and Luke writes about the generous repayment promised by the Lord, "Good measure, pressed down, shaken together, running over, shall they pour into your lap" (Lk 6:38). There is no danger that God will run out of an abundance of things with which he can reward all the just since he is the Lord of all things and can with a single word multiply and increase all things beyond measure. Neither is there the fear that he may make a mistake in checking on the number or value of merits. For he is all wise, and all things are open to his eyes. And he searches the reins and hearts of the servants who work well for him so that he knows their attitude, intention, zeal, and diligence in performing all their tasks. No one can suppose that God has the evil intention of cheating his servants and his sons of their just reward since he is trustworthy in all his words. Finally, he cannot die since he is preeminently immortal; since all things live for him, there is no danger that an early death will interfere in any way with a just recompense. Let it stand as fixed and settled that God the just judge will bestow a fitting reward for all the good works of all just men. Hence, it is perfectly safe to deal with God about work and reward, but it is dangerous and stupid to trust in men and to expect from them a just reward for one's labor.

Now let us compare rewards with rewards, divine with human, heavenly with earthly. What, I ask, can men give to those who work all day for them and pass whole nights without sleep and risk their very lives in battles? Oh, human blindness! What can they give except cheap and shoddy trifles, which will quickly fall apart? The rewards that God gives are great, sublime, and eternal. Yet the first are sought after, the latter spurned. Saint John Chrysostom, commenting on Matthew, compares the palaces, cities, and kingdoms of this world that men admire with the mud castles that children make out of clay.[2] Children make these tiny houses and buildings with great effort, but adults openly laugh at them, and often a father or a teacher, seeing little boys neglect their books and spend their time on these trifles, kick them all down, and what was built up with great time and effort is easily smashed down in a moment. The great palaces, towers, citadels, cities, towns, and kingdoms of mortals are only mud castles, if compared with heavenly and eternal goods, and are laughed at by the blessed angels looking down from heaven. Often our heavenly Father effortlessly turns them upside down so we can understand what clear folly they all are. Although few people notice this now, still everybody will understand it on the day of judgment when the knowledge will do little good. Saint Hilary, in his Commentary on chapter 10 of Matthew's Gospel, says the day of judgment will reveal that all these things were nothing and vanity.[3] But let us explain in more detail what are the rewards of heaven which most people now spurn for these trifling rewards of earth.

First, the heavenly kingdom will have most, or rather all, of the good things that can be desired. Everybody who lives in that kingdom will be happy—happiness is the sum total from adding all good things together. Therefore, wisdom and the virtues, the goods of the mind, will be there as well as such goods of the body as beauty, health, and strength and such external goods as riches, pleasure, and glory.

Second, all these will be there in the highest, most perfect, and most eminent degree. God now shows his power in the creation of the world from nothing, his wisdom in its governance and providence, and his charity and goodness in the redemption of the human race by the mystery of the incarnation and passion of his Son; he will show the magnificence of his glory and the munificence of his generosity in distributing rewards, palms, and crowns to those who will triumph over their enemy the devil. Wisdom then will not be speculation about the divinity revealed in created things, but the clear vision of God's essence, the cause of all causes, and the first and highest truth itself. The souls of the saints will shine from this brilliant vision with a light so resplendent that Saint John says of that future glory, "We shall be like to him, for we shall see him just as he is" (1 Jn 3:2). This highest wisdom gives rise to a charity, the queen of the virtues, so burning that it always clings to the highest good and neither wants to be nor can be separated from it. Thus the whole soul and all its faculties remain fixed in the best state. The body shines like the sun, as the Lord himself bears witness in saying, "Then the just will shine forth like the sun in the kingdom of their Father" (Mt 13:44). This will be its beauty. Its health will be immortality; its strength will include impassability; and lastly the body, which now is natural, will then be spiritual (1 Cor 15:44), that is, it will obey the wish of the spirit, surpassing the winds in agility and walking through walls with its subtlety. Their riches will lack nothing as they possess all things with God and in God, for he has placed them over all his goods (Mt 24:47). What shall I say about their pleasure, since it is written, "They shall be inebriated with the plenty of your house; and you shall make them drink of the torrent of your pleasure" (Ps 36:8)? What mind could conceive what a pleasure it is to enjoy the supreme good, to see beauty itself, to taste sweetness itself, to enter the joy of the Lord, that is, to partake of that pleasure which makes God happy? The honor and glory of the saints surpass all eloquence, for God himself will praise all the saints with the whole world, all men and angels as an audience, and he will crown them like victors, and they will be seated on the throne of Christ as participants in his kingdom, something that surpasses every dignity. Thus we read in Revelation, "He who overcomes, I will permit him to sit with me upon my throne; as I also have overcome and have sat with my Father on his throne" (Rv 3:21). The Prophet marveled at the loftiness of this honor when he said, "But to me your friends, O God, are made exceedingly honorable; their principality is exceedingly strengthened" (Ps 139:17).

If we add eternity like a wondrous seasoning to the number and excellence of these goods, who could grasp the greatness of heavenly happiness? But what we can hardly grasp by our thinking we will experience by our possession, if we some day reach that blessed fatherland by living a pious, just, and temperate life (Ti 2:12). Those goods will really endure forever which Christ's servants acquire through God's grace by now working a short while.

What do you say now, my soul? Will you choose to play children's games by building up mud castles and deprive yourself of the possession of a truly everlasting kingdom? Will you choose to delight in the pleasures of cattle, something the mind shudders to think of, when you are invited to indescribable joy with the angels? May your mercy, O Lord, keep this away from the soul of your servant. Rather "pierce my flesh with your fear" (Ps 119:120) and may obedience to your law ever grow sweet for me "above honey and the honeycomb" (Sir 24:27) so that crucifying my flesh with its vices and concupiscences (Gal 5:24), I may dare aspire to the lasting spiritual pleasures of your paradise. Grant, Lord, that your servant may follow in the footsteps of your Christ (1 Pt 2:21), who, "meek and humble of heart" (Mt 11:29), "when he was reviled, did not revile, when he suffered, did not threaten" (1 Pt 2:23), grant me to live "temperately and justly and piously in this world" so that I can with some confidence look for "the blessed hope and glorious coming of our great God and Savior, Jesus Christ" (Ti 2:12, 13).

CHAPTER FOUR

On the Depth of Justice with Which God Prepared Eternal Punishment for Sinners

Our remaining task is to consider the justice which God exercises by punishing sinners in the deepest abyss of hell. If we do this carefully and attentively, we can really understand how true is what the Apostle teaches in the Letter to the Hebrews, "It is a fearful thing to fall into the hands of the living God" (Heb 10:36).

Let us follow the order that we used for justice in rewarding the merits of the saints. God the just judge will have a record of all sins, even slight ones such as an idle word, for as we read in the Gospel, "But I tell you, that of every idle word men speak, they shall give an account on the day of judgment" (Mt 12:36). Men indeed do not punish many sins either because they cannot when the guilty fight back or flee, or because they do not know that the sins have been committed or they are not verified by proper witnesses, or because they are unwilling to punish them when they have been corrupted by bribes or overwhelmed with favors or depraved by their own malice. But God is omnipotent so that no one resists his power; he is everywhere so that no one can hide from him: "Whither shall I go from your spirit or whither shall I flee your face? If I ascend into heaven, you are there; if I descend to hell, you are present" (Ps 139:7, 8). Moreover, he is most wise and knows all things, even the hidden and obscure things in the deep recesses of the heart, nor does he lack witnesses to verify the crimes since for the Lord men's consciences take the place of a thousand witnesses. Lastly, no bribes or favors can corrupt God's justice since he has no need for our goods. The result is that no sin, neither the greatest nor the least, neither the most grave nor the slightest, can escape God's justice that avenges and punishes sin unless it has been previously washed away by repentance. To the degree that his mercy now abounds with forgiving, after this life his justice will be rigid and severe in punishing. Isaiah says of the present life, "In the acceptable time I have heard you, and the day of salvation I have helped you" (Is 49:8). Explaining this in his Second Letter to the Corinthians, the Apostle says, "Behold, now is the acceptable time; behold, now is the day of salvation (2 Cor 6:2). As for the future time after this life Zephaniah exclaims, "That day is a day of wrath, a day of tribulation and distress, a day of calamity and misery, a day of darkness and obscurity, a day of clouds and whirlwinds, a day of the trumpet and alarm" (Zep 1:15, 16).

Not only will all sins be punished, but they will be punished with horrible punishments which will be so massive that only a few can now imagine them. Just as the eye has not seen nor the ear heard nor has it entered into the heart of man what God has prepared for those who love him (1 Cor 2:9), so too the eye has not seen nor the ear heard nor has it entered into the heart of man what God has prepared for those who hate him. The punishments of sinners in hell will be many, terrible, and pure, that is, unmixed with any consolations, and what infinitely increases their misery, they will be everlasting.

They will be many, I say, because each of the faculties of the soul and each of the senses of the body will have its torturers. Weigh the words of the supreme judge's sentence which are found in the Gospel, "Depart from me, accursed ones, into the everlasting fire" (Mt 25:41). "Depart" he says, that is, move away from the fellowship of the blessed, deprived forever of the vision of God, which is the highest and essential happiness and ultimate end for which you were created. "Accursed ones," that is, cherish no further hope for any sort of blessing; you will be stripped of any life of grace, any hope of salvation; the water of wisdom will no more rain upon you, nor the dew of good inspirations. No longer will the ray of heavenly light enlighten you, nor will the grace of repentance sprout in you, nor the flower of charity nor the fruit of good works. "The Orient from on high" (Lk 1:78) will never again visit you from that moment on; you will lack not only spiritual goods but also physical ones, not only eternal ones but temporal ones. For you will have no riches, no pleasures, no solace, but you will be like the fig tree that I cursed, which immediately dried up roots and all (Mt 21:19).

"In the fire," that is, into the oven of blazing and inextinguishable fire which will take hold not of one member, but of all your members at the same time and burn them with the sharpest pain. "Everlasting," that is, into the fire which does not need firewood to keep burning forever, but is whipped up by the breath of God almighty so that as your guilt will never be destroyed, so there will never be an end to your punishment. Rightly then does the Prophet Isaiah cry, "Which of you can dwell with devouring fire? Which of you shall dwell with everlasting burnings?" (Is 33:14), as if he were saying no one at all could bear it patiently, but they would be forced against their will to bear it in impatience, anger, and despair. He adds, "Their worm shall not die and their fire shall not be quenched" (Is 66:24). Our Lord repeats these words more than once in Mark's Gospel (Mk 9:43, 45, 47). He includes the worm of conscience and of the memory of this time when sinners, had they wanted, could have escaped punishment with a little effort and enjoyed everlasting joys.

No one should think that the damned can find a little relief by walking about and changing their place; hear what the Lord himself says, "Bind his hands and feet and cast him forth into the darkness outside, where there will be the weeping, and gnashing of teeth" (Mt 22:13). Those wretches, bound hand and foot by eternal chains, will lie forever in the same place, deprived of the light of the sun, moon, and stars, scorched by burning fire, weeping and lamenting and gnashing their teeth in their fury and desperation.

In hell those who are thrust down into that place full of horror will suffer not only terrible pain, but also the extreme lack of all things, shame and disgrace full of acute embarrassment and confusion. In a flash they will lose their palaces, fields, vineyards, cattle, oxen, clothing, and lastly their gold, silver, and precious gems and will suffer such destitution that with the rich banqueter they will desire and beg for a drop of cold water and not be heard (Lk 16:24–26). Those proud and boastful men who in the present time put up with no injury and rank their dignity above everything else will see before the audience of the whole human race and all the angels, the largest audience that ever was or will be, all their crimes revealed and publicly exhibited, even those committed in the dark or hidden in the recesses of the heart, even the most shameful betrayals, robberies, incests, and sacrileges. As the Apostle says in his First Letter to the Corinthians, when the Lord comes to judge the world, he "will both bring to light the things hidden in darkness and make manifest the counsels of hearts; and then everyone will have his praise for God" (1 Cor 4:5), and doubtless every sinful and wicked man will also receive reproach from God. So great will be the shame and confusion of wicked men before that audience that Saint Basil does not fear to say in his commentary on Psalm 33 that this will be the heaviest of all punishments, especially for hypocrites, the proud, and all those who in their quest for glory made honor their God, or rather their idol, in this world.[4]

If what we have said about the loss of all goods, both heavenly and earthly, and about the bitter pains, ignominy, and shame were to have an end or at least were mixed with some sort of consolation or refreshment like all the miseries of this life, then they might be considered somewhat tolerable, but since it is absolutely certain and beyond any doubt that, just as the happiness of the blessed will continue forever without mixture of misery, so the unhappiness of the damned will last without any mixture of relief forever, that is, for world without end. They must be blind men and fools who do not make every effort to attain to the kingdom of heaven and heavenly happiness, regardless of any trials and dangers and shame and death, which the Apostle calls light and passing (2 Cor 4:17).

CHAPTER FIVE

Why the Punishments of the Damned Are Eternal

Perhaps somebody will wonder why the most merciful God has established such savage and lasting punishments for men's sins, which pass away instantly and do not seem all that serious. Let him hear what Saint Augustine says in his book *The City of God:* "Anyone who thinks that such damnation is excessive or unjust clearly does not know how to measure how great was the wickedness in sinning where it was so easy not to sin." He adds, "Who can sufficiently explain how much evil there is in disobeying in an easy matter a command that carried so much authority and threatened such dire punishment?"[5] Augustine is talking about the sin of the first man, but the same argument applies to all sins. If we weigh this on fair and true scales, we will find that every mortal sin is most serious for three reasons: It is a terrible thing for a creature to disobey his Creator since an infinite gap separates the dignity of the Creator from lowliness of creature. By nature the creature is a servant, and by nature the Creator is Lord. And whatever the creature is and has he owes to the Creator, though the Creator owes nothing to the creature. Second, even if the commands of the Creator were hard, still the creature should obey. But "his commandments are not burdensome" (1 Jn 5:3), and our Savior himself calls his yoke easy and his burden light (Mt 11:30). How great and inexcusable is the guilt when the little worms of the earth do not obey their Creator in such an easy matter. Moreover, if God had not threatened sinners with the punishment of eternal death, maybe man could have fabricated an excuse for his sin, but who will make excuses for his obstinacy in sin when he has been threatened so often and so clearly with eternal punishment by the prophets and apostles?

Lastly, if the guilt of the damned were not eternal, we might wonder why the punishment for sin was going to be eternal, but since the obstinacy of the damned is eternal, why should we wonder if the punishment is also eternal? But this will hardened in evil, which will be common to men who are damned and to the devils, this will, I say, which will ever remain stable and unmoved in its perversion and aversion from God, its highest good, makes holy men shrink in horror from mortal sin more than from the fire of hell. Listen to what the Englishman Eadmer writes about Saint Anselm in the second book of his biography. He says, "On my conscience as witness I do not lie that often we heard him [Anselm] under witness of truth assert that, if he saw bodily on one side the frightfulness of sin and on the other the pain of hell and was forced to be immersed in one of them, he would choose hell rather than sin. He also used to say something else perhaps no less surprising to some people, namely, that he would prefer to go to hell pure and innocent of sin than gain the kingdom of heaven defiled by the stain of sin."[6] If that holy man said and thought this because he was illumined by God and recognized that the gravity of sin was greater than the punishment of hell, how much more will God, who penetrates the evil, filthiness, and perversity of sin right to the bottom, judge justly that the punishment for sin which he himself established from all eternity is fair?

Make no mistake, my soul; be not deceived nor be like those

who "profess to know God but by their works they disown him" (Ti 1:16). Many people have faith, but a faith which is habitual rather than active, like a sword buried in its scabbard. If they believed actively and reflected with earnest faith that God is faithful and just and has really prepared punishments that are harsh, never-ending, and unmixed with consolation for the wicked, it would be impossible for them to act as they do and drink, as is said in Job (Jb 15:16), iniquity like water, that is, they commit so many grave sins with such ease, equanimity, and cheerfulness as if sinners deserved rewards rather than punishment. Do you, I say, trust firmly and realize in faith that in the present time God is the Father of mercies (2 Cor 1:3) and is prepared to forgive mercifully the sins of all who truly repent, but this same God after this life will indeed be a God of vengeance (Ps 94:1) and will require from sinners those punishments which he has prepared and commanded his prophets and apostles to preach and to hand down in writing for the memory of posterity? Thus it will be that, lifted aloft on the two wings of the fear of intolerable punishments and the hope of supreme rewards, you will pass safely through the dangers of the present life and attain to life and rest everlasting. Amen.

NOTES

Note to the Dedication

1. On Pietro Aldobrandini (1571–1621), see *Dizionario biografico degli Italiani* II, 107–112. He was made a cardinal together with Bellarmine in 1593 by his uncle Clement VIII, during whose pontificate he was a major figure.

Notes to the Introduction

1. When Bellarmine speaks of the Apostle, he is always referring to Saint Paul. When he speaks of the Prophet he is generally referring to David in the psalms. This was common usage in Bellarmine's time.

2. Saint Augustine, *City of God* [De civitate Dei] XIX, c. 19 [*PL* 41, 647–648].

3. Saint Augustine, *Confessions* [Confessionum libri tredecim] X, c. 40 [*PL* 32, 807].

4. Saint Gregory the Great, *Pastoral Care* [Regulae pastoralis liber] II, c. 5 [*PL* 77, 32–33].

5. Saint Bernard, *On Consideration* [De consideratione libri quinque] I, 1–9 *passim* [*PL* 182, 727–739].

6. The Gradual Psalms are Psalms 120–134.

Notes to Step I

1. Saint Basil's sermon is preserved in a Latin translation by Rufinus [*PG* 31, 1734–1744]; the words "Consider yourself" are attributed to Moses by Saint Basil; cf. col. 1734. Rufinus here follows the *Vetus Latina* for Dt 4:9, as does Saint Ambrose [*PL* 14, 273].

2. Saint Augustine, *Confessions* IX, c. 6 [*PL* 32, 769].

3. Saint Cyprian, *Testimonies against the Jews* [Testimoniorum libri tres adversus Judaeos] III, c. 4 [*PL* 4, 764].

4. *Enchiridion Symbolorum*, ed. A. Denzinger and A. Schönmetzer (Barcelona, 1963), n. 390; subsequent references will be to *DS*, with the appropriate number. Bellarmine is paraphrasing rather than quoting.

5. This citation seems based on *Homily 10 on the Six Days of Creation*, formerly attributed to Saint Basil [*PG* 29, 207].

6. Saint Augustine, *On Nature and Grace* [De natura et gratia] c. 70 [*PL* 44, 290].

Notes to Step II

1. Saint Gregory Nazianzen has only one sermon on Easter [*PG* 35, 395–402], which contains nothing on the idea of man as microcosm. Bellarmine seems rather to have had in mind Saint Gregory of Nyssa's *Third Sermon on Easter* [*PG* 46, 667], which touches on the microcosm theme.

2. Saint Jerome, *Commentary on Isaiah* [Commentariorum in Isaiam prophetam libri XIX] XI, c. 40 [*PL* 24, 420].

3. Saint Thomas Aquinas, *The Summa of Theology* [Summa theologiae] Ia, q. 50, a. 3.

4. Saint Dionysius, *The Celestial Hierarchy* [De hierarchia caelesti] c. 14 [*PG* 3, 321–326]. Dionysius, or Denis, the Areopagite is mentioned (Acts 17:34) as a convert of Saint Paul. An ancient tradition named him bishop of Athens; a much later tradition made him bishop of Paris. An unknown Syrian monk about A.D. 500 wrote several treatises, of which four survive, under Dionysius's name. These treatises, strongly influenced by the Neoplatonist philosopher Proclus, long remained influential. In his *Ecclesiastical Writers*, Bellarmine defends the authenticity of these works in the face of the objections of Erasmus and others.

5. Saint Thomas Aquinas, *The Summa of Theology* Ia, q. 50, a. 4.

6. Theodoret's *Religious History* [Religiosa historia] [*PG* 82, 1283–1496] is a series of biographical sketches of early Eastern monks and hermits. Bellarmine refers to the work in general rather than to a specific passage.

7. Saint Ignatius of Antioch, *Letter to the Romans* 5 [*PG* 5, 691–692].

8. The Roman Breviary for January 21, Feast of Saint Agnes, response to the second lesson of Matins.

Note to Step III

1. Saint Augustine, *Confessions* I, c. 1 [*PL* 32, 661].

NOTES

Notes to Step IV

1. Saint Augustine, *On the Predestination of the Saints* [De praedestinatione sanctorum] c. 8 [*PL* 44, 971].

2. Saint Augustine, *Confessions* IX, c. 1 [*PL* 32, 763].

3. The Roman Breviary, hymn at the beginning of Nones.

4. This famous statement stands at the beginning of Aristotle's *Metaphysics*.

Note to Step V

1. Saint Prosper of Aquitaine, *On the Vocation of All the Nations* [De vocatione omnium gentium] II, c. 26 [*PL* 51, 711].

Notes to Step VI

1. Saint Gregory the Great, *The Moral Commentary on Job* [Moralium libri in Iob] XXXII, c. 24 [*PL* 76, 668].

2. Saint Augustine, *Homilies on the Psalms* [Enarrationes in Psalmos]. On Psalm 70 (71), sermon 2, n. 5 [*PL* 36, 895].

3. Saint Augustine, *On Holy Virginity* [De sancta virginitate] c. 24, 25 [*PL* 40, 408–409].

4. Saint Augustine, *Confessions* X, c. 27 [*PL* 32, 795].

5. Saint Bonaventure, *Life of Saint Francis* [Vita Sancti Francisci] XII, 7.

6. Marcos da Silva, *The Chronicle and Institutions of the Order of . . . S. Francis* (St. Omers, 1618; photographically reprinted, Ilkey, Yorkshire, 1977), I, c. 30, p. 58.

7. Saint Bernard, *On Consideration* I, c. 2 [*PL* 182, 730, 731].

8. Alanus, *Second Life of Saint Bernard the Abbot* [Secunda vita Sancti Bernardi abbatis auctore . . . Alano] c. 21 [*PL* 185, 503–506]. Bellarmine used the same story of Duke William in his sermon "Caritas ignis," preached at Rome in 1582, *Opera oratoria postuma*, IX, 139. The same sermon, 132–141, has many parallels with step 6, chapters 3–6, of the *Ascent*.

Notes to Step VII

1. The distances and speeds postulated by Bellarmine's Ptolemaic cosmology and astronomy were numerically much smaller than those given by modern scientists but were still so large as to defy the human imagination. In contrasting medieval and modern cosmology, C. S. Lewis has observed, "Now of course this is a small distance compared with those of which modern astronomers talk. But we are here considering not the accuracy of the figure but its

imaginative and emotional impact. From that point of view I maintain that the difference . . . is wholly negligible" (*Studies in Medieval and Renaissance Literature* [Cambridge, 1966] pp. 46–47).

2. The pre-Socratic philosophers, especially Empedocles, developed a cosmology based on the four elements. Aristotle, followed by the Stoics, added ether as a fifth element. Aristotle argues for its circular motion in *De caelo* I, 2, 3.

3. Saint Augustine, *Letter* 55, 12–27 [*PL* 33, 210–218].

4. Saint Ignatius of Antioch, *Letter to the Romans* n. 6. [*PG* 5, 692].

5. Saint John Chrysostom, *Homilies on Matthew* [In Matthaeum Homiliae] Homily 8, 2 [*PG* 57, 84–85].

6. Bellarmine used the same simile of a chorus of young women dancing to illustrate the harmony of nature in a sermon of 1582, *Opera oratoria postuma*, IX, 146.

Notes to Step VIII

1. Here Bellarmine follows the Aristotelian and Thomistic rational psychology that was commonplace in his day.

2. Saint Augustine, *Confessions* VIII, c. 9 [*PL* 32, 758].

3. This verse began each of the seven hours in the priest's breviary.

4. Saint Bonaventure, *Life of Saint Francis* V, 8.

Notes to Step IX

1. From the Apostles' Creed.

2. Saint Augustine, *The City of God* XII, c. 9 [*PL* 41, 356].

3. Saint John Chrysostom, *Homilies on the Epistle to the Romans* [In Epistolam ad Romanos Homiliae] Homily 32, 2 [*PG* 60, 678].

Notes to Step X

1. Saint Bernard, *On Consideration* V, c. 13 [*PL* 182, 804–807]. Saint Bernard considers the length, breadth, height, and depth of God in turn, as does Bellarmine in Steps X to XV of the *Ascent*, but their development of the *topos* is very different.

2. Saint Augustine, *Letter* 140 (To Honoratus, On the grace of the New Testament) c. 20, n. 64 [*PL* 33, 566].

3. Saint Augustine, *Homilies on the Psalms*. On Psalm 113 (114), sermon 2, 11 [*PL* 37, 1486].

4. Saint Bernard, *Sermons on the Canticle*, Sermon 23, 16 [*PL* 183, 893].

5. Saint Augustine, *Confessions* IX, c. 10; X, c. 6 [*PL* 32, 774, 783]; *Homilies on the Psalms*. On Psalm 26 (27), sermon 2, 12 [*PL* 36, 205].

Notes to Step XI

1. Saint Augustine, *Homilies on John's Gospel* [In Johannis Evangelium Tractatus]. Homily 24, n. 1 [*PL* 35, 1593].

2. Modern scholars consider this letter spurious. For the text see *PG* 3, 1079–1082.

3. Saint Augustine, *Letter* 187 (To Dardanus) c. 6, 18 [*PL* 33, 839].

4. Saint John Chrysostom, *Homilies on Genesis* [In Genesim Homiliae] Homily 4, c. 1, 4–5 [*PG* 53, 43–44]. Bellarmine is paraphrasing Chrysostom here.

5. Ibid., Homily 6, 3 [*PG* 53, 57].

6. Ibid., Homily 7, 3 [*PG* 53, 64].

7. Saint Augustine, *Homilies on the Psalms*. On Psalm 56 (57), 1 [*PL* 36, 661].

8. Saint Leo the Great, Sermon 67, c. 6 [*PL* 54, 371].

Notes to Step XII

1. Saint Augustine, *City of God* XII, c. 1 [*PL* 41, 349].

2. Saint Augustine, *Letter* 211, 10 [*PL* 33, 962].

3. Saint Basil, *On Virginity*, c. 7. This work, printed in *PG* 30, 669–810, is no longer attributed to Saint Basil by scholars.

4. Scholars today believe that Daniel was indeed written after the events it seems to predict.

5. Saint Augustine, *City of God* II, c. 24 [*PL* 41, 72].

6. Saint Augustine, *On The Divination of Demons* [De divinatione daemonum] c. 3–6 [*PL* 40, 584–587].

7. Saint Gregory the Great, *Dialogues* [Dialogi de vita et miraculis patrum Italicorum] IV, c. 33 [*PL* 77, 376]. Bellarmine's quotation is not verbatim.

8. Saint Jerome, *Commentary on Jeremiah the Prophet* [Commentarii in Ieremiam Prophetam] III, c. 17 [*PL* 24, 819–820].

Notes to Step XIII

1. Galen (129?–199), the greatest Greek medical authority, saw the existence of a Creator reflected in the order of the universe. Cf. Galen, *De usu partium* I, 48; M. T. May, ed. and trans., *Galen on the Usefulness of the Parts of the Body* (Ithaca, 1968) I, p. 100.

2. Saint Augustine, *Confessions* IX, c. 6 [*PL* 33, 769].

3. From the "Exueltet," or prayer at the blessing of the paschal candle in the liturgy for Holy Saturday.

4. Alleluia verse from the Mass for the Assumption of the Virgin, August 15.

5. Collect, Mass for the seventh Sunday after Pentecost; the same idea is found in several hymns in the Roman Breviary.

6. Saint Augustine, *On Order* [De ordine] I, c. 1 [*PL* 32, 978].

7. Ibid. [*PL* 32, 979].

8. Saint Augustine, *On True Religion* [De vera religione] c. 22 [*PL* 34, 140].

Notes to Step XIV

1. Collect, Mass on the day of burial.

2. Saint Augustine, *Homilies on the Psalms.* On Psalm 85 (86), 5 [*PL* 37, 1086].

3. Saint Bonaventure, *Life of Saint Francis* X, 7 and 8.

4. Rufinus, *Ecclesiastical History* [Historia ecclesiastica] I, c. 36 [*PL* 21, 504].

Notes to Step XV

1. Saint Augustine, *On Nature and Grace,* c. 70 [*PL* 44, 290].

2. Saint John Chrysostom, *Homilies on Matthew's Gospel.* Homily 23, 9 [*PG* 57, 318–319].

3. Saint Hilary of Poitiers, *Commentary on Matthew's Gospel* [Commentarius in Matthaeum] 10 [*PL* 9, 972].

4. Saint Basil, *Homily on Psalm* 33 (34), 4 and 8 [*PG* 29, 359, 371].

5. Saint Augustine, *City of God* XIV, c. 15 [*PL* 41, 423].

6. Eadmer, *Life of Saint Anselm* [Vita Sancti Anselmi] II, c. 2 [PL 158, 89–90]. Bellarmine wrongly identifies the author of this work as Edinerus.

The Art of Dying Well

by

Saint Robert Cardinal Bellarmine, S.J.

DEDICATION

To Francesco Sforza,

Cardinal of the Holy Roman Church,

Bishop of Alba,

Robert Cardinal Bellarmine sends hearty greetings.

A few months ago I wrote a little work on the art of dying well both in order to prepare myself for my own coming death and in order to share willingly with my brethren and lords, as is my custom, what I found useful for this greatest of all tasks. However, I decided to dedicate this little work to you, Francesco Sforza, excellent Cardinal, for two reasons. My first reason was so that through you the holy memory of the supreme pontiff, Gregory XIII, might be commended to eternity. For you alone remain alive from all those excellent cardinals, by whose creation that wise pontiff adorned this college of ours, and you alone from the Roman nobility are related through marriage to the Buoncompagni family, itself a noble family. This same Gregory was not only a most gentle lord, but also a most loving father to this religious order of the Society of Jesus which has been my good mother for sixty years. For he gave many letters of commendation to the society, by which he either extended or increased the privileges granted to her by previous pontiffs. He also built at great expense the Roman College and with no less generosity gave the funds whereby the members of the college might be supported. This same holy pontiff built colleges in many places out of the desire for spreading the faith with which he ardently burned, especially the German and Hungarian Colleges at Rome, whose administration he wanted to be in the care of the Society of Jesus.[1] The Society celebrates the memory of this vigilant pontiff at Rome with anniversary Masses and eulogies. I thought it well to append to this letter the generous deeds of so great a pontiff toward the Society of Jesus so that they may also redound to the praise and honor of the illustrious prince, to whom I desire that my books, which are dedicated to him, be not unwelcome.

I now come to the second reason which especially moved me to dedicate these books to you, excellent Cardinal. The argument of the volume does not attract one to read, but rather deters especially men great in political or sacred princedoms. For this book does not contain a philosophical or oratorical or poetic art which might instruct the mind or polish the tongue or delight the ears, but exhorts to meditation on death and to thinking about things which are not generally pleasing to great men, such as poverty, humility, patience, and other true Christian virtues. Therefore, I chose you, a prince with a political and sacred princedom. And relying on your singular humanity, I have dedicated to you the books *The Art of Dying Well*, books of little erudition, but of great utility. And relying on your goodness, I conceived the good hope that these short books will be read by you and that there will be others who will do so in imitation of you. That will be something highly pleasing to me, and I do not think that it is I who have offered you a little gift, but rather that it is I who have received a great gift from you. Farewell.

PREFACE

As I was pondering in my customary retreat, in which I am free from public concerns and am free entirely to myself, what is the reason why so few are eager to learn the art of dying well, which ought to be well known to everyone, no other reason occurred to me than that, as the Wise Man says, the number of fools is infinite (Sir 1:15). For what greater folly can be thought or imagined than to neglect that art upon which depend the greatest and eternal goods and to master with great labor and to practice with much zeal many, almost innumberable other arts by which perishable goods are either preserved or increased. No one who is willing to consider attentively that in death one must render an account to God of all we have done, said, and thought, even of one idle word uttered, while the devil is our accuser, conscience is our witness, God is our judge, and the punishment of eternal death or an everlasting reward is awaiting us, will deny that the art of dying well is the most important of all the arts. We see every day that, while awaiting judgment about even the least matters, the litigants are without rest; one moment they visit the lawyers, the next the prosecutors, and then the judges and the judges' friends and relatives. And in death, while the case is pending before the supreme judge about everlasting life and death, the defendant, often unprepared or overcome by illness, hardly mentally competent, is forced to render an account of those things about which he had never thought when he was in good health. Hence, wretched mortals rush into hell in great numbers, and, as Saint Peter says, "If the just man scarcely will be saved, where will the impious and the sinner appear?" (1 Pt 4:18). Therefore, I considered it worthwhile to warn myself first of all and then my brethren to value highly the art of dying well. And if there are any who have not yet learned this art from other more learned teachers, let them not scorn what we have carefully gathered together about this art from the Sacred Books and from the writings of the masters of old.

But before we come to the rules of this art, I thought it valuable to investigate the nature of death, that is, whether it should be reckoned among the good or bad things. And indeed if death is considered alone, it is doubtless to be esteemed as an evil because it is opposed to life, which is undeniably good. Besides there is the fact that "God made not death, neither has he pleasure in the destruction of the living," but "by the envy of the devil, death came into the world," as the Wise Man teaches (Wis 1:13, 2:24). The Apostle Paul subscribes to this, when he says, "Through one man sin entered into the world and through sin death, and thus death has passed unto all men because all have sinned" (Rom 5:12). Certainly if God did not make death, death is not good, since everything that God has made is good, for Moses says, "God saw all the things that he had made, and they were very good" (Gn 1:31).

Although death is not good in itself, nonetheless the wisdom of God knew how, so to speak, to temper death so that from it there can arise many good things. Hence David sings, "Precious in the sight of the Lord is the death of his saints" (Ps 116:15), and the Church, speaking of Christ, says, "He destroyed our death by dying and restored our life by rising."[1] Certainly a death that destroyed death and restored life cannot but be very good. Hence, at least some death must be called good even if not every death. Therefore, Saint Ambrose did not hesitate to entitle his book *The Good of Death*, in which he shows quite clearly that, although born of sin, death has many good uses.[2]

There is another reason that shows that, although death is evil in itself, it can produce many good things by the grace of God. For we derive the first great good from death when it puts an end to the many and great miseries of this life. Holy Job expressly complains of the miseries of the present life. He says, "Man born of a woman, living for a short time, is filled with many miseries" (Jb 14:1). Ecclesiastes says, "I praised the dead rather than the living. And I judged him happier than them both, that is not yet born, nor has seen the evils that are done under the sun" (Eccl 4:2–3). Ecclesiasticus, however, adds, "Great labor is created for all men, and a heavy yoke is upon the children of Adam, from the day of their coming out of their mother's womb until the day of their burial in the mother of us all" (Sir 40:1). The Apostle also complains of the miseries of this life and says, "Unhappy man that I am! Who will deliver me from the body of this death?" (Rom 7:24).

Therefore, by these proofs from the words of God it is sufficiently established that death has in itself the ability to free man from the many miseries of this life. Second, death brings an excellent good, when it becomes the door from our prison to the kingdom. That was revealed by the Lord to John the Apostle and Evangelist when he was exiled for the faith on the island of Patmos. He says, "I heard a voice from heaven saying, 'Write: Blessed are the dead who die in the Lord henceforth. Yes, says the Spirit, let them rest from their labors, for their works follow them' " (Rv 14:13). Clearly the death of the saints is blessed, since it leads the soul forth from the prison cell of the flesh by the order of the heavenly king and brings it into the heavenly kingdom where, dead to their labors, the holy souls rest in comfort and receive for the reward of their good works the crown of the kingdom.

And death brings no small benefit to the souls who are led off to purgatory, since it frees them from the fear of hell and makes them certain of future everlasting happiness. Indeed, death's arrival seems to bring some benefit even to reprobates, when it separates them from the body and prevents the measure of their punishments from increasing any further. On account of these immense values death does not reveal to good people a dreadful and terrifying, but a gentle and friendly countenance. Thus the Apostle confidently cries out, "For me to live is Christ and to die is gain . . . desiring to depart and be with Christ" (Phil 1:21, 23). And in the First Letter to the Thessalonians he tells good Christians that they should not be saddened by the deaths of their dear ones or mourn them as dead, but look upon them as asleep (1 Thes 4:13). There lived a holy woman in the memory of our grandfathers, Catherine Adorni of Genoa, who so burned with the love of Christ that she longed with an incredible desire to be dissolved and go to her Beloved. Hence, as though captured by the love of death, she often praised it as most fair and beautiful, blaming in it only that it flees from those who seek it and seeks those who flee from it. Let the reader consult *The Life of Blessed Catherine of Genoa*, chapter VII.[3]

From what we have said we see that death, as the offspring of sin, is evil, but that by the grace of Christ, who deigned to undergo death for us, it has been rendered for us in many ways useful and salutary, lovable and desirable.

BOOK ONE

CHAPTER ONE

The first rule for dying well, which is that one who desires to die well should live well.

I now come to the rules of the art of dying well. We will divide this art into two parts. In the first part we give the rules that we should use while we are in good health. In the second we will give those that we will need when we suffer such a dangerous illness that death is probably imminent. In the first part we shall begin by providing the rules which pertain to the virtues, then those which pertain to the sacraments. For by these two we are especially helped both to live well and to die well. However, a general rule should, it seems, be set before these, namely, that one should live well if one desires to die well. For since death is merely the end of life, surely everyone who lives well up to the end cannot die badly, since he has never lived badly, just as he who has always lived badly dies badly, and one cannot fail to die badly if he has never lived well. We see this in all sorts of examples. For those who keep to the right path arrive without fail at the place where they are going. But those who wander from the right path will never find its end. And those who diligently apply themselves to the study of the sciences emerge in a short time as knowledgable or even as teachers. But those who frequent the schools, but do not prepare their minds to learn the disciplines, waste their time and effort.

Someone might raise as an objection the good thief who always lived badly, yet ended his life well and happily. That was not the case; rather the good thief lived piously and holily and for that reason met a good and holy death. Though he spent the greater part of his life in crime, nonetheless he spent another part of his life in such a holy manner that he easily rid himself of past sins and acquired extraordinary merit. For burning with love for God, he openly defended Christ from the calumnies of the wicked; and burning equally with love for neighbor, he admonished and corrected his own blaspheming companion and tried to recall him to a better life. For he was still living this mortal life when he said to his companion, "Do you not even fear God, seeing that you are under the same sentence? And we indeed justly, for we are receiving what our deeds deserved; but this man has done nothing wrong" (Lk 23:40–41). This same thief had not died, but was still living, when he cried out loudly, confessing and invoking Christ, "Lord, remember me when you come into your kingdom" (Lk 23:42). Thus he was apparently one of those who came to the vineyard last and received his reward before those who came first (Mt 20:8–9).

Hence, the statement is true and universal: One who lives badly, dies badly. Yet no one can deny that it is dangerous to put off conversion from sins to justice until the end of life, that they are far happier who have borne the yoke of God's law "from their youth" (Lam 3:27), as Jeremiah says, and that those are most happy in every respect who "were purchased from among men, the first fruits unto God and unto the Lamb," who not only "were not defiled with women," but "in their mouth was found no lie; they are without blemish before the throne of God" (Rv 14:4–5). Such was the Prophet Jeremiah and John, greater than a prophet, and especially the Mother of the Lord, and many other men and women, whom only God in his knowledge knows. Let our first thesis remain that the rule of dying well depends upon the rule of living well.

CHAPTER TWO

The second rule of the art of dying well, which is to die to the world.

Indeed for anyone to live well, he must, first of all, die to the world before he dies to bodily life. For all who live for the world are dead to God, and no one can begin to live for God unless he first dies to the world. This truth is proclaimed in Holy Scripture with such great evidence that only infidels and unbelievers could doubt it. And since two or three witnesses establish any claim (Dt 19:15; Mt 18:16; 2 Cor 13:1), I will produce the apostles, Saints John, James, and Paul, witnesses beyond all exception, in whom the Holy Spirit, who is the Spirit of truth, spoke most clearly. John the Apostle and Evangelist wrote and has Christ himself say, "The prince of this world is coming, and in me he has nothing" (Jn 14:30), where he understands by the prince of this world the devil, who is prince of all the wicked. And by this world he understands the assembly of all sinners who love the world and are loved by the world. A bit later he says, "If the world hates you, know that it has hated me before you. If you were of the world, the world would love what is its own. But because you are not of the world, but I have chosen you out of the world, therefore the world hates you" (Jn 15:18–19). And in another place, he says, "Not for the world do I pray, but for those whom you have given me" (Jn 17:9), where Christ clearly shows that by the word *world* is understood those who in the judgment will hear along with their prince, "Depart from me, accursed ones, into the everlasting fire" (Mt 25:41). Saint John also adds in his Letter, "Do not love the world, or the things that are in the world. If anyone loves the world, the love of the Father is not in him; because all that is in the world is the lust of the flesh, and the lust of the eyes, and the pride of life, which is not from the Father, but is from the world. And the world with its lust is passing away, but he who does the will of God abides forever" (1 Jn 2:15–17).

Now let us hear his fellow apostle, James, who speaks as follows in his Letter: "Adulterers, do you not know that the friendship of this world is enmity with God? Therefore, whoever wishes to be a friend of this world becomes an enemy of God" (Jas 4:4). Finally, let us hear Paul, the fellow apostle of both, the vessel of election.

Writing to all the faithful, in the First Letter to the Corinthians, he said, "You ought to have gone forth from this world" (1 Cor 5:10), and adds in the same letter, "When we are judged, we are being chastised by the Lord that we may not be condemned with this world" (1 Cor 11:32), where he clearly states that the whole world will be condemned on the last day. But by "world" he does not mean heaven and earth or all the men who are in the world, but only those who love the world. For just and good men, in whom there reigns the love of God and not the lust of the flesh, are indeed in the world, but not of the world. The unjust and wicked, however, are not only in the world, but also of the world. The love of God does not reign in their hearts, but the lust of the flesh, that is, wantonness, and the lust of the eyes, that is, avarice, and the pride of life, that is, becoming so puffed up in their minds that they raise themselves above others and imitate the arrogance and pride of Lucifer, not the humility and gentleness of Christ Jesus.

Hence, if anyone wants to master the art of dying well, he ought seriously, not in word and tongue, but in deed and truth, leave the world and even die to the world and say with the Apostle, "The world is crucified to me, and I to the world" (Gal 6:14). This endeavor is not a children's game, but something serious and difficult. And so, when asked whether those who are saved are few, the Lord answered, "Strive to enter by the narrow gate" (Lk 13:24) and more clearly in Matthew, "Enter by the narrow gate. For wide is the gate and broad is the way that leads to destruction, and many there are who enter that way. How narrow the gate and close the way that leads to life! And few there are who find it" (Mt 7:13–14).

To live in the world and to despise the goods of the world is something truly difficult. To see beautiful things and not love them, to taste sweet things and not to take delight, to despise honors, to seek labors, gladly to take the last place, to yield to all others the higher positions, and finally to live in the flesh as if without flesh, it seems, should be called an angelic rather than a human life. And yet in writing to the church of Corinth, in which almost all were living with wives and, hence, were not monks, not hermits, but, as we now say, laymen, the Apostle said, "But this I say, brethren, the time is short; it remains that those that have wives be as if they had none; and those who weep, as though not weeping; and those who rejoice, as though not rejoicing; and those who buy, as not possessing; and those who use this world, as though not using it, for this world as we see it is passing away" (1 Cor 7:29–31).

By these words the Apostle is urging the faithful to be alive to the hope of heavenly happiness and to be as little affected by earthly things as if they were not involved with them at all. Let them love their wives, but with as moderate a love as if they did not have them. If it is necessary to weep because of the loss of children or fortunes, let them weep as moderately as if they were not saddened or weeping. If joy presents itself because of earnings or honor acquired, let them rejoice as moderately as if they did not rejoice, that is, as if the joy were not theirs. If they buy a field or a house, let them be as affected by those things as if they did not possess them. Finally, the Apostle commands that we live in the world as if we were strangers or pilgrims, not citizens. This is more plainly stated by the Apostle Peter when he says, "I exhort you as strangers and pilgrims to abstain from carnal desires which war against the soul" (1 Pt 2:11). For this blessed prince of the apostles wishes us to live in our own city and home as if we were living in a foreign home and country, little worried whether there is a lack or an abundance in that place. He commands this so that we abstain "from carnal desires which war against the soul." For carnal desires do not readily arise when what we look upon does not really involve us. This then is what not being in the world means for those who are dead to the world and live only for God. For this reason they do not fear bodily death which brings them not loss, but gain, according to the words of the Apostle Paul, "For me to live is Christ and to die is gain" (Phil 1:21).

How many, I ask, will we find in our times so dead to the world that they have already also learned to die well to the flesh and thus have assured their salvation? I certainly do not doubt that in the Catholic Church, not only in monasteries and among clerics, but also in the world there are found many holy people, truly dead to the world, who have learned the art of dying well. But I also see that there are obviously many, not only not dead to the world, but immersed in the world and ardent lovers of pleasures, honors, and riches. Unless they decide to die to the world and really do die to the world, they will undoubtedly die a bad death and, as the Apostle says, "be condemned with this world" (1 Cor 11:32).

But the lovers of the world will perhaps say it is too difficult to die to the world while we are in the world and to pay no attention to those goods which God created for men to enjoy. So I answer them that God does not want or command us to completely neglect or cast aside wealth and honor and worldly goods. For even Abraham, a close friend of God, possessed vast riches. Also David and Hezechiah and Josiah, we read, were wealthy kings and also close friends of God, and we can say the same thing of many Christian kings and emperors. Therefore, the goods of this world, wealth, honors, and pleasures, are not completely forbidden to Christians, as is the immoderate love of things of this world which is called by John the Apostle "the lust of the flesh, the lust of the eyes, and the pride of life" (1 Jn 2:16). Abraham was certainly a very wealthy man, but he not only used his riches moderately, but was ready to cast aside everything immediately at a word from God. For he did not spare his only and good son whom he loved when God commanded that he be sacrificed by his father (Gn 22:1–19). How much more easily would he have cast aside all his wealth at a word from God? Abraham was indeed rich in possessions, but he was richer in faith and charity. He was not of this world; he was dead to the world. And the same can be said of other holy men who, though endowed with riches, power, and glory, even with kingdoms and empires, were poor in spirit. Dead to the world and living only for God, they had learned thoroughly the art of dying well.

Hence, it is not abundance of wealth, eminence of honor, or kingdoms and empires that make one to be of the world, even if he lives in the world, but "the lust of the flesh, the lust of the eyes, and the pride of life," which in a word is called desire and is opposed to divine love. So if anyone begins, with God's help, truly to love God for his own sake and his neighbor as himself, he will begin to leave the world, and as love increases, desire will lessen. He will begin to die to the world. For love cannot grow without desire lessening. Thus there will occur what seemed impossible when desire reigned. It will become quite easy for a man living in the world not to be of the world, as love grows and desire lessens. For what is an unbearable and hard burden for desire is for love a gentle yoke and light burden.

Thus our previous statement, that leaving the world and dying to the world is not a children's game, but something very serious and difficult, most accurately applies to those who have not experienced the power of the grace of God and tasted the sweetness of love and who are natural men without the Spirit. For once one has tasted the Spirit, all flesh loses its flavor. So everyone who seriously desires to master the art of dying, upon which depends eternal salvation and all true happiness, should not put off leaving the world and dying to the world, since no one can live for the world and for God and since no one can enjoy both earth and heaven.

CHAPTER THREE

The third rule of the art of dying well, which is the three theological virtues.

We maintained in the previous chapter that those who leave the world, but do not die to the world, cannot die well. Now we have to add what those who have died to the world must do in order to live for God. For dying well is only granted to those who have lived well, as we showed in the first chapter. The essence of living well is stated by the Apostle in the First Letter to Timothy in these words, "The purpose of this charge is charity from a pure heart and a good conscience and faith unfeigned" (1 Tm 1:5). The Apostle was aware of the Lord's answer to the man who had asked, "What must I do to gain eternal life?" (Lk 10:25). For the Lord answered, "If you wish to enter life, keep the commandments" (Mt 19:17). But Paul wanted to explain in the fewest words possible the purpose of the primary commandment, upon which depends the whole law as well as all understanding and fulfillment of the law and the way to eternal life. At the same time he wanted to teach the virtues necessary for perfect justice. Regarding these he said elsewhere, "So there abide faith, hope, and charity, these three; but the greatest of these is charity" (1 Cor 13:13). Thus he says, "The purpose of this charge is charity," that is, the purpose of all the commandments, whose observance is necessary for living well, lies in charity. And thus in order for one to have love of God, let him fulfill all the commandments that belong to the second tablet. The Apostle also explains this second part, which might appear rather obscure, when he says in the Letter to the Romans, "He who loves his neighbor has fulfilled the law. For 'You shall not commit adultery; you shall not kill; you shall not steal; you shall not speak false testimony; you shall not covet'; and if there is any other commandment, it is summed up in this saying, 'You shall love your neighbor as yourself.' Love of neighbor does no evil. Love therefore is the fulfillment of the law" (Rom 13:8–10). From this reasoning each person can understand for himself that all the commandments which refer to worshiping God are fulfilled in love alone. For as love of neighbor does not work evil toward the neighbor, so too the love of God does not work evil toward God. Hence, the fulfillment of the law, both with respect to God and with respect to the neighbor, is love.

The Apostle also explains what is true and perfect love both toward God and toward neighbor, when he says, "Charity from a pure heart, a good conscience, and faith not feigned." Regarding these words we follow Saint Augustine in the introduction to his homily on Psalm 31 and understand by good conscience the virtue of hope, which is one of the three theological virtues.[1] Hope is called good conscience because it arises from a good conscience, just as despair arises from a bad conscience. From this comes the saying of Saint John, "Beloved, if our heart does not condemn us, we have confidence toward God" (1 Jn 3:20). Therefore, there are three virtues in which consists the perfection of the Christian law: charity from a pure heart, hope from a good conscience, and faith not feigned. But as in the order of perfection charity is first, so in the order of generation faith is first, in accordance with the words of the same Apostle, "So there abide faith, hope, and charity, these three; but the greatest of these is charity" (1 Cor 13:13).

Let us begin with faith which is born first in the hearts of those being justified. Not without reason did the blessed Apostle add to "faith," "not feigned." For faith begins justification, provided it is true and sincere, not false and feigned. The faith of heretics does not begin justification, because it is not true, but false faith. The faith of bad Catholics does not begin justification, because it is not sincere, but feigned faith. It is called feigned in two ways: either when someone really does not believe, but feigns that he believes, or when he indeed believes, but does not live as he believes one should live. It seems that the words of Saint Paul in the Letter to Titus have to be understood in both ways, "They profess to know God, but by their works they disown him" (Ti 1:16). This is the way the Fathers, Saint Jerome in his commentary and Saint Augustine in *Homily* 31, dealing with the words of the Apostle, interpret them.[2]

In the light of this first virtue of the just man it is readily apparent that many do not live well and thus do not die well. I will not even mention unbelievers, pagans, heretics, and atheists, who certainly do not know the art of dying well. Among Catholics how many profess in words to know God, but deny it in actions? How many profess that Christ is the judge of the living and the dead and yet live as though they were going to have no judge? How many profess that the Mother of the Lord is a virgin and yet do not fear to blaspheme and call her a whore? How many praise prayer, fasting, almsgiving, and the other acts of the virtues, but practice all the opposite vices? I omit the rest which everyone knows. Let them not boast that they have unfeigned faith. Either they do not believe what they falsely say they believe, or they do not live as the Catholic faith commands that they should live. Let them acknowledge that they have not yet begun to live well. Let them not hope that they will die happily, unless, under the inspiration of the Lord's grace, they master the art of living well and of dying well.

The second virtue of the just man is hope, or a good conscience, as our teacher, the Apostle Paul, thought it should be called in this passage. This virtue arises from faith, for one who either does not know the true God or does not believe that he is powerful and merciful cannot hope in God. A good conscience is very important for exercising and strengthening hope so that it can be called not merely hope, but also trust. For with what attitude can one approach God and ask favors from him, if he is aware of a sin he has committed against God, but has not yet expiated by true penance? For who asks favors from an enemy? Who is confident of being helped by someone he is sure is angry with him? Hear what the Wise Man thinks of the hope of the wicked. "The hope of the wicked," he says, "is as dust, which is blown away with the wind, and as a thin froth which is dispersed by the storm, and a smoke that is scattered abroad by the wind, and as the remembrance of a guest of one day that passes by" (Wis 5:15). Such are the words of the Wise Man who wisely warns the wicked that their hope is fragile and not solid, short-lived and not long-lived. For they can in some fashion, while they live, hope that they will sometime do penance and be reconciled to God. But when death comes, unless God helps them with special mercy and inspires them to do penance, their hope will be turned to despair, and along with the other wicked men they will say what we read in the same passage: "Therefore we have erred from the way of truth, and the light of justice has not shined for us. What has pride profited us? Or what advantage has the boasting of riches brought us? All those things are passed away like a shadow" (Wis 5:6, 8–9). The Wise Man has wisely warned us that, if we wish to live well and die happily, we should not dare to cling even for a second to our sins, deceived by the empty hope that much of our life still lies ahead and that we will do serious penance in plenty of time. For this vain confidence has deceived and will continue to deceive many, unless they learn the art of dying well while there is still time.

There remains the third virtue, which is rightly called the queen of the virtues, namely, charity. With it no one perishes; without it no one lives, neither on the way nor in the fatherland. True charity is said to be that which arises "from a pure heart," not that a pure heart properly speaking generates charity. "For love is from God" (1 Jn 4:7), as Saint John says, and Saint Paul speaks even more clearly, "The charity of God is poured forth in our hearts by the Holy Spirit who has been given to us" (Rom 5:5). Charity is said to be from a pure heart, because charity is not kindled in an impure heart, but in one purified from errors by divine faith, according to the saying of the Apostle Peter, "But [God] cleansed their hearts by faith" (Acts 15:9), and in one purified from the love and desire of earthly things by divine hope. For as a fire is not kindled in green wood still full of sap, but in dry wood, so the fire of charity demands hearts purified from earthly love and from empty confidence in one's own abilities.

From this one can understand what is true charity as well as what is false and feigned charity. For if someone readily speaks of God and in his prayers feels compunction to the point of tears and does some good works, distributing alms and fasting at times, yet keeps in his heart a filthy love, vainglory, hatred for his neighbor, and other things of that sort that make a heart impure and unclean, he does not possess divine and true charity, but the empty form or image of charity. Hence, the Apostle was wise to mention not simply faith, hope, and charity, when he spoke of true and perfect justice, but said, "The purpose of this charge is charity, from a pure heart and a good conscience and faith unfeigned" (1 Tm 1:5). And the true art of living well and of dying happily consists in persevering in this true and perfect charity up to death.

CHAPTER FOUR

The fourth rule of the art of dying well, which contains three lessons from the Gospel.

Although what has been said about faith, hope, and charity might seem to be sufficient for living well, yet Christ himself has deigned to give us three lessons in the Gospel to teach these things more perfectly and more clearly. For in the Gospel of Luke, he says, "Let your loins be girded about and your lamps burning in your hands, and you yourselves like men waiting for their master's return from the wedding; so that when he comes and knocks, they may straightway open to him. Blessed are those servants whom the master, on his return, shall find watching" (Lk 12:35–7). This parable can be understood in two ways: as about preparation for the Lord's coming on the last day and for his coming on the day each of us dies. This latter explanation, which is that of Saint Gregory in his thirteenth homily on this Gospel, seems to be more to our point.[1] For awaiting the last day will only concern those who are still among the living. Yet the Lord gave the parable to the apostles and to all of us. Yet the apostles and the generation after them were certainly distant by many centuries from the last day. Furthermore, many frightening signs will precede the last day, as our Lord said, "There will be signs in the sun and moon and stars, and upon the earth distress of nations; men fainting for fear and for expectation of the things that are coming on the world" (Lk 21:25, 26). No certain signs will precede the Lord's coming at the particular judgment on the day each of us dies, and this is the coming that is meant by the oft-repeated words in Holy Scripture, that the Lord will come as a thief, that is, when he is least expected.

Let us then briefly explain this parable and realize that preparation for death is something necessary for all of us above all else. The Lord gives all of us three commands: first, that we have our loins girded; second, that we have lamps burning in our hands; and finally, that we keep watch and await his coming, although we do not know when he will come, just as almost all do not know of a thief's coming. Let us explain the words "Let your loins be girded." The literal meaning of these words is that we be ready and dressed to run to meet the Lord, when he calls us by death to the particular judgment. The image of girded loins is taken from the custom of men from the East who wore long garments which they gathered up and tied about their waist when they were about to run, so that the length of the garment did not impede their movement. Thus the Book of Tobit speaks of the angel Raphael, who was about to accompany the young Tobit, "Then Tobit going forth found a beautiful young man, standing girded, and as it were ready to walk" (Tb 5:5). And with that Eastern custom in mind, Saint Peter wrote, "Therefore, having girded up the loins of your understanding, be sober and set your hope perfectly, . . ." (1 Pt 1:13). And in the Letter to the Ephesians, Saint Paul says, "Stand, therefore, having girded your loins with truth" (Eph 6:14).

Having one's loins girded implies two things: first, the virtue of chastity; second, readiness to meet Christ as he comes for judgment, whether particular or general. The Fathers, Saint Basil, in explaining the fifteenth chapter of Isaiah, and Saint Augustine in his book *On Continence*, and Saint Gregory in his thirteenth homily on this Gospel, take the first interpretation.[2] The lust of the flesh, more than all other disturbances of the soul, impedes swift and unencumbered running to meet Christ as he comes, just as, on the contrary, nothing makes a man more free to follow Christ than virginal chastity. For we read in Revelation that virgins follow Christ "wherever he goes" (Rv 14:4), and the Apostle exhorts us, saying, "He who is unmarried is concerned about the things of the Lord. Whereas he who is married is concerned about the things of the world, how he may please his wife; and he is divided" (1 Cor 7:32, 33–34).

The second interpretation, which does not restrict girded loins to continence alone, but extends it to unencumbered service of Christ in all things, is Saint Cyprian's in the book *Exhortation to Martyrdom*, chapter eight, and it is followed by those who wrote commentaries on the Gospel of Luke.[3] Therefore, the meaning of this passage of the Gospel is that all concerns of this life, even the best and most necessary, should not so occupy our minds that they impede the primary consideration of meeting Christ, when he calls us by death to give an account of all our works, and also words and thoughts, even of idle words and useless thoughts. Therefore, when death comes unforeseen, what will they do who are wholly occupied in temporal things and have never for a moment thought of giving an account to God of all their works, all their words, all their thoughts, all their desires, and all their omissions? Are they going to run to meet Christ with their loins girded? Or will they not rather lie entangled and trapped in their filth, silent and despairing? What will they answer the judge when he says, "Why did you not heed my words with which I warned you? 'Seek first the kingdom of God and its justice, and all these things shall be given you besides' (Mt 6:33). And why did you not consider those words which are often publicly chanted for you in the church, 'Martha, Martha, you are anxious and troubled about many things; and yet only one thing is needful. Mary has chosen the best part, and it will not be taken away from her' (Lk 10:41–42). If I chided Martha's concern in wanting to serve me most faithfully, will your concern for amassing superfluous riches, for attaining dangerous honors, and for fulfilling harmful desires be able to please me, while in the meantime you forget the kingdom of God and its justice, which is necessary above all else?"

Let us come to the second duty of a diligent and faithful servant, "And let lamps be burning in your hands" (Lk 12:35). It is not enough for a faithful servant to have his loins girded that he may run to meet the Lord free and unencumbered. There is needed a burning lamp to show the way, since the Lord returning from the marriage feast is expected at night. Here the lamp means the law of the Lord which shows the right way: David says, "Your word is a lantern for my feet" (Ps 119:105). And in Proverbs, Solomon says, "The law is a light" (Prv 6:23). But this lamp does not give light and show the way if it is left in a room or at home. It has to be held in one's hands to show the right way. There are many who know the laws of God and of man, but commit so many sins or pass over good and necessary works because they do not carry a lamp in their hands, that is, they do not apply knowledge of the law to their works. How many learned men commit very grave sins, because, when they act, they do not consult the law of the Lord, but rather anger, or lust, or some other disturbance of the soul? If King David, when he saw Bathsheba naked, had consulted the law of the Lord, "You shall not covet your neighbor's wife" (Dt 5:21), he would never have fallen into so great a crime. But because he consulted the beauty of a woman, he, a man otherwise just and holy, forgot the law of God and committed adultery. Therefore, one has to have the lamp of the law of the Lord always in his hands, not hidden in a room, and one has to obey the words of the Holy Spirit, who commands that we meditate "on the law of the Lord day and night" (Ps 1:2). And with the Prophet himself we say, "You have commanded that your commandments be strictly kept. May my paths be guided to keep your justifications" (Ps 119:4–5). For he who always has the lamp of the Lord's law before the eyes of his mind runs with confidence to meet his Lord when he comes.

There remains the third and final duty of the faithful servant, namely, that he always be on watch, as he is uncertain when the Lord will come. He says, "Blessed are those servants whom the master, on his return, shall find watching" (Lk 12:37). The Lord did not will that all men should depart from life at a fixed time in their lives lest they spend all the preceding time in eating and drinking, in games and jokes, and in other evil works and then a little before death be converted to God. Therefore, divine providence willed that nothing be more uncertain than the hour of death. Some die in their mother's womb, others shortly after birth; some in extreme old age; others in the flower of youth. Again, some languish for a long time; others die suddenly. Some recover from a very serious and nearly incurable disease; others are only slightly ill, yet, when they seem safe from death, the strength of the disease grows and kills them. Our Lord said in the Gospel, pointing out this incertitude, "And if he comes in the second watch, and if in the third, and finds them so, blessed are those servants! But of this be assured, that if the householder had known at what hour the thief was coming, he would certainly have watched, and not have let his house be broken into. You also must be ready, because at an hour that you do not expect, the Son of Man is coming" (Lk 12:38–40). So that we might grasp the importance of being convinced of the uncertainness of the time when our Lord will come to judge, either at the death of each of us or at the end of the world, nothing is repeated more frequently in Holy Scripture—not only in the Gospels, but also in the Letters of the Apostles and in Revelation—than the word *watch* and the image of the thief, who usually comes, when he is least expected to come.[4]

From all of this one can understand how great is the negligence and ignorance—I do not want to say madness and folly—of the majority of men. We have been warned so often by the very Spirit of truth through the holy writers who cannot lie to prepare ourselves for death, as for a great and difficult effort. For upon it depends our everlasting and supreme happiness or our everlasting and supreme destruction. Yet there are few who are awakened by the words or rather the thundering of the Holy Spirit.

Someone will ask, "What advice do you offer us so that we may watch as we should, and by watching prepare ourselves to meet death happily?" Nothing more useful occurs to me than frequently to prepare ourselves for death by a serious examination of conscience. Catholics make an examination of conscience when they make the yearly confession of their sins. And when they grow ill, doctors are forbidden by a decree of the Sovereign Pontiff Pius V to visit the sick a second time, unless they have atoned for their sins by confession preceded by an examination of conscience.[5] Finally, there is almost no one in the Catholic Church who does not, when death is imminent, confess his sins after an examination of conscience. But what shall we say of those who are carried off by a sudden death? What of those who suffer madness or fall into delirium before confessing their sins? What of those who are overcome by the seriousness of their disease to the point that they cannot think of how many and of what sins they have committed? What of those who sin in dying or die in sinning, as those in an unjust war or in single combat or those killed when caught committing adultery?

In order to avoid these and like things prudently and religiously, nothing more useful can be devised than that those concerned about their eternal salvation diligently examine their conscience twice every day, that is, in the morning and in the evening. They should uncover what they did, said, desired, and thought at night or on the day before in which the stain of sin might be found. And if they should find something of the sort, especially if it seems mortal, they should not delay in seeking the remedy of true contrition, along with the resolution to approach the sacrament of penance at the first opportunity. And so they should ask God for the gift of contrition, ponder the gravity of their sin, and heartily detest their guilt; they should seriously weigh whom they, mere men and useless servants, have offended, namely, almighty God, the Lord of heaven and earth. Their eyes should not spare the tears, nor their hand cease beating the breast. Finally, they should form a true and effective resolution of never again provoking God by sinning and of never offending our good Father. If this examination is correctly made morning and evening, or at least once a day, it will be almost impossible to sin while dying or to die while sinning or to be caught off guard by delirium or madness or other such misfortunes. Thus we who are well prepared for death will neither be harmed by death's uncertainty nor lack the happiness of endless life.

CHAPTER FIVE

The fifth rule of the art of dying well in which is unmasked the error of the rich of this world.

To what we have said above, we should add the refutation of an error that is prevalent among the rich of this world and that greatly impedes a good life and a happy death. The error is that the rich think the wealth they possess is absolutely and unconditionally theirs, when they hold it by just title, and that they can, therefore, use it up or give it away or waste it as they please, and that no one may say to them, "Why do you act this way? Why do you dress so luxuriously? Why do you dine so lavishly? Why are you so prodigal in feeding dogs and hawks, or why do you lose so much money in games of chance and other pleasures?" For they answer, "What business is it of yours? I can do what I want with my own possessions." This error is undoubtedly very serious and particularly dangerous. Let us grant that the rich of this world are masters of their possessions in comparison with other men, but in comparison with God they are not masters, but administrators, or stewards, or overseers. I can show this by many proofs.

Hear the Royal Prophet. He says, "The earth is the Lord's and the fullness thereof, the world, and all they that dwell therein" (Ps 24:1), and elsewhere, "For all the beasts of the woods are mine, the cattle on the hills, and the oxen. If I should be hungry, I would not tell you, for the world is mine, and the fullness thereof" (Ps 50:10, 12). And in the First Book of Chronicles, when David offered for the building of the temple three thousand talents of gold and seven thousand talents of the purest silver and white marble in great abundance and when at the king's example the princes of the tribes offered five thousand talents of gold and ten thousand talents of silver and eighteen thousand talents of bronze and also one hundred thousand talents of iron, David said to God, "Yours, O Lord, is magnificence, and power, and glory, and victory; and to you is praise; for all that is in heaven, and in earth is yours; yours is the kingdom, O Lord, and you are above all princes. Yours are riches, and yours is glory; you have dominion over all. Who am I, and what is my people, that we should be able to promise you all these things? All things are yours; and we have given you what we have received of your hand" (1 Chr 29:11–12, 14). To these we can add the testimony of God himself, who speaks through the Prophet Haggai, "The silver is mine, and the gold is mine" (Hg 2:9). The Lord said this so that the people might understand that nothing at all would be lacking for the reconstruction of the temple, since he himself commanded that the temple be rebuilt who owns all the gold and silver in the world.

I add from the New Testament and from the words of Christ two more proofs. There is a parable in Luke about the unjust steward. The Lord says, "There was a certain rich man who had a steward, who was reported to him as squandering his possessions. And he called him and said to him, 'What is this that I hear of you? Make an accounting of your stewardship, for you can be steward no longer' " (Lk 16:1–2). By the term *rich man* was undoubtedly meant God who, as we have just mentioned, said through Haggai, "The silver is mine, and the gold is mine" (Hg 2:9). By the term *steward* or *administrator* as we read in the Greek texts, we should understand a rich man, for such was the explanation given this passage from Saint Luke the Evangelist by the Fathers, Saint John Chrysostom, in the *Golden Chain* of Saint Thomas, Saint Augustine in *Questions on the Gospels*, book two, question 34, Ambrose, Bede, Theophylact, Euthymius, and others.[1] Every rich man of this world, if he believes the Gospel, ought to admit that the wealth that he possesses, whether by a just or an unjust title, is not his own. If he possesses it by a just title, he is God's steward or administrator; if he possesses it by an unjust title, he is a robber and a thief. That a rich man in this world is not master of the wealth he possesses is evident from the fact that God removes from his stewardship the one accused of injustice before God by death of the body or by neediness. That is what the words mean, "Make an accounting of your stewardship, for you can be steward no longer." For God has many means of reducing the wealthy to need and thus removing them from their stewardship: shipwreck, robbery, hail, caterpillar, too much rain, too much drought, too many storms, and other things of this sort which are God's way of saying that "you can be steward no longer."

What the Lord says at the end of the parable, "Make friends for yourselves with the mammon of wickedness, so that when you fail they may receive you into the everlasting dwellings" (Lk 16:9), does not mean that we should give alms out of dishonestly gotten wealth, but that we should give alms out of wealth, which is not genuine wealth, but merely the shadow of wealth. Clearly that is the import of the same passage in the Gospel according to Luke, where the Lord says, "If you were not faithful in the wicked mammon, who will entrust you with the true mammon?" The meaning of these words is that "if you were not faithful in the wicked mammon," that is, if you were not faithful in false riches in generously giving them to the poor, "who will entrust you with" true riches, the riches of the virtues that make a man truly rich? Saint Cyprian explained this passage in this way in the sermon *On Work and Almsgiving*, and St. Augustine, in the second book of the *Questions on the Gospels*, question 34, explains it in almost the same way.[2] There he says that the mammon of iniquity are the riches which only the wicked and the foolish regard as riches, while just and wise men place no value on them and insist that only spiritual gifts are true riches.

Another Gospel passage from the same chapter sixteen of Saint Luke can be taken as a commentary on the parable of the unjust steward. The Lord says, "There was a rich man who wore purple and linen and daily feasted in splendor. And there was a beggar by the name of Lazarus who lay at his door covered with sores and longing to be fed with the scraps that fell from the table of the rich man. But no one gave them to him, and the dogs came and licked his sores. It happened that the beggar died and was carried by angels to the bosom of Abraham. But the rich man died and was buried in hell" (Lk 16:19–23). This rich banqueter was clearly one of those who thought themselves masters of their wealth, not stewards and administrators of God. And so he did not think that he sinned against God, if he wore purple and linen and feasted daily in splendor and fed many dogs and perhaps even clowns and actors. For he said in his heart, "I spend my own money. I do no one any harm. I do not violate God's laws; I do not blaspheme; I do not swear falsely; I observe the Sabbath. I honor my parents; I kill no man; I commit no adultery. I speak no false witness; I desire not my neighbor's wife or goods." But if that is so, why is he buried in hell? Why is he tortured by the fire of hell? We have to admit that all who say they are absolute masters of their own riches are mistaken. For if the rich banqueter had other more serious sins, Holy Scripture would have recalled them in some way. But since it says no more, we are clearly meant to understand that lavishly clothing the body with clothes of an exorbitant price, the vast daily expenditures on banquets, and the numerous servants and dogs, along with the merciless treatment of the poor man full of sores, is a sufficient cause for the rich man to be buried in hell and tortured by eternal flames.

So let it be a certain law of living well and also of dying well to think frequently, to consider seriously, and to reflect that an account will have to be given to God for the superfluous luxury in palaces, gardens, coaches, in the number of servants, in the cost of garments, in banquets, in amassing wealth, in other unnecessary expenses which greatly harm many poor and sick persons who lack what others have in abundance. Surely even now they cry out to God and will still cry to God on the day of judgment until these rich are handed over to be burned in unquenchable fire along with the wealthy banqueter.

CHAPTER SIX

The sixth rule of the art of dying well, in which are explained three moral virtues.

The three theological virtues, faith, hope, and love, contain all the rules of living well in a brief compendium and, consequently, all the rules of dying well. Yet for a better grasp of this most wholesome art the Holy Spirit, the primary author of all the Sacred Books, wanted to add three other virtues which wonderfully assist men to live and to die well. These are sobriety, justice, and piety. Of them the Apostle Paul says in the Letter to Titus, "For the grace of God our Savior has appeared to all men, instructing us, in order that, rejecting impiety and worldly lusts, we may live soberly and justly and piously in this world; looking for the blessed hope and glorious coming of our great God and Savior, Jesus Christ" (Ti 2:11–13). So the sixth rule of living well and dying well is "that, rejecting impiety and worldly lusts, we may live soberly and justly and piously in this world." Here is a summation of the whole divine law reduced to one remarkably short sentence of incredible brevity. "Turn from evil, and do good" (Ps 37:27), says the holy prophet David. In evil there are, according to Jeremiah, two factors: turning from God, and turning to creatures, "My people have done two evils. They have foresaken me, the fountain of living water, and they have dug for themselves cisterns, broken cisterns that can hold no water" (Jer 2:13). What should one do who wants to turn away from both evils? He will reject "impiety and worldly lusts." For impiety turns one from God, and worldly desires turn one toward creatures. As far as doing good is concerned, we fulfill the law when we live "soberly and justly and piously," that is, when we are sober toward ourselves, just toward our neighbor, and pious toward God.

I would like to develop this a little more fully so that this wholesome and short rule can be more easily reduced to practice. What is impiety? The vice opposed to piety. What is piety? A virtue or gift of the Holy Spirit by which we respect, worship, and revere God as our Father. We are commanded to reject impiety in order to "live piously in this world" or—what comes to the same thing—we are commanded to live piously in this world so as to reject all impiety. Why are the two mentioned when one is enough? The Holy Spirit spoke in this manner so that we might understand that, if we wish to please God, we have to cultivate a piety free from any impiety. For there are Christians who cultivate piety when they pray to God, when they attend the awesome sacrifice, and when they listen to a priest's preaching, but at other times they blaspheme God in jest, or swear by God without reason, or fail to keep vows made to God. What is this but to worship God piously and yet to act impiously toward God? Those who desire to live well so that they may be granted a good death should worship God with such piety that they reject all impiety—even every shadow, however thin, of impiety. It profits little to hear Mass daily and to venerate Christ in the sacred Mystery, if at other times you blaspheme against God with impiety or swear falsely by God.

One should also carefully note that the Apostle did not say "reject impiety," but "reject all impiety," that is, every kind of impiety, not merely terrible, but even mild impiety. This is directed against those who regard it as a slight matter to swear without need, to watch women in holy places with an impudent though not a lustful eye, to talk during holy Mass, and to commit all those kinds of sin, as if they did not believe that God is present and sees all and notes even the slightest sins. Our God is "a jealous God, visiting the iniquity of the fathers upon the children, unto the third and fourth generation of them that hate" him, "and showing mercy unto thousands to them that love him and keep his commandments" (Ex 20:5–6). The Son of God taught this by his own example. For he was meek and humble, and "when he was reviled, he did not revile, when he suffered, he did not threaten" (1 Pt 2:23). Yet when he saw "the sellers of doves and the money-changers sitting in the temple" (Jn 2:14), he burned with great zeal and cast the buyers and sellers out with a whip made from cords and overturned the tables of the money-changers. He said, "It is written, 'My house is a house of prayer,' but you have made it a den of thieves" (Lk 19:46). And he did this twice, once the first year of his preaching according to Saint John and once the last year according to the three other evangelists (Mt 21:12–13; Mk 11:15–17; Lk 19:45–46; Jn 2:14–17).

Let us turn to the second virtue, justice, which directs our actions toward our neighbor. The Apostle speaks of this virtue when he says, "To reject worldly lusts and live justly." Here also applies that general truth, "Turn from evil and do good" (Ps 37:27). For there cannot be true justice toward the neighbor where worldly lusts do not cease. What do worldly lusts mean but the lust of the flesh, the lust of the eyes, and the pride of life, which are not from God, but from the world or this age? Just as justice cannot be unjust, so worldly lusts can in no way be joined to true justice. A child of this world can simulate justice in word and tongue, but he cannot produce it in deed and truth. The holy Apostle not only wisely told us to live justly, but he previously told us to reject all worldly lusts. Thus he indicated that we must first tear out the poisoned root of concupiscence before a good tree can be planted in a goodly heart.

What it means to live justly scarcely needs to be questioned. Everyone knows that justice demands that we give to each his due. The Apostle says, "Render to all men whatever is their due; tribute to whom tribute is due; taxes to whom taxes are due; fear to whom fear is due; honor to whom honor is due" (Rom 13:7). To the prince we owe tribute, to parents honor, to masters fear. Thus speaks the Lord through Malachi, "If I then be a father, where is my honor? And if I be a master, where is my fear?" (Mal 1:6). To the seller is owed a just price; to the worker a just wage, and so on with others. Those whose job it is to distribute common goods have a greater, not a lesser, responsibility to distribute them in accord with distributive justice to the more deserving, not in accord with personal preference to those more closely related or better liked. If someone wants to learn the art of living well and of dying well, let him hear the Wise Man who, in the beginning of his Book, cries out, "Love justice, you that are the judges of the earth" (Wis 1:1), as well as Saint James, lamenting in his Letter, "Behold, the wages of the laborers who reaped your fields, which have been kept back by you unjustly, cry out; and their cry has entered into the ears of the Lord of Hosts" (Jas 5:4).

There remains the third virtue, sobriety, to which worldly desires are no less opposed than they are to justice. By sobriety we do not here understand only the virtue opposed to drunkenness, but the whole virtue of temperance or moderation that helps a man to apportion what is needed for the care and preservation of the body according to reason rather than desire. This virtue is rarely found among men, and worldly desires have apparently filled the homes of all the rich. Lovers of wisdom ought not to pay attention to what the foolish do, although they are very many and almost innumerable, but to what the wise do. Solomon was among the wisest and prayed to God: "Two things I have asked of you; deny them not to me before I die. Give me neither beggary nor riches; give me only the necessities of life" (Prv 30:8). The Apostle Paul was wise and said, "Having food and sufficient clothing, with these let us be content. For we brought nothing into this world, and certainly we can take nothing out" (1 Tm 6:8, 7). And that is the wisest of reasons. Why should we be concerned about superfluous riches when we cannot take them with us to that place where we arrive through death? Christ the Lord was not merely wiser than Solomon and Paul, but was the very wisdom of God, and he said, "Blessed are you poor, but woe to you rich!" (Lk 6:20, 24). Of himself he said, "The foxes have dens, and the birds of the air have nests, but the Son of Man has nowhere to lay his head" (Lk 9:58). If "in the mouth of two or three witnesses every word shall stand" (Dt 19:15; Mt 18:16), how much more ought the testimony of those truly wise men establish any claim. And if we add that wealth beyond our needs is not ours, but belongs to the poor, as the common opinion of the holy Fathers and scholastic Doctors holds, are they not fools who so carefully protect precisely what will damn them to hell at the judgment of God?

If anyone wants to master the art of living well and dying well, let him not follow the crowd which believes in or values only what it sees, but let him follow Christ and his apostles who taught by word and deed that we should not care for the things of the present, but await "the blessed hope and glorious coming of our great God and Savior, Jesus Christ" (Ti 2:13). For so great a thing it is that we hope for in our Lord Jesus Christ's glorious coming from heaven as judge that we should regard all the past glory and riches and joys of this world as naught, and those who want to trust fools in a matter of such vital importance rather than the wise should be judged most foolish and unhappy.

CHAPTER SEVEN

The seventh rule of the art of dying well, which is prayer.

Up to now we have drawn the rules of dying well from the three theological virtues, faith, hope, and charity, and from three moral virtues, sobriety, justice, and piety, concerning all of which the blessed Apostle Paul has warned us. Now I will add another rule from the three works of the virtues, prayer, fasting, and almsgiving, which we have learned from the angel Raphael. For we read in the Book of Tobit that the angel Raphael said, "Prayer is good with fasting and alms more than to lay up treasures of gold" (Tb 12:8). This trio of good works is the fruit of the three virtues, religion, mercy, and temperance, which have a great resemblance to piety, justice, and sobriety. Just as piety has to do with God, justice with the neighbor, and sobriety with oneself, so prayer, an act of religion, has to do with God, almsgiving, an act of mercy, has to do with the neighbor, and fasting, an act of abstinence, has to do with oneself. Many have written extensively on prayer. We will explain only three points in accord with the goal of this work, one on the necessity of prayer, another on the fruits of prayer, and a third on the manner of praying fruitfully.

The necessity of prayer is so evident in Scripture that there is nothing more clearly taught or shown. Although God knows what we need, as the Lord himself says in Matthew (Mt 6:8), he wants us to ask for such things and receive them by prayer as though by spiritual hands or by some other means suited for this. Hear the Lord in Luke, "You must always pray and not lose heart" (Lk 18:1). So too, "Watch, then, praying at all times" (Lk 21:36). Hear the Apostle, "Pray without ceasing" (1 Thes 5:17). Hear Ecclesiasticus, "Let nothing hinder you from praying always" (Sir 18:22). These directives do not mean that we should do nothing else, but that we should never forget this very wholesome practice and that we should often return to it, as Christ and his Apostle taught by their example. For the prayer of Christ and the Apostle did not prevent them from also teaching the people and confirming what they said by signs and miracles. Yet we can say that they prayed always because they prayed so frequently. This is how we interpret "My eyes are ever toward the Lord" (Ps 25:15), and "His praise shall be always in my mouth" (Ps 34:2), as well as the words of the Apostle, "And they were continually in the temple, praising and blessing God" (Lk 24:53).

The fruits of prayer are principally three: merit, satisfaction, and receiving what we ask for. We have Christ's words in the Gospel concerning merit, "Again, when you pray, you shall not be like the hypocrites, who love to pray standing in the synagogues and at the street corners, in order that they may be seen by men. Amen I say to you, they have received their reward. But when you pray, go into your room, and closing your door, pray to your Father in secret; and your Father who sees in secret will reward you" (Mt 6:5–6). By these words our Lord does not forbid that prayer be made in public, for he himself prayed publicly, before he raised Lazarus (Jn 11:41–42). But he forbids public prayer when it is done so that the one praying may be seen by many, that is, because of the desire for vainglory. Otherwise, we can pray even in the temple and find there the chamber of the heart and pray to our Father there "in secret." "He will reward you" refers to merit. For as he said of the Pharisee, "He has received his reward," that is, human praise, so of the one praying in the chamber of his heart and concerned only with God, we should understand that a reward will be given to him by the Father, "who sees in secret."

We know of satisfaction for past sins from the practice of the Church, in which, when a penance is imposed, prayer is always joined to almsgiving and fasting. In fact, almsgiving and fasting are often omitted, but prayer is never omitted. Finally, Saint John Chrysostom teaches in a beautiful manner the value of prayer for obtaining many favors in his two books *On Prayer*, where he uses the image of human hands.[1] Just as man, born naked and vulnerable and in need of everything, still cannot complain about his Creator, since he was given hands by which he can provide for himself food, clothes, shelter, protection, and everything else, so too the spiritual man can do nothing without God's help, but has the power of prayer, the best of all spiritual means, by which he can easily get everything else for himself.

Besides these three primary fruits there are many others. First, prayer enlightens the mind. For man cannot intently fix the eyes of the mind upon God who is light and not be enlightened by him. "Come to him," says David, "and be enlightened" (Ps 33:6). Second, prayer nourishes faith and trust. For the more frequently one converses with another, the more confidently he approaches him. Third, prayer kindles love and prepares the mind to receive greater gifts, as Saint Augustine says.[2] Fourth, prayer increases humility and holy fear. For one coming to prayer realizes that he is a beggar before God and, as a result, usually stands more humbly before him. And one who needs God's help in all things is most careful to avoid offending him. Fifth, frequent prayer leads to a contempt for all temporal things in the heart of the one who prays. For all earthly things inevitably become cheap and soiled for one who steadily gazes upon things heavenly and eternal, as Saint Augustine shows in book nine of *The Confessions*.[3] Sixth, prayer brings forth an incredible delight since by its means a man begins to taste the sweetness of the Lord. The greatness of his sweetness can be grasped from the fact that we know that some have not only spent whole nights, but were even able to spend whole days and whole nights in prayer without effort. Finally, besides its usefulness and pleasure prayer also confers upon one who prays no small dignity and honor. Even the angels honor the soul they see so readily and so frequently admitted to converse with the divine Majesty. Read Saint John Chrysostom in his first book on praying to God.[4]

We still have to say something about the manner of praying well, upon which especially depends the art of living well and, thus, the art of dying well. As the Lord says, "Ask, and it shall be given to you" (Lk 11:9) and also, "Everyone who asks receives" (Lk 11:10). In his Letter Saint James declares that this should be understood on the condition that we ask well. He says, "You ask and do not receive, because you ask amiss" (Jas 4:3). We may then draw the following conclusions: Those who ask well for the gift of living well certainly will receive it, and those who ask well to persevere in living well right up to death and thus to a happy death will without doubt receive this. Let us then explain briefly the conditions of praying well so that we may learn to pray well, live well, and die well.

The first condition is faith, for the Apostle says, "How then are they to call upon him, in whom they have not believed?" (Rom 10:14). Saint James agrees, "Let him ask with faith, without hesitation" (Jas 1:6). This necessity of faith should not be understood in the sense that we have to believe with certitude that God will do what we ask. For in that case faith would often be found to be false, and we would obtain nothing at all. We must believe that God is all-powerful, all-wise, all-good, and all-faithful and that he is able and knows and is ready to do what we ask, if it is fitting for him to give and expedient for us to receive what we ask for. This is the faith that Christ asked of the two blind men who wanted to be cured. "Do you believe that I can do this to you?" (Mt 9:28). With the same faith David prayed for his sick son, "Who knows whether the Lord may not give him to me?" (2 Kgs 12:22). His prayer shows that he did not believe with certitude that God would do what he asked, but that he could do so. Certainly the Apostle Paul prayed with similar faith that the thorn in his flesh be taken from him (2 Cor 12:8), since he prayed with faith and his faith would have been false if he had with certitude believed that God would do what he then asked. For he did not then obtain what he asked for. The Church prays with that same faith that all heretics, pagans, schismatics, and bad Christians repent, although it is certain that not all do so. On this point see Saint Prosper in his books *The Vocation of All the Nations.*[5]

A second and highly necessary condition of praying well is hope or trust. For although we should not by faith, an act of intellect, hold with certitude that God will do what we ask, yet through hope and trust, an action of the will, we ought to cling firmly to the divine goodness and trust with certainty that God will indeed do what we ask. This is the condition that the Lord sought in the paralytic to whom he said, "Take courage, son; your sins are forgiven you" (Mt 9:2). The Apostle demands the same condition of everyone when he says, "Let us therefore draw near with confidence to the throne of his grace" (Heb 4:16). And much earlier the

Prophet has the Lord say, "Because he hoped in me I will deliver him" (Ps 91:14). Because trust is born of perfect faith, when Scripture asks for faith in matters of moment, it adds something about trust. Thus we read in Mark, "Whoever says to this mountain, 'Arise, and hurl yourself into the sea,' and does not waver in his heart, but believes that whatever he says will be done, it shall be done for him" (Mk 11:23). The words of the Apostle refer to this faith that gives birth to trust: "If I have all faith so as to move mountains, . . ." (1 Cor 13:2). Thus John Cassian, in his *Conference on Prayer*, writes that it is a sure indication that one will obtain what he prays for if he prays with a firm confidence that he will receive what he asked for, does not at all hesitate to ask, and is flooded with spiritual joy while he prays.[6]

The third condition of praying well is charity, or that justice by which we are justified from our sins. For surely only God's friends obtain favors from him. David speaks to that effect in the psalms, "The eyes of the Lord are upon the just, and his ears unto their prayers" (Ps 34:16). And elsewhere, "If I have looked at iniquity in my heart, the Lord will not hear me" (Ps 66:18). In the New Testament the Lord says, "If you abide in me, and if my words," that is, my commandments, "abide in you, ask whatever you will, and it shall be done to you" (Jn 15:7). And the beloved disciple says, "If our heart does not condemn us, we have confidence toward God; and whatever we ask, we shall receive from him, because we keep his commandments and do those things which are pleasing in his sight" (1 Jn 3:21–22). Nor is this teaching contradicted by the fact that the publican asked of God pardon for his sins and went away justified. For a penitent sinner does not obtain his request as a sinner, but as a penitent. As a sinner he is an enemy of God, but as a penitent he is beginning to be a friend of God. Those who sin do what does not please God, but those who repent of their sins do what pleases God most.

The fourth condition of praying well is humility, for those who pray do not trust in their own justice, but in God's goodness. God says, "To whom shall I have respect, but to him that is poor and little, and of a contrite spirit, and that trembles at my words?" (Is 66:2). Ecclesiasticus adds, "The prayer of him who humbles himself shall pierce the clouds, and will not depart until the most High behold" (Sir 35:21).

The fifth condition is devotion, which causes the one who

prays to pray attentively, carefully, diligently, and ardently, not negligently, as most are accustomed to do. The Lord seriously rebukes those who pray with their lips alone. "This people," says the Lord through Isaiah, "honors me with their lips, but their heart is far from me" (Mt 15:8; Is 29:13). This virtue of devotion arises from a living faith that is not merely habitual, but really actualized. For those who ponder attentively and with firm faith the immensity of God's majesty, the extent of our own worthlessness, and the importance of what we are asking can hardly fail to come to prayer with the greatest humility, reverence, devotion, and ardor.

This is the right place to add two exceptional passages from the Fathers that bear witness to this. Saint Jerome says, in the *Dialogue against the Luciferians*, "I come to prayer. I would not pray if I did not believe. But if I really believed, I would cleanse that heart by which God is seen, I would beat my breast with my hands and water my cheeks with tears. My body would tremble; my face would grow pale. I would lie at my Lord's feet and bathe them with my weeping, dry them with my hair, and cling to the frame of the cross. I would not stop before I obtained mercy. But now during my prayer I often either stroll on the porch or compute interest or, distracted by a dirty thought, even do things too embarrassing to mention. Where is faith? Do we suppose that Jonah prayed in this fashion? or the three young men? or the thief on the cross?"[7] Saint Bernard, in the sermon on four ways of praying, says, "At the time of prayer we must enter the heavenly court, that court where the King of Kings is seated upon his throne of stars, surrounded by an innumerable and ineffable host of blessed spirits. With what great reverence and fear and humility ought that vile little frog draw near as it creeps and comes forth from its pond? How fearful, how suppliant, how humble and worried and utterly intent ought a wretched little man stand before the glorious Majesty in the presence of the angels, in the council and assembly of the just?"[8] Thus in all our actions we have great need of vigilance, but especially in prayer.

The sixth condition of praying well is perseverance, which the Lord recommends in two parables set forth in the Evangelist Luke. The first is about the man who went to his friend in the middle of the night to ask him for three loaves of bread. After he had been repeatedly refused because the time was not convenient, he finally obtained what he asked for because he persevered in asking (Lk 11:5–8). The second is about the widow who pleaded with the judge to do justice for her against her adversary. Although the judge was very wicked and neither feared God nor respected man, he was overcome by the perseverance and insistence of the woman and did justice for her against her adversary (Lk 18:1–8). From these parables the Lord concludes that we ought much more to persevere in prayer to God, who is just and good. Saint James adds that God "gives abundantly to all men, and does not reproach" (Jas 1:5), that is, he gives generously to all who ask for his gifts and does not reproach their persistence on the grounds that their asking often becomes a bother. For God is merciful beyond measure. In his explanation of the last verse of Psalm 65, Saint Augustine adds to the words "Blessed be God who has not turned away my prayer, nor his mercy from me": "If you see that your request has not been turned away, you can be sure that his mercy has not been taken from you."[9]

CHAPTER EIGHT

The eighth rule of the art of dying well, which is fasting.

We will now briefly treat of fasting in accord with the order set down by the angel. And leaving aside many points about fasting that theologians discuss, we will set forth only those which are pertinent to our topic. We have proposed to explain the art of living well insofar as it smooths the path for the art of dying well. For this art the same three points which we discussed in reference to prayer, that is, necessity, fruitfulness, and manner, seem sufficient. The necessity of fasting rests upon both divine and human law. The prophet Joel, who speaks for God, bears witness with regard to the divine law, "Be converted to me with your whole heart, in fasting, and in weeping, and in mourning" (Jl 2:12). The same point is made by the prophet Jonah, who bears witness that the people of Nineveh proclaimed a fast and the wearing of sackcloth to appease God; yet there was no positive law at that time concerning fasting (Jon 3:7). The same point can be seen in the words of the Lord in Saint Matthew, "When you fast, anoint your head and wash your face, so that you may not be seen fasting by men, but by your Father, who is in secret; and your Father, who sees in secret, will reward you" (Mt 6:17–18).

We will add one or two passages from the Fathers. In his *Letter to Casulanus*, Saint Augustine says, "I see as I reflect upon the Gospels and Letters of the Apostles and that whole instrument called the New Testament that fasting is commanded, but I do not find settled by command of the Lord or of the Apostles the days on which one should not fast or the days on which one should."[1] Saint Leo, in the *Fourth Sermon on the December Fast*, says, "Those things which bore the shapes of things to come were ended when what they signified was fulfilled. Yet the grace of the New Testament has not taken away the usefulness of fasts, but has embraced with pious observance abstinence as always profitable for body and soul. As the Christian retains, 'You shall adore the Lord God, and serve him alone,' and the other commandments like it, so no interpretation does away with what is commanded in the same books about the holiness of fasts."[2] By this Saint Leo did not intend to say that Christians should fast at the same times the Jews fasted, but rather that the commandment of fasting given to the Hebrews should be observed by Christians at the time and in the manner determined by those who preside over the Church. What they have determined is far too well known to need restatement here. So much for the necessity of fasting.

The fruitfulness and utility of fasting can easily be shown. First, fasting is highly useful for preparing the soul for prayer and the contemplation of heavenly things, as the angel Raphael pointed out when he said, "Prayer is good with fasting" (Tb 12:8). Moses prepared his soul by a fast of forty days before he dared to enter into conversation with God (Ex 24:18). So too Elijah fasted forty days in order to be able to converse with God as he did on Mount Horeb (1 Kgs 19:8). Daniel prepared by a fast of three weeks to receive God's revelations (Dn 10:3). So the Church instituted fasts on the vigils of the great feasts that Christians might be better prepared for devoting themselves to the things of God. The holy Fathers often preached on the usefulness of such fasting. Let the reader consult Saint Athanasius in the book *On Virginity*, Saint Basil, in his *First and Second Talks on Fasting*, Saint Ambrose, in the book *On Elias and Fasting*, and Saint Bernard, in the *Sermon on the Vigil of Saint Andrew*.[3] But I am going to quote a few but splendid words of Saint John Chrysostom from the *First Homily on Genesis.* He says, "Fasting is the food of the soul; it produces for it light wings so that it is carried aloft and can contemplate the heights."[4]

A second usefulness of fasting is to conquer the flesh, and on this basis fasting greatly pleases God. It pleases him that we crucify the flesh with its vices and passions, as the Apostle teaches in the Letter to the Galatians (Gal 5:24). He also spoke of this very reason, "I chastise my body and bring it into subjection lest perhaps after preaching to others I myself should be rejected" (1 Cor 9:27). Chrysostom and Theophylactus in their commentaries, and Saint Ambrose, in the *Letter to the Church of Vercelli*, interpret these words as referring to fasting.[5] This usefulness of fasting is proclaimed by the following Fathers: Saint Cyprian, in the *Sermon on Fasting*, Saint Basil, in his *First Talk on Fasting*, Saint John Chrysostom, in the *First Homily on Genesis*, Saint Jerome, in the *Letter to Eustochium*, *On the Preservation of Virginity*, and Saint Augustine in the tenth book, chapter 31, of *The Confessions.*[6] And the whole Church in the Office for Prime sings from the hymn of Saint Ambrose, "Scarcity of food and drink frightens the pride of the flesh."

The third usefulness of fasting is the worship of God. For God considers it an honor to himself when we fast for his sake. Thus the Apostle speaks in the Letter to the Romans, "I exhort you therefore, brethren, by the mercy of God, to present your bodies as a sacrifice, living, holy, pleasing to God—your spiritual service" (Rom 12:1). The Greek reads *logiken latreian*, that is, rational worship. Saint Luke speaks of this worship when he says of the widow, Anna, "She never left the temple, with fastings and prayers worshiping night and day" (Lk 2:37). And the great Nicean Council in canon five calls the Lenten fast a pure and solemn gift offered by the Church to God, as Tertullian also says in the book *The Resurrection of the Flesh*, where he calls "late and dry food" sacrifices pleasing to God.[7] And Saint Leo, in the *Second Sermon on the December Fast*, says, "For the perfect reception of all the fruits the sacrifice of continence is most fittingly offered to God, their giver."[8] Finally, Saint Gregory, in *Homily Sixteen*, writes that by the Lenten fast there is offered to God the tithes and first fruits of our life.[9]

The fourth usefulness of fasting is satisfaction for sins. Examples from Scripture show this. The Ninevites placated God by fasting, as Jonas testifies (Jon 3:7). The Jews did the same when by fasting with Samuel they placated God and brought back victory over the enemy (1 Sm 7:6). Achab, the wicked king, partially placated God by fasting and haircloth (1 Kgs 21:27). At the time of Judith and of Esther, the Hebrews found mercy before God by no other sacrifice than fasting, weeping, and lamentation. This same doctrine is constantly taught by the ancient Fathers. In his book *On Fasting*, Tertullian says, "As at first the use of food wrought destruction, so fasting now makes satisfaction."[10] Saint Cyprian, in the sermon, *On Apostates*, says, "Let us placate the anger and offense of God by fasting and weeping, as he himself warns us."[11] Saint Basil, in the *First Talk on Fasting*, says, "Penance without fasting is fruitless and pointless; through fasting satisfaction is made to God."[12] Saint John Chrysostom, in his *First Homily on Genesis*, says, "As an indulgent father, God found this cure for us which comes through fasting."[13] Saint Ambrose says in the book *On Elias and Fasting*, "Fasting is the death of guilt, the destruction of sins, the remedy unto salvation."[14] Saint Jerome says in his *Commentary on Jonah*, chapter three, "Sackcloth and fasting are the weapons of penance, the help against sins."[15] Saint Augustine, in his *Sermon* 60, *Of the Season*, says, "No one fasts for human praise, but for the pardon of sins."[16] Saint Leo, in the *Fourth Sermon on the September Fast*, says that God is placated by the sacrifice of fasting.[17] Saint Bernard, in the sixty-sixth of the *Sermons on the Canticle*, says, "I abstain at times, and my abstinence serves as satisfaction for sins, not a superstition for impiety."[18]

The fifth usefulness of fasting is that it is meritorious and very helpful for obtaining God's good gifts. Hannah, the wife of Elkanah, although she was sterile, merited by fasting to bear a son (1 Sm 1:7). Saint Jerome, in the second book of *Against Jovinianus* so interprets the words of Scripture, "But she wept and did not take food." "Hannah," he says, "merited to fill her belly that was empty of food with a son."[19] Sarah likewise is freed from the demon by a fast of three days, as is written in the book of Tobit (Tb 3:10). There is an outstanding passage on the merit of fasting in the Gospel. The Lord says, "But you, when you fast, anoint your head and wash your face, so that you may not be seen fasting by men, but by your Father, who is in secret; and your Father, who sees in secret, will repay you" (Mt 6:17–18). Those words, "he will repay you," mean that he will give you your recompense. For they are in contrast to the words "They disfigure their faces in order to appear to men as fasting. Amen I say to you, they have received their recompense"

(Mt 6:16). Thus the hypocrites in fasting receive their recompense, the praise of men, and the just in fasting receive their recompense, the reward of God.

Many clear statements of the holy Fathers illustrate this point. Saint Jerome says in the preface to his *Commentary on Saint Matthew* that Saint John the Evangelist, when about to write the Gospel, declared a great fast that he might merit the grace to write correctly, and on this point Venerable Bede followed Jerome in commenting on the first chapter of John.[20] Tertullian, in the book *On Fasting*, says, "Fasting merits from God knowledge even of the mysteries."[21] Saint Ambrose, in the *Letter to the Church of Vercelli*, says, "Who are these new teachers who exclude the merit of fasting?"[22] Saint Athanasius, in the book *On Virginity*, says, "Whoever is troubled by an unclean spirit ought to keep in mind that evil spirits leave those they afflict when they fast, since the evil spirits fear its power."[23] Saint Basil, in his *First Talk on Fasting*, says, "Fasting is useful for avoiding the evils and for attaining the goods of the next life."[24] Saint Gregory Nazianzen, in his *Talk in Praise of Saint Cyprian*, says, while listing the weapons by which a certain holy virgin repulsed the devil, "She cast at him the poison of fasting and sleeping on the ground."[25] Saint John Chrysostom, in his *First Sermon on Fasting*, says, "Fast because you have sinned; fast that you may not sin; fast that you may receive; fast that you may not lose what you have received."[26] Saint Jerome in the book *Against Jovinianus* deliberately undertakes a discussion of the merit of fasting.[27] And in homily sixty-two Augustine says, "Fasting is either a remedy or a reward," that is, it gains either the pardon of sins or the reward of the heavenly kingdom.[28] Saint Leo, in the *First Sermon on the September Fast*, says, "Through the humility of fasting we merit God's help against all our enemies."[29]

We have seen the necessity and the usefulness of fasting. There remains the manner, that is, we should briefly explain how to fast so that fasting is truly useful to us for living well and thus for dying well. For many fast on all the days appointed by the Church, for example, on vigils, on Ember Days, and in Lent. And there are those who voluntarily fast during Advent in order to prepare themselves for the birthday of the Lord, or on Friday in memory of the Lord's passion, or on Saturday in honor of the Virgin Mother of God. But whether their fasting truly obtains the fruits of fasting is a question that deserves asking. The primary goal of fasting is mortification of the flesh so that the spirit may emerge in greater strength. For this goal one has to eat little and inexpensive food. Mother Church indicates this when she commands that the body be fed not twice a day, but once, and not with meat and dairy products, but with herbs and vegetables and also other lighter foods. Tertullian expressed this in two words in the book *The Resurrection of the Flesh*, when he called the food of those fasting "late and dry food."[30] Surely this is not observed by those who on the day they fast eat no less in one meal than on other days at dinner and supper combined and who for the one meal prepare such expensive dishes of various kinds of fish and of other foods suited to tempt one to gluttony that they seem to prepare not a meal of mourners and penitents, but a marriage supper that will last much of the night. Those who fast in this manner surely do not obtain its fruit.

Nor do those obtain the fruit of fasting who, even if they eat less sumptuously and more soberly on fast days, do not refrain from games and jokes, from quarrels and arguments, from bawdy songs and immoderate joy, and—what is worse—from sins and crimes any more than on other days that are not dedicated to fasting. Hear what Isaiah the Prophet says of this sort of man, "Behold in the day of your fast your own will is found, and you exact of all your debtors. Behold you fast for debates and strife, and you strike with the fist wickedly. Do not fast as you have done until this day, to make your cry to be heard on high" (Is 58:3–4). The Lord rebukes the Hebrews because on the days of fast, which are days of penance, they want to do their own will, not the will of the Lord. They not only are unwilling to forgive the debts of their debtors, as they beg that their debts be forgiven by God, but they do not want to grant even a slight delay to their debtors. Likewise the time which those fasting ought to have spent in prayer to God was spent in lawsuits and arguments. Finally, not only did they not take time off for spiritual concerns, as they should have, but they added to their sins by wickedly striking their neighbor. Good men ought to avoid such conduct, if they want their fasting to be pleasing to God and useful to themselves so that they can hope for a good life and a happy death.

Of the three works which the angel Raphael praised in Tobit and proposed for imitation by all of us, almsgiving still remains to be treated.

CHAPTER NINE

The ninth rule of the art of dying well, which is almsgiving.

Concerning almsgiving there are three points that need brief explanation: the necessity, the fruit, and the manner. No one has ever doubted that there is a precept about giving alms. For even if we had nothing else, the sentence of the most just and highest judge is more than sufficient. For he will say to the wicked in the last judgment, "Depart from me, you cursed, into everlasting fire which has been prepared for the devil and his angels. For I was hungry and you did not give me to eat. I was thirsty and you did not give me drink. I was a stranger and you did not take me in. I was weak and in prison and you did not visit me" (Mt 25:41–43). A little later he adds, "As long as you did not do this to one of these little ones, you did not do it to me" (Mt 25:45). With regard to this passage we can infer that only those who are able to do so are bound to give alms. For we do not read that the Lord performed such works, but only that he ordered part of the money given to him be given to the poor. This can be gathered from that Gospel passage where, when the Lord said to Judas, "Do quickly what you are doing" (Jn 13:27), the disciples thought that the Lord had commanded that Judas give something to the needy from the purse which he carried.

Some theologians hold that this precept is contained under the commandment of the Decalogue, "Honor your parents," others under "You shall not kill." It is not necessary that this precept be contained in the Decalogue since almsgiving pertains to charity, and the commands of the Decalogue are precepts of justice. But if all the moral precepts can be reduced to the Decalogue, the opinion of Albert the Great is probable.[1] He subsumes the precept on almsgiving under "You shall not steal," since not giving to the poor what they deserve seems to belong to the genus of stealing. Yet the opinion of Saint Thomas Aquinas is more probable, since he reduces the precept to the first of the second tablet, "Honor your parents."[2] For honoring parents in that passage is not limited only to showing them reverence, but rather involves providing them what is necessary for life. And this is a sort of alms which we owe to our principal neighbor, as Saint Jerome explains in his commentary on the fifteenth chapter of Saint Matthew.[3] From this we gather that we owe alms to our other neighbors in need. Furthermore, the precept concerning alms is not negative, but affirmative. Among the precepts of the second tablet none is affirmative except the first, that is, "Honor your parents." But this is not the place to discuss this more at length. Enough then for the necessity of almsgiving.

The fruit of almsgiving is plentiful. First, almsgiving frees one from eternal death, whether it is done as satisfaction, or as a disposition for grace, or for some other reason. The Holy Scriptures clearly teach this. In the Book of Tobit we read, "Alms delivers from all sin and from death, and will not suffer the soul to go into darkness" (Tb 4:11) and in the same book the angel Raphael says clearly, "Alms delivers from death, and it is what destroys sins, and causes that one find mercy and eternal life" (Tb 12:9). Daniel said to King Nabuchodonosor, "Wherefore, O king, let my counsel be acceptable to you, and redeem your sins with alms, and your iniquities with works of mercy to the poor" (Dn 4:24).

Second, if an alms is given by a just man and out of true charity, it merits eternal life. Christ, the judge of the living and the dead, will be a witness to this truth, when in judgment he will say, "Come, blessed of my Father, take possession of the kingdom prepared for you from the foundation of the world. For I was hungry and you gave me to eat," and so on. Later he says, "As long as you did it to one of these least brothers of mine, you did it to me" (Mt 25:34–35, 40).

Third, alms has the power of a kind of baptism, that is, of destroying sins in both their guilt and their punishment, as Ecclesiasticus says, "Water quenches a flaming fire, and alms resists sins" (Sir 3:33). For water completely puts out a fire so that not even smoke remains. And the Fathers, Saints Cyprian, Ambrose, Chrysostom, and Leo teach the same thing. Saint Cyprian says in the sermon on alms, "As the fire of hell is put out by the bath of saving water, so by alms and just deeds the flame of sins is quieted."[4] Saint Ambrose says in *Sermon Thirty-One* says, "Alms is in a way another bath for souls, as the Lord says, 'Give alms, and all will be clean for you.' Yet—and we say this without departing from the faith—alms is a greater mercy than the bath. For the bath is given once and promises pardon once, but as often as you give alms, you merit pardon."[5] Saint John Chrysostom, in the twenty-fifth of the *Homilies on the Acts of the Apostles*, says, "There is not a sin that alms cannot clean away or that it cannot destroy."[6] Saint Leo, in the *Fifth Sermon on the Collects*, says, "Almsgiving removes sins by destroying death and puts out the penalty of perpetual fire."[7] This is indeed a great prerogative of alms and ought to inflame all to a love of alms. Yet this should not, it seems, be understood of just any almsgiving, but of that alone which proceeds from great contrition and from a great burning love. Such was the alms of Saint Mary Magdalene, who watered the Lord's feet with tears and with the alms of precious balm annointed those same feet.

Fourth, alms increases trust in God and produces spiritual joy. For although every good work bears this fruit, yet it fits almsgiving especially, since through it we offer a service pleasing to both God and neighbor and it is a work that is clearly and obviously recognized as good. Hence, we have the words of Tobit, "Alms shall be a great confidence before the most high God, to all that give it" (Tb 4:12), as well as the words of the Apostle, "You have had compassion of those in prison. Do not, therefore, lose your confidence" (Heb 10:34, 35). Finally, in the sermon on almsgiving, Saint Cyprian calls alms a great comfort to the faithful.[8]

Fifth, alms wins the good will of many so that they pray to God for their benefactors and obtain for them either the grace of conversion or the gift of perseverance or an increase in grace as well as of glory. For the words of the Lord can be understood in all these ways. "Make friends for yourselves from the mammon of wickedness, so that when you fail, they may receive you into everlasting dwellings" (Lk 16:9).

Sixth, almsgiving forms a disposition for the grace of justification. Solomon speaks of this fruit in Proverbs, when he says, "By alms and faith sins are purged away" (Prv 15:27). When the Lord had heard of the generosity of Zacchaeus who said, "Behold, I give one-half of my possessions to the poor; and if I have defrauded anyone of anything, I restore it fourfold," he said, "Today salvation has come to this house" (Lk 19:8, 9). Finally, in the Acts of the Apostles we read that Cornelius, who gave much alms, was told, though he was not yet Christian, "Your alms have gone up and been remembered in the sight of God" (Acts 10:4). In *The Predestination of the Saints*, Saint Augustine proves from that passage that by almsgiving Cornelius had obtained from God the grace of Christian faith and of perfect justification.[9]

Seventh and last, the giving of alms often is a cause of an

increase in temporal goods. The Wise Man asserts this when he says, "He that has mercy on the poor, lends to the Lord," and also, "He that gives to the poor, shall not want" (Prv 19:17, 28:27). The Lord taught the same thing by example when he ordered his disciples to distribute to the crowds the five loaves and two fish which were all they had. For as a result of his action they gathered up twelve baskets full of fragments of loaves and fish, which would be enough for them for many days (Jn 6:.1–15; Mt 14:13–24; Mk 6:31–44; Lk 9:10–17). Tobit, who generously shared his goods with the poor, also acquired great wealth in a short time. So too the widow of Zarephath, who gave a bit of flour and oil to the prophet Elijah (1 Kgs 17:10–16), received from the goodness of God the gift that her flour and oil lasted for a long time. Many further appropriate examples in writing are found in Gregory of Tours in the fifth book of the *History of the Franks*, in Leontius in *The Life of Saint John the Almsgiver*, and in Sophronius in *The Spiritual Meadow*.[10] Saint Cyprian also confirms this point in his sermon on almsgiving.[11] So does Saint Basil in his *Talk to the Rich*, where in a beautiful image he compares wealth to the water of wells which usually gushes forth ever fresher and more abundant, if it is frequently drawn upon, but decreases and goes bad if it is left untouched.[12] Wealthy misers do not like to hear and are skeptical about this sort of thing, but after this life they will understand and believe that it is true, when understanding and believing will be of no avail.

We have still to write something on the manner of giving alms. For giving alms in the right manner is necessary above all else if we are to live a pious and holy life and die a happy death. First, we must give alms with the right intention of pleasing God, not in order to win public approval. Our Lord clearly teaches this when he says, "When you give alms, do not sound the trumpet, and do not let your left hand know what your right hand is doing" (Mt 6:2–3). Saint Augustine explains this passage in his *Exposition of the Letter of Saint John*, where he understands left hand to mean the intention of giving alms for temporal honor or for any other temporal gain.[13] The right hand he interprets as the intention of giving alms for the sake of eternal life, the glory of God, and the love of the neighbor.

Second, alms should be given promptly and readily so that it does not seem torn from us by entreaties. It should not be put off from day to day if it can be given immediately. The Wise Man says, "Say not to your friend, 'Go, and come again, and tomorrow I will give to you,' when you can give at present" (Prv 3:28). Abraham, a friend of God (Gn 18:3ff.), asks strangers to stay with him without waiting for them to ask. His just nephew Lot does the same (Gn 19:2–3). So too Tobit does not wait for the poor to come to him, but seeks them out himself (Tb 1:6, 15, 19).

Third, alms should be given joyfully, not sadly. Ecclesiasticus says, "In every gift show a cheerful countenance" (Sir 35:11). And the Apostle says, "Not grudgingly or from compulsion, for God loves a cheerful giver" (2 Cor 9:7). Fourth, alms have to be given humbly so that a rich man understands that he receives more than he gives. On this Saint Gregory says, "It greatly helps to subdue the pride of the giver if, when he gives temporal things, he ponders carefully the words of the heavenly Teacher who says, 'Make friends for yourselves with the mammon of wickedness so that when you fail, they may receive you into the everlasting dwellings (Lk 16:9).' For if we acquire everlasting dwellings by their friendships, we ought surely, when we give, think that we are offering presents to our patrons rather than handouts to the needy."[14]

Fifth, alms should be given generously in accord with one's abilities. For Tobit, a remarkable almsgiver, teaches us so, when he says, "According to your ability be merciful. If you have much, give abundantly; if you have little, take care even so to bestow willingly a little" (Tb 4:8). And the Apostle teaches that alms should be given as a blessing, not as avarice (2 Cor 8:2, 14). And Saint John Chrysostom adds, "Almsgiving does not mean giving, but giving generously."[15] And in the same sermon he adds that those who wish to be heard when they say to God, "Have mercy on me, O God, according to your great mercy (Ps 51:1)," ought also to take pity upon the poor in accord with generous almsgiving.

Finally, it is most essential for one who wants to be saved and thus to die well to examine carefully, either by personal reading and meditation or with the help of truly learned and pious men, whether superfluous riches can be kept without sin or must be given to the poor and what wealth is to be called superfluous and what necessary. For moderate wealth is possibly superfluous for one person, while for another a vast amount of riches seems clearly necessary. Since this little work of mine neither needs nor has room for long and drawn-out scholastic questions, I will note here briefly the passages of the Holy Scriptures and Doctors, both ancient and more recent, and then put an end to this discussion.

The passages of Scripture are: Matthew 6:24, "You cannot serve God and mammon"; Luke 3:11, "Let him who has two tunics share with him who has none, and let him who has food do likewise." In Luke 12:20 the rich man who has so much that he hardly knows where to put it all is told, "You fool, this night do they demand your soul of you." Saint Augustine explains these words in the *Fiftieth Book of Homilies, Homily Seven*, that the rich man perished eternally because he kept superflous riches.[16]

The chief passages from the Fathers are the following: Saint Basil says in the *Talk to the Rich*, "Are you not a thief when you regard as your own what you have received to give away?" and a little later he says, "Why do you do injury to so many poor since you are able to give?"[17] Saint Ambrose in *Sermon* 81 says, " 'How is it unjust, if I carefully keep my own goods since I do not invade the property of others?' Oh, foolish saying! Your own goods, you say? Which ones?" and further on, "It is no less a crime, when you are able and have an abundance, to refuse to give to the needy than to deprive someone of his possessions."[18] Saint Jerome in the *First Letter to Hedibia*, the first question, says, "If you have more than you need for food and clothing, give it away and consider yourself owing a debt to that extent."[19] Saint John Chrysostom, in *Homily* 34, *To the People of Antioch*, says, "Do you own your own goods? The belongings of the poor have been entrusted to you, whether you possess them from just labor or as family inheritance."[20] Saint Augustine, in his homily on Psalm 147, says, "The superfluities of the rich are the necessities of the poor. When you have more than enough, you have what belongs to others."[21] Saint Leo, in the *Fifth Sermon on the Collects*, puts it this way, "Earthly and bodily resources come from the generosity of God so that he will rightly demand an account of those things which he has entrusted to us to give away as much as to possess."[22] Saint Gregory, in the third part of his *Pastoral Care*, the twenty-second admonition, says, "Those who neither desire the goods of others nor give of their own should be warned that the earth from which we are made is common to all men and that it also provides food for all in common. Those who make the common gift of God their own only foolishly think themselves innocent."[23] Saint Bernard, in the *Letter to Henry the Archbishop of Sens*, says, "It is ours," the poor cry, "that you spend; what you stupidly spend is cruelly taken from us."[24] Saint Thomas, in *The Summa of Theology*, says, "Goods which some have in abundance are owed by natural right to the sustenance of the poor," and later he says, "The Lord commands not only that a tenth part, but all that is superfluous be given to the poor."[25] Finally, the same author writing on the *Four Books of the Sentences*, testifies that this is the common doctrine of all the theologians.[26] I add here that, if one should wish to argue that what is superfluous need not be given to the poor in strict justice, he still cannot deny that it should be done out of charity. However, it matters little whether one goes to hell from a lack of justice or from a lack of charity.

CHAPTER TEN

The tenth rule of the art of dying well, which concerns the sacrament of baptism.

Having explained the main virtues which teach the art of dying well, let us now add a few words on the doctrine of the sacraments, which are equally helpful for happily mastering the art of dying well. The sacraments instituted by Christ number seven: baptism, confirmation, eucharist, penance, orders, matrimony, and extreme unction. They are like divine instruments which God uses to confer or increase or restore divine grace by the ministry of his servants so that men freed from being slaves to the devil and brought to the dignity of the sons of God might come to endless happiness with the holy angels. Our task is to show briefly from these seven sacraments who is advancing in the art of living well and who is failing in it. Thus one can gather who can hope for a happy death and who, on the contrary, ought to expect an unhappy death, unless he changes his life and conduct.

Let us begin with the first sacrament. Baptism is the first among the sacraments and is correctly called the gateway of the sacraments, since no one is fit to receive the other sacraments unless he has been baptized. In the sacrament of baptism the following rites are followed. First of all, the one to be baptized should profess the Catholic faith either by himself or through another. Then, he should renounce the devil, his pomps and his works. Third, he should be baptized in Christ, and in that baptism he is transferred from slavery to the devil over to the grace of the sons of God. All his sins are wiped away, and he receives the heavenly gifts by which he is made an adopted son of God, an heir of God, and a co-heir of Christ. Fourth, he is given a white robe and ordered to keep it pure and clean up to death. Fifth, he is given a lighted candle which signifies good works which he ought, while he lives, to add to his innocent manner of life, which the white robe just received signifies. For the Lord says this in the Gospel, "Even so let your light shine before men, in order that they may see your good works and give glory to your Father in heaven" (Mt 5:16).

These are the main rites that the Church uses in conferring baptism. I omit the others which are of no concern to our topic. Each person can see from these whether he has lived well from the reception of baptism up to the present. I strongly suspect that there are only a few who have done all that they promised to do or ought to do. For "many are called, but few are chosen" (Mt 20:16, 22:14), and "How narrow the gate and close the way that leads to life!" (Mt 7:14).

Let us begin with the Creed. How many are the rustics and beggars and workers in the lower trades who do not remember or who have never learned or who know only how to utter the words, but do not understand the Creed? Yet in baptism they answered through sponsors that they believed in the individual articles. If Christ is to dwell in our heart through faith, as the Apostle Paul says (Eph 3:17), how will he dwell in the hearts of those who can barely form the words on the tongue and have nothing at all in the heart? And if God purifies our hearts through faith, as the Apostle Peter says (Acts 15:9), how impure will their hearts be who have not received the faith of Christ in the heart, although they have received baptism in the flesh? I speak of adults, not of children. The latter are justified by habitual faith, hope, and charity, but when they grow up, they must learn the Creed and believe the Christian faith in their heart unto justice and confess it on the lips unto salvation, as the Apostle clearly says in his Letter to the Romans (Rom 10:10).

Let us turn to the second rite. All Christians either themselves or through sponsors, when asked if they renounce the devil, his pomps, and his works, answer, "I do renounce them." But how many make this renunciation in words, but not in deeds? Or rather how few are there who do not love and follow the pomps and works of the devil wholeheartedly? Yet God sees all and will not be mocked. Hence, anyone who desires to live well and to die well ought to enter into the chamber of his heart and, without deceiving himself, seriously and attentively weigh and ponder whether he takes delight in the pomps of this world or in the works of the devil, which are sins, and gives place to them in his heart in both word and deed. Thus either a good conscience will console him, or a bad conscience will bring him to repentance.

In the third rite we see God's beneficence so sublime, so profound, and so utterly clear that, if we spent whole days and whole nights in admiring it and in thanking God for it, we could still offer nothing worthy of it. Good God, who can conceive, who is not stunned, who is not wholly turned to tears, if he realizes that man justly condemned to hell suddenly passes through baptism from wretched captivity to a right to the blessed kingdom? Yet the greater this gift is, the more we should detest the ingratitude of most men. Many hardly attain the use of reason and they begin to renounce—so to speak—this wonderful gift of God and surrender themselves into slavery to the devil. What does it mean to follow from early adolescence the lust of the flesh, and the lust of the eyes and the pride of life but to make a treaty of friendship with the devil and to deny Christ really and truly? Rare are they who, aided by God's singular help, carefully guard the grace of baptism and begin to bear the Lord's yoke "from their youth," as Jeremiah says (Lam 3:27). But unless we either carefully preserve the grace of baptism or again renounce the devil through true penance and return to the service of Christ and persevere in it until death we can neither live well nor escape a bad death.

The fourth rite is the reception of the white robe which the baptized is ordered to wear until he comes into the Lord's presence. This rite signifies that we ought to preserve most carefully the innocence of life received by the grace of baptism right up until death. But who can tell how great are the snares of the devil, the constant enemy of the human race, who wants nothing more than to sprinkle that garment with every sort of stain? So very few who live longer escape the filth of sins. And holy David proclaimed those blessed who remain spotless along the way (Ps 119:1). As it is more difficult to walk along a dirty road without stain, so the palm and crown of an innocent life will be the more glorious. Hence, all who want to live well and to die well ought to strive mightily to keep white the garment of innocence. But if it should become stained, they ought to wash it again and again in the blood of the Lamb, with true contrition and tears of repentance. When holy David had wept long over his sin, he came alive again with hope of pardon, and in thanking the Lord, he said with confidence, "You will sprinkle me with hyssop, and I will be cleansed. You will wash me, and I will be made whiter than snow" (Ps 51:9).

The final rite is the reception of the lighted candle and the carrying of it in one's hands. This signifies, as we said above, the good works that should be added to innocence of life. By his own example the Apostle teaches the good works to be performed by those reborn through baptism in Christ, when he says, "I have fought the good fight, I have finished the course, I have kept the faith. For the rest, there is laid up for me a crown of justice, which the Lord, the just Judge, will give to me on that day" (2 Tm 4:7–8). These few words sum up all the good works that are to be done by those reborn through baptism in Christ. For we have to fight bravely against the temptations of the devil, who "as a roaring lion, goes about seeking someone to devour" (1 Pt 5:8). We have to finish the race of good works by keeping the commandments of the Lord, according to the words of the Psalm, "I have run the way of your commandments, when you enlarged my heart" (Ps 119:32). We have to keep faith with our Lord by multiplying our talents, or by cultivating the vineyard, or in the stewardship entrusted to us, or in the task of governing of our family, or in any other business committed to us by the Lord. God in his wisdom willed to admit us as adopted sons to a heavenly inheritance. But in order for that to take place for his greater glory and ours, his divine wisdom chose to have us merit the heavenly inheritance, that is, eternal beatitude, by good works performed by his grace and our free will. Thus that rich and glorious inheritance will not be given to sleepers, men of leisure, or men of play, but to those who watch and toil and persevere in good works until the end of life.

Therefore, let each examine his works and weigh his life and character if he wants to live well and die happily. If his conscience bears witness that he has fought the good fight against vices and concupiscence and all the temptations of the ancient serpent, that he has happily finished the race in all the commandments and ordinances of the Lord without blame, and that he has kept faith with the Lord in all tasks and offices entrusted to him, let him rejoice in security and say with the Apostle, "There is laid up for me a crown of justice, which the Lord, the just judge, will give to me" (2 Tm 4:8). But if he carefully examines his conscience and it bears witness that in the fight with the enemy of the human race he was badly wounded and that the flaming arrow penetrated to the soul itself not once, but often, and that in the race of good works he often failed, not only not running swiftly, but even sitting down or lying down on the way out of weariness, and that finally he did not keep faith with the Lord in business entrusted to him, but either vainglory or respect for persons or something else of this sort carried off part of the earnings, let him have recourse to the remedy of penance and to God himself as physician and not put off this greatest of all tasks to another time, because we know not the day nor the hour of death.

CHAPTER ELEVEN

The eleventh rule of the art of dying well, which is confirmation.

After the sacrament of baptism there comes the sacrament of confirmation. We can draw from it a lesson no less suited for living well than we drew from baptism. Although the sacrament of baptism is more necessary than the sacrament of confirmation, the sacrament of confirmation has greater dignity. This can be seen from the minister, the matter, and the effect. The ordinary minister of baptism is the priest or deacon and, in time of need, anyone. The ordinary minister of confirmation is the bishop and, by permission of the sovereign pontiff, a mere priest. The matter of baptism is ordinary water; the matter of confirmation is precious oil mixed with balm and consecrated by the bishop. The effect of baptism is the grace and the character such as is needed to bring forth a spiritual child, according to the words of Saint Peter, "Crave, as new born babes, pure spiritual milk" (1 Pt 2:2). The effect of confirmation is the grace and the character such as is needed for creating a Christian soldier to fight against invisible enemies, according to the words of Saint Paul, "Our wrestling is not against flesh and blood, but against the Principalities and the Powers, against world-rulers of this darkness, against the spiritual forces of wickedness on high"

(Eph 6:12). Finally, in baptism infants are given a taste of salt; in confirmation a slap is given so that the soldier of Christ might learn to fight not by striking, but by suffering.

To better understand the task of the person anointed with chrism, that is, of the soldier of Christ, we have to see what the apostles received in their confirmation, which was given to them on the day of Pentecost. The apostles were not confirmed, strictly speaking, by the sacrament of chrism, but received from Christ, the prince of priests, the effect of the sacrament without the sacrament. They received three gifts: wisdom, eloquence and charity in the highest degree, and the gift of miracles, which was highly useful for converting unbelievers to the faith. These gifts were signified by the tongues of fire which appeared on the day of Pentecost and by the great noise which was heard at the same time. The light of the fire signified wisdom, the heat of the same fire charity, the shape of tongues eloquence, and the great noise the gift of miracles. The sacrament of confirmation we receive does not bring with it the gift of various languages or the gift of miracles because these were necessary for the conversion of unbelievers, not for the assistance and perfection of the apostles themselves. But it does bring the gift of charity, which is "patient and kind" (1 Cor 13:4), and as a sign of this patience, which is a very rare and very precious virtue, the bishop publicly gives a slap to the confirmed person. Thus he may understand that he has been made a soldier of Christ not for striking, but for suffering, not for inflicting injuries, but for bearing them. For in the army of Christ one fights not against men whom we see, but against demons we do not see. For in this way Christ our commander-in-chief, nailed to the cross, fought and conquered, defeating the powers on high. And in this way the newly confirmed apostles fought, when, after being severely beaten with whips in the council of the Jews, they "departed from the presence of the Sanhedrin, rejoicing that they had been counted worthy to suffer disgrace for the name of Christ" (Acts 5:41). The grace of the sacrament of confirmation enables a man who is unjustly struck not to think of revenge, but to rejoice that he suffers injustice for justice's sake.

Let the person confirmed enter into his own heart and look carefully to see whether he finds in his heart the gifts of the Holy Spirit, especially wisdom and courage. Let him see whether he has received the wisdom of the saints, which values highly eternal goods and despises temporal ones, and the courage of Christ's soldiers who suffer injustices more willingly than they do injustice. And so that he may not be deceived, let him get down to what he does and examine his conscience. For if he truly finds that he is quick to give alms and not to amass wealth, and if he does not think of revenge when he has suffered injustice, but readily and willingly forgives injustice, he can rightly exult in spirit that he holds in his heart the pledge of the spirit of the adopted sons of God. If after receiving the sacrament of confirmation he does not find that he is less lustful, less greedy, less angry, less impatient, and if he really finds it difficult to tolerate a gold or silver coin leaving his purse to relieve the poor, and if, on the other hand, he sees that he eagerly seizes upon every opportunity for gain, and if he knows that he is quick to anger, swift to revenge, and, even if asked by friends to forgive an offense, he does not allow himself to give in, what can he gather but that he received the sacrament, but did not receive its grace?

I mention the above for those who come, as adults, to receive this sacrament. For, with regard to those who receive confirmation in their youth and are hardly capable of deceit, we are supposed to believe that the gifts and virtues are infused, since there is nothing to prevent this. Nonetheless, we have to fear for them lest by later sins and the long postponement of penance they extinguish the Spirit received in confirmation, that is, they lose the grace of the Holy Spirit. For this is how we interpret what the Apostle says, "Do not extinguish the Spirit" (1 Thes 5:19). For one extinguishes the Holy Spirit to the extent that he can when he extinguishes the grace of God in himself.

Hence, he who desires to live well so that he may get to die well should greatly value the grace of the sacraments, which are vessels of heavenly treasure. And he should especially value those sacraments which, once lost, cannot be found in any way. Such is the sacrament of confirmation, in which there is received an incomparable treasure of good things. For although the character of the sacraments cannot be destroyed, the character without the gifts of grace does not bring comfort, but increases the punishment of confusion.

CHAPTER TWELVE

The twelfth rule of the art of dying well, which is the eucharist.

The most holy eucharist is the greatest of all the sacraments. It contains not only grace in great abundance, but the very source of grace. In order that a Christian live well with respect to this sacrament and in his time die well, two things are needed: One, that he receive this sacrament at some time, since our Lord said, "Unless you eat the flesh of the Son of Man, you shall not have life in you" (Jn 6:54). Second, that he eat this excellent food worthily, since the Apostle says in the Letter to the Corinthians, "He who eats and drinks unworthily, without distinguishing the body of the Lord, eats and drinks judgment to himself" (1 Cor 11:29). There is some question about how often it is good to take this food and about what is to be regarded as sufficient preparation to approach this heavenly banquet worthily or at least not unworthily.

Regarding the first question we know that there have been many different customs in the Catholic Church. In the Church of the first centuries the faithful received the Body of the Lord very frequently. For Saint Cyprian in his sermon *On the Lord's Prayer*, which is sixth in order, explains those words, "Give us this day our daily bread," as being about the eucharist, and teaches that the eucharist ought to be received daily, unless one is legitimately prevented.[1] Later, when charity cooled, many put off holy communion for whole years. Therefore, Pope Innocent III promulgated the decree that at least every year during the Easter season all men and women are bound to receive the holy eucharist.[2] The more common opinion of the Doctors seems to be that it is far better for lay people not to be obliged to approach the most holy eucharist every Sunday and on the more important feasts. Well known among the writers on this subject is that opinion supposedly uttered by Saint Augustine, "The daily reception of the Eucharist I neither praise nor blame; yet I urge and exhort that you receive communion every Sunday."[3] Although *The Book of Church Dogmas*, from which this statement is taken, does not seem to be Saint Augustine's, yet it stems from an ancient author and is not contrary to the doctrine of Saint Augustine who clearly teaches in his *Letter to Januarius* that neither those who think they should receive communion daily nor those who think that they should receive communion less frequently are mistaken.[4] Certainly the teacher of this doctrine would not blame those who chose a middle position, namely, that they should approach this sacrament at least every Sunday. Saint Jerome approved the same position, as can be seen from his *Commentary on the Letter to the Galatians*, where in explaining the fourth chapter he speaks as follows: "Though we may always fast or always pray and joyfully celebrate the Lord's day with the reception of the Lord's body, the Jews are not permitted thus to sacrifice a lamb," and so on.[5] The same opinion found favor with Saint Thomas in the third part of *The Summa of Theology*, Question 80, Article 10 (toward the end).[6]

As far as preparation for receiving such a great sacrament is concerned, so that one receives it unto salvation, not unto judgment and condemnation, it is first of all required that the soul be alive by the life of grace and not dead by the death of mortal sin. For it is called food and is given in the form of bread precisely because food is not for the dead, but for the living. "He who eats this bread," says the Lord in John, "shall live forever" and in the same passage he says, "My flesh is food indeed" (Jn 6:59, 56). The Council of Trent added that, to prepare to receive this heavenly banquet worthily, one stained with mortal sin should not be content with contrition alone, but should seek to expiate his sins by the sacrament of penance, provided that he has access to a confessor.[7] In second place, since this sacrament is not only food, but medicine, and the best and most effective medicine against all the diseases of the vices, the sick person should desire good health and want to be cured of all the diseases of the vices, especially the main ones, which are wantonness, avarice, and pride. Saint Ambrose teaches that the eucharist is medicine in the fifth book of *The Sacraments*, chapter 4: "He who has a wound needs medicine; it is a wound because we are under sin. The medicine is a heavenly and venerable sacrament."[8] Saint Bonaventure in the second book of *The Progress of Religious*, chapter 78, says, "Let him who regards himself as unworthy reflect that he needs and must seek a physician the more he feels he is sick."[9] And Saint Bernard, in the sermon *On the Lord's Supper* advises his brothers to attribute it to the Blessed Sacrament when they experience in themselves the lessening of evil inclinations and other ailments of the soul.[10]

Finally, the Blessed Sacrament is not only food for those on this pilgrimage and medicine for the ill, but is also the wisest and most loving physician. Hence, one should receive it with the greatest joy and reverence. And the abode of the soul should be decorated with every kind of virtue, especially with faith, hope, charity, devotion, and piety, as well as with the fruits of the good works of prayer, fasting, and almsgiving. The sweet guest of our soul who does not need our goods asks for these ornaments. Besides, the physician who visits us is also the King and God whose purity is infinite and requires the purest abode. Hear Saint John Chrysostom in *Homily 66, To the People of Antioch*; he says, "To what shall we compare the purity that one who enjoys that sacrifice ought to possess? Should not the hand that breaks this bread and the mouth that is filled with spiritual fire be more resplendent than any ray of the sun?"[11]

Now let whoever desires to live well and to die well enter into the chamber of his heart and, with his door closed, alone with his heart alone, in the presence of God, who searches the loins and heart, let him consider carefully how often and with what preparation he partakes of the sacrament of the Lord's Supper. And if he finds that by God's grace he partakes frequently and salutarily and thus is well nourished and is gradually being cured of the diseases of the vices and daily grows more and more in the virtues and in good works, let him rejoice with fear and continue to serve the Lord in a fear that is chaste and filial, not servile. But if he is one of those who are content with annual communion and do not think any more of this most salutary sacrament and, having forgotten to eat this life-giving bread, are growing fat and heavy, as their souls grow gradually weaker and dry up, let him realize that he is very unwise and far removed from the kingdom of God. For annual communion was prescribed by the ecumenical council not as at most an annual event, but as at least an annual occurrence, if one does not want to be thrown out of the Church and handed over to Satan. Hence, these persons generally receive their Lord in the sacrament not with the love of a son, but with the fear of a slave. And soon afterward they return to the cornhusks meant for the swine, to the delights of the world, to temporal gain, to their ambitions for ephemeral honors, so that in death they hear with the rich banqueter, "Son, remember that you in your lifetime have received good things" (Lk 16:25). But if there should be anyone who frequents the mysteries either every Sunday or even daily, if he has the office of priest, and yet does not guard against mortal sins and does not practice good works and has not truly left the world, but, like others who are of the world, longs for financial gain, takes delight in the snares of the flesh, and craves for positions of honor and dignity, he certainly eats the Lord's flesh unto his own judgment. And the more often he unworthily handles the sacred mysteries, the more he imitates Judas the betrayer, of whom the Lord said, "It were better for that man if he had not been born" (Mt 26:24). Yet no one should despair of salvation as long as he lives. Let him who in the chamber of his heart ponders his years and deeds and recognizes that he has hitherto run astray from the path of salvation realize that there is still time to come to his senses, if he only desires to do penance in a serious way and to return to the path of truth.

I want to add at the end of this chapter what Saint Bonaventure wrote in the *Life of Saint Francis* concerning the marvelous piety and love of this holy man for the holy eucharist so that his ardor might warm our tepidity or coldness. He says, "He burned with reverence for the sacrament of the Lord's body with a fervor of all his being, dazed with wonder, especially over that most loving kindness and most kind love. Often he partook so devoutly that he made others devout, when, as if drunk in spirit at the sweet taste of the immaculate Lamb, he was almost completely caught up into an ecstasy of mind."[12] Far removed from such piety are not merely many lay communicants, but also many priests who celebrate and perform something so holy with such unbelievable haste that they do not seem to know what they are doing and do not allow others to consider a little more attentively so great a reality.

CHAPTER THIRTEEN

The thirteenth rule of the art of dying well, which is penance.

There follows the sacrament of penance, which principally involves three virtues on the part of the one who receives it: contrition in the heart, confession on the lips, and satisfaction in deed. For those who correctly perform these three undoubtedly obtain pardon for their sins. But we must see and most carefully consider whether the contrition is true, the confession complete, and the satisfaction full.

Let us begin with contrition. The Prophet Joel cries out, "Rend your hearts, and not your garments" (Jl 2:13). When the Hebrews wanted to manifest sorrow, they tore their garments. But the holy prophet warns that, if we wish to manifest true and inner sorrow before God for sin committed, we should rend our hearts. And the Prophet David adds that we should not only rend, but also crush and, so to speak, reduce them to dust. "A contrite and humbled heart, O God, you will not despise" (Ps 51:19). These images clearly show that to please God by penance it is not enough to say in words, "I am sorry for my sin." Rather, we need the deep and profound sorrow from the heart that can hardly be found without sobs and tears and sighs. It is amazing how severely the holy Fathers speak of true contrition. Saint Cyprian says in the sermon *On Apostates*, "Let us weep as abundantly as we have sinned greatly. Let careful and long treatment not be lacking for a deep wound. Let penance be no less than the sin. We ought to pray and beg more insistently, pass the day in mourning, spend nights in watching and tears, fill every moment with tears and laments, lie on the ground and cling to the ashes, turn about in haircloth and dirt."[1] Clement of Alexandria in Eusebius's *History* calls penance "a baptism of tears."[2] Saint Gregory Nazianzen, in the *Second Homily on Baptism*, says, "I welcome penitents if I see them wet with tears."[3] Theodoretus, in the *Epitome of Divine Decrees*, in the chapter on penance, writes that wounds received after baptism are curable, but not as before, by the easy task of the bath of regeneration, but by many tears and hard labors.[4]

All the holy Fathers have written thoughts like these on the genuineness of contrition. Now very many approach confession who show little or no contrition. Yet those who truly want to be reconciled with God and to live well so that later they may die well ought to enter into their heart and, with the door closed to all disturbance, meditate on these and similar thoughts: Alas! What have I done, poor wretch that I am! I have committed this outrage and that. First, I have offended that sweetest Father, the author of every good, who has loved me so much, who has surrounded me on every side with his gifts. There are as many signs of his love as I see good things in myself and others. What shall I say of my Christ? He loved me when I was an enemy and handed himself over for me as "an offering and a sacrifice to God to ascend in fragrant odor" (Eph

5:2). And am I so ungrateful and wretched that I do not cease from offending him? How great is my cruelty! My Lord was beaten with rods, crowned with thorns, fixed to the cross with nails in order to heal my former sins and crimes. And I do not cease a moment from adding new ones. Naked on the cross he cried out that he thirsted for my salvation, and I continue to offer him gall and bitter vinegar to drink. Who will explain to me the greatness of the glory from which I fell when I committed this or that mortal sin? I was an heir of the kingdom of heaven, of blessed eternal life; from this great and splendid and immense happiness in every respect I fell wretchedly through that brief pleasure or through those words even of blasphemy against God which brought me no good. And from that great happiness to what fate have I descended? To captivity to the devil, my cruelest enemy! And as swiftly as that foul wall of my body, which every moment threatens ruin, will break down, so swiftly and without any remedy I shall descend into the eternal fire. Alas, wretched me! Perhaps tomorrow, perhaps this night I shall begin to dwell in those endless fires. But above all these my heart is twisted and torn by the ingratitude of myself, the worst son and servant, toward the best and most loving Father and Lord. For the more he heaped his gifts upon me, the more I offended him by my sins.

If you want to ponder carefully these and similar things, locked in the chamber of your heart, whoever you are who deign to read this little book, I surely hope that you will obtain from the good Lord the gift of contrition. David once entered as a penitent into the solitude of his heart after having committed adultery and, as soon as he felt contrition, he began to wet his bed with tears (Ps 6:7). Peter entered into his own heart as a penitent after denying Christ and immediately "wept bitterly" (Mt 26:75). That sinful woman entered into her heart as a penitent and immediately "began to bathe the feet of Jesus with her tears, and wiped them with the hair of her head" (Lk 7:38). Hence, these are the fruits of holy contrition which are only born in the solitude of the heart.

Now let us say a few things about confession. I see many men approach this most salutary sacrament with no fruit or very little. And for no other reason than because they do not enter into their heart when they prepare for making their confession. There are some who so negligently approach this task that they can only say in a general and confused fashion that they have violated all the commandments or have committed all the mortal sins. They deserve only a general and confused absolution. In fact they do not deserve even such an absolution. For they confess what perhaps they did not do and do not confess what they really did. There are others who learned to state their sins individually and in order, but take no account of the quality of the person, of the place or the time, of the number and of those other things which are called circumstances. This is a remarkable and dangerous negligence. For it is one thing to strike a cleric, another to strike a layman. Excommunication is attached to the first striking, not to the second. It is one thing to have intercourse with a virgin; it is quite another thing to do it with a religious nun, still another with a married woman, and yet another thing with a prostitute. It is one thing to do it once; quite another to fall into the same sin ten times. The sin is the same, but multiple. Finally, there are some—and this is more astonishing—who think that internal sins, such as desires of fornication, adultery, murder, and theft, are not sins if they are not carried out in deed. They do not even count wanton looks and lascivious words as sins. And yet the Lord himself speaks clearly when he says, "Anyone who so much as looks with lust at a woman has already committed adultery with her in his heart" (Mt 5:28). If one wants to consult his conscience and make a profitable and salutary confession, he must first find some book on the manner of properly confessing sins, or he should at least consult a good and learned confessor. Then he should enter into his heart and examine his conscience, not lightly and rapidly, but carefully and earnestly. Let him carefully search his thoughts, desires, words, and deeds as well as omissions, and let him open his conscience to a good and experienced physician of souls. Let him humbly seek absolution from him, ready to fulfill the penance that the confessor thinks should be imposed.

There remains satisfaction. Those wise men who have gone before us took much greater account of this than many of us seem to do. Since they seriously believed that one could make satisfaction to God much more easily here on earth than in purgatory, they imposed long and heavy penalties. As far as duration is concerned, they imposed penances of seven, fifteen, or thirty years, sometimes even for a whole lifetime. As to the quality, they imposed frequent fasts and even more frequent prayers. They forbade the use of baths, horses, chariots, and expensive clothes; they ordered abstinence from games, jokes, and theaters. Finally, their whole life was taken up in the grief and sadness fitting penitents. I will give an example.

In the Tenth Council of Toledo we read that the bishop of Bracchara, called Potamius, who was once defiled by a woman's touch (such is the Council's language), locked himself in a prison under no pressure from others and did nine months of penance. And then he made known by his own letter his sin and his freely undertaken penance to the council of bishops. But the council decreed that he should continue to do penance for the rest of his life, although the council still claimed that it dealt with him more humanely and mercifully than the rules and severity of the ancients would allow.[5] Such was the severity of old. But we are now so weak and delicate that the imposition of a fast on bread and water for a few days along with the recitation of seven psalms and litanies on the same number of days and the distribution of a few coins in alms to the poor seems to be severe, even if it is imposed as penance for many sins and crimes. But we shall severely pay in purgatory for having been easy upon ourselves here, as the justice of God demands, unless the power of true contrition flowing from burning love is so great that it is able to obtain from the mercy of God remission of all sin and punishment. A heart truly contrite and humble really arouses the mercy of God our Father in a marvelous way. For the sweetness and goodness of the Father cannot refrain from going forth to the prodigal but truly repentant son, and embracing and kissing him. He will give him the ring of peace, wipe away the tears of sorrow, and fill him with tears of joy sweeter than all honey (Lk 15:11–32).

CHAPTER FOURTEEN

The fourteenth rule of the art of dying well, which is the sacrament of orders.

The last two sacraments that we will briefly consider do not concern all Christians. The one pertains to clerics, namely, the sacrament of orders; the other to laymen, namely, the sacrament of matrimony. Of the first let us speak briefly, not mentioning everything about the sacrament, but only that which has to do with the art of living well and dying happily.

There are seven orders, four minor and three major. Of these, the highest, which is called the presbyterate, is divided in two. There are greater priests who are called bishops, and lesser ones who are priests. All of these orders are preceded by first tonsure, which serves as the doorway to all orders and is what really makes one a cleric. Because what is required of clerics with regard to living piously and religiously is required all the more of those in minor or major orders and especially of priests and bishops, I will be content to consider and explain briefly those things which concern clerics.

There are two points that need explanation regarding them: first, the ritual itself by which one becomes a cleric; then, the office which clerics enjoy in the Church. The ritual by which one becomes a cleric can be grasped from *The Pontifical Book*.[1] First the hairs of the head are clipped. This rite signifies the laying aside of superfluous thoughts and desires, such as, the thoughts and desires of temporal things, of wealth, honors, pleasures, and other things of that sort. They are told to say, as their hairs are clipped, the verse of the fifteenth psalm, "The Lord is the portion of my inheritance and of my cup; it is you who will restore my inheritance to me" (Ps 16:5). Then the bishop orders that a white surplice be brought out, and he clothes the new cleric with it, saying the words of the Apostle to the Ephesians, "May the Lord clothe you with the new man, which has been created according to God in justice and holiness of truth" (Eph 4:24). The new cleric is not assigned any office, but in accord with custom, his role is to serve the priest when he says Mass privately.

Let us now consider the height of perfection required in a cleric. And if so much is required in a cleric, how much more is required in an acolyte, in a subdeacon, in a deacon, in a priest, in a bishop? My mind trembles at the thought of it, since one hardly finds in many priests what is properly demanded in a single cleric. The cleric is bidden to cast aside superfluous thoughts and desires which are proper to worldly men, that is, to men who belong to this world, who are of this world, and who constantly think and desire the things of the world. The good cleric is bidden to seek no other portion or inheritance but God, so that God is his sole portion and his inheritance and he is said to be and truly is the portion and inheritance of God alone. Oh, the height of clerical perfection that renounces the whole world to possess God alone and to be, in turn, possessed by God alone! This is signified by those words of the psalm, "The Lord is the portion of my inheritance and of my cup." "The portion of my inheritance" is said to be that portion of an estate which falls to each brother during its division. Hence, the sense of those words is not that a cleric should want part of his inheritance to be God and another part to be earthly wealth. Rather, he should desire from the heart to transfer his whole portion, that is, whatever could belong to him from this world, to God by a good act of will. There seems to be a difference between "cup" and "inheritance," for a cup has to do with pleasures and delights while an inheritance has to do with wealth and honors. Thus the complete meaning is: Lord, my God, from this time whatever riches or delights or other temporal goods I could have hoped for in the world, I desire to possess wholly in you alone. You alone will more than suffice in place of all these things. And since an abundance of heavenly goods cannot be had here on earth, the good cleric continues praying and says, "It is you who will restore my inheritance to me." What on your account I have rejected and cast aside, either giving to your poor or pardoning for your sake those who have taken them away, you faithfully keep for me and will restore at the proper time, not in its corruptible form, but in yourself who are the inexhaustible font of all goods.

But lest anyone want to contest this explanation of ours, we will add two witnesses beyond all exception, namely, Saint Jerome and Saint Bernard. In his Letter to Nepotianus, *On the Life of Clerics*, Saint Jerome says, "Therefore, let a cleric who serves the Church of Christ translate his title. And once he has translated the word, let him strive to be what it says. For if he is called *kleros* in Greek, he is called *sors* (lot) in Latin. They are called clerics, either because they are of the Lord's lot or because the Lord is their lot, that is, the portion of clerics. But whoever is either the portion of the Lord or has the Lord as his portion ought to prove himself such as to possess the Lord or to be possessed by the Lord. He who possesses the Lord and says with the Prophet 'The Lord is my portion' can have nothing apart from the Lord. But if he wants to have something else besides the Lord, the Lord will not be his portion. For example, if he wants to have gold, silver, possessions, and fancy clothes, the Lord will not deign to be his portion along with those other portions."[2] Thus wrote Saint Jerome, and if anyone wants to read his whole letter, he will find that he demands a very great degree of perfection in clerics. Now here is Saint Bernard, who not only approves the opinion of Saint Jerome, but at times uses his words without mentioning him. Thus he speaks in that long sermon on the words of Saint Peter found in the Gospel of Saint Matthew: "Behold, we have left all" (Mt 19:27). He says, "A cleric who has a portion on earth will not have a portion in heaven. If a cleric has anything besides the Lord, the Lord will not be his portion." And a little later he states what a cleric may keep for himself from church goods: "Not to give to the poor what belongs to the poor is recognized to be a crime equal to sacrilege. The powers of churches snatch from the patrimony of the poor with sacrilegious cruelty whatever ministers and managers, not indeed lords and owners, accept beyond food and clothing."[3] That is what Saint Bernard says; with Saint Jerome he says not what is false, but what is perfect.

Next comes the rite of vesting with the white surplice, along with the words of the Apostle, "Put on the new man, which has been created according to God in justice and holiness of truth" (Eph 4:24). For it is not enough that clerics do not abound with riches. Men who are vowed to the service of the altar, on which the Lamb without stain is daily offered, must also lead an innocent and spotless life. But to put on the new man is nothing more than the stripping off of the conduct of the old Adam who ruined his life and the putting on of the conduct of the new Adam, that is, Christ, who was born in a new way of a virgin and started a new life in justice and holiness of truth, not only in moral justice, but also in true and supernatural holiness. Such justice and holiness Christ revealed in himself, who, as the Apostle Peter bears witness, "did no sin, neither was deceit found in his mouth" (1 Pt 2:22). I wish that we would have many clerics of that sort who would reveal in their actions and their lives what they profess with the white vestment!

Finally, it is the office of clerics to assist devoutly, seriously, attentively, diligently, and with angelic purity at the divine sacrifice in which the Lamb of God is daily offered. I know there are many pious clerics in the Church; however, I not only know but have very often seen impudent men serve at the Lord's altar whose eyes wander about as though they were not performing something awesome and divine, but common and ordinary. Perhaps a sin so grave inheres not in the server alone, but also in the priest celebrating the sacrifice when at times he hurries and behaves so undevoutly that he seems not to know what he is doing. Let them hear what Saint John

Chrysostom says about the time of celebrating Mass. He says in the sixth book of *On the Priesthood*, "During that time the angels assist the priest, and the whole order of heavenly powers is heard, and the place near the altar is full of choirs of angels in honor of him who is offered in sacrifice."[4] We can readily believe this just on the basis of the greatness of the sacrifice which is offered. Let them hear also Saint Gregory; in the fourth book of the *Dialogues* he says, "Who among the faithful can doubt that in the very hour of sacrifice the heavens are opened at the word of the priest, the choirs of angels are present, the lowest are coupled to the highest, the earthly are joined to the heavenly, and one reality is made from things visible and invisible?"[5] If the celebrating priest and the serving cleric seriously weighed these things, how could they perform something so great in the manner they do? Oh, what a sad and deplorable sight it would be if we had the eyes of our mind opened to see the priest touching the divine mysteries, surrounded on every side by choirs of angels struck with awe and trembling at what he does and crying out in wonder with spiritual cries! And yet the priest in their midst is utterly cold and, as if stupid, pays no attention to what he does, does not understand what he says, and thus hastens on to the end, confusing signs and rushing over words so that he seems not to know what he is doing. At times the clerical server looks about hither and yon and chats away with someone. Thus is God mocked, thus are the sacred mysteries scorned, thus heretics are given matter for criticism. Wherefore, I warn and urge all major and minor clerics that, being dead to the world, they live for God alone, not pursuing an abundance of temporal possessions, but preserving innocence with great zeal and treating the divine mysteries with the reverence they deserve, while they bring others to treat them so as well. Thus they will gain great confidence for themselves before the Lord and will constantly fill the Church with the good odor of Christ.

CHAPTER FIFTEEN

The fifteenth rule of the art of dying well, which is on matrimony.

There follows the sacrament of matrimony with its twofold institution both as a civil contract of the natural law and as a sacrament of the law of the Gospel. We will speak briefly of each institution, not in general, but only for the purpose of living well so that we may later die well. Marriage was first instituted by God in the earthly paradise, for the words of God, "It is not good for man to be alone; let us make him a help like unto himself" (Gn 2:18), can only be understood to refer to a help for the procreation and education of children. For, as Saint Augustine correctly teaches, men need the help of women only in bearing and educating children. In other matters men are better helped by other men than by women.[1] Hence, shortly after the creation of woman Adam said under divine inspiration, "A man shall leave father and mother, and shall cleave to his wife" (Gn 2:24), and our Saviour attributes these words to God in Matthew, when he says, "Have you not read that the Creator, from the beginning, made them male and female, and said, 'For this cause a man shall leave his father and mother, and cleave to his wife, and the two shall become one flesh?' Therefore now they are no longer two, but one flesh. What therefore God has joined together, let no man put asunder" (Mt 19:4–6). The Lord attributed those words to God, because Adam did not speak them on his own, but under God's inspiration. And this was the first institution of matrimony.

The second institution, or rather the elevation of matrimony to the eminence of a sacrament, is found in the Apostle in these words of the Letter to the Ephesians, " 'For this cause a man shall leave his father and mother, and cleave to his wife; and the two shall become one flesh.' This is a great mystery—I mean in reference to Christ and to the Church" (Eph 5:31–32). Saint Augustine teaches that matrimony is a true sacrament in the book *The Good of Marriage*. He says, "In our marriages the holiness of the sacrament counts more than fertility of the womb."[2] And in chapter 24 he says, "The good of marriages among all nations and all peoples lies in the purpose of generating and in the fidelity of chastity. The good of marriage among the people of God lies also in the holiness of a sacrament."[3] And in the book *On Faith and Works,* he says, "In the city of the Lord and on his holy mountain, that is, the Church, there is commended not only the bond of matrimony, but also its sacrament."[4] But this is not the place to discuss these matters in detail. What is needed here is an explanation of how men and women joined in matrimony can live so that they may be confident that they will die well.

There are three goods of marriage if it is properly used: offspring, fidelity, and the grace of the sacrament. One must seek the generation of children and their good education if he wants to use matrimony well. On thc other hand, one gravely sins in not seeking offspring from marriage, but only the pleasure of the flesh. Thus one of the sons of the patriarch Judah, by the name of Onan, was seriously reproached in the Holy Scripture because during intercourse with his wife he spilled his seed on the ground to prevent sons from being born (Gn 38:9). For that is not the use but the abuse of marriage. If at times good couples are burdened by many children whom they find difficult to feed because of poverty, the remedy that is morally good and pleasing to God is to sleep in separate beds by mutual consent and to spend their time in prayer and fasting. For if it is pleasing to God that spouses grow old in a virginal manner according to the example of the Virgin Mother of God and Saint Joseph, whose manner of life was imitated by the Emperor Henry and his wife, Cunagunda, by King Edward and his wife, Egdida, by Count Elzear and his wife, Dalphina, and many others, why should it displease God or men that, after having had children, spouses cease by mutual consent from the marriage act so that they may spend the remaining part of their life in fasting and prayer?

It is also a grave sin if anyone already married neglects children born to him and permits them to go without a good upbringing or the necessities of life. There are many examples of this sort of thing in sacred and profane history, but since I am aiming at brevity, I will be content with one found in the First Book of Kings. God himself speaks as follows: "In that day I will raise up against Eli all the things I have spoken concerning his house; I will begin, and I will make an end. For I have foretold unto him, that I will judge his house forever, for iniquity, because he knew that his sons did wickedly, and did not chastise them. Therefore have I sworn to the house of Eli, that the iniquity of his house shall not be expiated with victims nor offerings forever" (1 Sm 3:12–14). The Lord foretold this and a little later brought it to fulfillment. For the sons of Eli were killed in war, and Eli himself, falling backward from his stool, broke his neck and perished miserably (1 Sm 4:11, 18). If Eli, otherwise a just man and judge of his people, perished miserably with his sons and lost the governance of his people because of the sins of sons whom he did not raise as he should have, and did not chastise when they later had become worse, what will happen to those who not only do not try to raise their children well, but even entice them to sin by the bad example of their lives? Certainly they ought to expect nothing but a horrible end for themselves and for their children, unless they become wise and do fitting penance for their sins.

The second good of marriage is fidelity, wherein the spouses understand that their bodies are not their own, but the spouse's. And as one cannot deny to the other what is owed, so one cannot give his body to another than his spouse. A symbol of this is the wedding ring. This teaching is found clearly in the Apostle. He says, "Let the husband render to the wife her due, and likewise the wife to the husband. The wife has not authority over her body, but the husband; the husband likewise has not authority over his body, but the wife. Do not deprive each other, except perhaps by consent for a time, that you may give yourselves to prayer" (1 Cor 7:3–5). This is the apostolic teaching that Christian spouses ought carefully to observe, if they want to live well and to die well. For adulterers, if their sin is made public, are readily punished by judges; in other cases relatives or family members do away with them for the sake of honor. But secret adulterers, who are more numerous, will be condemned to eternal punishments by the most just and omnipotent Judge, from whom secrets are not hidden.

The third and finest good is the grace of the sacrament which God himself pours into the hearts of good spouses, if they are found well-disposed and prepared when the wedding is legitimately celebrated. Besides the other goods which it brings, this grace is a wonderful help for building love between spouses, even though differing talents, habits, diseases, and dispositions of body and soul can easily breed hostility. Above all it is the imitation of the marriage of Christ with his Church that makes a marriage sweet and blessed. The Apostle speaks of that marriage in his Letter to the Ephesians, "Husbands, love your wives, just as Christ also loved the Church, and delivered himself up for her, that he might sanctify her, cleansing her in the bath of water by means of the word of life, in order that he might present to himself the Church in all her glory, not having spot or wrinkle" (Eph 5:25–27). The same blessed Apostle also warns wives, "Let wives be subject to their husbands as to the Lord; because a husband is head of the wife, just as Christ is head of the Church, being himself savior of the body. But just as the Church is subject to Christ, so also let wives be to their husbands in all things" (Eph 5:22–24). Finally the Apostle concludes, "Let each one of you also love his wife just as he loves himself; and let the wife respect her husband" (Eph 5:33). If this apostolic teaching is carefully weighed and observed, it will make happy marriages on earth and in heaven.

Let us briefly explain this whole apostolic doctrine of Paul. First the Apostle urges husbands to love their wives "as Christ also loved the Church." Certainly Christ loved the Church with the love of friendship, not with the love of desire. He sought the good of the Church, the benefit of the Church, the salvation of the Church, not some benefit or some pleasure of his own. Thus a husband is not imitating Christ when, captured by love of his wife's fairness, he loves her because of her exceptional beauty, or because of a dowry of thousands of gold pieces, or because of a rich inheritance. For such a husband does not love his spouse, but loves himself and desires to satisfy the lust of his flesh or the lust of his eyes, which is called avarice. Thus Solomon, at first wise, but at the end foolish, loved his wives and concubines not with the love of friendship, but with the love of desire, seeking not to do good for them, but to satisfy his carnal lust. Blinded by that lust, he was not afraid to sacrifice to foreign gods, lest he spoil his enjoyment in the least.

That Christ sought not himself in his marriage with the Church, that is, his own benefit or pleasure, but the good of the Church, is clear from the following words, "And he delivered himself up for her, that he might sanctify her, cleansing her in the bath of water by means of the word of life." It was true and perfect love to hand himself over to punishment for the eternal salvation of the Church, his spouse. Not only did Christ love the Church with the love of friendship rather than of lust, but he loved her with an endless rather than a temporary love. For as he never set aside the human nature he once took to himself, so also he joined to himself the Church as his bride by the bond of indissoluble marriage. "Yea I have loved you with an everlasting love" (Jer 31:3), he says through Jeremiah the prophet. Although the marriage of Hebrews and pagans can be dissolved in certain cases, a marriage that has been consummated between Christians is utterly indissoluble, because it is a sacrament signifying the marriage of Christ with the Church, and that marriage is utterly indissoluble.

Afterward the same Apostle adds an instruction for wives and teaches that they should be subject to their husbands as the Church is subject to Christ. Jezebel did not observe this commandment; she wanted to rule over her husband and destroyed herself and him with all their children (1 Kgs 21; 2 Kgs 10). And would that there were fewer wives among us who strive to rule over their husbands! But perhaps it is the fault of the husbands who do not know how to maintain their primacy. Certainly Sarah, the wife of Abraham, was so subject to her husband that she called him her lord. She said, "I am grown old, and my lord is an old man" (Gn 18:12). Saint Peter praised this virtue of Sarah when he said in his First Letter, "The holy women were subject to their husbands. So Sarah obeyed Abraham, calling him lord" (1 Pt 3:5–6). However, it seems strange that the Apostles Peter and Paul everywhere teach that husbands should love their wives and that wives should fear their husbands, or what comes to the same thing, that they should be subject to them. Should not a wife also love her husband? Ought she not love her husband and be loved by him? She ought, of course, to love her husband and be loved by him. But she ought to love with fear and reverence so that love does not interfere with fear. Otherwise a wife turns into a tyrant. Dalilah surely mocked her husband, Samson, otherwise so strong, treating him not as her husband, but as her servant (Jgs 16:4ff.). And in the third book of Esdras the story is told of the king who, ensnared by love of his mistress, allowed her to sit on his right and to take the crown from his head and place it on her own and to slap the king himself (3 Ezr 4:29–32).[5] And so it is not strange that the first woman was told by the Lord, "And you shall be under your husband's power, and he shall have dominion over you" (Gn 3:16). Hence, a husband needs much wisdom in order to both love and guide his wife and also to admonish, teach, and, if need be, correct and improve her. He must do this while he truly loves her as a part of his body and makes her to love him in return and convinces her that she is equally loved by her husband and admonished out of love, not out of hatred. We have the example of Saint Monica, the mother of Saint Augustine. Though she had a violent and pagan husband, she put up with him so shrewdly and piously that she was loved by him and he was converted eventually to Christ. Consult the *Confessions* of Saint Augustine.[6]

CHAPTER SIXTEEN

The sixteenth rule of the art of dying well, which is on the sacrament of extreme unction.

There remains the last sacrament, which is called extreme unction. From it we derive a highly useful lesson, not only for the end of life, but for its whole course. In this sacrament all the parts of the body are anointed, in which reside the five senses of the body, and it is said with reference to each, "May God pardon you whatever sins you may have committed through sight," and so of the rest of the senses. We gather from this that the five senses are the gates through which sins of all kinds enter into the soul. So if anyone carefully guards these gates, he will easily avoid a great number of sins, and thus he will live well and die happily.

We will speak briefly on the custody of these five gates. That the eye is the gate through which there enter sins which pertain to lust, Christ, the teacher of all, showed when he said, "Anyone who so much as looks with lust at a woman has already committed adultery with her in his heart. So if your right eye is an occasion of sin to you, pluck it out and cast it from you; for it is better for you that one of your members should perish than that your whole body should be thrown into hell" (Mt 5:28–29). We know that the old men who saw Susanna naked immediately blazed with lust for her and thus suffered a wretched death (Dn 13:1–64). We know that even David, an especially close friend of God, fell into adultery from merely the sight of Bathsheba in her bath and that murder and innummerable losses followed (2 Sm 11:1–27). Natural reason too supports this, for a woman's beauty in a way forces a man to love her and the beauty of a man also forces a woman to love him. And that love does not abate until it comes to sexual intercourse because of the lust that is left in us from original sin. The holy Apostle deplores this evil, when he says, "I see another law in my members, warring against the law of my mind and making me prisoner to the law of sin that is in my members. Unhappy man that I am! Who will deliver me from the body of this death? The grace of God through Jesus Christ our Lord" (Rom 7:23–25).

What remedy shall we find for such a serious temptation? The remedy is at hand and easy enough with God's help if one wishes to use it. The remedy is found in Saint Augustine's *Letter* 109, which contains the rule for nuns.[1] This holy Father speaks to his nuns as follows: "If your eyes shall fall upon anyone, let them be fixed upon no one." For a mere glance is almost inevitable, but it cannot or at least usually does not strike the heart unless it is prolonged. And so if one deliberately accustoms himself not to gaze at a beautiful person, even if he should accidentally come upon such persons, but immediately turns aside his eyes out of a good habit, no danger will befall him. Saint Augustine spoke the truth when he said that it is not a glimpse, but a lingering gaze that is dangerous. And this is what holy Job teaches by his example, when he says, "I made a covenant with my eyes, that I would not so much as think upon a virgin" (Jb 31:19). He does not say there, "I made a covenant" that I would not see, but "that I would not so much as think upon a virgin." That means: I will not cling so long to the sight of a virgin that the sight penetrates to the heart and I begin to think of her beauty and gradually to desire her company and embrace. And he gives the best reason, the sort it was fitting for such a holy a man to give, "For what part should God have in me?" (Jb 31:2). He so much as said, "My part and all my good is God, indeed the greatest good, a better than which cannot be thought. But God loves only the chaste and the just." Here also belongs the Lord's admonition, "If your eye is an occasion of sin to you, pluck it out" (Mt 5:29), that is, so possess it as if you did not possess it. And thus accustom yourself to refrain your eyes from such sights as if you were blind. Those who from early youth begin to exercise care about this matter do not find it hard to flee and avoid sins of this sort for the rest of their lives. On the other hand, those who have developed bad habits, can, although with difficulty, change their conduct with the help of God's grace and escape this most dangerous snare.

Someone might object as follows. Why did God create beautiful women and handsome men if he did not want them to be seen and loved? The answer is easy and twofold. God created men and women for the sake of marriage. Thus God spoke in the beginning, "It is not good for man to be alone; let us make him a help like unto himself" (Gn 2:18). A man does not need the help of a woman except for giving birth to and educating children, as we said above in accord with the teaching of Saint Augustine in his book *The Literal Meaning of Genesis.*[2] But man and woman would not readily come together nor willingly live together through all of life were it not for the beauty that wins their love. Hence, since a woman was made beautiful so that she might be loved by her husband, she ought not to be loved with a love leading to intercourse except by her husband. Thus it is said in the law of the Lord, "You shall not covet your neighbor's wife" (Dt 5:21). And to husbands the Apostle says, "Husbands, love your wives" (Eph 5:25). Moreover, there are many good and beautiful things which should not be sought by everyone, but only by those for whom they are suitable. Eating meat and drinking wine are good for the healthy, but not for the ill. So too the beauty of men and women will be safely loved after the resurrection when we will be truly healthy, because then we mortals will no longer be burdened by the sickness of carnal lust. So it should not seem strange that everyone is now permitted to enjoy the sight of the sun and moon and stars and flowers and other beautiful things of that sort which do not feed the sickness of lust, while everyone is not permitted to gaze upon beautiful women or handsome men lest that gaze might increase and feed the sickness of lust.

After the sense of sight there comes the sense of hearing, which should be guarded just as well as the sense of sight. And the tongue, the instrument of speech, should be classed with the ears. For words, whether good or bad, do not reach hearing unless they are sounded on the tongue. And unless the tongue is carefully guarded, it is the cause of very many evils. Thus Saint James proclaims, "If anyone does not offend in word, he is a perfect man," and a little later, "Behold, how small a fire—how great a forest it kindles! And the tongue is a fire, the very world of iniquity" (Jas 3:2, 5–6). The holy apostle makes three points in this passage. First, to guard the tongue well is a most difficult task, and thus there are only a few perfect men who know how to guard the tongue well. Second, an immense evil can quickly spring from a wicked tongue; he explains this point by the comparison with the spark of fire which, unless it is quickly put out, can devour a large forest of trees. Thus one word spoken unguardedly can stir up suspicions of a crime, from which there follow hostilities, fights, quarrels, murders, and the destruction of whole families. Lastly, Saint James teaches that a bad tongue is not just one evil, but includes a multitude of evils. Thus he calls it a world of iniquity. For through it evil deeds are prepared, such as fornication and thefts, or are committed, such as perjury and false witness, or are defended, such as an evil man excusing the sin he committed or claiming a good he did not do. Again the tongue is rightly called a world of iniquity because by the tongue man sins against God by blasphemy and perjury, against his neighbor by detraction and anger, against himself by boasting that he has done good works which he really has not and saying that he has not done evil deeds which in fact he did do.

I want to add to this testimony of the Apostle James that of David the prophet in the first of the Gradual Psalms. He says, "O Lord, deliver my soul from wicked lips, and a deceitful tongue" (Ps 120:2). If the holy king feared for himself a wicked and deceitful tongue, what ought private men do, and even more if they are not merely private, but poor, weak, and obscure? The Prophet adds, "What shall be given to you, or what shall be added to you, to a deceitful tongue?" (Ps 120:3). The words are obscure because of the peculiarity of the Hebrew language, but the meaning seems to me to be: Not without cause do I fear for myself a wicked and deceitful tongue, because such a tongue is so great an evil that no evil seems to add to it. The Prophet continues and says, "The sharp arrows of the mighty, with coals that lay waste." These words express in an elegant comparison the great evil of a deceitful tongue. The Prophet compares it to a flaming arrow shot by a mighty arm. First, arrows strike from afar and travel with such speed that they can hardly be avoided. Second, the arrows to which the deceitful tongue is compared are said to be shot by a powerful and strong arm. Third, he adds that the arrows are sharp, that is, well polished and sharpened by an experienced craftsman. Finally, he says that they are like coals that lay waste, that is, flaming so that they can destroy anything however hard. And yet a wicked and deceitful tongue is not so much like the arrows of men as like the arrows shot from heaven, such as the heavenly bolts of lightning which nothing whatsoever can withstand. Thus the Prophet describes a deceitful and wicked tongue so that no evil can be thought to be great enough to be compared to it.

To make all this better understood, I will add two examples from Scripture. The first is of wicked Doeg the Edomite, who accused the priest Ahimelech in the presence of King Saul of having conspired with David against the king. This was sheer calumny and falsehood. Yet because the king was ill-disposed toward David at that time, he readily believed it all and ordered not only that Ahimelech the priest, an innocent man, be killed, but also all the other priests—as many as eighty-five men—who did nothing at all to offend the king. Nor was King Saul content with that slaughter; he ordered that everyone who dwelled in the priestly city of Nob be killed. And he was not content to take his anger out on all the men and women, but did so also against children and infants. He even extended his cruelty to animals, cows and cattle and asses (1 Sm 22:9–19). It is possible that David referred to this deceitful and wicked tongue of Docg the Edomite in the psalm whose verse we were expounding. This example clearly shows the power of deceitful and wicked tongues for evil.

We will take the second example from the Gospel according to Saint Mark. When the daughter of Herodias danced before Herod the tetrarch and his princes, the girl's dance so pleased Herod that he swore before them all that he would give the girl whatever she asked, even half of his kingdom. This stupid and rash oath was the cause of many evils. First, the daughter of Herodias asked her mother what she should request of him, and she told her to ask for the head of John the Baptist. She requested this, and soon the head of our Lord's precursor, torn from his body, was brought forth on a platter (Mk 6:14–29). How great are these evils! The mother sinned seriously by asking for something unjust. Herod the tetrarch sinned just as seriously in ordering the death of the innocent man who was the Lord's precursor, who was more than a prophet, a greater than whom had not come forth among those born of woman, and one whom he knew to be a just and holy man. He did this without grounds, without trial, at the time of a solemn meal, at the request of a dancing girl.

But let us hear the evils of punishment as we have heard the evils of sin. A little later Herod was stripped of his kingdom by the Emperor Caius [i.e., Caligula] and banished into permanent exile. Thus he who had sworn that he would give half of his kingdom exchanged the whole of it for permanent exile, as Josephus bears witness in *The Antiquities*.[3] The daughter of Herodias, who caused the death of Saint John the Baptist by her dancing, was crossing a frozen river when the ice broke and she fell entirely into the water except for her head, which was cut from the body and danced on the ice. Everyone understood why she perished so wretchedly. Herodias herself, overcome with grief, soon met her death and followed her daughter to the torments of hell. These tragic events were recorded by Necephorus Callistus in his *History*.[4] See how many evils of sin and of its punishment followed upon Herod the tetrarch's stupid and rash oath.

Let us proceed to the remedy that wise men ought to apply to the sins of the tongue. The holy Prophet, David, indicates in the beginning of Psalm 38 the remedy he used. He says, "I said, 'I will take heed to my ways that I sin not with my tongue' " (Ps 39:2), that is to say, "I will carefully guard my ways to escape sins of the tongue. For I will neither speak nor think nor do anything without previously weighing what I am about to do or say or think." For these are the ways by which men walk in this life. And so the remedy for harmful words, and not only for harmful words, but for harmful deeds, desires, or thoughts, is to consider and to weigh beforehand what I am about to do, say, think, or desire. It is a distinctive mark of a human person not to act rashly, but to reflect upon what is to be done and to do it if it agrees with right reason and not to do it if it does not. And what we said regarding action ought to be applied to speech, desire, and other acts of the rational soul.

Even if some are unable to weigh beforehand all that they are about to do or say, at least there should not be a wise man desirous of eternal salvation who does not daily approach God in prayer the first thing in the morning before he takes up the tasks of this life and ask that his ways, his deeds, his words, his desires, and his thoughts be directed to the glory of God and the salvation of his soul. Then when the day is over before he gets into bed for sleep, he should examine his conscience and ask himself whether he offended God in thought, word, deed, or desire. And if he should find some offense against God, especially a mortal one, he should not close his eyes for a night's rest unless he has been reconciled with God by true penance and has made a true and firm resolution to guard his way so that he does not sin again with his tongue or in his actions or by his desires. This should suffice for guarding the tongue.

With reference to the sense of hearing just a few things remain to be said. If the tongue is checked by the bridle of reason from breaking forth into wicked words, there will be almost nothing which can harm the sense of hearing. There are four kinds of speech to which we should close our ears so that they do not pierce our senses so as to infect the heart. The first place is occupied by words against the faith, which are listened to readily enough because of human curiosity. Yet if they penetrate within, they remove from the heart the faith which is the root and source of all goods. Among the words of unbelief there are none more dangerous than those which deny either the providence of God or the immortality of the human soul. For those words lead not so much to heresy as to atheism and open the gate fully to every outrage. The second kind of evil words lies in detraction, which utterly destroys brotherly love and is listened to eagerly enough by the curious. Holy David, who was a man according to God's heart, says in the psalms, "The man that in private detracted his neighbor, him did I persecute" (Ps 101:5). And since detractions are frequently heard in banquets, Saint Augustine placed the following verses on the wall of his dining room:

Whoever enjoys attacking with words
the lives of those not here,
should know that he is not welcome
at this table.

This is reported by Possidius in the *Life of Saint Augustine.*[5] The third kind of evil words consists of flattery. Flattery is willingly listened to, and yet it makes one puffed up and proud. Pride is the queen of the vices and most hateful to God. The fourth kind of evil words pertains to wantonness and is found in lovers' talk and lascivious songs. Nothing sweeter is heard by those who love this world, though nothing is more harmful than such words. Lascivious songs are like the songs of the Sirens, who gave men pleasure in order to cast them into the sea and devour them.

Against all these dangers the salutary remedy is to have good friends and to have the foresight to stay away from the wicked. For strangers are hesitant to introduce words of detraction, heresy, flattery, or lasciviousness before persons they have not previously met or with whom they are not familiar. Thus Solomon instructs his son in the beginning of Proverbs and states the first rule as follows, "My son, hear the instruction of your father," and so on. "If sinners shall entice you, consent not to them. If they shall say: 'Come with us, let us lie in wait for blood, let us hide snares for the innocent without cause; let us swallow him up alive like hell, and whole as one that goes down into the pit; we shall find all precious substance, we shall fill our houses with spoils; cast in your lot with us, let us all have one purse.' My son, walk not with them," and so on. "They themselves lie in wait for their own blood, and practice deceits against their own souls" (Prv 1:8, 10–15, 18). Thus this counsel of the wisest of men can apply a remedy to the sense of hearing so that it is not easily harmed by evil words. This is especially true if we add the words of the Lord, who was wiser than Solomon and openly declared that a man's enemies were members of his own household (Mt 10:36). So much for the sense of hearing.

The third sense is smell, about which almost nothing need be said. For the sense of smell has to do with odors, and they do not play a major role in harming the soul. Precious fragrances are a concern for only a few, and the common ones, such as the scents of flowers, roses and lillies, are harmless.

I come to the fourth sense, which is called the sense of taste. Sins which enter through that gate to harm the soul are generally of two sorts: gluttony and drunkenness. But from these many others arise. We have the Lord's warning about gluttony and drunkenness in Luke: "Take heed to yourselves lest your hearts be overburdened with gluttony and drunkenness" (Lk 21:34). We have also the warning of the Apostle in the Letter to the Romans, "Not in carousing and drunkenness" (Rom 13:13). Those two sins are counted in Holy Scripture with the deadly sins, as the Apostle says in his Letter to the Galatians, "Now the works of the flesh are manifest, which are immorality, uncleanness, licentiousness, idolatry, witchcrafts, . . . murders, drunkenness, carousings, and suchlike. And concerning these I warn you, as I have warned you, that they who do such things will not attain the kingdom of God" (Gal 5:19–21).

This is not the only punishment for these sins. Gluttony and drunkenness weigh down the heart so that it cannot rise up to ponder and obtain the things of God. Our Lord taught this point, and Saint Basil explains it in his *First Homily on Fasting* with two apt comparisons.[6] The first uses the sun and fog. For just as thick fog which rises from damp ground blocks the sky with clouds and prevents the rays of the sun from reaching us, so too gluttony and drunkenness stir up smoke and fog within us that obscure the sky of reason and snatch from us the rays of divine light. A second comparison is drawn from smoke and bees. For as bees, the producers of honey, are driven from their hives by smoke, so too the wisdom of God which, like a bee, brings forth in our souls the honey of virtue and grace and consolations, is driven out most easily by gluttony and drunkenness.

Furthermore, gluttony and drunkenness harm the health of the body. Antiphanes, a skilled physician, as Clement of Alexandria reports in the second book of *The Teacher*, claimed that the one cause of almost all the diseases was the quantity and variety of foods.[7] Saint Basil, on the other hand, in his *First Homily on Fasting*, thought that abstinence should be called the mother of good health.[8] And all physicians everywhere use fasting for restoring health to ill bodies and prescribe abstinence from wine and meat. Besides this, gluttony and drunkenness not only harm the integrity of soul and body, but generally family property as well. Gluttony and drunkenness have made many rich men poor and many masters slaves. Gluttony and drunkenness have deprived many poor beggars of the alms of the rich. For those who are not content with modest food and drink easily spend all their wealth on their own pleasures so that nothing is left for their needy brethern. Thus are fulfilled the words of the Apostle, "One is hungry, and another drinks overmuch" (1 Cor 11:21).

Let us leave this aside to get to the remedy. The example of all the saints can be a remedy against gluttony and drunkenness. I omit the holy hermits and monks, about whom Saint Jerome wrote in his *Letter to Eustochium on the Preservation of Virginity* that for them to eat something cooked was a luxurious diet.[9] I pass over Saint Ambrose who, according to the testimony of Paulinus in his biography, fasted every day except solemn feasts and Sundays.[10] I pass over Saint Augustine who, according to the testimony of Possidius in his biography, had on his table vegetables and herbs, and occasionally meat for the sake of guests and the ill.[11] I pass over the other saints. If anyone carefully weighs what the Lord of all and the Father of all did when he took upon himself the task of feeding his people in the desert, he will surely master the art of sobriety in a wonderful manner. For during forty years God who alone is powerful, wise, and good, who had the power, the knowledge, and the will to provide for his chosen people in the best manner, rained manna upon them from heaven and drew water from the rock. But manna was a food resembling bread made of wheat and honey, as is reported in the Book of Exodus (Ex 16:31). See how simply the most wise Lord wanted his people to take their meals. Bread was their food, water their drink. And yet all were sound and healthy until they began to be caught by the desire of meat.

In accord with the example of the Father, the Son of God, Christ Jesus, "in whom are hidden all the treasures of wisdom and knowledge" (Col 2:3), when he wanted to prepare a combined dinner and supper for many thousands, offered them pieces of bread and fish along with water to drink. The Lord Christ prepared a banquet for his hearers with such sobriety not just when he was still mortal, but even after his resurrection, when "all power in heaven and on earth" had been "given to" him (Mt 28:18), he offered his disciples a meal of only fish and bread on the shore of the lake. There was no mention of wine or anything else. Oh, how far removed are the plans of God from the plans of men! The King of heaven and earth enjoys simplicity and is delighted with sobriety; he is first of all concerned with enriching, filling, and delighting the soul. But men prefer to listen to their lust and to the devil, to their enemy rather than to God, unless we should say with the Apostle that the God of carnal men is their belly (Phil 3:19).

There remains the sense of touch, which is both the most crass and the liveliest of all. Through this, works of the flesh enter to stain the soul and at the same time to corrupt other persons, deeds which the blessed Apostle enumerates as follows: "The works of the flesh are manifest, which are immorality, uncleanness, licentiousness" (Gal 5:19). By three words the Apostle indicates all kinds of wantonness. And there is no need to go further in explaining these matters, which are better unknown among the faithful and whose names should never even be heard. Thus the same Apostle writes to the Ephesians: "But immorality and every uncleanness, let it not even be named among you, as becomes saints" (Eph 5:3).

As remedies against all these sins the following occur to me, and they are the very ones that physicians use for curing the sick. For physicians first start with fasting or abstinence; they forbid those who show signs of illness to eat meat and to drink wine. Likewise the person given to wantonness ought to abstain from excessive food and excessive drink. The Apostle prescribed that for Timothy. He says, "Use a little wine for your stomach's sake and your frequent infirmities" (1 Tm 5:23), that is, use wine because of the weakness of your stomach, but only a little, so as to avoid wantonnness, for in wine is wantonness (Eph 5:18). Second, physicians of the body employ bitter potions, bloodlettings, and other such things hostile to nature. So holy men said with the Apostle, "I chastise my body and bring it into subjection, lest perhaps after preaching to others I myself should be rejected" (1 Cor 9:27). For this reason the hermits and monks of old set up a form of life utterly opposed to the delights and pleasures of the flesh, in fasting, watches, prostrations on the ground, in scourgings and in hair cloth, not out of hatred for the body, but out of hatred for the wantonness of the flesh. I will mention but one of many examples. Saint Hilarion, as Saint Jerome reports in his biography, when tempted with lustful thoughts, said, addressing his body, "I will fix you so that you do not fight back, and I will not feed you with barley, but with straw. I will crush you with hunger and thirst so that you think of food rather than lasciviousness."[12] In addition, physicians of the body prescribe moderate exercise, such as walking or a ball game or something of that sort, to preserve health. The very same is highly conducive to preserving the health of the soul, for instance, if a man desirous of eternal salvation would give an hour a day to meditating on the mysteries of the redemption or the four last things or other topics of devotion. But if the meditation does not succeed as desired, he should at least spend some time each day in reading the Holy Scripture or pious books or lives of the saints.

Finally, an especially efficacious remedy for all temptations of the flesh and sins of wantonness is to flee idleness. For no one is as subject to filthy thoughts as one who has nothing to do and wastes his time, either looking out the window or chatting and playing with friends. On the other hand, none are more free from dirty thoughts than those who are busy the whole day in the toil of cultivating the fields or in practicing various arts. For this reason Christ, our teacher, chose poor parents so that they would prepare their food by their own labor, and he himself, before he went to take up the work of preaching, wanted to have as his foster father a woodworker and assisted him in that art. For they said of him, "Is he not the carpenter, the son of Mary?" (Mk 6:3). I wanted to add this so that workers and farmers would not regret their lot, since the Wisdom of God chose that lot for his mother and saintly foster father, not because they had need of this remedy, but so that he might warn us, who are weak, to flee idleness, if we wish to avoid many sins.

NOTES

Note to the Dedication

1. Gregory XIII, Ugo Buoncompagni, fostered the German, Greek, and English Colleges in Rome, but Ludwig von Pastor notes, in *The History of the Popes* (Volume XX, p. 586 [St. Louis, 1930]), "Gregory's generosity was displayed in the fullest way in the case of the college which held the first place among the educational and instructional institutions in Rome, the Roman College of the Jesuits." The Jesuit Gregorian University in Rome still honors the name of Gregory XIII.

Notes to the Preface

1. From the Roman Missal, the first Preface for Easter.
2. Saint Ambrose, *The Good of Death* [De bono mortis], passim [*PL* 14, 567–596].
3. The life of Saint Catherine of Genoa to which Bellarmine refers is probably that of Cattaneo Marabotto, *Vita della beata Caterina Adorni da Genova* (Venice, 1601).

Notes to Chapter Three

1. Saint Augustine, *Homilies on the Psalms*. On Psalm 31, Sermon 2, 5 [*PL* 38, 261].
2. Ibid., 6–8 [*PL* 38, 261–263]; and Saint Jerome, *Commentary on the Letter to Titus* [Commentariorum in epistulam ad Titum liber unus] c. 1, v. 16 [*PL* 26, 611–612].

NOTES

Notes to Chapter Four

1. Saint Gregory the Great, *Homilies on the Gospels* [XL Homiliarum in Evangelia libri duo] I, Homily 13 [*PL* 76, 1123–1127].

2. Saint Basil, *Commentary on Isaiah* [Enarratio in Isaiam Prophetam] c. 15 [*PG* 30, 638]; Saint Augustine, *On Continence* [De continentia] c. 7 [*PL* 40, 359–360]; Saint Gregory, *Homilies on the Gospels* I, Homily 13, c. 1 [*PL* 76, 1123].

3. Saint Cyprian, *Exhortation to Martyrdom* [De exhortatione martyrii] c. 8 [*PL* 4, 687–688].

4. Such references are indeed abundant: Mt 24:2, 25:13; Mk 13:33, 35, 37; Lk 21:36; 1 Cor 16:13; 1 Pt 4:7, 5:8; 1 Thes 5:6; Col 4:2; Rv 3:3, 6:15.

5. This decree of Pius V pertained only to clerics.

Notes to Chapter Five

1. Saint John Chrysostom, in Saint Thomas Aquinas, *The Golden Chain* [Catena aurea] on Luke 16; Saint Augustine, *Questions on the Gospels* [Quaestionum Evangeliorum libri duo] II, qu. 34 [*PL* 35, 1348–1349].

2. Saint Cyprian, *On Work and Almsgiving* [Liber de opere et elymosynis] c. 8 [*PL* 4, 631]; Saint Augustine, *Questions on the Gospels* II, qu. 34 [*PL* 35, 1349].

Notes to Chapter Seven

1. Saint John Chrysostom, *Two Books on Prayer*, apparently, *Homilies on the Incomprehensibility of God* [De incomprehensibili] IV, 5, and V, 6 [*PG* 48, 734, 743–744]. Bellarmine tells us in his *Ecclesiastical Writers* that he used the five-volume edition of Saint John Chrysostom published in Venice in 1574.

2. Saint Augustine, *The Lord's Sermon on the Mount* [De sermone Domini in monte] II, c. 7 [*PL* 34, 1280–1281].

3. Saint Augustine, *The Confessions* IX, c. 1 and c. 10 [*PL* 32, 763, 773–775].

4. Saint John Chrysostom, *On Praying to God* I, apparently, *Homilies on the Incomprehensibility of God* IV, 5 [*PG* 48, 734].

5. Saint Prosper, *The Vocation of All the Nations* I, c. 4 [*PL* 51, 650–651].

6. John Cassian, *Conference on Prayer* [Collatio IX. De oratione] c. 32 [*PL* 49, 808–809].

7. Saint Jerome, *Dialogue against the Luciferians* [Dialogus contra Luciferianos] c. 15 [*PL* 23, 178].

8. Saint Bernard, *Sermon* 25 [Sermo XXV. De obsecratione, oratione, postulatione et gratiarum actione] 7 [*PL* 183, 609].

9. Saint Augustine, *Homilies on the Psalms.* On Psalm 65, 24 [*PL* 38, 801].

Notes to Chapter Eight

1. Saint Augustine, *Letter* 36 (To Casulanus) c. 11 [*PL* 33, 147].

2. Saint Leo, *Fourth Sermon on the December Fast* [Sermo XV. De jejunio decimi mensis IV] c. 2 [*PL* 54, 175].

3. Saint Athanasius, *On Virginity* [De virginitate, sive de ascesi] [*PG* 28, 251–282]; Saint Basil, *First and Second Talks on Fasting* [De jejunio. Homiliae I et II] [*PG* 32, 163–198]; Saint Ambrose, *On Elias and Fasting* [De Elia et jejunio] [*PL* 14, 731–764]; Saint Bernard, *Sermon on the Vigil of Saint Andrew* [In vigilia Sancti Andreae Apostoli] [*PL* 183, 501–504].

4. Saint John Chrysostom, *Homilies on Genesis*. Homily 1 [Homiliae in Genesim. Homilia Prima] 4 [*PG* 53, 25].

5. Saint John Chrysostom, *Commentary on the First Letter to the Corinthians* [In Epistolam Primam ad Corinthios. Homilia XXIII] 2 [*PG* 61, 189–190]; Theophylactus, *Commentary on the First Letter to the Corinthians* [Expositio in Epistolam I ad Corinthios] [*PG* 124, 678]. Saint Ambrose, *Letter to the Church of Vercelli* [Epistola LXIII] 7 [*PL* 16, 1242].

6. Saint Cyprian, possibly: *On Work and Almsgiving* [*PL* 4, 625–646]; Saint Basil, *First Talk on Fasting* [*PG* 31, 163–184]; Saint John Chrysostom, *Homilies on Genesis*. Homily 1 [*PG* 53, 21–26]; Saint Jerome, *Letter to Eustochium, On the preservation of virginity* [Epistola XXII. Ad Euchstochium. De custodia virginitatis] [*PL* 22, 394–425]; Saint Augustine, *Confessions* X, c. 31 [*PL* 32, 797–799].

7. The Council of Nicea, canon 5 (Sacrorum Conciliorum . . . Amplissima Collectio, ed. J. D. Mansi [Paris and Leipzig, 1901] II, 687); Tertullian, *The Resurrection of the Flesh* [De resurrectione carnis] c. 8 [*PL* 2, 852].

8. Saint Leo, *Second Sermon on the December Fast* [*PL* 54, 172].

9. Saint Gregory, *Homilies on the Gospels* I, Homily 16, 5 [*PL* 77, 1137].

10. Tertullian, *On Fasting* [De jejuniis] c. 3 [*PL* 2, 1009].

11. Saint Cyprian, *On Apostates* [De lapsis] c. 29 [*PL* 4, 504].

12. Saint Basil, *First Talk on Fasting* [*PG* 31, 167].

13. Saint John Chrysostom, *Homilies on Genesis*. Homily 1, 1 [*PG* 53, 21].

14. Saint Ambrose, *On Elias and Fasting* c. 2 [*PL* 14, 733].

15. Saint Jerome, *Commentary on Jonah* [Commentariorum in Jonam Liber] c. 3 [*PL* 25, 1140].

16. Saint Augustine, *Sermon* 60, *Of the Season* [Sermo LX, De Tempore]; now listed as *Sermon* 62 and attributed to Caesarius of Arles, c. 2 [*PL* 39, 1865].

17. Saint Leo, *Fourth Sermon on the September Fast* c. 6 [*PL* 54, 447].

18. Saint Bernard, *Sermons on the Canticle*. Sermon 66 [Sermones in Cantica: Sermo LXVI] 6 [*PL* 183, 1096].

19. Saint Jerome, *Against Jovinianus* [Adversus Jovinianum] II, 15 [*PL* 23, 322].

20. Saint Jerome, *Commentary on Saint Matthew, Preface* [Commentariorum in Evangelium Matthaei. Prologus] [*PL* 26, 119]; Venerable Bede, *An Explanation of John's Gospel* [In S. Joannis Evangelium Expositio] c. 1 [*PL* 92, 637].

21. Tertullian, *On Fasting* c. 11 [*PL* 2, 1015].

22. Saint Ambrose, *Letter to the Church of Vercelli* 16 [*PL* 14, 1245].

23. Saint Athanasius, *On Virginity* c. 7 [*PG* 28, 259].

24. Saint Basil, *First Talk on Fasting* [*PG* 31, 163–184]; this does not seem to be a direct quotation.

25. Saint Gregory Nazianzen, *Talk in Praise of Saint Cyprian* [Oratio XXIV. In laudem s. Cypriani] 11 [*PG* 35, 1182].

26. Saint John Chrysostom, *Sermon on Fasting;* the translators have not been able to verify this reference.

27. Saint Jerome, *Against Jovinianus* I, c. 3 [*PL* 23, 224].

28. Saint Augustine, *Sermon* 62; now listed as *Sermon* 142 and attributed to Caesarius of Arles, c. 1 [*PL* 39, 2022].

29. Saint Leo, *First Sermon on the September Fast* c. 1 [*PL* 54, 437–438].

30. Tertullian, *The Resurrection of the Flesh* c. 8 [*PL* 2, 852].

Notes to Chapter Nine

1. Saint Albert the Great, *Commentary on the Four Books of the Sentences* [Commentarii in Quattuor Libros Sententiarum] IV, d. 15, a. 16.

2. Saint Thomas Aquinas, *The Summa of Theology* [Summa Theologiae] IIa–IIae, q. 32, a. 5.

3. Saint Jerome, *Commentary on Saint Matthew* II, c. 15 [*PL* 26, 109–110].

4. Saint Cyprian, *On Work and Almsgiving* c. 2 [*PL* 4, 626].

5. Saint Ambrose, *Sermon* 31; this sermon is now attributed to Maximus of Turin, *Sermon* 22a; cf. *Sermo* XXIIa, 4 in *Corpus Scriptorum Ecclesiasticorum Latinorum*, vol. 23, p. 374.

6. Saint John Chrysostom, *Homilies on the Acts of the Apostles* [In Acta Apostolorum. Homilia XXV] c. 3 [*PG* 60, 196].

7. Saint Leo, *Fifth Sermon on the Collects* [Sermo X. De collectis V.] c. 11 [*PL* 54, 165–166].

8. Saint Cyprian, *On Work and Almsgiving* c. 26 [*PL* 4, 645].

9. Saint Augustine, *The Predestination of the Saints* [De predestinatione sanctorum] I, c. 7 [*PL* 44, 969–970].

10. Gregory of Tours, *The History of the Franks* [Historia Francorum] V, 20 [*PL* 71, 339–340]; Leontius, *The Life of Saint John the Almsgiver* [Vita sancti Joannis Eleemosynarii] [*PG* 93, 1613–1660]; Sophronius, *The Spiritual Meadow* (Beati Johannis Eucratae, *Pratum Spirituale*) [*PG* 87, Pt. 3, 3058–3062, 3090].

11. Saint Cyprian, *On Work and Almsgiving* [*PL* 4, 631–632, 638–639].

12. Saint Basil, On the sayings in Luke's Gospel, "I will tear down my barns and build larger ones" (*In illud dictum evangelii secundum Lucam:* "Destruam horrea mea, et majora aedificabo:" *iterum de avaritia*) 5 [*PG* 31, 271].

13. Saint Augustine, *Exposition of the Letter of Saint John* [In espistolam Joannis ad Parthos tractatus decem] tr. 6 [*PL* 35, 2020–2021].

14. Saint Gregory, *Moral Commentary on Job* XXI, c. 19 (old c. 14) [*PL* 76, 207].

15. Saint John Chrysostom, *Homily* 37, *To the People of Antioch*. Bellarmine tells us in his work *Ecclesiastical Writers* that he used the 1574 edition of Saint

John Chrysostom's works published in Venice. In that edition there were eighty homilies listed as given to the people of Antioch.

16. Saint Augustine, *Sermon* 36 [Sermo XXXVI] 9 [*PL* 38, 219].

17. Saint Basil, *On the Saying in Luke's Gospel*, "I Will Tear Down My Barns and Build Larger Ones," c. 7 [*PG* 31, 275–278].

18. Saint Ambrose, *Sermon* 81; this sermon is now identified as the sermon of Saint Basil referred to in the preceding note, although it is not an exact quote [*PG* 31, 275–276].

19. Saint Jerome, *First Letter to Hedibia* [Epistola CXX. Ad Hedibiam] c. 1 [*PL* 22, 985].

20. Saint John Chrysostom, *Homily* 34, *To the People of Antioch.*

21. Saint Augustine, *Homilies on the Psalms.* On Psalm 147, c. 12 [*PL* 38, 1922].

22. Saint Leo, *Fifth Sermon on the Collects*, c. 1 [*PL* 54, 164–166].

23. Saint Gregory, *Pastoral Care* III, c. 21 [*PL* 77, 87].

24. Saint Bernard, *Letter* 42, To Henry, Archbishop of Sens [De moribus et officio episcoporum epistola 42, seu tractatus ad Henricum senonensem archiepiscopum] c. 7 [*PL* 182, 815].

25. Saint Thomas Aquinas, *The Summa of Theology*, IIa–IIae, q. 66, a. 7, and q. 87, a. 1.

26. Saint Thomas Aquinas, *Commentary on the Four Books of the Sentences* [Commentarii in Quattuor Libros Sententiarum] IV, d. 15.

Notes to Chapter Twelve

1. Saint Cyprian, *On the Lord's Prayer* [De dominica oratione] c. 18 [*PL* 4, 548–549].

2. The Fourth Lateran Council c. 21; *DS* 812.

3. Bellarmine is referring to Gennadius of Marseilles, *De ecclesiasticis dogmatibus liber* c. 53 [*PL* 58, 994].

4. Saint Augustine, *Letter* 118 (now: 54), To Januarius, c. 3 [*PL* 33, 201–202].

5. Saint Jerome, *Commentary on the Letter to the Galatians* [Commentarium in Epistolam ad Galatas] II, c. 4 [*PL* 26, 405].

6. Saint Thomas, *The Summa of Theology* III, qu. 80, a. 10.

7. The Council of Trent, Session 23, Canon 11; *DS* 1661.

8. Saint Ambrose, *The Sacraments* [Liber de sacramentis] V, c. 4 [*PL* 16, 472].

9. Saint Bonaventure, *The Progress of Religious* [De profectu religiosorum] II, c. 79.

10. Saint Bernard, *On the Lord's Supper* [Sermo in coena Domini] c. 3 [*PL* 183, 272–273].

11. Saint John Chrysostom, *Homily* 66, *To the People of Antioch.* Cf. n. 15 under Chapter IX above.

12. Saint Bonaventure, *Life of Saint Francis* [Legenda sancti Francisci] IX, c. 2 [*Opera omnia*, XIV (Paris, 1868)].

NOTES

Notes to Chapter Thirteen

1. Saint Cyprian, *On Apostates* c. 35 [*PL* 4, 507].

2. Saint Clement of Alexandria, in Eusebius of Caesarea, *Ecclesiastical History* [Historia ecclesiastica] III, 23, 18 [*PG* 20, 263–264].

3. Saint Gregory Nazianen, *Second Homily on Baptism* c. 1 [*PG* 36, 365].

4. Theodoretus, *Epitome of Divine Decrees* [Haereticarum fabularum compendium] V, ch. on penance [*PG* 83, 551].

5. Tenth Council of Toledo (*Sacrorum conciliorum . . . Amplissima Collectio*, ed. J. D. Mansi [Paris and Leipzig, 1901], XI, 41).

Notes to Chapter Fourteen

1. *The Pontifical Book* [Pontificialis ordinis liber] was the collection of prayers and rites used in ordinations; it was first compiled in the tenth century. It was revised and approved for use in Rome in 1486 and had just been imposed on the Latin Church in 1596.

2. Saint Jerome, *Letter* 52, To Nepotianus [Epistola LII. De vita clericorum et monachorum] c. 5 [*PL* 22, 531].

3. Saint Bernard, *Declamation of "Behold we have left everything,"* a work of the Abbot Gaufridus, but culled from the sermons of Saint Bernard [Gaufridi Abbatis Declamationes de Colloquio Simonis cum Jesu, ex S. Bernardi sermonibus collectae] cc. 9 and 17 [*PL* 184, 443, 449].

4. Saint John Chrysostom, *On the Priesthood* [De sacerdotio] VI, c. 4 [*PG* 48, 681].

5. Saint Gregory, *Dialogues* IV, c. 58 [*PL* 77, 425–428].

Notes to Chapter Fifteen

1. Saint Augustine, *The Literal Meaning of Genesis* [De Genesi ad Litteram] IX, c. 7 [*PL* 34, 397].

2. Saint Augustine, *The Good of Marriage* [De bono conjugali], 18 [*PL* 40, 388].

3. Ibid. 24 [*PL* 34, 394].

4. Saint Augustine, *On Faith and Works* [De fide et operibus] 7 [*PL* 40, 203].

5. 3 Esdras 4:29–32. This book is one of the pseudohistorical apocrypha of the Old Testament; it was definitively removed from the canon by the Council of Trent.

6. Saint Augustine, *The Confessions* IX, c. 9 [*PL* 32, 772–773].

Notes to Chapter Sixteen

1. Saint Augustine, *Letter* 109 (now: 211), 10 [*PL* 33, 961].
2. Saint Augustine, *The Literal Meaning of Genesis* IX, c. 7 [*PL* 34, 397].
3. Josephus, *The Antiquities* XVIII, 5.
4. Nicephorus Callistus, *History of the Church* [Ecclesiasticae Historiae libri decem et octo] I, c. 20 [*PG* 145, 691–694].
5. Possidius, *Life of Saint Augustine* c. 22 [*PL* 32, 52].
6. Saint Basil, *First Homily on Fasting* 9 and 11 [*PG* 31, 179, 183].
7. Clement of Alexandria, *The Teacher* [Paedagogus] II, c. 1 [*PG* 8, 379–380].
8. Saint Basil, *First Homily on Fasting* 7 [*PG* 31, 174].
9. Saint Jerome, *Letter to Eustochium on the Preservation of Virginity* [*PL* 22, 394–425].
10. Paulinus of Milan, *Life of Ambrose* [Vita sancti Ambrosii] 34 [*PL* 14, 42].
11. Possidius, *Life of Augustine* c. 22 [*PL* 32, 51].
12. Saint Jerome, *Life of Saint Hilarion* [Vita s. Hilarionis Eremitae] 5 [*PL* 23, 32].

BOOK TWO

The Art of Dying Well As Death Draws Near

CHAPTER ONE

The first rule of the art of dying well, as death draws near, which is to meditate on death.

In the beginning we divided the art of dying well into two parts. In the first part were set down the rules of dying well which pertained to the time of our lives when death could still seem far off. In the second part, which we are now taking up, we will set down the rules which pertain to death as already present or soon to come. Death is said to be imminent or at the door when we are worn out by old age, as the Apostle says, "That which is obsolete and has grown old is near its end" (Heb 8:13), or when a grave and, in the judgment of physicians, very dangerous disease attacks an old man, an adult, a youth, or a child. The first rule of this second group is, in our opinion, meditation on death. For when we are in the prime of life, death hardly moves us at all, however diligently and attentively we consider it, since it seems far off and thus less frightening. But when it seems to be almost here, so that it is almost tangible, then a consideration of it truly affects and greatly profits us. All the arts are better learned by practice than by instruction, and those who died, if not often, at least twice, clearly died happily. Such were

Blessed Christina and Drithelmus the Englishman, whom I mentioned in my book *The Mourning of the Dove*, and that hermit whose life John Climacus recounts and of whom we shall say a few words at the end of this chapter.[1] We who are allowed to die but once have no better path open to us than to meditate and consider what occurs at death.

First, we should consider that in death the soul is separated from the body, but that the soul is not snuffed out and the body does not die and return to dust without any hope of resurrection. If that were to occur, as atheists believe, they would apparently be right who said, "Let us eat and drink; for tomorrow we shall die" (Is 22:13). This is a very old proverb as one can see from Isaiah, chapter 22, and from the Apostle in the First Letter to the Corinthians, chapter 15 (1 Cor 15:32). There are some among us who say they believe, but deny it by their deeds, as one can see from the fact that, even in extreme old age, they do not think of death, just as if they were never going to die or as if they thought that with the death of the body the soul utterly perished as well. Despite their ravings, the separation of the flesh from the soul, as of a wife from her husband, is a temporary divorce, not a permanent repudiation. For the soul is immortal, and the flesh will without doubt rise on the last day.

If we are wise Christians, we ought to think often of our own approaching death. The whole of our existence depends upon our dying well. In this life the passage from virtue to vice is not difficult, nor with the grace of God is the passage from vice to virtue. He who is today an heir of the kingdom of heaven can fall by sin tomorrow from the heritage of the sons of God and become deserving of eternal fire. So too, under the inspiration of God's grace, one who is a slave of the devil can be freed from that servitude and again be numbered among the sons of God and heirs of the heavenly kingdom. But one who dies an enemy of God and deserves eternal fire will be an enemy of God forever and handed over to eternal fire. On the other hand, one who dies a friend of God and an heir of the kingdom of heaven will never be able to fall from that height of grace and glory. Thus all our happiness or unhappiness depends on a good or bad death. And so who but someone clearly stupid and without the least judgment will dare to pass from this life by death without first having used all his diligence to learn to die well and to prepare himself to meet death?

A second consideration about death can be highly useful.

Death is most certain, as the Prophet says, "Who is the man that shall live, and not see death?" (Ps 89:49), and as the Apostle agrees, "It is appointed unto men to die once and after this comes the judgment" (Heb 9:27); nonetheless, nothing is more uncertain than the day or the hour. Scripture itself proclaims this, "Watch therefore, for you know neither the day nor the hour" (Mt 25:13). For many are snatched off in infancy; others arrive at a decrepit old age. Some die as youths, others as adults. But what is worse, many die so suddenly that they do not have time to call upon God and commend their spirit to the divine mercy. Divine providence brings this about in accord with the richness of his wisdom precisely so that none of the elect should dare to cling even for a moment to the filth of mortal sin. Hence, my reader, should your conscience accuse you of mortal sin, do not dare to wait until tomorrow or even delay until the end of the day or even of an hour without at least expressing hatred for your sin before God with a humble and contrite heart.

A third consideration will be no less useful. In the morning, before you go out for the day's work, and in the evening before you settle down for a night's rest, lest death come and find you unprepared, you should carefully examine your conscience to see whether you did anything during the night or during the day just past that might seem to be a sin, especially a mortal sin. And if you find nothing, thank God the author of all goods. But if you find some offense against God, repent seriously and from the heart, confess it to a priest as soon as you can, and gladly accept and faithfully perform the penance he imposes. This method of examining one's conscience at least twice in the day is a marvelous help against death ever finding us unprepared.

A fourth consideration, no less useful than the others, is that which Ecclesiasticus mentions: "In all your works remember your last end, and you shall never sin" (Sir 7:40). For how could anyone sin in his work if he weighs whatever he does upon the scales of God's judgment that will occur at death? Here there belongs that saying of the man who died twice, whom John Climacus mentions in his *Ladder*, step six. Thus he speaks: "I will not omit telling the story of that hermit who dwelled in Horeb. After having lived for a long time most negligently and taking no care for his soul, he eventually came down with a disease and was brought to the point of death. Although he had completely departed from the body, he returned to himself after an hour and begged all of us to depart forthwith. The entrance of the cell was blocked with rocks, and he remained inside for twelve years, saying not a word to anyone and not tasting anything but bread and water. He sat there and pondered in awe what he had seen in his ecstasy. And he was so absorbed in thought that he never changed the expression of his face, but constantly stricken with awe, he poured forth in silence a flood of fervent tears. When he was close to death, we entered after breaking open the door. And when we humbly asked of him a word of instruction, we heard from him only this: 'No one who truly bears with him the memory of death will ever be able to sin.' "[2] That is what he says. Let the reader realize that this is history, not a fable, and written by a man who was holy and who wrote what he saw with his own eyes and heard with his own ears.

From this we can easily see how important it is to meditate on death and never drive its presence from our memory. This man was previously negligent in seeking his own salvation, but by the great mercy of God he tasted death and, rising from the dead, he constantly meditated on death for twelve years, while he bewailed his sins with continuous tears. And those sins which he thought slight and venial before his first death, once he had tasted the bitterness of death, he judged to be very serious and deserving twelve years of tearful expiation. He is a true commentator on the words of Scripture, "In all your works remember your last end, and you shall never sin" (Sir 7:40). If the constant memory of one of the last things brought such great profit to that monk, that by twelve years of penance he avoided the endless punishment of hell and earned the glory of the kingdom without end, what should the constant memory of the four last things, namely, death, judgment, hell, and paradise, do for us? Would that many would realize and desire to experience the whole of this profit!

CHAPTER TWO

On the second rule of the art of dying well, as death draws near, which is on the last judgment.

The second of the last things is judgment, which is twofold: the particular judgment at which individual souls are judged as soon as they leave the body, and the general judgment which will take place on the last day. Both are frightening and terrifying for the wicked, but pleasant and glorious for the just. It is highly useful for those who want to die happily to think attentively and frequently of each of them. No one is permitted to deny that the particular judgment will take place immediately after the death of each of us, since the Council of Florence declared against the heretics that those who depart this life stained with mortal sin descend at once to hell-fire, that those who die without mortal sin, but with the debt of temporal punishment, are taken to purgatory, and that those who after the reception of Baptism are found free from sin and the debt of punishment rise immediately to eternal happiness.[1]

One may believe, however, as the theologians teach, that the sentence of Christ the Judge is either indicated by the angels or revealed by God to the minds of the souls and that good souls either rise to heaven or descend to purgatory in the company of angels, while the souls of the reprobate are snatched by demons and plunged into hell.[2] This judgment can occur in a moment, since the Judge is present who, since he is both God and man, knows everything according to the form of man. Saint Peter spoke the truth to Christ, "Lord, you know all things" (Jn 21:17). There is present the accuser, the devil, who is called in Revelation "the accuser of our brethren" (Rv 12:10), and rushes to the dying like a wolf or lion or dog to its prey. There is present the witness, the soul's conscience, which, once freed from the body, can no longer be deceived by ignorance or forgetfulness, but knows itself thoroughly and sees whether it is pleasing to God or hateful to God. Thus nothing prevents the judgment from taking place immediately and being immediately executed. Yet this judgment can be called private if it is compared with the public and general one which will take place on the last day in the presence of all angels and men.

We must mention the reasons for the necessity of a second

judgment for those who were already not only judged, but also rewarded or punished. The first reason relates to God. For some see many just men unjustly treated by the wicked and also many wicked men abounding in temporal goods, and they suspect that God either does not see these things or does not care. And so, in order that the whole human race may understand that the world is justly governed by God, God has decided to render rewards to the good and punishments to the wicked on the last day in the presence of all the angels and men. Thus all will be forced to say and proclaim, "You are just, O Lord, and just are your judgments" (Rv 16:5, 7).

The second reason is that Jesus Christ, who was judged unjustly and subjected to severe and shameful punishment before men, might be seen before the whole world as judging all the wicked from his lofty throne in order to fulfill what was written in the Book of Job, "Your cause has been judged as that of the wicked. Cause and judgment you shall recover" (Jb 36:17). Thus the ignominy of the passion of the Son of God will be justly compensated for by the glory of his judging on the stage of the whole world, and then the words of the Apostle will be fulfilled, "At the name of Jesus every knee should bend of those in heaven, on earth, and under the earth" (Phil 2:10).

The third reason is that the retribution of the just might be complete. For the reward of justice is honor and glory. And since many highly just men were publicly put to death as criminal and wicked, it is fitting that their justice be proclaimed on the stage of the whole world. The martyrs of the Lord especially belong to this multitude of saints, for they will stand crowned before the eyes of their pagan persecutors and heretical princes and kings.

The fourth reason is for the confusion of the hypocrites. For there are some who die with the aura of sanctity, although they are really wicked. Such are the heretical Calvinists and Anabaptists, and such were those of whom Saint Cyprian writes in the book *The Unity of the Catholic Church*, "Even if they are handed over to the flames and fires and are burned, or even if they are tossed to the beasts and lay down their lives, there will be no crown of faith, but the punishment of perfidy. Nor will there be a glorious death in religious virtue, but a perishing in desperation."[3] Thus at least in the general judgment hypocrisy must be publicly uncovered.

The fifth reason is that bodies and souls may be judged together. In the particular judgment, only the soul is judged and receives its reward or punishment, but in the general judgment the whole of man will appear. And since souls sinned or did good with their bodies, it is fitting that after the resurrection souls along with their bodies receive rewards or punishments. The sixth and final reason is that, beyond having the good and bad deeds which we did in this life rewarded and punished, the good or evil effects of our right and wrong actions that continue on to the end of the world may publicly obtain praise or blame.

Let us illustrate this point by examples. Pious men have built hospices in which many recover their health, monasteries in which many are instructed in piety, and schools in which many are educated in the disciplines, and these works last for a long time. Others write books useful for spreading wisdom or for the various arts or for piety or for other good works, by which many profit and help their neighbor in every age. But there are bad men who destroy many others by writing dirty or seditious or heretical books. By building theaters for the games of gladiators or for obscene comedies or in other ways, many others harm their neighbor for a long time after they have died. At the end of the world, when all the series of events will come to an end and the merits, whether good or bad, of all men will be brought to completion, it will then be fitting that the sentence of the supreme, most powerful, and most just Judge be pronounced for all on that day which will be the most memorable of all that have passed since the beginning of the world.

These then are the reasons why, besides the particular judgment which will take place at the death of individuals, we should look for a general judgment at the end of the world. We have still to mention who will be the Judge in this terrible judgment, from where he will arrive, to what place he will come, whom he will judge, and what will be the Judge's sentence. The Judge without doubt will be our Lord Jesus Christ. For he says in Saint Matthew, "When the Son of Man shall come in his majesty, and all the angels with him, then he will sit on the throne of his glory; and before him will be gathered all the nations," and so on (Mt 25:31–32). The same thing is confirmed by the Apostles Peter, Paul, and John. In the Acts of the Apostles, Peter says, "He it is who has been appointed by God to be judge of the living and of the dead" (Acts 10:42). The Apostle Paul also says in Acts, "God has fixed a day on which he will judge the world with justice by a Man whom he has appointed . . . by raising him from the dead" (Acts 17:31). In his

Gospel the Apostle John speaks as follows, "He has granted him power to render judgment, because he is the Son of Man" (Jn 5:27), and in the same chapter, "Neither does the Father judge any man, but all judgment he has given to the Son" (Jn 5:22).

He will come from heaven for judgment, and he will come near to the earth as far as the air so that he can be seen and heard by all men who will be on earth. Hear Christ himself in Matthew, "You shall see the Son of Man coming upon the clouds of heaven" (Mt 26:64). Hear the Apostle Paul writing to the Thessalonians. He says, "They will be caught up together with them in clouds to meet the Christ in the air" (1 Thes 4:17), and the Prophet Joel had predicted the same thing, "I will gather together all nations, and will bring them down into the valley of Josaphat; and I will plead with them there" (Jl 3:2). The words "into the valley of Josaphat" are correctly interpreted to mean that the great judgment of all men will take place there, both because the Hebrew word *Josaphat* properly signifies the judgment of God, and because the valley of Josaphat is near Jerusalem on the east side of the temple, as Saint Jerome states in his commentary on the third chapter of Joel.[4] No place could be more suitable than that for such a great judgment. For from there one can see Jerusalem where Christ preached, and from there one can see also Mount Calvary where Christ was crucified for the redemption of the human race as well as Mount Olivet, where the victor over death ascended into heaven. To Josaphat Christ will come upon the clouds of heaven with all his angels, numbering at least "thousands of thousands, and ten thousand times a hundred thousand," as Daniel writes (Dn 7:10). I said "at least" because the opinion of Denis the Areopagite and of Saint Thomas is that the number of the holy angels surpasses that of all bodily things.[5] In the company of Christ will be the whole multitude of holy men and women in glorious bodies, of whom it is said in Revelation, "I saw a great multitude which no man could number, out of all nations and tribes and peoples and tongues" (Rv 7:9).

In this judgment there will be a spectacle such as has not been seen since the beginning of the world and will never be seen again. All the wicked will be subject to the sentence of eternal death. In their bodies that they have taken up again, they will stand on the earth, naked and downcast with the deepest and most incredible sadness, having been summoned by the angels from all corners of the earth to the valley of Josaphat and its vicinity. Their number will be far greater than the number of the saints, since the Lord himself said, "Many are called, but few are chosen" (Mt 20:16, 22:14) and, "Close is the way that leads to life! And few there are who find it; broad is the way that leads to destruction, and many there are who enter that way" (Mt 7:14, 13). If it is true, as it most surely is, that the number of holy men and women cannot be counted, then how much more uncountable will be the mob of reprobates? Added to them will be the evil spirits, who are also most numerous.

After all these arrangements, before the sentence of the Judge is pronounced, the books of records will be opened, as can be seen from Daniel the Prophet and Saint John (Dn 7:10; Rv 5:9, 20:12). The Apostle Paul explains the nature of these books which will be opened in the judgment when he says to the Corinthians, "Pass no judgment before the time, until the Lord comes, who will both bring to light the things hidden in darkness and make manifest the counsels of hearts" (1 Cor 4:5). For God will pour forth such light that it will make manifest the consciences of all the wicked. Thus all on that stage will see the consciences of all others as well as their deeds, words, thoughts, and desires. Oh, what a spectacle it will be to see the consciences of hypocrites, of liars, of traitors, of scoffers, who made nothing of swearing falsely by all that was sacred! Because of this publication of the crimes and outrages of all men, and the resulting anticipation of the sentence to come, there will occur what is described in Revelation, "The kings of the earth, and the princes, and the tribunes, and the rich, and the strong, and everyone, bond and free," will hide "themselves in the caves and in the rocks of the mountains. And they [will say] to the mountains and to the rocks, 'Fall upon us, and hide us from the face of him who sits upon the throne, and from the wrath of the Lamb; for the great day of their wrath has come, and who is able to stand?' " (Rv 6:15–17). The Lord predicted the same thing in the Gospel, when he said to the pious women, as he carried the cross on his shoulders, "Daughters of Jerusalem, do not weep for me, but weep for yourselves and for your children. For behold, days are coming in which men will say, 'Blessed are the barren, and the wombs that never bore, and breasts that never nursed.' Then they will begin to say to the mountains, 'Fall upon us,' and to the hills, 'Cover us!' " (Lk 23:28–30). And at the end, the sentence of the Judge will be pronounced, as he says, "Come, blessed . . . depart from me, accursed ones" (Mt

25:34, 41), and the just will enter eternal life, and the unjust eternal fire.

I beg my readers to consider and reconsider frequently and attentively that they too will be on that stage. Now when there is time, let them seriously weigh what they should do. And they should not protest that the day of judgment is still far off and there is no need to be tormented beforehand as if the day of the Lord were already here. For even if the general judgment is far off, the particular judgment is not. It is at hand and clearly stands at the door. And the sentence of the general judgment will be just the same as the sentence of the particular judgment. Thus a wise person ought in every way to prepare himself to hear the sentence of the particular judgment, as if it were to be heard today or tomorrow. For the hour of judgment is no more distant than the hour of death, and the hour of death cannot be far for an old man or one suffering from a serious illness. And so, in awaiting such a judgment, in which will be decided a matter of supreme importance, one ought seriously to implore the Advocate, who also will be the future Judge. "We have an advocate with the Father, Jesus Christ the just," as John the Apostle teaches us (1 Jn 2:1). Thus we ought also to beseech the friends of the Advocate, especially the most merciful Virgin, the Mother of the Advocate, and the angels and saints. It is fitting that we approach the Advocate and the friends of the Advocate not merely with words, but also with gifts. For the saints do not refuse gifts which profit not them, but the poor of Jesus Christ. For the blessed in heaven have no need of our gifts.

CHAPTER THREE

The third rule of the art of dying well, as death draws near, which is on hell.

After the consideration of death and judgment it is good to ponder very carefully the tortures of hell as well as the joys of heaven. For these are the two of the last things, one of which will befall each of us as Christ pronounces judgment. These two are opposed as contraries such that one must render us wretched, the other happy. But since we have written on each of them near the end of our book *The Ascent of the Mind to God*, and we wrote again on the joys of paradise in the whole book *The Eternal Happiness of the Saints*, and on the tortures of hell in the second book of *The Mourning of the Dove*, and we have spoken to the people on all the last things in extemporaneous Latin homilies which we have set down in writing, it seems good merely to mention the main topics so that the reader can carefully and profitably think and meditate upon them, while he awaits death and prepares himself to accept it with joy.[1]

Thus we have undertaken the brief consideration of three points concerning the unhappy state of those condemned to hell: the place, the time, and the manner. The place is the depth, the time is eternity, the manner is punishment without limit. The place, I say, is the depth, since on account of the immense crimes by which they offended the divine majesty, the reprobate will be imprisoned in the deepest part of the earth, which is furthest distant from the royal palace which is in the heavens. This is fitting to punish appropriately the pride of the devil and of proud men. For the devil said, "I will ascend into heaven, I will exalt my throne above the stars of God, . . . I will be like the Most High," and he was told, "You shall be brought down to hell, into the depth of the pit" (Is 14:13–15). The same thing will happen to all men who are children of pride.

From this first woe of the reprobate there follow three others: darkness, tight confinement, and need. Since hell is in the center of the earth where the rays of the sun and the moon and the stars cannot penetrate, there can be no light in it, except that of the sulfurous flames which serve not to lessen, but to increase the punishment. For that light will give them sight of the demons, their most cruel enemies, and of those men, whether friends or relatives, who were the cause of their damnation. They will see their own nakedness, their deceitfulness, their chains, their torments, all of which they might well wish not to see. Certainly they will not see anything good from which they might derive consolation. Oh, darkness not dark! Darkness because it hides everything good, and yet not dark because it makes visible everything evil.

The confines of hell are so narrow that they can scarcely hold the bodies of the many damned. For the earth is almost an indivisible point in comparison with the immensity of the heavens, and hell encompasses not the whole of it, nor a half, but only the center. Moreover, the number of those damned exceeds the number of those saved, of whom we read in Revelation, "I saw a great multitude which no man could number" (Rv 7:9). And so who can grasp the tightness of the confines of hell? Let the great kings, Nabuchodonosor, Darius, Alexander, Julius Caesar, and others, whom the globe could hardly contain, go there and broaden the boundaries of hell, if they can, so that they may lie a little more comfortably and be tortured a little less. Oh, vanity of vanities! Mortals strive to extend and broaden all their fields, their rules, their kingdoms, so that for a little while they might boast of their many subjects, and there never occurs to them the narrowness of the confines of hell that awaits them where they will be forced to dwell, not for a little while, but forever, whether they like it or not.

And what shall I say of the incredible neediness of the damned? Needy with respect to everything good, they who inhabit hell will be rich only in their abundant punishment. In hell rich men will remember the abundant delights of their life on earth, whether in food or drink or in expensive clothes, or in hunting or fowling, in gardens and vineyards, in theaters and various games. But this memory will only increase their pain as they see themselves in hell lying naked, despised, wretchedly stripped of their goods and fortunes. Then they will say what we read in the Book of Wisdom, "What has pride profited? Or what advantage has the boasting of riches brought us? All those things are passed away like a shadow" (Wis 5:8–9).

Let us get to the second point, namely, time. How long will the exile of hell last? Would that it would last no longer than our stay in this life has lasted! But there will be no comparison. For after time there will be no more time, but eternity. Thus the stay of the wicked in the torments of hell will last as long as the eternity of God, which, as it lacks a beginning, will also lack an end. The damned will be tortured as long as the blessed are in joy. Finally, the reprobate will be dead as long as God himself lives, and unless God were to cease to be what he is, the reprobate will not cease to be in the pains in which they are. O death-dealing life! O deathless death! If you are life, how do you kill? If you are death, how do you last? You ought to be called neither death nor life, since each of them has something good. Life has quiet, and death an end. But you are neither quiet nor do you have an end. What shall we say that you are but that totality of evil that neither life nor death has? It would be greatly to our advantage if we could even moderately fathom what eternal punishment is. This realization alone, as a sort of bridle, would check the passions of all and would so temper our life that we would all seem to be not merely Christians, but even the holiest of hermits.

Of the three points for consideration there remains only the manner, namely, that the punishment is without limit. For the punishment of hell is not a single punishment, but the sum total of all punishments. In hell every power of the intelligent soul is tortured along with all the senses, whether internal or external, and not one after the other. Rather all these pains launch their attack upon a man at once. As here on earth we never experience the total good of the blessed, so we never experience the utter evil of the damned. For when one has pains in his eyes, he does not at the same time suffer pain in his teeth, and one who is pained in his teeth is not also suffering in his eyes, and so on with the rest. But in hell terrible pains will have to be endured simultaneously in all our members, since the fire of hell will envelop our whole body and torture the whole of it with great violence and yet never consume it.

"Depart from me, accursed ones," says the Judge, "into the everlasting fire which was prepared for the devil and his angels" (Mt 25:41), and Isaiah says, "Their worm shall not die, and their fire shall not be quenched" (Is 66:24)—words which our Lord repeated three times in one chapter of the Gospel according to Mark (9:44–46, Vulgate) in order to impress clearly on our hearts that the punishment of hell is fire that will last eternally and that the whole body will be most cruelly racked with bitter pain through all eternity. Those who have seen a man here on earth burned with fire after a just judgment could hardly bear the sight of such a punishment, even though it is quickly finished. But if a man, however guilty, should last a whole day in the fire, surely no one could bear such a horrible sight. Let each say to himself: If I cannot endure the burning of a living man who is nothing to me, how will I bear the burning of my own body for one hour, or day, or month, or year? And if this strikes me as too ghastly even to think about, with what folly do I expose myself to such a great danger as burning for eternity? If we do not believe this, where is our faith? If we believe it, where is our good judgment? Our prudence? If we are of sound mind and have faith in the Holy Scriptures, how can it be that we are not stirred by the threat of such massive danger? Let one who desires to be saved enter into his heart. After he has considered all these matters with great attention, let him behave so that death finds him ready and the fire of hell may not get him, but so that he may deserve to enter happily into the joy of the Lord.

CHAPTER FOUR

The fourth rule of the art of dying well, as death draws near, which is the glory of the blessed.

There remains the glory of the blessed, which occupies the final place among the four last things. On this topic I shall consider only the three points that I considered in the previous chapter on the punishments of hell: the place, the time, and the manner. The place of the glory of the blessed is the heavenly paradise; the time is eternity; the manner is happiness exceeding all limit.

Let us begin with the first. The place of the heavenly paradise is high above all the mountains of the earth, above all the elements, above all the stars. Thus in the Holy Scriptures the kingdom of heaven is called "the house of God, the city of the great king, the city of the living God, the heavenly Jerusalem" (Gn 28:17; Mt 5:35; Heb 12:22). The sublime location of the heavenly city shows us that this place has many privileges and prerogatives over all the other places in this whole world. First, the higher a place is in this universe, the larger and more spacious it is, since the shape of the universe of created things is seen to be round, with the earth occupying the center of the world and the highest heaven containing in its embrace the last or highest sphere of almost infinite width.

Thus just as the place of the blessed is the highest, so it is the most spacious. So too, on the contrary, as the place of the damned is the lowest, it is also the smallest of all. Further, the highest place is also the purest. For certainly water is purer than earth, and air than water, and fire than air, and heaven is purer than fire, and the fiery heaven than the starry heaven. Finally, the highest place is also the safest; no evil can approach that place and no scourge draw near to his dwelling (Ps 91:10). Thus the seat of the blessed is most spacious; the blessed can freely move about from one place to another.

And there is no danger of their becoming tired since by the gift of agility they can move from place to place in a moment. What a pleasure it will be to move from the east to the west, from the south to the north, to circle the whole globe in a moment, while those who have perished remain in one place in hell for all eternity, bound hand and foot! An even greater pleasure lies in store for the blessed when they enjoy the pure air of heaven, which neither darkness nor fogs nor mists nor blasts of wind nor any pestilence can mar. Meanwhile, the inhabitants of hell, wretched beyond all measure, are forced to lie in that place full of horror in the black fog and smoke of the seething furnace with no hope of a purer air. What shall I say of the city on high, most safe from all betrayal or any evil because of its lofty height? "Praise the Lord, O Jerusalem," says David, "praise your God, O Sion. Because he has strengthened the bolts of your gates" (Ps 147:1–2). This reference to fortifying the gates does not mean what it sounds like; for in Revelation it is said of that city: "And its gates shall not be shut by day; for there shall be no night there" (Rv 21:25). Therefore, God "strengthened the bolts of the gates" of the heavenly Jerusalem, by making it unable to be stormed because of its height. And if the dragon fought with Michael in heaven, he did not rise up from the underworld to heaven, but he was created in heaven and rebelled against his Creator before he was confirmed in grace. Puffed up with pride, he tried to be equal to the Most High. But because the heavenly Jerusalem was founded in peace, the enemy of peace could not remain there, but immediately fell "as lightning from heaven" (Lk 10:18), and he could thereafter not set foot in the place. And from that time no one is admitted to dwell in the heavenly Jerusalem unless he is founded and solidly confirmed in perpetual peace.

Having covered the topic of place, we will now say a few things on time. The time of dwelling in the heavenly Jerusalem since the fall of the devil is time without time, that is, perpetual duration without the passage of days and nights, for in Revelation the Angel "swore by him who lives forever and ever, . . . that time shall be no longer" (Rv 10:6), and according to the Gospel, when the last day is over, the Lord will say, "And these," namely, the wicked, "will go into everlasting punishment, but the just into everlasting life" (Mt 25:46). The only difference will be that the wicked will suffer eternity against their will and seek death and not find it, whereas the just will find nothing more pleasant than that blessed eternity, that is, life without fear of dying and standing without fear of falling.

There remains for us to explain briefly the manner in which the blessed will dwell in paradise after the resurrection. And I think one thing can be said with certitude, that all the good things which are desired on earth, mixed as they are with many evils, will be possessed by the blessed in heaven to a greater degree and without any admixture of evil. The things counted as goods upon earth are honor, power, riches, and pleasures. We might find the honor of the blessed in heaven utterly unbelievable, if he who cannot lie had not asserted it. Listen to Christ the Lord, who is Truth, speaking in the Revelation of blessed John, "He who overcomes, I will permit him to sit with me upon my throne; as also I have overcome and have sat with my Father on his throne" (Rv 3:21). What more, I ask you, could be added to this glory? The throne of the Son of God is surely placed highest in heaven, and he who sits on it can be considered to have attained, indeed, an honor beyond belief. What hosannas, what praises will resound before God and the angels in heaven when a man, once mortal and fragile, will be placed by the hands of God upon the throne of the Son of God, who is "Prince of the kings of the earth" (Rv 1:5) and "King of kings and Lord of lords" (Rv 19:16)? Surely nothing can be added to such an honor.

The power of the blessed person will be great almost beyond what we can imagine. The promise of Christ is found in the Gospel passage concerning the faithful servant, "Amen I say to you, he will set him over all his goods" (Mt 24:47). These words clearly mean that in heaven the faithful servant will share the power God has over all creation. And how great is the power of God over creatures? Utterly the greatest and beyond comparison. Thus the saints will be called and will really be kings of the whole world, not for a few years, but for all eternity. And this is the sentence which Christ, the supreme judge, will pronounce for the just, "Come, blessed of my Father, take possession of the kingdom prepared for you from the foundation of the world" (Mt 25:34).

Concerning the riches of the blessed it should satisfy everyone to know that there will be abundant riches lasting forever, as the Prophet says, "Glory and wealth shall be in his house" (Ps 112:3) and, "God will be all in all" (1 Cor 15:28), as the Apostle says in the Letter to the Corinthians. Theophylactus as well as Saint Augustine explain these words so that the sense is: "God will be all in all," because now one thing is for us food, another drink, another clothing, still another a house, and yet others wealth, pleasure, honor, and power. But in heaven after the resurrection God will be for all the blessed food, drink, clothing, house, wealth, pleasure, honor, and power.[1] Thus for the blessed in heaven everything will be precious, everything incorruptible, everything divine. Saint Jerome adds in the Letter to Amandus that God will be for all the blessed not only all corporeal, but also all spiritual things, for now all divine graces are not given to everyone.[2] Rather to one is given wisdom, as to Solomon, to another goodness, as to David, to still another patience, as to Job. But when the end of all things has come, then all will be in all so that each saint will possess all the virtues and gifts. What, I ask, would a miser in this world not give in order to possess all riches? What would the lover of pleasure not give in order to attain all the pleasures he desires? What would an ambitious man not give to receive all the honors and dignities that he seeks? And yet these are temporal goods that will soon perish, and what is worse, after a short time they will be exchanged for everlasting poverty, pain, and shame. Why then do we not seek God, in whom we will possess all spiritual and corporeal goods for all of eternity?

Finally, what shall we say of the joy and pleasure of the blessed? Isaiah and Paul exclaim and say, "Eye has not seen nor ear heard, nor has it entered into the heart of man, what things God has prepared for those who love him" (Is 64:4; 1 Cor 2:9). For the just who love him, God has truly prepared in the heavenly fatherland joy, happiness, pleasure, delight, sweetness, and contentment, such as no mortal has ever tasted or has been able to attain in thought. To produce delight three things are needed: the power, the object, and the union of the power with the object. And the greater these are, the greater is the delight produced. No power in created things is greater, more lively, and more capable of delight than the rational will. No object is more outstanding, more lovable, and more sweet than the essence of the Creator. David says, "O taste and see that the Lord is sweet" (Ps 34:9). The Wise Man says, speaking of the sun and the stars, "With whose beauty, if they, being delighted, took them to be goods, let them know how much the Lord of them is more beautiful than they: for the first author of beauty made all those things" (Wis 13:3). No more intimate union can be conceived than that of God with the rational will, as the Apostle says, "He who cleaves to the Lord is one spirit with him" (1 Cor 6:17). The joining of bodies generally takes place on the surface, without penetrating to the interior, and yet bodily pleasure so greatly affects men that they are reduced in a sense to insanity. What contentment, then, what sweetness will the soul taste when it is joined so intimately with God who is infinite sweetness that it becomes one spirit with him? Words fail me here to express what I ponder with myself in thought.

And note that all human pleasure which arises from created things lasts either for but a moment or at most very briefly. But the pleasure which arises from the union of the human spirit with God who is infinite sweetness will never be limited at all. Yet such madness rules many men that they prefer sordid, small carnal pleasures that last at most for a brief time to the very great and pure pleasures that will last without doubt for all of eternity. And that should suffice here for the four last things.

CHAPTER FIVE

The fifth rule of the art of dying well, as death draws near, which is making a will.

After a consideration of death drawing near and the other last things, it follows that those who are preparing to depart from this world should put their house in order. Thus Isaiah warned Hezechiah, saying, "Put your house in order, for you shall die and not live" (Is 38:1). Religious are free from that bother, since they can say with the apostles, "Behold, we have left all and followed you" (Mt 19:27). One of these was Saint Augustine, of whom Possidius writes in his *Life*, "He did not make a will, because as one of Christ's poor he did not have the wherewithal to make one. For though he was a bishop, yet like a religious he kept nothing of his own."[1]

A will should be made at the beginning of an illness, unless one has wisely already done so. Those who do not think of making a will unless they are forced by relatives or friends when disease weakens them are making a foolish mistake. For at that time either their minds begin to wander, or at least they do not arrange their affairs with the wisdom they would have possessed in good health.

They must first of all consider repaying their debts, if they are burdened by any. Then they should leave their wealth to the people to whom they see that it rightly belongs. They should not allow themselves to be drawn to persons they love more, if this should be somehow contrary to justice. In matters which depend upon their choice, let them first consider the glory of God, then the needs of their neighbor. If they should have superfluous riches which, as such, ought to have been distributed to the poor long ago, let them not suppose that their conscience is clear because they confessed this to a priest along with their other sins and obtained absolution, unless they have given the order that those possessions be given to the poor or they themselves immediately do this. For it is the common opinion of the Fathers and of the principal scholastic Doctors that superfluous goods are owed to the poor. We have written on this point in the previous book, chapter nine, and need not repeat it here. Concerning the goods which can be given away by their free choice, let them consult pious men as to the works of charity more pleasing to God in terms of time and place. For in one place the building of a church or a cemetery will be more urgent; elsewhere the placement of poor virgins in matrimony; still elsewhere the urgent need is the number of sick in the hospital or of poor beggars in the streets; and in another place it is the redemption of captives. Finally, in this sort of distribution there is no better rule than "sincere faith and clear foresight," as Saint Ambrose writes, or "charity with prudence and prudence joined with charity," as Saint Gregory puts it.[2]

It is important that the alms, which the living give or which the dying order to be given, are given or are ordered to be given when the one giving or ordering them given is pleasing to God. Then almsgiving wins great merit for the donor, and such good almsgivers are welcomed "into the everlasting dwellings" by good friends, according to the promise of Christ in Luke (Lk 16:9). If alms are given or ordered to be given by a wicked man, they are without avail unto eternal life regardless of other merits. For they do not bring it about that the donors are received into the eternal dwellings. Hence, advice should be sought from a prudent confessor or friends by a man who realizes that he made a will while he lay in the filth of mortal sin, so that after making a new complete and truthful confession he might approve and ratify the whole disposition he made in his will, especially concerning the giving of alms after his death either to the church or to the poor.

Finally, we should add that one who has bestowed many gifts on his neighbors in his will should not forget his own soul, especially since it is possible that he may be carried off to purgatory rather than going directly to heaven. Thus he would be prudent and pious in ordering a portion of the alms to be given to priests for offering sacrifices to the Lord for his soul. "It is a holy and wholesome thought to pray for the dead, that they may be loosed from sins," as is said in the Book of Maccabees (2 Mc 12:46). From that passage Saint Augustine argues that the souls of the dead are helped even more by the sacrifice of the Body of Christ, if they were helped by the sacrifices of animals in the Old Testament.[3]

CHAPTER SIX

The sixth rule of the art of dying well, as death draws near, which is concerning the confession of sins.

After having considered the four last things and put one's house in order, it is necessary that an old man or one suffering a serious illness should put aside all other concerns and seriously attend to the proper reception of the sacrament of penance. For it often happens that at a time when the sacrament of penance is needed more, it is not received as properly. For because they are prevented by pain and weakness or by failing judgment or by fright at the nearness of death or by the love of dear ones whom they leave against their will, those who suffer from a serious illness make a rather imperfect confession of their sins and find it very difficult amid such difficulties to stir up in themselves true and perfect contrition.

I can bear witness to this difficulty which the sick especially suffer. For I once visited a friend, a rich nobleman, who fell into a deadly illness after committing a grave sin, and I said to him that nothing could be more salutary for him at the moment than true penance and contrition for his sins, since God never despises a humble and contrite heart. He answered, "What is contrition? I do not understand what you are asking of me." I replied, "I ask that you be sorry in the sincerity of your heart for having offended God and that you resolve, if you should live longer, never again to offend God. Let all this come from a true love of God who has given you countless gifts, while you in your ingratitude repaid him with injuries in exchange for his gifts." He answered, "I do not understand; I am not capable of such things." And thus he died, leaving us clear enough signs of his damnation. These and like examples warn us that, while we are in good health, we should unburden our conscience and do true penance, as if that confession would be our last.

Nonetheless, in a grave illness sacramental confession should be made with as much diligence as possible, and contrition should be especially aroused from true sorrow for past sins and a firm purpose of sinning no more, if one should live longer. Penance should be done not only for sins committed, but also for good works omitted to which we were obliged by our office or by charity. For many assess accurately enough the sins committed against God or neighbor, but readily forget or neglect their omissions. I can offer here a fairly useful example.

A very learned and pious bishop was sick unto death. A priest who was a mutual friend of ours came to him, and from him I got this story. The priest asked the bishop whether his conscience was sufficiently at peace. He answered that by the grace of God he could not recall anything serious which he had committed against God since his last confession. The priest asked further whether his conscience did not reproach him with any omissions, since the Apostle so carefully admonished his bishop, Timothy, "I charge you, in the sight of God and Christ Jesus, who will judge the living and the dead by his coming and by his kingdom, preach the word, be urgent in season, out of season; reprove, entreat, rebuke with all patience and teaching" (2 Tm 4:1–2). When he heard this, the good bishop groaned and said, "Indeed, omissions frighten me very much." He said that, and from his eyes poured forth rivers of tears.

For those who are preparing to die well contrition is especially necessary. For confession without contrition or at least true attrition does not suffice for salvation. Even satisfaction without contrition is of no avail and can hardly be made by one who is ill. Contrition which includes charity can lead to salvation even without confession and satisfaction, when these cannot be made. For, as we said just before, "A contrite and humbled heart God will not despise" (Ps

51:19). Thus we believe that the sick should earnestly seek to have contrition. We have a marvelous example of this in the Father, Saint Augustine. According to his biographer, Possidius, he ordered in his final and fatal illness that the penitential psalms of David be written out for him.[1] And lying in bed during those days of his illness he gazed upon the pages set against the wall and read them and wept continually and abundantly. He avoided being distracted by anyone. Almost ten days before he left his body, he asked his friends that no one enter his room except at the hours when the doctors came to see him or when meals were brought to him. Thus he was free for prayer all the remaining time. O blessed and wise man! After having received baptism and the forgiveness of sins of his past life, he lived forty-three years. During that time he assiduously preached the word of God until his last illness, wrote countless books highly useful to the whole Church, and lived an innocent and holy life without complaint. Yet in extreme old age and illness he allowed many days for contrition and penance so that he might weep continually and abundantly in reading the penitential psalms. Those two words, continually and abundantly, should be well noted. For he did not devote a day or an hour to contrition, but wept over his sins often and abundantly for many days. What kind of sins did that very holy man weep over? I imagine, only venial sins, so that he might go right to heaven, free not only from the flames of hell, but also from the fire of purgatory. And if a holy and wise man continually and abundantly wept over venial sins for so many days, what should they do who ought to make satisfaction to God not only for venial sins, but also for mortal sins?

Thus the ill, whose death is near, should really prepare themselves before they are sick so that in old age or illness they do not have to expiate serious sins, but only do penance for lesser offenses. They should strive to fortify themselves by communion and anointing against the snares of the devil so that, under the guidance of God and with the companionship of their guardian angel, they may happily arrive at the heavenly fatherland.

CHAPTER SEVEN

The seventh rule of the art of dying well, as death draws near, which is on holy viaticum.

The early Christians, in administering holy viaticum and the sacred anointing to the sick, first anointed the sick with extreme unction and then offered them the most holy Body of Christ. And in order to bring forth one or two proofs, there is in the writings of Lawrence Surius, in the first volume, *The Life of Saint William*, the archbishop of Bourges, who lived in the time of Pope Innocent III. In it we read, "He received the sacrament of anointing humbly and devoutly; after he had received it, he asked that he be immediately given the most holy eucharist so that, protected by such a guide for the journey, he might more safely pass through the ranks of the enemy."[1] The same thing is told of Saint Malachi, in his life written by Saint Bernard, namely, that he received the eucharist as viaticum after extreme unction.[2]

Besides these two proofs, which show the relation between extreme unction and the eucharist, two others can be offered which teach that viaticum was last, even though no mention was made of extreme unction. In *The Life of Ambrose*, written by Paulinus, we read that viaticum was given to Saint Ambrose when death was already imminent, so that he might breathe forth his spirit as soon as he had received viaticum.[3] Simeon Metaphrastes writes exactly the same thing of Saint John Chrysostom in his biography of that man.[4] Thus it is clear that among the early Christians the last sacrament was the viaticum of the Body of the Lord.

Now we first strengthen the sick with sacred viaticum, and then after several days, with the disease progressing, we anoint with holy oil. Each of these ways of proceeding has its reasons. The ancients thought that the venerable sacrament of holy oil was instituted both for recovering good health and for removing sins or the remains of sins. For thus Saint James speaks, "Is anyone among you sick? Let him bring in the presbyters of the Church, and let them pray over him, anointing him with oil in the name of the Lord. And the prayer of faith will save the sick man, and the Lord will raise him up, and if he be in sins, they shall be forgiven him" (Jas 5:14–15). Thus the ancients, hoping for bodily health for the sick person from the holy anointing, did not put off this sacrament until the doctors saw there was no hope of recovery. Rather, when the doctors diagnosed the disease as dangerous, they immediately had recourse to the holy anointing. The same point is illustrated by what Saint Bernard wrote in the *Life of Saint Malachi*, namely, that, when that holy man became gravely ill, he came down on foot from his bedroom which was in the upper part of the house to the church in order to receive first extreme unction and then viaticum.[5] And after the reception of these sacraments he returned on foot, unassisted, to his room and bed. Nowadays when the sick hear extreme unction mentioned, they think that their life is over. For that reason relatives and friends postpone this sacrament as long as possible to avoid frightening the sick.

Another reason which moved the ancients to anoint the sick first and then offer them viaticum was that sins are forgiven in the sacrament of extreme unction, as we have already heard from Saint James. Thus extreme unction is called by some of the ancients the penance of the sick. Forgiveness of sins and penance is rightly placed first as a preparation or disposition for the lofty sacrament of the eucharist, which demands special purity.

Finally, the sacrament of the Lord's Body is the conclusion and, so to speak, the seal of all the sacraments. For those who are baptized as adults, such as Jews or Turks, are confirmed immediately after Baptism and are admitted to the sacrifice of the Mass and receive holy communion. So too penitents, upon completing their penance, always approach the eucharist, at least according to the ancient custom. Those who receive minor or major orders also receive holy communion. Finally, those who are joined in matrimony strengthen and confirm that sacrament with the sacrament of the eucharist. In our time the order has been reversed and not without good reason. For it often happens that extreme unction is postponed for a long time in order not to frighten the sick. And the danger is that the sick person in the meantime may either lose the use of his reason or be rendered incapable for some other reason of properly receiving the most holy eucharist. Thus we now give viaticum first. For it is better that these sacraments be administered to the sick in reverse order than that they lose the salutary benefit of one of them. For extreme unction can be conferred upon a sick person even in his death agony when he no longer understands or is aware of what is going on around him, provided only that he is still alive. For the dead are incapable of receiving any sacrament. This should suffice for the order of conferring sacraments upon the sick.

I come now to bringing the precious Body of Christ to the sick in a beneficial manner. First I will explain what should be done for the sick person before the sacrament is brought to him; then what the sick person himself ought to do in the presence of Christ's Body; and finally, how he should conduct himself once refreshed by that rich food.

As for the first point, I would suggest, unless something more useful should occur to the spiritual father, that the sick person carefully consider the words of Saint Thomas:

O sacred banquet,
In which Christ is eaten,
The memory of his passion is recalled,
The mind is filled with grace,
And the pledge of future glory is given us!

Thus he will first consider carefully that the holy eucharist is offered to us on our pilgrimage as food so that we do not faint on the path to the fatherland, especially at that time when, tired by a long journey, our forces are apt to wane. But this food is called a banquet and a sacred banquet at that. For although it is given in the form of bread alone, it is yet a whole and great banquet and not an ordinary, but a sacred one, not for the body, but for the soul. And there is added: "In which Christ is eaten," because beneath the species or accidents of bread there is the Body of Christ united with his soul and divinity. And thus it is a very great and most precious reality, a huge and very sweet banquet surpassing every savor of sweetness, but suited for nourishing and delighting the soul, not the body.

The fruit and usefulness of this food is explained by the words "The memory of his passion is recalled, the mind is filled with grace, and the pledge of future glory is given us." The first fruit of this banquet is the memory of the passion of Christ. The Body and Blood of the Lord is consecrated under the two species of bread and wine. Thus the species of bread represents the Body separated from the Blood, and thus dead, and the species of wine represents the

Blood separated from the Body, although under both species Christ is whole and living. The Lord willed that these mysteries preserve in us the constant and daily memory of his venerable passion by which we have escaped every evil and attained every good. Thus the Lord himself said to his apostles, speaking of this sacrament, "Do this in remembrance of me" (Lk 22:19), and the Apostle Paul, explaining these words of the Lord, says, "As often as you shall eat this bread and drink the cup, you proclaim the death of the Lord, until he comes" (1 Cor 11:26). That is, as often as you approach this most holy mystery, you will recall that Christ the Lord laid down his life for you. And this commemoration will last until the second coming of the Lord, that is, until the end of the world. The Lord wanted us to be continually mindful of his passion and death, because he knew that remembering it would be most useful for us, so that, mindful of his wonderful love toward us, we would place all our hope in him in life and in death. For what could he refuse to those for whom he so readily laid down his life?

The second fruit of this heavenly banquet, mentioned in the words "The mind is filled with grace," is a singular privilege of the sacrament of the eucharist, when it is received with proper preparation. For bodily food is something that is eaten and carried to the stomach and yet refreshes, nourishes, strengthens, and invigorates all the members; and excessive abstinence from food not only leaves the stomach empty, but weakens, wears down, and makes all members deformed and feeble and ultimately kills. Similarly, this divine food refreshes, nourishes, and strengthens all the spiritual powers of the soul. With this holy food the memory is filled by the grace of the sweetest recollection of God's gifts, especially of the Lord's passion, by which we have been freed and saved. By this same food the intellect is filled with the grace of faith, not merely habitual, but also actual. Faith purifies the heart from many errors and fills the mind with the understanding of things of God, which gives birth to an incredible joy. Finally, by this food the will is filled with the grace of most certain hope and most ardent love. Since love is the queen of the virtues, it draws to itself all of the virtues, by the possession of which a man emerges as most rich in the wealth of heaven. Thus by this most divine sacrament the mind is filled with grace.

Next, "the pledge of future glory is given us" through this same salutary sacrament. The metaphor of a pledge is used because men cannot refuse something promised when a pledge has been left as a guarantee of keeping the promise. The Lord left his Body in the eucharist as a pledge of heavenly beatitude. Thus one who dies after having received the Body of the Lord with due purity and reverence will show the pledge and will be permitted to enter the happiness of heaven. The pledge is shown by one who dies united with Christ by true charity, which is left in the soul by worthy reception of this salutary sacrament. For then the soul leaves the body as a bride "leaning upon her beloved" (Sg 8:5).

This is what Saint John wrote in Revelation when he said, "Blessed are the dead who die in the Lord" (Rv 14:13), that is, blessed are the dying who die joined to the Lord as members to the head. "No one has ascended into heaven except him who has descended from heaven: the Son of Man who is in heaven" (Jn 3:13). Christ the Son of Man does not ascend without his body, of which he is the head. Moreover, only those die in the Lord who, when they die, cling to the Lord as members to the head. And all those who worthily receive the Lord a little before death do cling to the Lord.

Thus far we have considered the preparation of the sick person for receiving viaticum before the viaticum is itself present. As soon as the sacred viaticum is brought, the sick person should, as best he can, arise and adore his Lord, either falling to his knees or at least by a bowing of the head. For the Lord often provides strength so that even the dying can at that time arise and genuflect. That is what we read of Saint William, Archbishop of Bourges. "But when he learned that his Lord and Creator had come to him, he immediately leapt from his bed with his strength restored, as though all the fever had left him, to the amazement of those standing about, especially since he seemed close to his last breath. With a lively step he goes to meet his Savior, love providing strength, and on bended knee, he adores him, all aflood with tears. So that he might genuflect more often, he frequently kneels and gets up. With complete devotion he commends his agony to him, praying that he might deign to cleanse whatever remains to be cleansed, lest the wicked enemy find anything in him."[6]

I would recommend that, before the sick person receives the Body of the Lord, he recite or listen to those verses of Saint Thomas Aquinas which profess faith and arouse hope and kindle love. They are:

Devoutly I adore you, hidden God,
Who truly lie beneath these forms;
To you my heart is wholly subject,
Since it wholly faints, in contemplating you.

Sight, touch, and taste are in you misled,
Only hearing can be safely trusted.
I believe whatever the Son of God has said,
No word is truer than the word of Truth.

Only the divinity was hidden on the cross;
Here the humanity is concealed as well.
Yet believing and confessing both,
I seek what the penitent thief sought.

I do not see the wound, as Thomas did,
Yet I confess that you are my God.
Make me ever more believe you,
Have hope in you and love you.

O memorial of the death of the Lord,
Living Bread, offering life to man.
Allow that my mind live from you
And that you always taste sweet to it.

Good Pelican, Jesus Lord,
Cleanse me, unclean as I am, by your blood,
Of which one drop could save
The whole world from every sin.

Jesus, whom I gaze upon now veiled,
I beg that what I thirst for may occur,
That, seeing you with face unveiled,
I may be blessed by the sight of your glory. Amen.

When he has recited or listened to these verses, after making the ordinary confession, which begins, "I confess to almighty God," and receiving the absolution and blessing of the priest, let him say, "Lord, I am not worthy," and then let him add with the greatest humility and devotion, "Into your hands, O Lord," and so on, and then receive in confidence the holy and heavenly food.

Once viaticum has been received, there remains thanksgiving for so great a gift of God. Besides vocal prayers which can be recited from pious prayerbooks, it is most beneficial for the one who has received viaticum to enter into the chamber of his heart and therein meditate in silence on the sweet words of the Lord Jesus found in Revelation, "Behold, I stand at the door and knock. If any man opens his door to me, I will come in to him and will sup with him, and he with me" (Rv 3:20). These words apply to those who return from holy communion. For the Lord, who instituted this sacrament in the form of a banquet, wants nothing more than that Christians approach this banquet. This is indicated by the words, "Behold, I stand at the door and knock," that is, I invite myself to a common feast that I may at the same time be fed. "If any man opens the door to me," assenting to the good desire I have inspired so that we may feast together, "I will come in to him" through the communion of the holy banquet, "and I will sup with him, and he with me." For God is said to sup with us when he is delighted by our spiritual progress, according to the words of the Prophet, "The Lord shall rejoice in his works" (Ps 104:31). And in the same place, "Let my speech be acceptable to him, but I will take delight in the Lord" (Ps 104:34). These words express the mutual delight and the sweet feast of God with the soul and of the soul with God. For God takes delight in the spiritual progress of the soul, and the soul takes delight in the gifts received from God. The chief among these is that God himself deigns to become glued in a way to the soul by this magnificent sacrament.

Let the faithful soul ponder after he has received viaticum how sweet and how fruitful it is to have Christ as its guest, while the sacred species remain, not merely as God, but also as man, to be able to deal confidently with him and share with him its dangers and trials in leaving the body, to commend himself to him wholeheartedly and to ask of him to hold back the tempter, to send his holy angel as companion and to bring him to the harbor of safety.

CHAPTER EIGHT

The eighth rule of the art of dying well, as death draws near, which is on extreme unction.

The last sacrament is the sacred anointing which can bring great consolation if its power is understood and the sacrament itself is received at the proper time. The effects of this sacrament are two, as we said in the previous chapter: the health of the body and the remission of sins. We will briefly discuss each of these. Regarding the first effect Saint James says: "Is any one among you sick? Let him bring in the presbyters of the Church, and let them pray over him, anointing him with oil in the name of the Lord. And the prayer of faith will save the sick man" (Jas 5:14–15). That is surely a clear and solid promise.

There are two reasons why the sick nowadays so seldom get well after having received this anointing: One is that these days that sacrament is given to the sick later than it should be. For we should not expect miracles from this sacrament, such as there would be if the one breathing his last should suddenly recover. But if this sacrament is conferred on the sick when they first become seriously ill, we would often see health restored not in an instant, but in due time. This is the reason why extreme unction is not conferred upon those who are put to death by an executioner for crimes committed. For they can be freed from the danger of death only by the most obvious miracle. The second reason is that it is not always good for the sick person to be freed from his illness; rather it is better for him to die. The prayer of the Church that is said in this anointing does not ask unconditionally for the health of the sick man, but only if it is profitable for his eternal salvation that he get better at that time.

The second effect of this sacrament is the remission of sins. Saint James speaks as follows: "And if he be in sins, they shall be forgiven him" (Jas 5:15). Since the remission of original sin properly pertains to baptism and since the remission of actual sin pertains both to baptism, if the ones baptized are adults, and to the sacrament of penance, theologians teach that the sins which are forgiven in the sacrament of extreme unction are the remains of sins. And these fall into two categories. Sometimes the remains of sins refer to the mortal and venial sins themselves which were committed after the reception of the sacrament of penance and which were not later confessed. This might happen from ignorance if the penitent did not know that they were mortal sins or from forgetfulness if they did not come to mind so that the sick person did not seek out a confessor to whom he might confess them. The sacred anointing wipes away these remains of sin. And of this kind of sin Saint James states, "And if he be in sins, they shall be forgiven him." The Councils of Florence and of Trent teach this clearly.[1]

The second kind of remains of sin is a sort of horror and torpor, or sadness and grief, which comes over the sick. And to this the promise of Saint James refers, "And the Lord will raise him up" (Jas 5:15). For this sacrament cheers up the sick when they see the divine promises which are expressed in this venerable sacrament. And for this reason it should not be postponed until the last moment when the sick person hears and understands nothing.

The usefulness of this sacrament can be seen from the very form of the words. For the priest anoints with the holy oil mainly the five parts of the body in which are found the five senses, namely, the sense of sight, the sense of hearing, the sense of smell, the sense of taste, and the sense of touch. Meanwhile the priest says, "May the Lord pardon you whatever sins you may have committed by sight, hearing," and so forth. And since that prayer is the form of the sacrament, it doubtless brings about what the words mean, unless something on the part of the recipient impedes this.

The great generosity and kindness of our God is readily seen in this sacrament by one who considers the great multitude of sins that flows from these five fountains of sin. For this reason, when Saint Malachi, an Irish bishop, whose life was written by Saint Bernard, had for a few hours delayed administering the sacrament of extreme unction to a noblewoman who was ill and she meanwhile died, he was seized with such sorrow that he lay the whole night in the room of the deceased with his priests, in prayer and grief, blaming himself that that good woman had not recovered her health by the sacrament of extreme unction or received so great a forgiveness of her sins from the generosity of the Lord.[2] Because that holy bishop was a friend of God, he obtained from his Lord by his prayers and tears that the woman rose, and she was anointed with great devotion by the holy man and received both of the effects of the sacred anointing. For she clearly got well and lived on for many years and did not lose, as we piously believe, the pardon of her sins. This example of this great man faithfully committed to writing by another holy man can easily persuade us all of how we ought to treasure this venerable sacrament.

CHAPTER NINE

The ninth precept of the art of dying well, as death draws near, which is on the first temptation of the devil, that is, on heresy.

As death approaches, the devil, our adversary, "as a roaring lion" (1 Pt 5:8), is true to his nature and swiftly runs to the prey and attacks the dying with all his might in that final struggle. He usually begins the battle with a temptation about faith. For the things which we believe not only surpass the senses, but also natural reason. And that very faith is the foundation of our justification. When that foundation is destroyed, the whole structure of good works collapses. This temptation is easily the most serious, because our struggle is with an opponent not only most learned and intelligent, but accustomed to this sort of battle from the beginning of the world. He seduced all the founders of the heresies, of whom many were very fine and wise men. Thus the Apostle rightly warns us, "For our wrestling is not against flesh and blood," that is, against men, "but against spiritual forces of wickedness on high" (Eph 6:12), that is, against demons who are spirits, and spirits most wicked and most sly and who see us from the airy heaven. Our weapons in this battle will not be disputations, but simple belief in the truth. For thus the princes of the apostles teach us. The Apostle Peter says, "Your adversary the devil, as a roaring lion, goes about seeking someone to devour. Resist him, steadfast in the faith" (1 Pt 5:8–9). And the Apostle Paul says, "In all things taking up the shield of faith, with which you may be able to quench all the fiery darts of the most wicked one" (Eph 6:16). Thus according to the teaching of the apostles we should not dispute with the devil, but with the shield of faith seize all his darts and turn them back again, even though they seem to be lighted and burning, that is, effective and subtle.

Pietro Barozzi, the bishop of Padua, gives us a dreadful example in the three books he wrote on the manner of dying well.[1] In the second book he speaks as follows: "As I have heard, there were once two very learned men, easily the best in disputation of all who were from the same college, and also men of good conduct and very religious. One of these died and afterward appeared all in flames to the survivor as he was studying Sacred Scripture in his library. He was terrified at what he saw and inquired about the reason for such a great punishment. Groaning and grieving, the other answered: 'When I was about to leave this life, the old enemy came to me. And since he knew that I was quite learned, he began to ask me about my faith and what I believed. I replied that I believed in the contents of the Apostles' Creed. He asked me to clarify for him some things which seemed a little obscure. I explained to him what I had read in the Athanasian Creed. For I did not think that it could be put more clearly or truly. Then he said, "It is not as you think. What pertains to the Father is partially clear and true, but partially obscure and false. For he is eternal, but he is not always Father as he is always God. First he is God, later Father." When I cried out that that was heretical doctrine and the teaching of the devil, he said, "This is not a matter to be settled by shouting, but by reasons, if we are guided by the desire to discover the truth. I can easily state the reasons for my opinion. And you will free me from a great error if you can explain the reasons for yours." And I, poor wretch, trusted more than I should have in my talent and learning, and I began to dispute with him as I would with the rest of men. At last by the many arguments he raised against me and—what amazed me more—by proofs from Sacred Scripture he gradually led me to such terrible error that I thought neither the Son nor the Holy Spirit was God. Meanwhile, death seized my soul and presented it to the Judge such as it was. I was ordered by him to depart into this fire. Though it is the most raging fire, I would think it somewhat bearable if it would only end after ten million years. But it is eternal, and greater than any human era has seen. Thus I regret almost every hour the knowledge that cast me down to this dreadful destruction.' Saying this, he vanished.

"The other was startled both by the strangeness of the event and by the loss of his friend, but as soon as he came to his senses, he reported what he had seen to his closest friends and asked their advice in this matter. Their common decision was that each should commit himself to the faith which the Catholic Church holds. A little later he came down with an illness from which he was to die. And the ancient enemy, encouraged by reason of his success in the earlier debate, approached him as well. He asked about his faith and what he believed. He answered that he believed whatever the Church, his mother, believes. Again the ancient enemy asked what holy mother, the Church, believes. And he said, 'What I believe,' and in this fashion, in the hearing of those standing about, as if he were being questioned by someone, he kept saying, 'I believe what the Church believes, and the Church believes what I believe,' until he breathed his last. Thus it happened that, after having mocked the wiles of the enemy, he went off to heaven. After a few days, much changed in bodily appearance, he appeared to his friends whose advice he had sought in this matter. He thanked them for their counsel in virtue of which he ascended to the kingdom of heaven. We have considered it worthwhile to describe these events as they occurred so that everyone might learn by the misfortune or success of these men that one must not dispute with the devil about the faith, but that it is enough to commit oneself to the faith which the Catholic Church holds." This is what Barozzi said, to which we add nothing.

CHAPTER TEN

The tenth rule of the art of dying well, as death draws near, which is on the second temptation, that is, on despair.

The second temptation is usually one of despair, by which the devil often troubles not only bad men, but at times also some very good ones. He easily throws very wicked men into the pit of despair when death threatens. For he casts before their eyes all the sins which they committed while they lived. Venerable Bede writes of a certain soldier in the fifth book of the history of his people.[1] His words are: "There was in the time of Conrad, who reigned after Edilred, a layman who held a military office. But his interior neglect of himself was as displeasing to the king as his external efforts were pleasing. The king, therefore, constantly warned him to confess his sins and to leave his evil ways before he lost all time for repenting and amending his life by the sudden arrival of death. Although he was frequently warned, he spurned the words of salvation, promising that he would do penance later. Meanwhile, coming down with an illness, he took to his bed and began to suffer agonizing pain. The king came to see him—for he loved him much—and urged him even then to do penance for his sins before he died. But he said that he did not wish to confess his sins at that time, but after he had recovered from his illness, so that his companions would not reproach him for doing out of fear of death what he was unwilling to do when he was well. He spoke bravely in his own opinion, although he was pitifully seduced by the deceit of the devil, as became clear later. When the illness grew worse and the king came again to visit and instruct him, he shouted out suddenly in a wretched cry, 'What do you want now? Why have you come here? For you no longer can help me or save me.' But the king said, 'Do not speak like that. Come to your senses.' And he replied, 'I am not out of my mind. Rather, I have my bad conscience clearly before my eyes. A few minutes ago two handsome youths came in and sat next to me, one at my head, the other at my feet. The one brought forth a beautiful booklet, but very small, and he gave it to me to read. I looked and found written in it every good deed I have done. And they were few and trivial. Suddenly an army of evil and terrifying spirits arrived. Then the one who seemed most important because of his dark countenance and lead position brought forth a volume terrifying to see, enormous and almost too heavy to carry. He ordered one of his companions to give it to me to read. When I read it, I found that all my sins, not only those I committed by word and deed, but also those I committed by the slightest thought, were unmistakably described in horrid script.' Thus the poor wretch spoke in his despair, and not long after he died. The penance that he could have done in a short time with the fruit of forgiveness, he now performs eternally to no avail, while subjected to punishment." Thus Venerable Bede spoke. There we clearly see that our enemy, the devil, first got the poor soldier not to do penance out of hope for a longer life and then reduced him to despair.

There is another example in the same author in the following chapter, where he speaks as follows. "I knew a brother whom I wish I had not known. I could even mention his name, if that were of any use. He was placed in a well-known monastery, although he lived shamefully. Stricken with a sickness and brought unto the point of death, he called the brethren. Much saddened and like one damned, he began to report that he saw hell opened and Satan plunged into the depth of Tartarus, while Caiphas and the others who killed our Lord were given over with him to the flames of vengeance. 'In their proximity,' he said, 'I see a place of eternal damnation prepared for me, alas! poor wretch that I am.' Hearing this, the brothers began to exhort him earnestly to do penance then while he was still in the body. He answered them, 'I have no time now to change my life, for I see that my judgment has already been decided.' Saying that, he departed without viaticum, and his body is buried in the farthest reaches of the monastery."[2] Thus spoke Bede. What that poor monk says, namely, that he did not have time to change his life, he says not out of truth, but from the devil's persuasion. For the Holy Spirit clearly proclaims through the prophet Ezechiel that God is always ready to welcome those who turn from sin to penance (Ez 18:21–23, 33:11–16). Pope Saint Leo teaches this even more clearly in the Letter to Theodore, the bishop of Frejus, in these words, "We cannot set measures for or limit the time of God's mercy. Conversion to God suffers no delays, as the Spirit of God says, through the prophet: When you turn and grieve, then you will be saved."[3]

I will add an example or two to show that even very good men are tempted by the devil to the sin of despair as they leave this life. There is found in the writings of Lawrence Surius *The Life of Count Elzear*, who lived in virginity with his wife Dalphina, and who after his holy death was renowned for many signs and miracles. Yet he suffered very serious temptations in leaving this life. The author writes as follows in the last chapter. "Finally, in the agony of death, he appeared exceedingly frightened, and from this we gather that he was in great turmoil over some accusations that were made against him. He cried out in his struggle, 'Great is the power of the demons. But the power and merits of the most holy Incarnation and Passion of Jesus Christ utterly overcomes it.' Crying out again after a little while he said, 'I have clearly won.' Again after a little time, he said with a great shout, 'I commit myself wholly to the judgment of God.' And having said that, he appeared composed and, blessed with a healthy glow and beauty and grace, he gave up his spirit."[4]

A much more frightening example is found in John Climacus, who reports that a certain very venerable monk, by the name of Stephan, having lived around forty years in the desert, known for his fasts, vigils, tears, prayers, and other virtues, finally came to death.[5] When he came to his final agony, he was charged with many sins by the demons in order that they might bring him to despair. He was suddenly filled with amazement and began to answer with open eyes and a clear voice, at times like this: "It is true, it is really true. But I have destroyed the sin by penance and tears." At other times he said, "You have correctly accused me; I have nothing to say in response." And thus he died, leaving it in doubt whether he was saved or rejected. These and other such examples warn us to cleanse our conscience carefully before that hour and never to lose confidence in the Lord's mercy.

CHAPTER ELEVEN

The eleventh rule of the art of dying well, as death draws near, which is on the third temptation, that is, on hatred for God.

Our adversary, the devil, not only strives as much as he can to rob the dying of faith and hope and to lead them into heresy and despair, but endeavors to separate God's friends from his friendship and to lead them into hatred for God and into blasphemies and the arts of magic. These men generally do not fear death or the pains of hell. For they hope to live a merry life in hell as companions of the demons whom they suppose are ruling in hell. Grillandos writes of this in the book *Fortunetelling*, question nine, number two, and Martinus del Rio borrows from him in the sixth book of *Magical Investigations*, chapter one, section three.[1] These authors say, as witches have often admitted after they have been captured, that the devil aims and works at nothing else than persuading them to persist in their opinion up to death. Even as they are brought to the place of punishment and the fire is lit, the devils promise they will openly snatch their bodies from the noose and from the flames and will cause them to feel no pain from contact with the flames. They promise that, even if it should happen that they die by the fire, their death will be free from torment and they will depart from the miseries of this life and be transferred into the happiness of the future life without feeling the punishment. They promise them they will be like the demons, endowed with the same strength, knowledge, riches, power, and pleasure that the devil himself possesses and enjoys. Thus the lying devil deceives them.

There are still others who, although they are not strictly speaking witches or magicians, are nonetheless so blinded by greed that they are only a little different from the infidels. Not without reason did the blessed Apostle call greed slavery to idols (Eph 5:5; Col 3:5).

I myself once visited a sick person close to death, and when I began to talk about preparations for leaving this life, he answered bravely and fearlessly, saying, "I wanted, sir, to speak with you, not on my behalf, but on behalf of my wife and children. For I am on my way to hell, and there is nothing you can do for me." He said this calmly, as if he were speaking of a trip to a villa or town. The devil had so subdued his soul that he had no desire or wish to be delivered from him. Though he was not a magician or a necromancer, he was, nonetheless, practicing a very dangerous art. Intent upon gain by fair means or foul, he seemed to have forgotten not only God, but also his own soul. The result is that I was helpless in trying to recall him to a better life despite all I said. Someone may want to know what art he practiced. I will tell you it so that his destruction may help other men of the same profession to come to their senses. He was a lawyer, one of those who do not care very much whether they undertake to defend a just or an unjust cause. And at times these men injure both parties, while they fill their purses.

I will add another example since I am on this topic. When a highly learned lawyer was speaking to me, explaining the merits of a certain case, I interrupted and said, "You seem to me to favor an unjust cause." Agreeing, he answered, "I am not an advocate for truth or for justice, but for my client. My duty is to expound the merits of the case I have undertaken to defend. Let the judge look to the party for whom he should decide." I said, "I do not want you to believe me, but Saint Thomas Aquinas, a supreme and most holy teacher. For in the Second Part of *The Summa of Theology*, he speaks as follows: 'I respond. One must say that it is wrong to cooperate with someone in doing evil, by advising, or aiding, or consenting in some way or other. For advising and helping is in some fashion doing, and the Apostle says in writing to the Romans that not only they who commit sin, but also those who approve of them (Rom 1:32) are worthy of death. Thus, as was said above, all such persons are bound to restitution. However, it is clear that an advocate offers aid and advice to him whose cause he defends. Hence, if he knowingly defends an unjust cause, he undoubtedly sins gravely and is bound to the restitution of the loss which the other party incurs unjustly by reason of his help. But if he defends an unjust cause in ignorance, thinking that it is just, he is excused in accord with the manner in which ignorance is able to excuse one.'[2] That is what Saint Thomas says. Cardinal Cajetan explains the final words of Saint Thomas as follows: 'Whoever has defended either a just cause or an unjust cause, although he does not know it to be unjust, not because of ignorance, but with ignorance which does not excuse, unjustly defends the cause. Those who do not make the effort to discern and investigate whether they are undertaking a just or an unjust cause are clearly neglecting to get the knowledge that they are bound to have.'[3] That is Cajetan's view."

To these temptations we can add another which helps more than it harms, although the devil uses it to do harm. For the enemy of the human race is in the habit of appearing with a terrifying countenance to the dying so that, if he cannot deceive them, he might at least impede them from alacrity and eagerness for prayer. Thus Severus Sulpicius relates that the devil appeared to blessed Martin as he was dying, and Saint Martin said to him, "Why are you here, you cruel beast? You are going to find nothing bad in me."[4] Venerable Peter Damian also writes in *The Life of Saint Odilo* that shortly before his death the devil appeared to blessed Odilo, looking dreadful, and blessed Odilo, we read, said of him, "In the very hour of my decision, in that corner (for he pointed out the place with his finger) I saw a certain shape cruel and terrifying, which endeavored to horrify and frighten me with his cruel visage. But with the power of Christ comforting me, it could not harm me by any attack."[5] Saint Adelinus, bishop of Sagium, writes in Lawrence

Surius in *The Life of Saint Opportuna*, that the devil appeared to her as she was dying in the guise of the blackest Ethiopian, whose hair and beard appeared to drip hot and molten pitch.[6] His eyes were as flaming iron which comes forth from the furnace shooting out many sparks. From his mouth and nostrils there came forth flames and sulphuric smoke.

The angel of the Lord explains why God permits holy men to be tried by such visions, in *The Life of Saint Aichard*, which survives in Lawrence Surius for the fifteenth of September.[7] For when the devil was in a certain monastery, intent upon plunder, the holy guardian angel of that monastery said to the devil, "You will have here a task fruitful for the monks, but not profitable for you. For them it will serve as expiation; for you it will serve as confusion." The devil answered, "Am I obliged to assist these or any Christ-worshipers toward salvation?" The angel answered, "In this respect you are obliged to help them, because, if there is anything in them that ought to be pruned away, it will be removed by the fear of seeing you." Then a little later the same angel said to Saint Aichard about the devil, "Do not fear his countenance. No power is given him in this Christian family for working harm, except that the sight of him strikes a wholesome fear into the souls of those about to leave their bodies, so that if there is something in them that ought to be pruned away, it will be removed by fright over that terrible sight."

CHAPTER TWELVE

The twelfth rule of the art of dying well, as death draws near, which is on the first remedy against the temptations of the devil.

In the preceding chapters we have explained four temptations which often seriously trouble the dying. Against these temptations two kinds of remedies can be applied. One is for those who have the use of their reason and can hear and understand what is said to them. The other is a general remedy for all and most safe and useful.

As far as the first one goes, if the temptation attacks the Catholic faith, it is in no way helpful, as we said above, to dispute with the devil. Generally the sick who are tempted are to be warned that, if the temptation concerns the nature of God who, according to the faith, is one in essence and three in persons, they should consider how little we know not merely about spiritual, but even about bodily creatures. In fact, many men find it hard to believe that single stars of the sky are larger than the whole orb of the earth; yet mathematicians easily prove that it is utterly true. But if such a bodily matter is not understood by learned men who still believe that it is so, why should they not believe what God himself revealed about his nature through the apostles and prophets and confirmed with many great signs and miracles?

But if the temptation concerns those things which we believe God has done and does every day, such as, above all, the changing of bread and wine into the Body and Blood of Christ, while the accidents of bread and wine remain, one has to make use of examples of the many kinds of things we believe God has done, though we cannot account for any of them. Who can comprehend that the whole world was made out of nothing by the mere command of God? And yet many who believe this cannot be brought to believe the mystery of the eucharist. Likewise, who can believe that the bodies of all the dead that have been reduced to ashes or to dust or have been devoured by beasts or turned into plants will rise up in a moment by the word of the Lord? And yet all Catholics readily believe this and profess it in the Creed. Even Job believed this a few thousand years ago. For he said, "I know that my Redeemer lives, and in the last day I shall rise out of the earth. And I shall be clothed again with my skin" (Jb 19:25–26). On the basis of these and other such marvelous works of God which surpass our understanding, other things which the Catholic Church proposes for our belief can be easily accepted, since the Church is, by the testimony of the Apostle, "the pillar and mainstay of the truth" (1 Tm 3:15). These and similar things can be proposed to those who are tempted about faith.

To those who suffer temptations about hope we should propose the clearly infinite magnitude of God's mercy which surpasses by far the number and mass of all sins. For the Holy Spirit speaks through David as follows: "The Lord is gracious and merciful, patient and plenteous in mercy. The Lord is sweet to all, and his tender mercies are over all his works" (Ps 145:8–9). Likewise we should propose the propitiation of the Mediator, of which Saint John says, "He is a propitiation for our sins, not for ours only but also for those of the whole world" (1 Jn 2:2). We should also propose the power of penance, which, if it comes from a truly contrite heart, never will meet with rejection from God. For the Prophet wrote most truly: "A contrite and humbled heart, O God, you will not despise" (Ps 51:19). We should also propose the example of the prodigal son, who had barely uttered the words, "Father, I have sinned against heaven and before you" (Lk 15:21), when suddenly his father's heart was touched and he rushed to embrace his son. And he ordered that he be clothed in an expensive robe and that a ring be put upon his finger and that a splendid banquet be prepared, because his son had been lost and was found.

Finally, we should propose the example of Saint Paul, who, while he was still persecuting the Church, was touched by the grace of God and transformed from a persecutor into an apostle. He himself wrote that that had happened so that all sinners might be converted by his example and that no one, however wicked, should despair of God's mercy. He says, "This saying is true and worthy of entire acceptance, that Jesus Christ came into the world to save sinners, of whom I am the chief. But for this reason I obtained mercy, that in me first Christ Jesus might show forth all patience, as an example to those who shall believe in him for the attainment of life everlasting" (1 Tm 1:15).

Those who are tempted by the demon with a grave temptation against the love of God and are stirred up to a hatred of God and a love of the devil should first be instructed that the devil is a liar, as our Lord says, "When the devil tells a lie he speaks from his very nature, for he is a liar and its father" (Jn 8:44). Where the expression "and its father" means that the devil is the father of lies, as Saint Augustine and Saint John Chrysostom teach.[1] For the devil told the very first lie when he said to Eve and through her to Adam, "No, you shall not die the death" (Gn 3:4). For God had told Adam that he should not eat of the forbidden tree, if he wished never to die. The devil, however, said that they should eat and that they would not die. Thus the devil deserves no trust since he is a liar and the father of lies.

Second, the devil has already been condemned to eternal fire with all his followers. For the Lord will say on the day of judgment,

"Depart from me, accursed ones, into the everlasting fire which was prepared for the devil and his angels" (Mt 25:41). Those are mistaken who subject themselves to the devil in the hope that they will reign with him after death in the underworld and will enjoy the greatest wealth and pleasures. Finally, experience shows that all the promises of the devil are false. For we have as yet found no one who has received the immense treasure the devil has promised. Nor have we found that anyone condemned to prison or to galleys or even to death by legitimate authority has been rescued by the devil.

If these three examples were seriously weighed by greedy men, there would probably be few or none at all who would dare to leave God, true and truly omnipotent and all-wise and all-good, for the most deceitful and most stingy and most miserable devil.

On the fourth temptation there is nothing for us to say, since it has already been sufficiently established that that temptation is more helpful than harmful for those who are dying. Yet if anyone wishes a remedy from Scripture for bearing it more easily, let him read or have someone read, while that horrible vision lasts, Psalm 27, which begins, "The Lord is my light and my salvation" (Ps 27:1).

CHAPTER THIRTEEN

The thirteenth rule of the art of dying well, as death draws near, which is on the second remedy against the temptations of the devil.

Having explained the first remedy against each kind of temptation of the devil, we will now explain the second remedy, which will be common to all temptations. This great and salutary remedy lies in prayer, whether it is the prayer of the sick person for himself or the prayer of others for him or the prayer of both the sick person and of others present. For it is certain that the prayer of those who fear God is of great value, especially since we know well that the devil can tempt someone only as much as the Lord allows him. For the devil is like a roaring lion or mad dog tied with an iron chain. He cannot bite at will, but only as God, who holds the chain in his all-powerful hand, allows him to bite. Saint Augustine stresses this, in explaining the words of the Psalm, "Say to my soul: I am your salvation" (Ps 35:3). Bringing forth the example of Job, he says, "God showed in the case of that holy man, Job, that the devil himself does not have the power of taking away these temporal things, unless he has received it from that supreme power. The devil could envy the holy man, but could he harm him? He could accuse him, but could he in any way condemn him? Was he able to take anything away? Could he harm even a nail or a hair, if he had not said to God, 'Send forth your hand'? What does 'Send forth your hand' mean? Grant the power. He received the power, and he tempted Job. Yet it is the one tempted who triumphs; the temptor is overcome. For although God permitted the devil to take away Job's possessions, he did not himself interiorly abandon his servant, but made for himself out of the soul of his servant a sword for overcoming the devil. How strong is he? I mean the man. Although he was conquered in paradise, he conquers on the dunghill. The one who was conquered there by the devil through the woman here conquers the devil and the woman."[1]

The same point that Saint Augustine makes, namely, that the devil can do nothing unless God allows it, Saint Anthony and Saint Francis teach by example. Saint Athanasius, who wrote a biography of Saint Anthony, speaks as follows: "Surrounded by a multitude of demons, Anthony used to say, as if he were mocking his enemies, 'If you had some power, one of you would suffice for battle, but since you are broken because the Lord has removed your strength, you try to strike terror by your multitude. The very fact that you don the forms of irrational beasts is proof of your weakness.' Again he would say with confidence, 'If you have any power, if the Lord has given you any power over me, devour what has been given you. But if you are powerless, why are you struggling in vain? For the sign of the cross and faith in the Lord is a wall for us that cannot be stormed.' "[2]

Saint Bonaventure tells almost the same thing of Saint Francis. He says, "Seeking lonely places, he would go to abandoned wildernesses to pray at night where he frequently withstood terrible attacks of demons who, obviously fighting among themselves, were striving to distract him from the pursuit of prayer. But, armed with heavenly weapons, the more violently he was attacked by his enemies, the more he was rendered strong in virtue and fervent in deed, confidently saying to Christ: 'Under the shadow of your wings protect me from the face of the wicked who have attacked me.' To the demons he said, 'Do whatever you will to me, evil and deceitful spirits. For you can only do what the hand of God allows, and I stand ready to bear with all joy everything which he decided should be inflicted.' Unable to bear such constancy of mind, the proud demons left in confusion."[3] We have laid down as a solid foundation that the devil can do only what God permits; therefore, we can have no doubt that fervent prayer to God whether by the sick person or by those present is very effective, especially if those who are praying are friends of God.

We have a marvelous example of this in Saint Gregory in the Fourth Book of the *Dialogues*. He says that he encountered this example in his monastery and that he spoke of it in a sermon to the people. "That man," he says, "whom I remember having spoken of in homilies to the people, was a very restless lad, by the name of Theodore, who followed his brother into my monastery more out of necessity than out of choice. It greatly distressed him if someone said something on behalf of his salvation. Not only could he not do good; he could not even bear hearing it. With oaths and anger and ridicule he swore that he would never take the habit of the holy rule. However, during the plague that recently killed off many of the people of this city, he was stricken in the groin and brought close to death. And when he was drawing his last breath, the brethren gathered to help his passing with their prayers. His body was already dead in its extremities; only in his breast was there left the warmth of life. The brethren began to pray for him all the more urgently when they saw that he was now quickly passing away. Then suddenly he began to shout at the brethren present there and to interrupt their prayers with loud cries, saying, 'Go away, go away. I have been given to the dragon to devour, and because of your presence he cannot devour me. He has already got my head in his mouth. Leave so that he does not torture me more, but does what he is going to do. If I have been given to him to devour, why should I suffer delay because of you?' Then the brethren began to say to him, 'What is it that you are saying, brother? Make the sign of the holy cross.' He answered, 'I want to make the sign of the cross, but I cannot, as I am pressed down by the scales of this dragon.'

When the brethren heard this, they prostrated themselves on the ground and began to pray with tears more fervently for his rescue. And, behold, the sick man suddenly began to cry out, 'Thank God, behold, the dragon, who had taken me to devour, has fled; driven out of me by your prayers, he could not stay. Only intercede for my sins, because I am ready to be converted and leave completely the life of the world.' Thus the man who was, as we said, already dead in the extremities of his body was restored to life and was wholeheartedly converted to God. And after his conversion he was long afflicted with trials; then finally his soul was freed from his flesh."[4] Those were the words of Saint Gregory.

Therefore, those who are present at a deathbed should learn not so much to speak with the sick person as to pray ardently for him to God. Nor should one admit just any sort of person to visit the sick person in his last moments, but only pious and good men who have much influence with God by their prayers. For the constant and fervent prayer of the just man has much influence with God (Jas 5:16). And as the devil, because he has little time, makes every effort he can in that hour, so faithful friends ought much more to help by prayers and tears their brethren departing this present world.

CHAPTER FOURTEEN

The fourteenth rule of the art of dying well, as death draws near, which is about those who die, not from ordinary illness, but from some other cause.

Thus far we have explained how those who die from a long illness ought to prepare for death. It is now appropriate to say what they should do who face the danger of death not from long illness, but from some other cause. There are three kinds of men whom the danger of death threatens apart from ordinary illness. For some death comes unforeseen and yet certain; such are those taken by heart attack or struck by lightning. For others death comes neither unforeseen nor certain, but as highly likely; such are those who wage war with the enemy or struggle with the waves and blasts of wind on the high sea. For others death comes neither unforseen nor uncertain; such are those who are put to death by the executioner after the sentence of the judge.

The men of the first class have no other remedy but the daily or even continual recollection of death. The very solemn warning of the Lord and Savior, "Watch, for you know neither the day nor the hour," (Mt 25:13) properly applies to them. It is a grave but valuable necessity that forces us to what is best and most profitable for us. If the Lord would say, "Watch, naked in the cold air until you freeze and expire with your flesh broken open on all sides," as the Forty Martyrs had kept watch, should we not do so in order to come safely and joyously to eternal happiness? And if he should say, "Watch, naked and bound to a gridiron, until, consumed in deep and bitter pain by the burning fire set beneath it, you pass from this life," as we read was done to Saint Lawrence, should we not readily do so in order to avoid the pit of eternal fire?

But the Lord, our God, does not give such an order to all of us, but he orders us to watch lest, while we sleep, the thief in the night should come and steal the gold of charity, the precious gems of chastity, the treasure of faith, or the other goods of true virtue while we sleep in sin. Thus, overcome by the deadly sleep of sin and caught off guard by death, we would suffer the loss of the heavenly kingdom and be cast into the pit burning with inextinguishable fire. Some die so suddenly that no assistance can be provided them. Granted, they are few; how do you know that you will not be among them? And if you are one of those few, what will the multitude of those who have escaped such danger matter to you? And so, while you can still escape such a terrible evil, listen to the advice of God our Father crying out and saying, "Watch, watch, you know neither the day nor the hour."

For the second sort of men, who either die a sudden death in war or perish at sea, lost in the waves during a violent storm, three things are necessary if they are to die a happy death. The first is that they do not go to war unless they are sure that the war is just. Or, if they do not take to arms willingly, but forced by their prince, at least they should not know that the war is unjust. For Saint Augustine teaches this in the book *Against Faustus the Manichee*.[1] For he writes that the situation of the prince who commands is different from that of the soldier who obeys. And he teaches that the prince may not fight a war unless he knows that the war is just, but that a soldier may, provided that he does not know that the war is unjust. The second is that in war they observe the laws of Saint John the Baptist, who, when asked by soldiers what they should do in order to be saved, answered, "Plunder no one, accuse no one falsely, and be content with your pay" (Lk 3:14). The last is that they do not permit mortal sin ever to cling to their hearts. Otherwise it will be easy for death that carries off many in battle to find them unprepared and hand them over to eternal death to suffer endless torture. Thus soldiers stationed in camps are in great danger of losing eternal life unless they are ever on guard and fight no less against the demons tempting them to sin than against mortal foes fighting for temporal glory.

These same points can be addressed to those who sail the sea amid danger. They ought first of all to avoid undertaking a voyage for a bad end, such as, to capture and to rob whomever they come upon, as pirates do. Second, if the voyage is undertaken for the sake of waging war, they should also observe the laws we have received from the holy precursor of our Lord. Finally, they should not dare to offend God by a mortal sin, since they are no further away from death than their ship is from the waters.

Men of the third sort can be called fortunate, if they know what is good for them. For they are put to death after being condemned either justly or unjustly. If justly, death can assist them in making satisfaction before God, provided they seriously detest their sins and freely accept death to expiate their sins. If they are unjustly put to death and forgive from the heart those who were the cause of their undoing, they are imitators of the Redeemer, who prayed to his Father for those who crucified him, saying, "Father, forgive them, for they do not know what they are doing" (Lk 23:34). Consider too that they suffer far less in death than those who suffer a long and serious illness. Furthermore, since their senses are unimpaired and their mind is undamaged, they can more easily put forth effort on the proper reception of holy confession and the sacrament of our Lord's Body and on prayers than can those who are kept in bed, preoccupied with bearing various pains and with their natural strength usually weakened or even exhausted. Finally, in many places learned and pious men aid with much care and concern men who are about to be executed and teach them how to prepare for meeting death in a holy way so that, as they begin to die to mortal life, they may begin to live unto blessed immortality.

CHAPTER FIFTEEN

The happy death of those who have learned the art of dying well.

Having explained the rules of the art of dying well, there remains one thing more, namely, that we briefly explain the usefulness of this art. The task is easy and yet of great import. For one who dies well, dies a happy death. But he who dies well does not merely die a happy death, and he who dies a bad death does not merely die unhappily. One who dies well passes from a deadly and miserable life to a life that is eternal and blessed in every way. And one who dies badly passes from a life that seems long and happy to a life full of every labor and pain and that will never come upon an end of toil. Thus it is better called eternal death than life. For they will be men damned, who have died to face every labor and pain.

Holy Scripture clearly teaches us that it will be so. Of those who die well Saint John says in Revelation, "I heard a voice from heaven saying, 'Write: Blessed are the dead, who die in the Lord henceforth. Yes, says the Spirit, let them rest from their labors, for their works follow them' " (Rv 14:13). There are some authors who think that this statement applies only to the martyrs, but the more common and more correct interpretation teaches that the words of Saint John apply to all the saints who die piously in Christ. Certainly Saint Bernard says this in his letter, which is entitled *On the Maccabees*, " 'Blessed are the dead, who die in the Lord.' Not only those who die for the Lord, as the martyrs, but those who die in the Lord, as the confessors, will doubtless be happy. Thus two things, in my opinion, make death precious, the life one leads and the reason one dies, but the latter more so than the former. Yet the most precious death will be that commended both by the life led and the reason one dies."[1] Besides this, the Church, which is the best interpreter of the Scriptures, bids that the reading in Masses for all the dead be taken from that passage of Revelation. Saint John, therefore, says, "Blessed are the dead who die in the Lord," that is, blessed are all those who, when they die, are found "in the Lord," that is, are found joined to the Lord by true charity as living members of the head, which is Christ. Thus Saint Luke wrote of Saint Stephan's death, "He fell asleep in the Lord" (Acts 7:59), that is, joined to the Lord as a member to the head.

Saint John explains as follows why those who have died in the Lord are happy, "Yes, says the Spirit, let them rest from their labors." For the Holy Spirit clearly states that in the death of the saints all their laborious works are finished and endless peace begins and that not only do all labors cease, but there begins a most happy life filled with every kind of pleasure, because their works follow them. For works that are good and deserving of all consolation and pleasure, not for a time, but eternally, do not remain on earth, but follow the saints into heaven, according to the words of the Prophet, "He has distributed, he has given to the poor; his justice remains forever and ever" (Ps 112:9). The riches of a holy man are left on earth, or rather are consumed on earth, but the justice, generosity, and mercy by which earthly riches are shared with the poor "remains forever and ever." And it not only remains, but also makes a man most rich since he distributed his perishable wealth to the needy on earth. Not only do deeds of generosity follow them, but also works of wisdom, works of faith, of hope, and of love, works of fear of the Lord, of temperance, and of fortitude, works of chastity and works of religion. Finally, all good works follow them and gain for them ample and endless rewards. Thus he who has died well is indeed most happy, since he gains rest from all labors and the sum of all goods for eternity. Besides this true testimony of Scripture there are the visitations of the saints who are often present to good men as they die, in order to console and help them in their departure from the body and to hold in check the demons who are accustomed to strike terror at that time. Such a visitation is not the least of the joys of those who die a holy death.

I could here recount many stories, but I will be content with the examples extant in the *Dialogues* of Saint Gregory. Thus in the fourth book Blessed Gregory speaks of Ursinus the priest. "Ursinus the priest was near death when he began to cry out with great joy, saying, 'Welcome, my lords, why have you deigned to come to your little servant? I am coming, I am coming, I give thanks.' When he repeated this again and again, those who were present asked him to whom he was saying this. He answered them in wonder, saying, 'Don't you see the holy Apostles gathering here? Don't you see Blessed Peter and Blessed Paul, the princes of the apostles?' Turning to them, he said again, 'I come, behold, I come,' and in the midst of those words he gave up his spirit. And by following them he testified that he truly saw the holy apostles. And it generally happens that great saints see visions at death lest they fear the penal sentence of their death, and while the company of the citizens from above is revealed to their mind, they are released from the chain of their flesh without the exhaustion of pain and fear."[2]

Saint Gregory also relates in the following chapter of the same book that the martyrs Saint Juvenal and Saint Eleutherius came with great splendor to Probus, the bishop of the church of Riete, as he was dying, and that soon venerable Probus was released from the flesh and went off to heaven with those who came to him.[3] In the following chapter this author says that Saint Peter appeared to Saint Galla, a servant of God, as she was ill and near to death, and indicated to her that all her sins had been forgiven so that she might depart from the world in safety.[4] In the next chapter he reports that, when Servulus, a paralytic, was dying, songs of angels were heard in heaven and a marvelous odor was poured forth.[5] In the following chapter he tells that for Romula, a servant of God, an immense number of holy souls came to her from heaven in a light incalculably bright and with the sweetest fragrance.[6] In the next chapter he reports that his aunt, Tharsilla, first saw Pope Felix, a relative of hers, appear to her and say, "Come, for I welcome you in this mansion of light." And then she was suddenly overtaken by fever and, as she neared her end, she saw Jesus coming to her and, stretching out toward him, she expired.[7] And so sweet was the smell left in that place that its very sweetness showed that the source of all sweetness was there. He also writes in the following chapter that the Mother of God, the Blessed Virgin, appeared with a chorus of virgins to a girl, Musa, and brought her as she died to the kingdom of heaven.[8] Finally, he writes in the next chapter that holy angels were present to Stephen as he died.[9]

Thus from the testimony of Saint Gregory we know that not only angels, but also martyrs who have gone before, or the princes of the apostles, or the queen of heaven, or even Christ himself, the king of eternal glory, often assist good men and women as they leave this life. Only those who have been permitted to experience such great favors of God can say how great is this happiness, how great the glory, how great the joy of the heart for those who have learned to live well and to die a happy death.

CHAPTER SIXTEEN

The unhappy death of those who have neglected the art of dying well.

The Lord said of Judas the traitor, "It were better for that man if he had not been born" (Mt 26:24). We can conceive of no greater unhappiness than that of a man who veers away by sin from the end for which he was created. If other things, whether brute animals or plants or inanimate things, do not attain their ends, they still suffer no trouble once they cease to be. But if a man veers away from his end, which is life that is happy and endless, he does not stop existing and living, but leads a life worse than all death so that he constantly seeks death and never finds it. Hence, he who does not strive with all his strength to come to eternal happiness is more foolish than every fool and sillier than every dunce, since no one can fail of eternal happiness without falling into the abyss of eternal damnation.

To grasp correctly this matter of the highest moment I thought it worthwhile to consider briefly the words of the Apostle Paul, which are found in the Second Letter to the Corinthians: "For our present light affliction, which is for the moment, prepares us for an eternal weight of glory that is beyond all measure in sublimity; while we look not at the things that are seen, but at the things that are not seen. For the things that are seen are temporal, but the things that are not seen are eternal" (2 Cor 4:17–18). These golden words of the Apostle are fully disclosed to the spiritual man, and by them the spiritual man most easily learns the art of living well and the art of dying well. But for the carnal and natural man these words are mere darkness and, indeed, Cimmerian darkness, as if they were Hebrew or Arabic for one who speaks Latin or Greek.

The spiritual man gathers from these words that the tribulations undertaken for the sake of God, however severe, are very light and brief, even though they have to be borne for many years, since everything that has an end cannot be really long. He realizes that with God these tribulations produce merit of such great worth that with it one may purchase an immense and everlasting treasure of glory and of all goods. Wise men conclude from this that they should fear not tribulations, but sins, and that they should value highly not temporal goods, but eternal goods. Consequently, they live well on earth in order to reign happily in heaven, and in this way they live holy lives and die happy deaths.

But natural men, who do not have the spirit, who verbally profess that they believe "but by their works they disown" (Ti 1:16) the words of the divine Scripture, invert the words of the Apostle and say, if not aloud, at least in their heart, that need, ignominy, injuries, and tribulations are most serious and should be avoided and repulsed by every resource of their wit, even if it is necessary to lie, to cheat, to commit murder, to offend God, and after death to suffer hell. For who knows, they say, whether there is a hell anyway? And who has seen the eternal weight of glory? But we know by experience that need, ignominy, and injuries are bad; we know it with certitude; we touch it with our hands. The world and those who are of the world do not say such things aloud, but bear witness to them by their deeds, and that is the reason why a large number of men live badly and die most unhappily.

And to provide an example or two of the unhappy death of a man who has been lost, there is in Saint Gregory, in the fourth book of the *Dialogues*, the example of a certain Chrisorius. He was one of those whom I described just before, a man of politics, wise and well suited, as Saint Gregory says, for things of the world, yet proud and greedy.[1] When he reached the end of his life, he saw with open eyes the foulest spirits standing in his presence and violently threatening that they would snatch him off to the gates of hell. He began to tremble, to grow pale, to perspire, and to plead with loud cries for a respite, shouting and saying, "A respite at least until morning, a respite at least until morning." But while he was shouting that, he was torn in the midst of those cries from the abode of his flesh. It is obvious, of course, that he saw those things not for his own sake, but for our sake, so that his vision might be of profit to us. It often happens this way with those who want to put off their conversion to the final hour of life, and of their number are those who, as the Saint

Gregory teaches in the beginning of the fourth book, do not readily believe what they do not see, or, if they do believe, they do not believe strongly enough to make them live a good life.

Saint Gregory provides a second example in the same book about a certain hypocritical monk who was believed to be fasting, although he was eating and drinking in secret.[2] Saint Gregory writes that he had been condemned to hell while he was confessing his sin, although without repentance. For God willed that his hypocrisy be revealed. And he did not grant him the grace of repentance so that others might learn not to postpone confession and repentance until the end of life.

Having dealt with those who culpably did not learn the art of living well and thus did not have a happy passage from this life, I return to the words of the holy Apostle Paul, which are filled with salutary mysteries and lessons.

First of all, it is worth noticing how emphatically the Apostle makes light of his own merits, that is, his labors undertaken for Christ, and extols the glory of the kingdom of heaven, which is the reward of merit. He says, "Our present light affliction, which is for the moment" (2 Cor 4:17). Here he is making light of his own merits. The Apostle toiled with all his strength for about forty years. For, when he was called by Christ and came to his service, he was a young man. For he is so described in the Acts of the Apostles: Those stoning Stephan "laid down their garments at the feet of a young man named Saul" (Acts 7:58). But he lived in the service of Christ into old age, as he writes of himself to Philemon, "Since you are, as Paul, an old man" (Phlm 9). Thus the Apostle Paul spent in Christ's service all the years of his young manhood and of his maturity and a part of his old age, and he still says that the tribulations which he had constantly from his conversion up to his martyrdom were momentary. And what he says is true, if they are compared to an eternity of endless happiness. Nonetheless, considered by themselves, they lasted a long time.

He joins lightness with brevity in saying, "Our present light affliction which is for the moment." But he himself indicates how cruel and harsh those tribulations were, when he says in the First Letter to the Corinthians, "To this very hour we hunger and thirst, and we are naked and buffeted, and have no fixed abode. And we toil, working with our own hands. We are reviled and we bless, we are persecuted and we bear with it, we are maligned and we entreat, we have become as the refuse of this world, the offscouring of all, even until now" (1 Cor 4:11–13). He adds the following in the Second Letter to the Corinthians, "In many more labors, in prisons more frequently, in lashes above measure, often exposed to death. From the Jews five times I received forty lashes less one. Thrice I was scourged, once I was stoned, thrice I suffered shipwreck, a night and a day I was adrift on the sea; in journeying often, in perils from floods, in perils from robbers, in perils from my own nation, in perils from the Gentiles, in perils in the city, in perils in the wilderness, in perils in the sea, in perils from false brethren; in labor and hardships, in many sleepless nights, in hunger and thirst, in fastings often, in cold and nakedness" (2 Cor 11:23–27). These are the tribulations that he calls light. Although in themselves they are severe, the love of Christ and the greatness of the reward makes them seem with good reason to be very light.

The Apostle adds the greatness of the reward, saying: It "prepares for us an eternal weight of glory that is beyond all measure in sublimity." Here, in accord with the custom of Holy Scripture to adapt itself to our capacity, the Apostle uses the image of bodily greatness to describe the reward of our labors. For a bodily reality is said to be large when it is lofty and long-lasting and wide and deep. He says the loftiness of the happiness of the blessed is "beyond all measure in sublimity," that is, the reward of our labors will be sublime beyond measure, that is, most high, so that no greater honor, dignity, or sublimity can be thought. He calls its length "eternal," for it will have no end, and in comparison all duration can be called brief and momentary. Its width and depth he describes as a "weight of glory." The word *glory* means that happiness will be like splendor or light that is everywhere diffused and fills everything. The word *weight* indicates the depth of something solid and full, that is not superficial and empty, but most solid and full. Thus the happiness of the saints will be something sublime beyond all limit and measure, that is, eternal and most solid and full.

But because natural men, such as are the citizens of this world, do not understand these things, he adds, "We look not at the things that are seen, but at the things that are not seen. For the things that are seen are temporal, but the things that are not seen are eternal." This is the true and entire reason why so few learn the art of living and dying happily and well: because they either do not consider at all or do not seriously consider those things which are not seen and which are eternal. They are wholly occupied in considering the beauty and utility of bodily and passing things which are seen. Therefore, there is only one difference between brute beasts and natural men who lack the Spirit. The former consider only what is present because they do not have a mind capable of reason, by which alone future and everlasting things can be considered; whereas, carnal and natural men do not think about and do not consider future and everlasting things, because they are caught by the bird-lime of concupiscence and refuse to turn their minds from present things and to turn them toward things to come, which are alone truly great, valuable, and everlasting. This should suffice for the first consideration of the Pauline statement.

The second consideration, no less useful and salutary, applies to those who have gone down to hell. For punishment has opened the eyes of their mind which in this world had been closed by sin. They are the ones who most clearly realize that the goods of this world, that is, riches, honors, pleasures, kingdoms, and empires, were for them momentary and light and that, on account of them, nonetheless, they lost goods that are most eminent and everlasting goods. Hence, they groan unceasingly and find no consolation because, while they were on earth, they were stupid enough to lose goods having "an eternal weight of glory beyond all measure in sublimity" for the sake of fragile and perishing goods that are not so much goods as shadows of heavenly goods.

Let us listen to the words of the foolish in the Book of Wisdom. For the Holy Spirit wanted to report in this Book of Wisdom their words which are surely useless to them, but which can be beneficial for us if we so wish. "Therefore we have erred from the way of truth, and the light of justice has not shined unto us, and the sun of understanding has not risen upon us. We wearied ourselves in the way of iniquity and destruction, and have walked through hard ways, but the way of the Lord we have not known. What has pride profited us? Or what advantage has the boasting of riches brought us? All those things are passed away like a shadow, and like a post that runs on, and a ship that passes through the waves, whereof, when it is gone by, the trace cannot be found, nor the path of its keel in the waters; or as when a bird flies through the air, of the passage of which no mark can be found" (Wis 5:6–11). Such are the Wise Man's words. From this we gather that natural men will do penance in hell, not only because they have lost great, eternal goods on account of small, temporal ones, but also because they completely wore themselves out in the labor of acquiring and keeping goods that will perish. And it is obviously true and a frequent occurrence that those who condemn temporal goods live more joyfully and happily than those who have an abundance of riches and honors.

Certainly the Apostle Paul, whose words we have set out to explain, says of himself, "I am filled with comfort, I overflow with joy in all our troubles" (2 Cor 7:4). In *The Life of Saint Anthony*, Saint Athanasius reports that Anthony never seemed sad although he had given up all his temporal goods.[3] The same thing can be said of all the saints, however much they were poor and however much they labored in prayer and fasting and mortification of their flesh. Thus those who have no fear of losing everlasting goods in order to acquire, preserve, and increase temporal goods, not only utterly lose everlasting goods, but to a large extent surrender internal joy and consolation because of those temporal goods. Thus, in seeking earthly happiness, they lose happiness on earth and in heaven.

And so is it not right that we who are still on the journey begin to grow in wisdom by the example of those who have preceded us? Surely, if someone warns us while on a trip that a road we have set out on does not lead to where we want to go, but to a precipice or a den of thieves, we would all welcome the warning with gratitude and take another road immediately. But if we react this way in a bodily or temporal danger, it is surely right that we do so even more willingly and quickly in a danger that is both spiritual and corporeal, temporal and everlasting.

Finally, there remains for us to consider those men who are so carnal and natural that they do not place much value on the loss of eternal life and the heavenly glory that surpasses all understanding. They should be warned that, if they do not place great value upon heavenly glory which they have never seen, they should at least not despise fire and sulphur and other bodily punishments which they do know and which will be found in hell in their fiercest form. For pleasure of the flesh which is present, light, and for the moment will produce in the wicked an eternal weight of misery beyond all measure in the depth of hell (2 Cor 4:17). And Christ the Lord will make this evident on the last day in a few words, saying, "Depart from me, accursed ones, into the everlasting fire which was prepared for the devil and his angels" (Mt 25:41).

But blessed John in the Book of Revelation explains more extensively what sort of torments have been prepared for the devil and his angels and those men deceived and seduced by the devil. In the Book of Revelation we read as follows about the devil, the prince of the wicked, "And the devil who deceived them was cast into the pool of fire and brimstone, where are also the beast and the false prophet; and they will be tormented day and night forever and ever" (Rv 20:9–10). And in the following chapter he says of the rest who are condemned to hell, "But as for the cowardly and unbelieving, and abominable and murderers, and fornicators and sorcerers, and idolators and all liars, their portion shall be in the pool that burns with fire and brimstone, which is the second death" (Rv 21:8). Here only the first group needs explanation, for the rest clearly involve sins. Saint John calls "cowardly" those who do not dare to resist the tempter, whether the devil or man, but immediately yield and consent to him. Saint James writes to these people, "Resist the devil, and he will flee from you" (Jas 4:7). There are many, even countless men who have not learned to fight the battles of the Lord and without any resistance accept wounds from the devil and die the first death, which is mortal sin. And because they are also cowardly in doing penance, not daring to chastise and subdue their body, they also fall into the second death, which is hell. Thus John correctly put the cowardly in first place, because cowardice leads a countless number of men to hell.

How will carnal men respond at this point? By our own experience and that of others we have all learned that temporal goods are momentary and light, but Holy Scripture, in which there can be no falsity, clearly bears witness that the torments of hell are most grievous and will last without end. From this it follows that the summation of the whole art of dying well is the content of the three following propositions or the conclusion of the following argument.

CHAPTER SEVENTEEN

A summation of the whole art of dying well

Both the consolation and the tribulation of the present life are momentary and slight, while both the consolation and tribulation of the life to come are everlasting and immense. Thus those who despise the consolation and tribulation of the life to come are fools. The first proposition of this argument is known by experience, the second is well known from the Scripture of the Holy Spirit, and the third follows from the preceding two. Thus, if anyone wants to master easily and quickly the art of dying well, he should not be content with reading this book or others like it, but should carefully consider the great difference between the momentary and the everlasting, between the slight and the immense, not once, but often, and not with an eye on learning, but with the intention of living well and dying happily. If he wants to be solidly confirmed in this highly useful truth, he should consider the examples of those who went before us, whether they were wise or foolish, that is, whether they died happily by living well or perished eternally by living badly. In order to spare the readers the task of finding examples, I will offer three pairs of examples, the first of kings, the second of ordinary men, and the third of clerics. I will take them all from Scripture.

The first will be the example of Saul and David. When Saul, the first king of the Hebrews, was a poor man not living a public life, he was so good that, as Scripture bears witness, there was none better than he among the children of Israel. After he was made king, he changed his life and conduct so that there was then no one worse than he. He pursued David, who was innocent, to the point of death, simply because he suspected that he would succeed him on the throne. Finally, after he had reigned twenty years, he was killed in battle and went to hell. After Saul's long pursuit, the faithful and good David was declared king, and he justly governed the realm for forty years, during which he suffered many trials and finally died in peace.

Now let us compare the consolations and tribulations of each and see which of them learned the art of living well and dying well. The pleasure of ruling, which is usually very great, Saul possessed neither clearly nor firmly while he lived because of the hatred with which he pursued David. Thus he tasted the sweetness of his twenty-year reign along with the bitterness of envy. After those years had passed, all the joy of life fled from him, and pure and everlasting disaster took its place. And now for almost two thousand and seventy years his nobler part, that is, the soul, has lived in pains of the greatest sort and—what is worse—of endless duration. On the other hand, David lived seventy years and reigned for forty. Though he experienced tribulations that were neither slight nor few, he also received from God's revelations frequent great consolations, which he expressed in his delightful psalms. After his death he went to refreshment, not to punishment, since he entered into the bosom of Abraham with the holy patriarchs. After the resurrection of Christ the Lord he rose to the kingdom of heaven with Christ himself.

Now let the reader judge whether wicked men's passing from the body, although they might be kings and emperors, is not truly unhappy and the passing of just men, even if they are kings and emperors, is far happier. Saul, as I said, reigned for twenty years; after death he remained over two thousand years in the fire of hell without any comfort. What comparison is there between twenty years and two thousand? Who would chose twenty years of the highest and purest pleasure if he knew with certainty that, because of that pleasure, he would remain for over two thousand years in a blazing furnace? Would there be any man so senseless as to want to undergo the greatest of all torments for years, not let us say for two thousand years, but for two hundred, so that afterward he might enjoy for twenty years even the greatest pleasure? But what if we add that the torment of hell will last not two thousand years, but will have no end? Surely the eternity alone of the torments that will last without any cessation and without any respite is sufficient to bend a heart of iron and a breast of bronze to repentance. The reader himself can apply the same consideration to David's momentary and slight tribulation and to the immense and everlasting pleasure, which he obtained after his death in the heavenly kingdom, although the torments of hell move us more than the joys of paradise.

The second example will be that of Lazarus and the banqueter from the Gospel of Saint Luke (Lk 16:19–31). The wealthy banqueter, who "used to clothe himself in purple and fine linen, and who feasted every day in splendid fashion," rejoiced for a short time with his friends. In contrast, Lazarus, a beggar, lay sick, at the gate of the rich man, "covered with sores, and longing to be filled with the crumbs that fell from the rich man's table, and no one gave them to him" (Lk 16:19–21). But soon everything was changed: The rich banqueter died and went down to hell; Lazarus died and was borne by angels to a place of refreshment and the bosom of Abraham. After his brief comfort the rich man began to be tortured in the flames of eternal fire and is even now being tortured there and will be tortured there without any respite or pause forever and ever. Good and patient

Lazarus, after his brief trial, entered into rest in the bosom of Abraham, and after the resurrection of Christ he will journey to the heavenly and happy kingdom where he will be blessed without end. Surely, if we had lived at that time, few if any of us would have wanted to be like Lazarus, but all or almost all of us would have wanted to be like the rich man. Yet now we all regard Lazarus as most happy and the rich man as most wretched. Why, therefore, while we have the option, do we not choose the virtue of Lazarus rather than the vices of the rich man? We need not blame riches, for Abraham and David and many other saints were wealthy. But we should condemn overindulgence, luxury, vanity, lack of mercy, and the other vices which brought the rich man to hell. Nor do we consider in Lazarus only his poverty and sores; we praise his patience and piety. It is truly amazing that, although we know all these things and judge the rich man a fool and Lazarus a wise man, we still find many who do not hesitate to imitate the rich man in their life, although they can be sure that their punishment will be similar to that of the man whose vices they chose to imitate.

There remains the third example, of Judas the traitor and Saint Matthias who replaced Judas as an apostle. Judas was surely unhappy in this world and even unhappier in the next. He followed our Lord and Savior for three years, seeking to fill his purse by sacrilegious theft. He was not content with the money he received from the communal alms, but under pressure from the disease of greed, he went so far as to sell our Lord and Master. A little later he was reduced to despair by the devil; he gave back the money, hanged himself, and lost at once both temporal and eternal life. This is why the Lord pronounced that terrible sentence about Judas, "It were better for that man if he had not been born" (Mt 26:24). Saint Matthias, who succeeded Judas, that is, after having been elected to his position, underwent slight labor for a short time along with an abundance of heavenly delights. But now with all labor and pain ended, he reigns in heaven, happy with Christ, whom he most faithfully served on earth.

This comparison of Judas with Matthias applies to bishops and religious. For Judas was an apostle of Christ and, thus, named a bishop. Saint Peter interprets the words of the psalm, "And his bishopric let another take" (Ps 109:8; Acts 1:20), as speaking of Judas and Matthias. And Judas was numbered among religious men, since Saint Peter says of all the apostles, "Behold, we have left all and followed you; what then shall we have?" (Mt 19:27). When Judas, the most unhappy of all men, had fallen from the high state of perfection, he lost even the small gain he had so wickedly acquired by giving it back. Having become his own executioner and having been condemned to everlasting punishment, he can serve as an example for all clerics and religious so that they see how they should walk and what danger threatens them if they do not measure up to the perfection of their state by living a holy life. For by dying, Saul and the banqueter went from temporal happiness to everlasting bitterness. Judas had no temporal happiness, but only a shadow or a hope of happiness, and yet he killed himself and came to a destruction that was everlasting and more horrible than was the destruction of Saul and the banqueter. But even if Judas surpassed all mortals in the acquisition of riches and later came to eternal poverty and the pains of hell that are to last without end, as indeed did happen, what would the mass of wealth have profited him?

Therefore, let the argument stand firm and true, which we set out at the beginning of this chapter and which we now repeat in the words of the Apostle: "For our present light affliction, which is for the moment, prepares for us an eternal weight of glory that is beyond all measure in sublimity; while we look not at the things that are seen, but at the things that are not seen. For the things that are seen are temporal, but the things that are not seen are eternal" (2 Cor 4:17–18).

NOTES

Notes to Chapter One

1. *The Mourning of the Dove* c. 9, where he cites Venerable Bede's *Ecclesiastical History of England* [Historia Ecclesiastica] V, c. 12 [*PL* 95, 247–252].
2. John Climacus, *The Ladder of Divine Ascent* [Scala Paradisi], Step VI [*PG* 88, 797–798].

Notes to Chapter Two

1. The Council of Florence, *DS* 1304–1306.
2. Cf. Saint Thomas, *Commentary on the Four Books of the Sentences* IV, d. 47.
3. Saint Cyprian *The Unity of the Catholic Church* [De catholicae ecclesiae unitate] [*PL* 4, 527].
4. Saint Jerome, *Commentary on Joel* [Commentariorum in Joelem] c. 3 [*PL* 25, 979].
5. Saint Denis the Areopagite, *The Celestial Hierarchy* I, c. 14 [*PG* 3, 321–322]; Saint Thomas, *The Summa of Theology* Ia, q. 50, a. 3.

Notes to Chapter Three

1. *The Ascent of the Mind to God; The Eternal Happiness of the Saints; The Mourning of the Dove; Sermons on the Four Last Things*. For the first three cf. *Opera Omnia*, Volume VI (Naples, 1862) 205–396; for the fourth, cf. *Trattai delli quattro novissimi e della miseria dell' humana vita*, trans. from Latin by Count Camillo de' Arbieri (Rome, 1621); these are extracts from Bellarmine's *Conciones habitae Lovanii ante annos circiter quadraginta* (Cologne, 1605).

Note to Chapter Four

1. Theophylactus, *Commentary on the First Letter to the Corinthians* [Expositio in Epistolam I ad Corinthios] c. XV, v. 28 [*PG* 124, 767–768], and Saint Augustine, *The City of God* XXII, c. 30 [*PL* 41, 801–802].

2. Saint Jerome,, *Letter* 55 (To Amandus) [Epistola LV] c. 5 [*PL* 22, 564–565].

Notes to Chapter Five

1. Possidius, *Life of Saint Augustine* c. 31 [PL 32, 64].

2. Saint Ambrose, *The Duties of Ministers* [De officiis ministrorum] II, 28, 142 [*PL* 16, 150]; the translators have not been able to locate the reference to Saint Gregory.

3. Saint Augustine, *On Caring for the Dead* [De cura pro mortuis gerenda ad Paulinum] c. 1 [*PL* 40, 593].

Note to Chapter Six

1. Possidius, *Life of Saint Augustine* c. 31 [*PL* 32, 63–64].

Notes to Chapter Seven

1. Lawrence Surius, *The Life of Saint William, Archbishop of Bourges*, Tome I, for January 10; Surius's many-volumed work on the lives of the saints (*De probatis sanctorum historiis* [Cologne, 1570–1575]) was revised in 1617–1618 by another Carthusian.

2. Saint Bernard, *Life of Saint Malachi* [Vita sancti Malachiae] XXXI, 71 [*PL* 182, 1115].

3. Paulinus of Milan, *Life of Ambrose* c. 47 [*PL* 14, 46].

4. Simeon Metaphrastes, *Life of Saint John Chrysostom* [Vita S. Joannis Chrysostomi] c. 61 [*PG* 114, 1206].

5. Saint Bernard, *Life of Saint Malachi* XXXI, 71 [*PL* 182, 1115].

6. Lawrence Surius, *The Life of Saint William*, Tome I, for January 10.

Notes to Chapter Eight

1. The Council of Florence, *DS* 1324–1325; the Council of Trent, *DS* 1696, 1717.

2. Saint Bernard, *Life of Saint Malachi* XXIV, 53 [*PL* 182, 1103–1104].

NOTES

Note to Chapter Nine

1. Pietro Barozzi, *The Way to Die Well* [De modo bene moriendi] (Venice, 1531).

Notes to Chapter Ten

1. Venerable Bede, *The Ecclesiastical History of England* V, c. 13 [*PL* 95, 252–253].
2. Ibid., c. 14 [*PL* 95, 254].
3. Saint Leo, *Letter* 108 (To Theodore, Bishop of Frejus) [Epistola ad Theodorum, episcopum Foroiuliensem. Epistola CVIII] 4 [*PL* 54, 1013].
4. Lawrence Surius, *The Life of Count Elzear*, Tome V, for September 27, last chapter.
5. John Climacus, *The Ladder of Divine Ascent*, Step 7 [*PG* 88, 813–814].

Notes to Chapter Eleven

1. Paolo Grillando, *Liber de hereticis et sortilegiis* (Lyons, 1536); Martinus del Rio, S.J., *Disquisitionum magicarum libri VI* (1599).
2. Saint Thomas, *The Summa of Theology* IIa–IIae, q. 71, a. 3.
3. Thomas de Vio Cajetan, *Commentary* on *the Summa of Theology* IIa–IIae, qu. 71, a. 3; Cajetan's *Commentary* is printed in the Leonine edition of the works of Saint Thomas. Cf. *Sancti Thomae Aquinatis Opera Omnia*, Volume 9 (Rome, 1897).
4. Sulpicius Severus, *The Life of Saint Martin* [Vita Sancti Martini. Epistola tertia] XI, 2 (*PL* 20, 159).
5. Peter Damian, *The Life of Saint Odilo* [Vita s. Odilonis] [*PL* 144, 944].
6. Lawrence Surius, *The Life of Saint Opportuna.*
7. Lawrence Surius, *The Life of Saint Aichard*, for September 15.

Note to Chapter Twelve

1. Saint Augustine, *Homilies on John's Gospel*, Homily 42, 14 [*PL* 35, pt. 2, 1705]; and Saint John Chrysostom, *Homilies on John*, Homily 54, 3 [In Joannem Homilae. Homilia 54] [*PG* 59, 299].

Notes to Chapter Thirteen

1. Saint Augustine, *Homilies on the Psalms*, On Psalm 34, Sermon 2, 7 [*PL* 38, 327].
2. Saint Athanasius, *The Life of Saint Anthony* [Vita sancti Antonii] 9 [*PG* 26, 858].
3. Saint Bonaventure, *The Life of Saint Francis* X, 3.
4. Saint Gregory, *Dialogues* IV, c. 38 [*PL* 77, 389–392].

Note on Chapter Fourteen

1. Saint Augustine, *Against Faustus the Manichee* [Contra Faustum Manichaeum] XXII, c. 75 [*PL* 42, 448].

Notes to Chapter Fifteen

1. Saint Bernard, *Letter* 98 (To Someone Unknown, Concerning the Maccabees) [Epistola XCVIII. Ad ignoratum, de Machabaeis] 8 [*PL* 182, 234].
2. Saint Gregory, *Dialogues* IV, c. 11 [*PL* 77, 337–338].
3. Ibid., c. 12 [*PL* 77, 337–340].
4. Ibid., c. 13 [*PL* 77, 339–342].
5. Ibid., c. 14 [*PL* 77, 341–344].
6. Ibid., c. 15 [*PL* 77, 343–348].
7. Ibid., c. 16 [*PL* 77, 347–348].
8. Ibid., c. 17 [*PL* 77, 347–350].
9. Ibid., c. 19 [*PL* 77, 352].

Notes to Chapter Sixteen

1. Saint Gregory, *Dialogues* IV, c. 28 [*PL* 77, 391–394].
2. Ibid., c. 28 [*PL* 77, 393–394].
3. Saint Athanasius, *The Life of Saint Anthony*, possibly c. 14 [*PG* 26, 863–866].

Index to Preface and Introduction

Index to Texts

Other Volumes in this Series

Julian of Norwich • SHOWINGS
Jacob Boehme • THE WAY TO CHRIST
Nahman of Bratslav • THE TALES
Gregory of Nyssa • THE LIFE OF MOSES
Bonaventure • THE SOUL'S JOURNEY INTO GOD, THE TREE OF LIFE, and THE LIFE OF ST. FRANCIS
William Law • A SERIOUS CALL TO DEVOUT AND HOLY LIFE, and THE SPIRIT OF LOVE
Abraham Isaac Kook • THE LIGHTS OF PENITENCE, LIGHTS OF HOLINESS, THE MORAL PRINCIPLES, ESSAYS, and POEMS
Ibn 'Ata' Illah • THE BOOK OF WISDOM and Kwaja Abdullah Ansari • INTIMATE CONVERSATIONS
Johann Arndt • TRUE CHRISTIANITY
Richard of St. Victor • THE TWELVE PATRIARCHS, THE MYSTICAL ARK, and BOOK THREE OF THE TRINITY
Origen • AN EXHORTATION TO MARTYRDOM, PRAYER, AND SELECTED WORKS
Catherine of Genoa • PURGATION AND PURGATORY, THE SPIRITUAL DIALOGUE
Native North American Spirituality of the Eastern Woodlands • SACRED MYTHS, DREAMS, VISIONS, SPEECHES, HEALING FORMULAS, RITUALS AND CEREMONIALS
Teresa of Avila • THE INTERIOR CASTLE
Apocalyptic Spirituality • TREATISES AND LETTERS OF LACTANTIUS, ADSO OF MONTIER-EN-DER, JOACHIM OF FIORE, THE FRANCISCAN SPIRITUALS, SAVONAROLA
Athanasius • THE LIFE OF ANTONY, A LETTER TO MARCELLINUS
Catherine of Siena • THE DIALOGUE
Sharafuddin Maneri • THE HUNDRED LETTERS
Martin Luther • THEOLOGIA GERMANICA
Native Mesoamerican Spirituality • ANCIENT MYTHS, DISCOURSES, STORIES, DOCTRINES, HYMNS, POEMS FROM THE AZTEC, YUCATEC, QUICHE-MAYA AND OTHER SACRED TRADITIONS
Symeon the New Theologian • THE DISCOURSES
Ibn Al'-Aribī • THE BEZELS OF WISDOM
Hadewijch • THE COMPLETE WORKS
Philo of Alexandria • THE CONTEMPLATIVE LIFE, THE GIANTS, AND SELECTIONS
George Herbert • THE COUNTRY PARSON, THE TEMPLE
Unknown • THE CLOUD OF UNKNOWING
John and Charles Wesley • SELECTED WRITINGS AND HYMNS
Meister Eckhart • THE ESSENTIAL SERMONS, COMMENTARIES, TREATISES AND DEFENSE
Francisco de Osuna • THE THIRD SPIRITUAL ALPHABET
Jacopone da Todi • THE LAUDS
Fakhruddin 'Iraqi • DIVINE FLASHES
Menahem Nahum of Chernobyl • THE LIGHT OF THE EYES

John Climacus • THE LADDER OF DIVINE ASCENT
Francis and Clare • THE COMPLETE WORKS
Gregory Palamas • THE TRIADS
Pietists • SELECTED WRITINGS
The Shakers • TWO CENTURIES OF SPIRITUAL REFLECTION
Zohar • THE BOOK OF ENLIGHTENMENT
Luis de León • THE NAMES OF CHRIST
Quaker Spirituality • SELECTED WRITINGS
Emanuel Swedenborg • THE UNIVERSAL HUMAN AND SOUL-BODY INTERACTION
Augustine of Hippo • SELECTED WRITINGS
Safed Spirituality • RULES OF MYSTICAL PIETY, THE BEGINNING OF WISDOM
Maximus Confessor • SELECTED WRITINGS
John Cassian • CONFERENCES
Johannes Tauler • SERMONS
John Ruusbroec • THE SPIRITUAL ESPOUSALS AND OTHER WORKS
Ibn 'Abbād of Ronda • LETTERS ON THE SŪFĪ PATH
Angelus Silesius • THE CHERUBINIC WANDERER
The Early Kabbalah •
Meister Eckhart • TEACHER AND PREACHER
John of the Cross • SELECTED WRITINGS
Pseudo-Dionysius • THE COMPLETE WORKS
Bernard of Clairvaux • SELECTED WORKS
Devotio Moderna • BASIC WRITINGS
The Pursuit of Wisdom • AND OTHER WORKS BY THE AUTHOR OF THE CLOUD OF UNKNOWING
Richard Rolle • THE ENGLISH WRITINGS
Francis de Sales, Jane de Chantal • LETTERS OF SPIRITUAL DIRECTION
Albert and Thomas • SELECTED WRITINGS

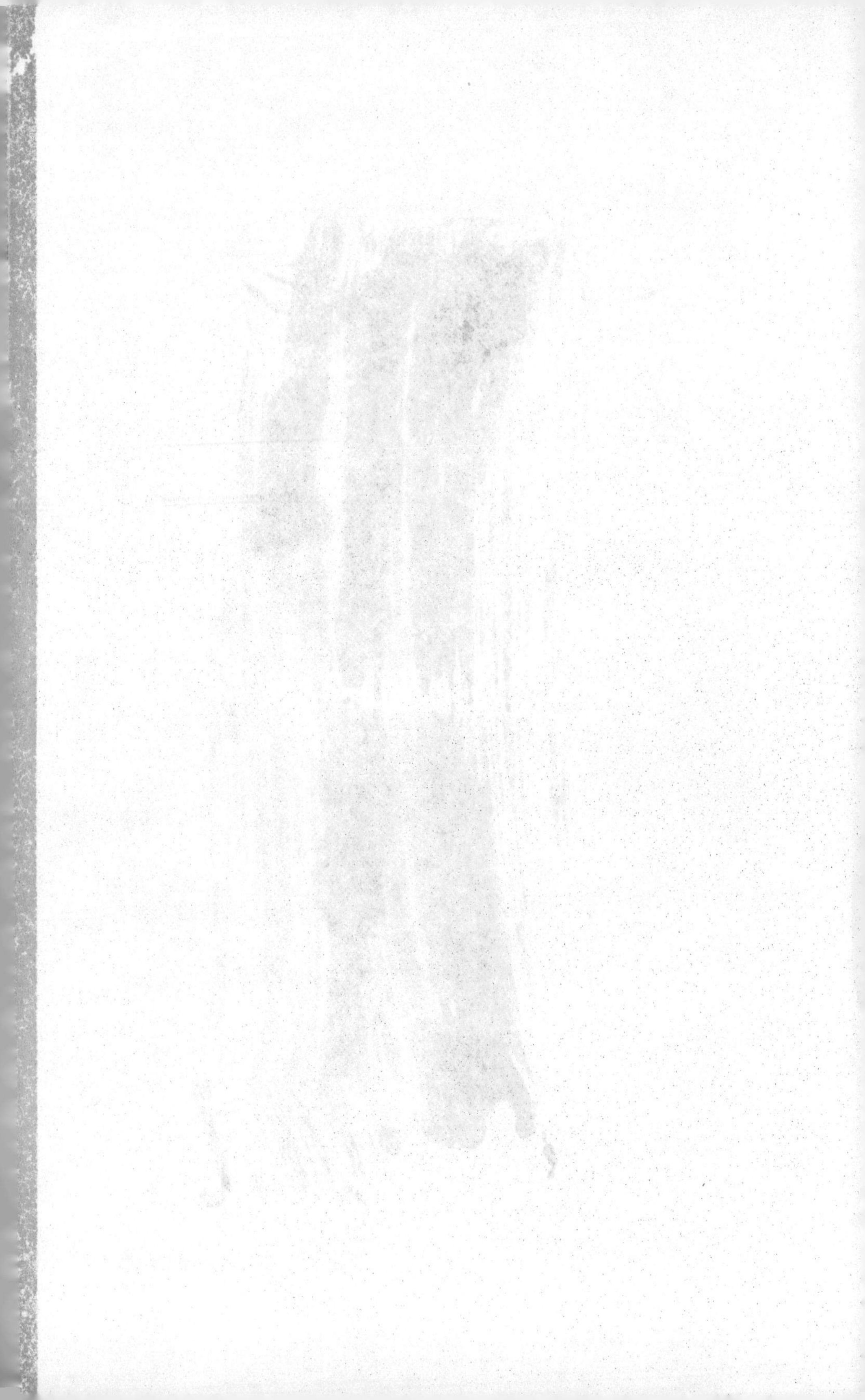